Robust Java

Exception Handling, Testing, and Debugging

Robust Java

Exception Handling, Testing, and Debugging

Stephen Stelting

Prentice Hall PTR, Upper Saddle River, NJ 07458
www.phptr.com

Acquisitions Editor: *Gregory G. Doench*
Editorial Assistant: *Raquel Kaplan*
Production Supervision: *Mary Sudul*
Page layout: FAST*pages*
Cover Design Director: *Jerry Votta*
Cover Designer: *Anthony Gemmellaro*
Art Director: *Gail Cocker-Bogusz*
Manufacturing Manager: *Alexis R. Heydt-Long*
Marketing Manager: *Chris Guzikowski*
Sun Microsystems Press Publisher: *Myrna Rivera*

First Printing

ISBN 0-13-100852-8

Sun Microsystems Press

A Prentice Hall Title

To my parents, family, and friends, thank you all.
You've given me the greatest gift in the world:
the gift of your friendship and support.

contents

Part 3
Effective Use of Exceptions, Errors, and Handling 239

Chapter 13   Testing 289

Chapter 14   Debugging 313

"All undetectable errors will be treated as if no error occurred."
—*Technical reference from a major*
computing company (attributed)

"The goal of Computer Science is to build something that will last—
at least until we've finished building it."
—*Anonymous*

"As soon as we started programming, we found to our surprise that it wasn't as easy to get programs right as we had thought. Debugging had to be discovered. I can remember the exact instant when I realized that a large part of my life from then on was going to be spent in finding mistakes in my own programs."
—*Maurice Wilkes (attributed)*

Wouldn't it be a wonderful world if everything always went as you planned? Wouldn't it be great if every project you started was a total success, if every hiking trip was bright and sunny, if you won every contest that you entered? Wouldn't it be incredible if you were instantly a master at everything you tried? Whether you decided to build a new deck for your house, a catamaran, or a space shuttle, everything was always guaranteed to be an instant success. What a great world it would be....

In the meantime, we have to live in the real world. And in *this* world, things sometimes go wrong. Not always, but often enough that it makes sense to have a fallback plan sometimes. You start to build your deck, but you keep the phone number for a carpenter nearby just in case. When you go on a hike, you hope for good weather, but you bring along a poncho in case it rains. In extreme cases you might even bring:

- A poncho (for rain)
- A parka (for cold)
- Suntan lotion (for sun)
- Water
- Insect repellent
- A first aid kit
- A map
- A compass
- Mountain climbing rope

- Emergency flares
- Sled dog team
- Oxygen equipment

OK, the last few items on the list might be a *little* far fetched, but some of us like to be prepared. It's the same way for software—we want to design our code to plan for problems. Rather than assuming that everything will run perfectly every time, we should work out what can go wrong, and develop an approach to address potential problems.

How should your applications respond if there's a problem in code? Well, it depends. You don't always respond the same way when things don't go as planned in everyday life—why would you want your code to behave that way? Think about it: what would happen if you just smiled and laughed every time something went wrong? People would walk all over you. On the other hand, if you yelled and threw heavy objects every time something didn't go as planned, people might accuse you of overreacting. Clearly, we need to have some kind of strategy for our software to help us decide when to ignore problems and when to throw the heavy objects.

It's entirely appropriate for software systems to follow different strategies depending on the category or type of error. Usually, you need to take different approaches to fix the problems that can occur; it's rare to find a "one size fits all" solution for the code you write. In some cases, you may be able to ignore the error case. In other cases, you may decide you have to take action. In any event, establishing a plan for handling errors is one of the hallmarks of a well-written application. With a good exception handling strategy, you can't guarantee that everything will always go according to plan ... but you have a "plan B" (and possibly C, D and E) in case something goes wrong.

Why It's Important to Know This Stuff

All right, why did I write this book? I've taught a lot of people about Java over the years, and I've noticed that many of my students never really had a good reference on how to deal effectively with errors in their Java code. For many years, you were lucky to find a Java book with a full chapter on the subject. As a result, a generation of Java developers has had to manage exception handling in their code as best they could. In a sense, I can understand why the subject has been so neglected. Dealing with error scenarios in code is a lot like going to the dentist. We know that it's something we have to do, but we don't particularly look forward to it.

At the same time, it is a vitally important topic. The way in which we handle errors has a direct, bottom-line impact on whether our code will run or not. It directly affects vital aspects of software such as maintainability. And it *definitely* makes a big difference in how easy it is to test and debug our code. Who hasn't stayed up late working on a project, desperately trying to make sense out of someone else's code? As the hours stretch slowly outward into morning, who hasn't felt a twinge of helpless panic when faced with code that makes about as much sense as the programmer who wrote it after a dozen cups of coffee and two sleepless nights? Who hasn't felt the rush of terror when faced with a production problem, aware that an application's source code is hiding (yes, hiding) erroneous assumptions, faulty logic and mishandled errors somewhere deep inside? You can directly trace a lot of these problems to mistakes in dealing with exceptions and errors in code.

Of course, exception and error handling isn't the *only* thing responsible for errors and maintainability problems in code. But it *does* have a major impact in more applications that you might think. There have been many code examples, even in well-designed systems and books on "correct" Java coding, where you can find programming gems like this one:

```java
try{
  operationA();
  component.operateB();
}
catch (Exception e){}
```

The problem, of course, is that it's easy to write code like the example above. It's a quick, simple way to get a class to compile. If you've never read much about exceptions, it might seem OK. If you've never had to maintain the code, it might seem like a pretty good idea. To developers who work in production support, it usually means pure terror.

Robust Java is intended to teach you what you need to know about exceptions, errors and handling—to help you learn to write truly robust, maintainable code. I spent the last year and a half of my life working on this project because I wanted to give developers a good, practical reference about how to deal with problems that can occur in their code. This book should be a good, practical resource for you that will lead to a better understanding of the topic, and ultimately to better practices in the software development community.

Part of this book is based on writing effective code, and part is based on showing you how to apply that knowledge. It takes an interesting mix of skills to write truly robust software systems. To be effective, to write really robust Java code, you need a good foundation understanding of what exceptions are and how they work. You need to understand how to write effective exception handling code. You need some grounding in software design, so that you can structure your code to effectively deal with exceptions and errors. You need to know a little about the APIs, to understand how and why code can fail. Finally, you need exposure to topics like architectural decisions and design patterns, so that you can develop an application that will stand the test of time. Ultimately, all of these skills come in handy as you develop a software system.

This book is not:

- A catalog of Java exceptions and errors
- A substitute for thought and reasoning
- A methodology or silver bullet

This book isn't meant to document all of the exceptions thrown by every method in the Java APIs. If I had tried to do that, this book would be longer than the collected works of Isaac Asimov. Also, I'd be so old by the time I was done that I would have forgotten what I was writing about. It's much more useful to talk about ways that code can fail, and to provide an overview of common errors that can occur in an API or application.

I'm a great believer in the benefits of applied reasoning, especially in a field like ours. This book contains a number of best practices. Some of them are widely documented. I've seen others mentioned in e-mail discussions or documented as lessons learned in development projects. However, keep in mind that any best practice is ultimately a suggestion. Suggestions have to be understood and intelligently applied, or they have little practical benefit. Ultimately, the best "best practices" won't do you much good if you apply them indiscriminately. This means you should think about how to apply the practices to your own projects, and do so when it makes good sense to you as a developer.

The approaches described in this book are not silver bullet solutions to all your problems. There is not such thing as a silver bullet in our business. Never has been, never will be. This book can make your code more solid, more maintainable, easier to test, easier to debug. But I know of nothing in this universe that will make all of the problems in a software project go away.

How this Book Is Organized

I believe this topic really depends on a full spectrum of software development skills. The act of creating a really robust software system depends on skills in development, design and architecture. Because of this, I wrote *Robust Java* in three parts.

Part 1 focuses on the mechanics of exceptions and exception handling in Java—the "nuts and bolts" of dealing with errors in code. This section gives you a good idea of what exceptions really are, how they are produced, and how they can be used within a system. It also describes some best practices for developers, and presents general APIs and techniques used in almost every type of exception handling. This is general material that relates to any Java developer. The topics are intended to give the reader a well-rounded view of how exceptions fit into the Java, acting as a foundation for the next two parts of the book.

Part 2 focuses on design concepts associated with exception handling. It discusses how to incorporate exception handling into your software design, and introduces the concept of "failure mode analysis." We spend a lot of time in this chapter looking at commonly-used Java APIs. This section provides a perspective on what exceptions are produced in a given API and why. Since exception handling tends to be so vital in complex multi-tier systems, this section provides a special focus on Java's distributed APIs and the J2EE architectural framework.

Part 3 covers the topics related to using exceptions, errors and handling effectively over the full lifecycle of software development. It covers software architecture, design patterns, testing and debugging. The intent is to carry the topic beyond the basic discussion about exception handling to how to produce well-architected systems, systems that are effectively maintainable over the long term. Part of this section focuses on possible design patterns that tend to be well-suited for exception handling frameworks. Part examines the impact of exception handling strategies on the overall system architecture. And part of this section discusses the closely-related tasks of testing and debugging.

To Find Out More

Education is a constant process. If I've learned anything from seven years as a technical instructor, it's that lesson. It's helpful to read the stuff that's in this book, but it's also important to try out code, read articles and have discussions. Software developers, like most professionals in engineering, tend to follow a "learn by doing" model at least some of the time. It's usually important to have a number of follow-on sources for information, questions and so on.

There are a bunch of good additional resources for this book. If you want to look at related material, take a look at the bibliography. I've also set up a Web site for *Robust Java*. You can find it at:

```
http://talk-about-tech/robustjava
```

The site provides discussion forums, code examples and additional topics of interest for the book. Take a look, let me know what you think and what you'd like to see. I hope to see you there!

There's something about the end of a writing project that makes a person get misty eyed and philosophical. Sitting in my favorite coffee shop, I can't help but think back a couple of years to when I started to write this book. When I co-authored *Applied Java Patterns*, I promised myself that I'd learn from the experience. The *next* time, I said I would carefully budget my time. I would work out a detailed outline and stick to it throughout the project. I would produce regular, incremental deliverables. Naturally, I broke all those promises. It's taken me about six months longer than I'd planned, and the book is much longer than I'd originally imagined.

I'm constantly amazed that it's even possible to transform a tangled mass of ideas, musings and code examples into a polished, coherent book. Maybe one person can do it on his own, but I doubt it. I know that I certainly don't have the patience for the job. If I didn't have the ongoing support of a wonderfully talented team, I would have given up long ago and spent all my time playing "Ratchet and Clank." So, to the people who have made *Robust Java* possible, you have my heartfelt thanks.

For Greg Doench, editorial wonder worker:
In the technical publishing business, editors are the ultimate champions of a book. They fight long and hard to get the advertising, editing and production resources that a book needs if it's going to succeed. I'm extremely grateful for all Greg's help and support in assisting me to navigate the waters of the publishing industry and make this book a reality.

For Brian O'Donnell, Mike Ernest and Natalie Levi, my talented technical reviewers:
Thank you so much for your honest, objective feedback. In this business, it's always good if a technical book actually makes sense. Thank you for helping me find a way to translate my thoughts into something resembling normal human speech.

For Mary Sudul, Robin Carroll, and Carol Cramer of the prolific Prentice-Hall production department:
My sincere thanks for your help and support. I appreciate all your hard work on a tight schedule; you've helped us turn a manuscript into something we can all be proud of.

For Wayne and Peggy Kovsky, organizers of the Colorado Software Summit:
Thanks for your ongoing support over the years. In my opinion, you've got one of the best, most informative Java conferences in the world. Thanks also for your interest in this work. Several of the chapters in this book are based around topics that I first

presented at the conference. For details on the Summit and its great technical presentations, take a look at **http://www.softwaresummit.com**.

Since this book covers a lot of material, I'd like to give special thanks to the following people for their inspiration, help and advice on specific parts of this book:

J. Keith Ratliff and Simon Roberts, for their inspiring work on J2EE architectures for Sun's SL425 course.

Bryan Basham, for his substantial insight into J2EE Web tier technologies.

Kathy Sierra, for most of the inspiration on EJB technologies.

Many thanks to Karen Sutherland and Mary Grinham, my managers at Sun, for their ongoing support and encouragement.

I'd like to thank my fellow instructors at Sun Microsystems and our partner organizations. You're an amazing bunch of folks. It's a great honor to be a part of such a talented, dedicated and dynamic team. Thanks also to my students. Over the years, you've helped me broaden my own horizons through questions and discussions. I hope to be able to pass along some of the things we've learned to others.

Finally, to all the coffee shops of the world, you have my thanks. I would have slept most of my life away if it weren't been for you, and this book would probably still be unfinished. As it is, I'm hyper but happy.

part 1

Fundamentals of Exceptions and Exception Handling

chapter 1

Introducing Exceptions

Introduction

Suppose we wanted to write a program in Java that would read in a line of text that a user typed and print it back out to the terminal again. A basic echo program, to check on Java's I/O capabilities. In a world without exceptions, where our code was guaranteed to run perfectly,[1] we might write something like the following program:

```
1   import java.io.*;
2   public class BuggyEchoInput{
3       public static void main(String [] args){
4           System.out.println("Enter text to echo");
5           InputStreamReader isr = new InputStreamReader(System.in);
6           BufferedReader inputReader = new BufferedReader(isr);
7           String inputLine = inputReader.readLine();
8           System.out.println("READ: " + inputLine);
9       }
10  }
```

Fairly simple, right? In the BuggyEchoInput class, we declare a main method on line 3. On line 4, we prompt a user to enter text. Lines 5 and 6 set up a `Buffere-dReader` object that is connected to an `InputStreamReader`, which in turn is connected to the standard input stream, `System.in`. On line 7, we read a line of text, and on line 8, we print it using the standard output stream, `System.out`.

There's just one problem with the BuggyEchoInput class: we don't live in a perfect world. There are a bunch of assumptions that we have to make if it's going to properly read input when we call the `readLine` method on line 7. We assume that the keyboard is functional, that communication between the keyboard and the computer is working properly. We assume that the keyboard data can be transferred from the oper-

---

1.   If you ever find that world, let me know. I want to rent a timeshare there.

ating system to the Java Virtual Machine, and from there to our `BufferedReader`, `inputReader`.

Most of the time, these assumptions will probably be valid. Occasionally though, there could be a problem somewhere along the line. Java uses exceptions as a way to ensure that we're aware of the possibility of an error and that we take steps to correct the potential failure in our code. In this example, if we tried to compile the program shown above, we'd get the following message:

```
BuggyEchoInput.java:7: unreported exception java.io.IOException;
   must be caught or declared to be thrown
            String inputLine = inputReader.readLine();
                                                    ^

1 error
```

What's the meaning of this compiler error? Basically, we're being told that the `readLine` method call on line 7 can fail. If it does, it will produce something called an `IOException` to document the failure. The compiler error is telling us that we need to change our code to address this potential problem.

Actually, we can get the same information from the HTML Java documentation. If we opened a browser to the Java document page for the `BufferedReader` class and browsed to the method readLine, this is what we'd see (Figure 1-1):

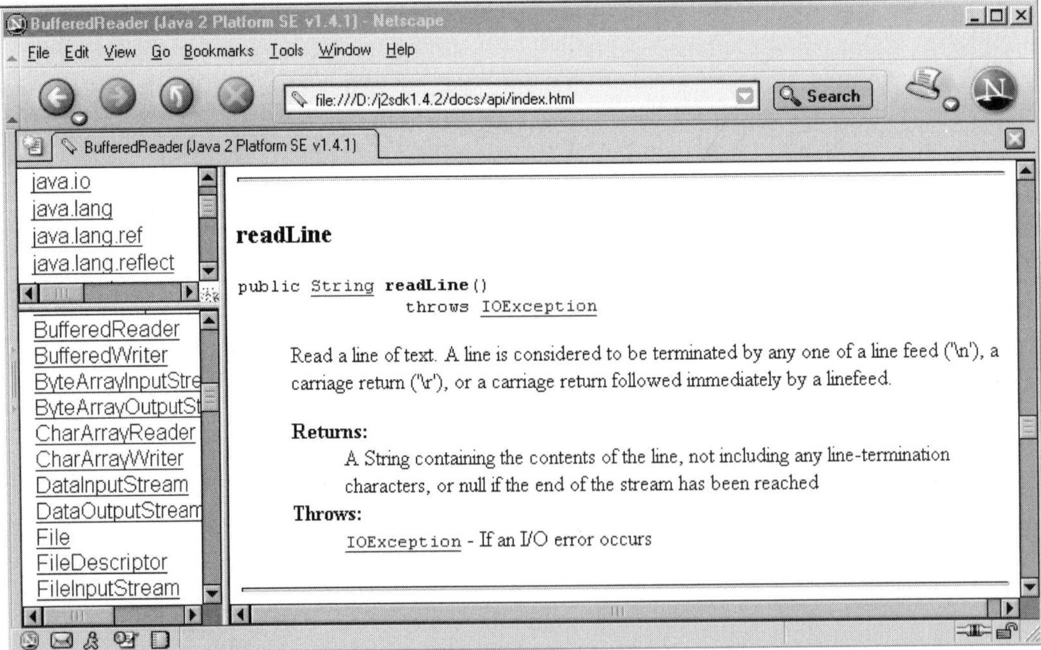

Figure 1-1

Java Documentation entry for the `BufferedReader` method `readLine`.

As you can see, Figure 1-1 also shows that the method can sometimes produce an `IOException`. So, knowing that we have a potential problem, what are our options? As the compiler indicated, we can "catch" or "declare" the `IOException`. Catching the exception means that we intercept the error when it's produced by the `readLine` method, which allows us to fix or document the problem. Declaring the exception means we indicate that our method can cause an `IOException`, so any code that calls the method will be notified that the exception may be produced. This suggests that we're not handling the exception, but passing it along to whatever code called our method in the first place.

If we decided to catch this exception, we'd need to add a special "handling code block" where we could receive and act on the `IOException`. If we chose that approach, our echo program would look like this:

```
1   import java.io.*;
2   public class EchoInputHandle{
3       public static void main(String [] args){
4           System.out.println("Enter text to echo");
5           InputStreamReader isr = new InputStreamReader(System.in);
6           BufferedReader inputReader = new BufferedReader(isr);
7           try{
8               String inputLine = inputReader.readLine();
9               System.out.println("READ: " + inputLine);
10          }
11          catch (IOException exc){
12              System.out.println("Exception encountered: " + exc);
13          }
14      }
15  }
```

The addition of the code blocks with the "try" and "catch" keywords (lines 7, 10, 11 and 13) indicate that we plan to attempt to read input. If we succeed, everything runs fine. If there's a problem while reading input, we will catch the problem (represented as an `IOException` object) and take some action in response. In this case, we print out the exception.

If we chose to declare the `IOException` rather than catch it, we would specifically indicate that our method (in this case, the main method) can fail, and specifically that it can produce an IOException. This choice would result in a program that looked like this:

```
1   import java.io.*;
2   public class EchoInputDeclare{
3       public static void main(String [] args) throws IOException{
4           System.out.println("Enter text to echo");
5           InputStreamReader isr = new InputStreamReader(System.in);
```

```
 6              BufferedReader inputReader = new BufferedReader(isr);
 7              String inputLine = inputReader.readLine();
 8              System.out.println("READ: " + inputLine);
 9          }
10      }
```

In this case, we don't take any action to recover from a possible failure of the `readLine` method. We document that an `IOException` can be produced in our own method, and that anyone who calls our method should be prepared to deal with this possible problem.

This chapter provides detail on the foundation concepts we've briefly illustrated in this example program. We describe exceptions, explain how they are produced, describe the base class hierarchy, and explain the rules behind catching and declaring exceptions.

Concept of Exceptions

One way to look at an exception is to think of it as a kind of message. Whether or not we're directly aware of the fact, most applications in Java and other programming languages use messages all the time. They're especially common in graphical user interfaces (GUIs), where they're often used as a way to send information about events— some kind of data relating to user interaction with the application, like clicking on a button or typing in a text box.

In a sense, exceptions are messages that communicate information about some problem in the system, a failure case, an action that hasn't gone as planned. They hold that information so that it can be passed from one part of an application to another.

Why should a programming language do this? Why not just handle failure cases when and where they occur in our code? There are a couple of reasons to use exceptions. Sometimes, we want to communicate error information within a system so that it's possible to have some kind of uniformity in dealing with problems. You often see this kind of strategy used in enterprise frameworks and distributed systems.

In other cases, you have several possible ways to fix a problem, but you don't know which one to use. In these cases, it's reasonable to delegate the task of handling the exception to the code that calls your method. The caller usually has more context about the source of the problem or the business operation that led to the exception, so it will often be better able to decide on the right way to recover. You frequently see this kind of strategy used in APIs or low-level utility classes.

In order for exceptions to be useful to communicate information in Java, they need to have a framework that is common to any kind of generic message system. Figure 1-2 shows the basic messaging framework and how it relates to exceptions:

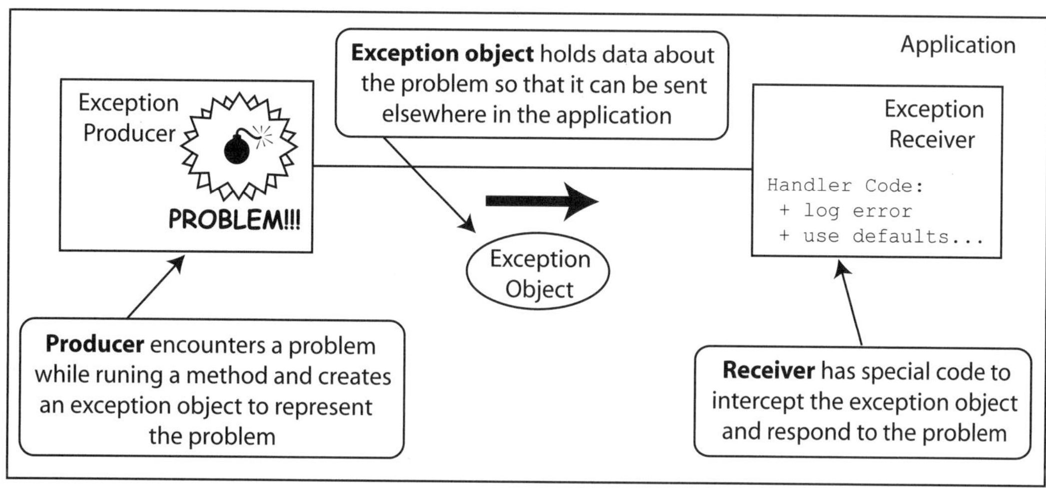

Figure 1–2
Generic Messaging Framework.

As you can see, the exception must be produced in some class or object within a running Java application. The exception object will be produced in a method of the "sender" when a failure case occurs. In some cases, the failure might represent some problem encountered in Java code; in others, it might actually correspond to an error in the JVM or the underlying hardware or operating system.

In the example at the beginning of this chapter, the exception "producer" is the `BufferedReader` used to read in a line of text.[2] The `IOException` object is created in the method `readLine` if the failure condition occurs. Of course, exceptions are presumably generated for a reason; there must be some original failure condition that causes the producer to create and propagate the exception object. The important thing to recognize is that the exception producer gives application code a chance to address problems by converting the root cause of an error into a message—a Java language exception object.

The exception itself represents the message—the "payload" of data passed from sender to receiver. First and foremost, exceptions convey useful information based on their class type. In many cases, the class of an exception object is all that's needed to identify the base cause of failure and correct a problem. In addition, exceptions also carry additional data as properties that may be useful. Data such as an exception message or a root cause of failure falls into this category.

---

2. Actually, the true point of failure is the read method of the `System.in` object. The read method is ultimately called to get keyboard input from the user, and it generates the `IOException` which is propagated by the `readLine` method.

A message needs to have a receiver in order for its information to do any good. This is especially important when dealing with exceptions. Without a receiver for an exception, it's impossible to recover from the underlying problem that produced the exception in the first place.

Where is the exception "receiver" in our example? In our own code. Take another look at the try-catch structure in the `EchoInputHandle` application. The catch block acts as the receiver for the exception that could potentially result when we read input. In our example, we document the problem in our catch block by printing out the exception in `String` form.

The Exception Class Hierarchy

Now that we have a general perspective on what exceptions are, let's take a closer look at their class hierarchy in Java. Figure 1-3 illustrates the classes that are central to how exceptions are categorized in Java.

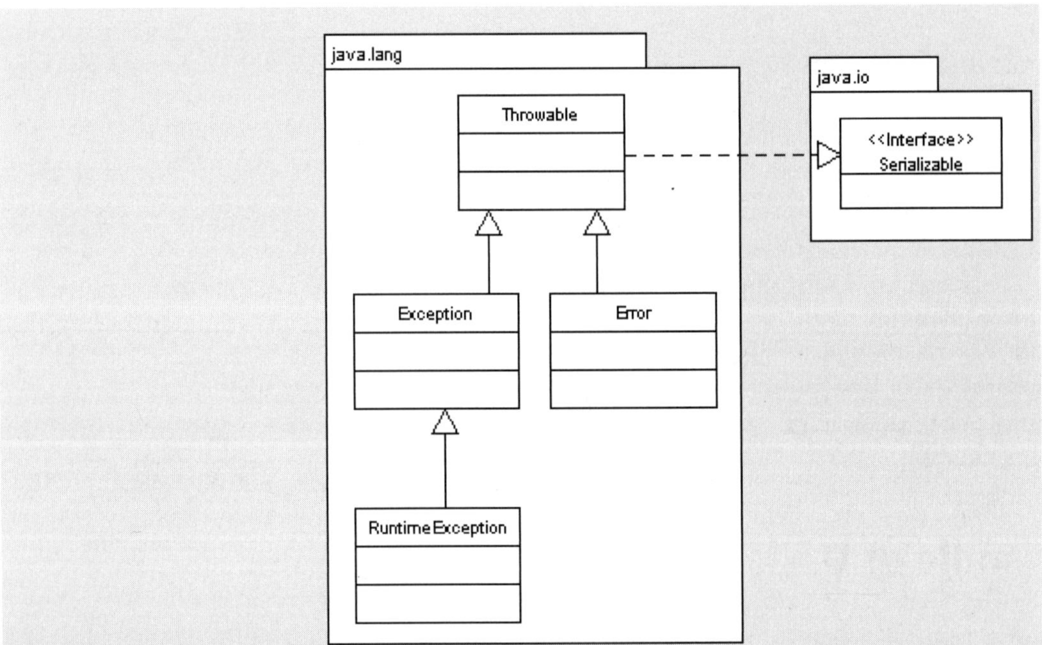

Figure 1-3
The Java exception class hierarchy.

Java categorizes all its exceptions according to a common ancestor, Throwable. Throwable specifies common traits of anything that represents a problem within code that can be transmitted through a Java application using the exception propagation mechanism.

Throwable has two important subclasses: Exception and Error. Both of these classes represent a major subcategory in Java exception handling. In other words, there are a number of subclasses for each branch that represent specific kinds of Exception and Error types.

Exceptions represent potentially recoverable, predictable problems within an application. According to the Java API documentation, they indicate conditions "that a reasonable application might want to catch." Generally speaking, most exceptions represent problems of mild to moderate severity.

What's more, an exception tends to be produced under specific circumstances—we can pinpoint an exception's location to a specific method or operation performed in our code. The `IOException` in our `EchoInput` class is an example of an exception. Remember that the exception could be produced when attempting to call the `readLine` method.

Errors, on the other hand, represent a more serious problem in a running application. The Java API documentation describes an error as "a subclass of Throwable that indicates serious problems that a reasonable application should not try to catch. Most such errors are abnormal conditions."

Many errors are not due to anything we as programmers have done in our code. Instead, they represent problems that have taken place in the JVM as it runs. The `OutOfMemoryError`, for instance, occurs when the JVM no longer has the memory resources it needs to continue operation.

In addition, the Exception class has an important subclass called RuntimeException. RuntimeException and its subclasses represent exceptions that can occur due to the "normal operation of the Java Virtual Machine." Examples that would result in a runtime exception would be trying to use a null-valued object reference (`NullPointerException`), dividing a number by zero (`ArithmeticException`), or overstepping the boundaries of an array (`ArrayIndexOutOfBoundsException`).

Handle or Declare Options for Exceptions

Recall that we had two choices when dealing with the possible failure scenario in our code example. In cases where we call a method that can potentially result in an exception, we can catch the exception or we can declare that our method throws the exception. This is commonly known as the "handle or declare" rule.

How does the Java compiler know that we need to follow the handle or declare rule in our code? Remember that the method signature for `readLine` in the `java.io.BufferedReader` class indicated that the method call could throw an `IOException`.

Handling Exceptions: `try`, `catch` and `finally`

If we opt to catch an exception, we must add an exception handler block to our code. There are potentially three parts to this Java structure, each marked with a Java keyword. The example below demonstrates a `try-catch-finally` code structure:

```
 1   import java.io.*;
 2   public class EchoInputTryCatchFinally{
 3       public static void main(String [] args){
 4           System.out.println("Enter text to echo");
 5           InputStreamReader isr = new InputStreamReader(System.in);
 6           BufferedReader inputReader = new BufferedReader(isr);
 7           try{
 8               String inputLine = inputReader.readLine();
 9               System.out.println("READ: " + inputLine);
10           }
11           catch (IOException exc){
12               System.out.println("Exception encountered: " + exc);
13           }
14           finally{
15               System.out.println("My job here is done.");
16           }
17       }
18   }
```

try blocks

When you enclose one or more statements within a `try` block, you flag those statements as potentially throwing exceptions. The compiler puts a special structure in place to evaluate all statements within the block with the explicit understanding that exceptions may be produced. So what happens when you have code in place to test for a possible problem? What can you do afterward? What choices do you have?

catch blocks

One option is to define a block of code to handle problems if they arise. This is the purpose of the `catch` block. The `catch` block acts as a receiver for exceptions produced in the `try` block. The basic rule is that once an exception is produced, execution halts within the `try` block and the JVM will look for a matching `catch` block.

Notice in the example above that the catch block at line 11 takes an argument of type `IOException`. The `catch` block performs an `instanceof` test on the exception: if the thrown exception is the same class or a subclass of `IOException`, the code block will be run. In a `try-catch` structure, it's possible to have multiple `catch` blocks. In that case, an exception will be handled by the first matching catch block.

`finally` blocks

Another possibility is to define a block of code that will always be run, regardless of the outcome of the attempt to run the code in the `try` block. The `finally` code block satisfies this requirement. Under every normal circumstance, the `finally` block will be run. It will be run whether or not the `try` block ran to completion, whether or not an exception was produced, and whether or not a generated exception was handled in a `catch` block.

Rules about `try-catch-finally`

1. A `try` block must always be followed by a `catch` or `finally` block. A `try` block may have both `catch` and `finally`, but must have at least one.
2. The order of the blocks is enforced: if your code uses both `catch` and `finally` blocks, the `catch` block must always follow the `try` block.
3. There can be no statements between a `try` block and its corresponding `catch` or `finally` blocks.
4. A `catch` block is associated with a specific exception class type.
5. A `try` block may have multiple `catch` blocks. In that case, the first matching block will be executed. This leads to a rule of thumb: always organize handling blocks from the most specific to the most general.
6. A `finally` block will always be executed to completion, except in the following situations:
   a. The JVM is prematurely terminated (`System.exit(int)` is called).
   b. An unhandled exception is thrown while in the `finally` block.
   c. The computer is unplugged, catches fire, or is stepped on by Godzilla.
7. You can nest `try-catch-finally` structures.
8. You can re-throw an exception in a `try-catch-finally` structure.

Declaring Exceptions

If you choose to declare an exception, you must add it at the end of your method's signature block, after the input section. An example of an exception declaring method is shown below:

```
1 public void errorProneMethod(int input) throws java.io.IOException{
2     // Code for the method, including one or more method
3     //   calls that may produce an IOException
4 }
```

When you do this, you ensure that the declared exception will be passed on to the caller of the method. Moreover, it tells the compiler that any callers of the method should also obey the handle or declare rule.

Rules about Declared Exceptions

1. You must declare any checked exceptions that your method can throw.
2. You may declare unchecked exceptions, but are not required to.
3. Calling methods must follow the handle or declare rule for any checked exceptions.

   If you override a method, you cannot declare different exceptions than the method you override. Any exceptions that you declare must be the same classes or subclasses of the ones declared in the overridden method.[3]

Checked and Unchecked Exceptions

There's a big distinction in the Java language between checked and unchecked exceptions. Any checked exception is verified by the compiler, which will enforce the handle or declare rule for any method declaring that it throws such an exception.

Unchecked exceptions, on the other hand, are *not* subject to the handle or declare rule. You are not bound to take any corrective action when such an exception is produced, and the compiler will not check to see if you have addressed such an exception. There are two main classes that define the unchecked exceptions: RuntimeException and Error.

The main reason that the Error subclasses are unchecked is that they can be produced at unpredictable moments of time. The `OutOfMemoryError` can occur anytime that a Java application runs out of memory; it's generally not due to a specific call made within the application, but to a problem within the JVM itself. Additionally, since Error classes generally represent severe problems that an application may not be able to address, these classes are treated as unchecked exceptions.

Why are the RuntimeException classes unchecked? Well, one reason is that runtime exceptions, being produced as a result of normal JVM operation, can happen virtually all the time. They're usually due to a specific operation (unlike Errors), but the operations tend to occur frequently in a Java application. Think about this: what would your code look like if you had to write exception handling code to check for null references every time you used an object? Your application would quickly turn into a single, *very* large `try-catch` block! For this reason, a runtime exception is free from compiler checks and the handle or declare rule.

Another reason that the RuntimeException classes are unchecked is that they're intended to represent problems that you should never *have* to handle as exceptions. You can handle a `NullPointerException` within a try-catch structure, but it's simpler and less expensive to test for a null value before using a reference. Likewise, you can check for a 0 value during division and avoid an `ArithmeticException`.

---

3. Of course, you don't have to declare any exceptions if your method doesn't throw any exceptions.

The API for Exceptions

Actually, all the behavior for Exceptions and Errors in Java is centralized in the Throwable class. The API for this class is provided in Table 1-1.

Table 1-1   **The API for java.lang.Throwable**

```
public class Throwable implements Serializable
```

Constructor Summary
```
Throwable()
```
   Constructs a new throwable with null as its detail message.
```
Throwable(String message)
```
   Constructs a new throwable with the specified detail message.
1.4 `Throwable(String message, Throwable cause)`
   Constructs a new throwable with the specified detail message
   and cause.
1.4 `Throwable(Throwable cause)`
   Constructs a new throwable with the specified cause and a
   detail message of (cause==null ? null : cause.toString())
   (which typically contains the class and detail message of cause).

Method Summary
```
Throwable fillInStackTrace()
```
   Fills in the execution stack trace.
1.4 `Throwable getCause()`
   Returns the cause of this throwable or null if the cause is
   nonexistent or unknown.
1.1 `String getLocalizedMessage()`
   Creates a localized description of this throwable.
```
String getMessage()
```
   Returns the detail message string of this throwable.
1.4 `StackTraceElement[] getStackTrace()`
   Provides programmatic access to the stack trace information
   printed by printStackTrace().
1.4 `Throwable initCause(Throwable cause)`
   Initializes the cause of this throwable to the specified value.
1.1 `void printStackTrace()`
   Prints this throwable and its backtrace to the standard error
   stream.
```
void printStackTrace(PrintStream s)
```
   Prints this throwable and its backtrace to the specified print
   stream.
```
void printStackTrace(PrintWriter s)
```
   Prints this throwable and its backtrace to the specified print
   writer.
1.4 `void setStackTrace(StackTraceElement[] stackTrace)`
   Sets the stack trace elements that will be returned by
   getStackTrace() and printed by printStackTrace() and related
   methods.
```
String toString()
```
   Returns a short description of this throwable.

Notice that the class definition of Throwable implements the Serializable interface; that means, of course, that every Exception and Error in the language implements Serializable as well.

What does this mean in practical terms? It means that it's possible to use a stream in Java to send an exception to some other destination. The other destination could be a file, providing the capability for persistent storage. It could also be another JVM, allowing an exception to be sent across a network connection in a distributed system. This is an important feature and it will be used (and useful) as we begin to discuss exceptions in distributed systems and APIs.

Basically, Throwable allows you to hold three pieces of information you can think of as properties: Message, Stack Trace and Cause. Table 1-2 provides summary information for each of these properties:

Table 1–2   **Properties for the Throwable Class**

Name	Class	Description	Read-Write
Message	String	Descriptive text providing detail about the exception.	R (can only be set in constructor)
Stack Trace	StackTraceElement [ ]	A record of all method calls leading to this.	R-W
Cause	Throwable	The root cause that produced this exception.	R-W (can only be set once)

Message provides a more detailed description about the problem associated with the exception, and can be set in two of the constructors. It can be retrieved with a call to the method `getMessage`.

Stack Trace provides a record of the call stack associated with an exception—the series of places in application code where this particular exception caused code execution to halt. We provide more detail on stack traces in Chapter 3, but for the time being, think of this property as providing a detailed record of every point in your application where execution stopped when this exception was thrown. Methods that are associated with the stack trace are `getStackTrace` and `setStackTrace`, as well as `fillInStackTrace` and all of the `printStackTrace` methods.[4]

The **Cause** property is a newly introduced feature in JDK1.4. Basically, it provides a way to designate another Throwable object as the "root cause" of the current exception. We examine the use of cause in Chapter 3. The `getCause` and `initCause` methods provide a way to set and get this property, and two of the constructors also allow for a value for cause to be set.

In addition to these three properties, the Throwable has the methods `toString` and `getLocalizedMessage`. The `toString` method is overridden from the Object

---

4. The `getStackTrace` and `setStackTrace` methods are a new addition in JDK1.4, as is the class StackTraceElement.

class, and returns the exception class name and, if not null the message string. The method `getLocalizedMessage` simply returns the value of the message string.

Summary

In this chapter, we got a general introduction to exceptions and their use in Java. The focus has been on explaining the basic nature of exceptions, how they work, what their general structure is, and what responsibilities we have for dealing with exceptions in our code.

Reasonable follow-on questions for this chapter are: How can we effectively use this knowledge in the code we write? What options do we have when working with exceptions? What are rules of thumb and best practices for dealing with exceptions in our applications? These topics are the subject of Chapter 2, Exeption Handling Techniques and Practices.

Exception Handling Techniques and Practices

Introduction

Chapter 1 provided a general introduction to exceptions. It described them, talked about their structure and capabilities, and explained how they worked in Java applications. Of course, knowing what exceptions *are* doesn't really help you deal with them in the code you write. To effectively work with exceptions in your applications, you need to know what a reasonable response would be for your code if something goes wrong. That means you need to have some idea of what you can do—what your options are and why you'd choose one alternative over another. You have to answer questions like:

- What kinds of options are open when you handle exceptions?
- What are best practices for exception handling?
- What things do you want to avoid in exception handling code?

We answer these questions in this chapter and discuss standard application responses for exceptions and weigh pros and cons of various choices. We also look at the best and worst practices when dealing with exceptions.

When to Handle and When to Declare

Based on Chapter 1, you know that you have two general choices when you call an exception-throwing method in your code: you can either handle or declare the exception. Although this chapter focuses on handling options, it's fair to start things off with a fundamental question:

When should we handle an exception, and when should we declare it?

A pretty simple question . . . if only there were a simple answer! Generally, you declare exceptions when you want or need to pass the information along—to send the error message to another part of the running system. Normally, you do that when you don't have the capability of dealing with the exception locally, or when the exception affects more of an application than a single method. If you wanted to sum all that up, a fairly good rule of thumb is:

Handle an exception when you can, declare an exception when you must.

Sounds good; now, what does it mean? Basically, a method should only pass an exception to its caller when it doesn't have the information, context or resources to deal with the exception on its own.

As an example, think about a client application that needs to contact a server. For the sake of argument, let's say the client has a utility class called ClientNetwork to manage the communication with the server. When the client wants to connect to a server, it calls the following method to establish a communication link:

```
public void connect(String server, int port) throws java.io.IOException
```

Notice that the connect method throws an `IOException`. If this method call fails, what should the client application do? Well, according to the previous principle, you should handle the exception in the code if you know how to deal with this failure. For instance, if you had a back-up server, you could try to connect to it instead.

There are lots of ways to deal with the problem in this example, though. If you couldn't connect to the server, you could:

- Wait for awhile, then try to connect again.
- Try to connect to the same server on a different port.
- Try to connect to a different server.
- Pop up a dialog box and ask the user what to do.
- Display a message saying that the connection attempt failed.

Since there are so many ways to respond to this problem, you might want to delegate the decision to the caller of the method. If you did this, you could declare the exception, and it would be passed to the method's caller. The caller would have the responsibility for choosing the right course of action. This example provides a good illustration of the challenges you sometimes face when trying to decide whether to handle an exception or declare it.

Advantages of handling the exception within the connect method are that the handler code is co-located with the source of the exception. That can be a big plus, especially for more complex applications. In the long run, it can make the code much easier to maintain. Additionally, callers of this method won't need to have handler code, which means that they'll be simpler.

Of course, there's also a downside to handling the exception locally; it makes the code of the connect method less generic, more tied to a specific client implementation. It also forces you to write a certain level of application logic into the method, which increases the method's complexity. For that reason, as well as for promoting greater application flexibility, you might want to declare the exception.

Standard Exception Handling Options

The previous example showed a few common choices for handling exceptions in code. Let's take a look at the "long list" now. Let's see what standard choices there are when dealing with exceptions in a catch block.

Normally, there are nine ways you can respond to most error conditions that you catch in a block of handler code:

1. Log the exception or relevant information.
2. Ask the user or application for input.
3. Use default values or alternate data.
4. Forward control to some other part of the application.
5. Convert the exception to another form.
6. Ignore the problem.
7. Retry the action.
8. Take an alternate or recovery action.
9. Prepare the system for shutdown.

Keep in mind that you're not limited to a single option in your handling code. In some cases, the best course of action may be to do a few of these things. For example, if a client fails to connect to a server, the proper course of action may be to log the problem and then to retry with a pause.

1. Log the exception and any relevant information

Logging is one of the most useful tools for effective exception handling. Logging acts in support of longer-term system development and maintenance, helping in such tasks as system recovery, testing and debugging. There are quite a few ways to manage logging in Java. Generally speaking, when you want to log information, you can use some or all of the following:

- The standard output or standard error streams.
- A custom logging class.
- The Java Logging API.

Logging to Standard Output and Standard Error

For simple logging tasks, you can use `System.out` or `System.err`, the standard output and standard error streams:

```
1   System.out.println("User error: replace user and continue");
2   System.err.println("Press any key. Go on. I dare ya.");
```

Since the System class lets you redirect either output to another destination through the method calls `System.setOut(PrintStream)` and `System.setErr(PrintStream)`, you can fairly easily adapt the streams for things like basic file output:

This kind of functionality tends to be useful for local logging in simple applications. It takes a fair amount of work to adapt these capabilities to a more complex application. Additionally, some kinds of Java code (especially server-side components, like Enterprise JavaBeans) don't allow you to direct output to these locations, since they are run within a JVM on a server. These provide direct logging methods within the API.

Logging through a Custom Logging Class

Some applications require greater flexibility or configurability of logging capability. In these cases, it may be appropriate to develop a logging resource for the system—a class that can receive application-wide calls and log them to a central location. Such a class is often implemented as a static resource or as a Singleton,[5] to ensure that it is universally available in a system without requiring other objects to hold its reference.

```
 1   import java.io.*;
 2   import java.util.*;
 3
 4   public class CustomLogger{
 5     private static final String DEFAULT_FILE = "exceptions.log";
 6     private static final String FILE_KEY = "application.logfile";
 7     private static CustomLogger instance = new CustomLogger();
 8     private PrintWriter outputLog;
 9     private CustomLogger(){
10       String filename = System.getProperty(FILE_KEY, DEFAULT_FILE);
11       try{
12         outputLog = new PrintWriter(new FileWriter(filename, true));
13       }
14       catch (IOException exc){
```

---

5. The Singleton design pattern ensures that there can only be a single instance of an object in a runtime environment.

```
15          exc.printStackTrace();
16      }
17    }
18    public static CustomLogger getInstance(){
19      return instance;
20    }
21    public void log(String message){
22        logMessage(new Date() + "    " + message);
23    }
24    public void log(Throwable error){
25      StringBuffer message = new StringBuffer(new Date() +
26        " ERROR: " + error.getClass().getName() +
27        System.getProperty("line.separator"));
28      message.append(error);
29      logMessage(message.toString());
30    }
31    private void logMessage(String message){
32        outputLog.println(message);
33        outputLog.flush();
34    }
35 }
```

Logging classes are useful in medium to larger applications, both local and distributed, and generally have a high degree of reusability. However, JDK1.4 introduced an alternative that is usually more flexible and easier to use than a custom logging class—the Logging API.

Logging with the Java Logging API

In JDK1.4, Sun introduced the Logging API to promote flexible, effective logging of errors, messages and notifications. You can usually perform simple logging tasks by using a few classes in the java.util.logging package. For example, if you want to send a message to standard output, the code would look like this:

```
3  Logger logException = Logger.getLogger("basic.exception.example");
4  logException.log(Level.WARNING, "Unable to find configuration file.");
```

Setting up a human-readable log file isn't much more complicated:

```
3  Logger logException = Logger.getLogger("exception.example");
4  try{
5    Handler fileOut = new FileHandler("exc.err", true);
6    fileOut.setFormatter(new SimpleFormatter());
7    logException.addHandler(fileOut);
8  }
```

```
 9  catch (IOException ex){
10    // In this example, ignore the possible IOException for the Handler
11  }
12  // Additional application code...
13  logException.log(Level.WARNING, "Exception generated");
```

Of course, these are basic demonstrations. It's possible to use the Logging API to develop extremely sophisticated frameworks for large-scale applications. Chapter 5 describes how to use the Logging API in greater detail.

2. Ask the user or application for input

For problems that occur "close" to an end user, it may be a good idea to let the user decide how to respond to a given problem in the application. Frequently, this is managed through a GUI that allows the user to make choices or input information. In simple failure scenarios, the user may only need to decide on an appropriate course of action, while more involved problems may involve adding additional or alternate information. Many GUIs use a dialog box to prompt the user for a decision. In AWT, you can use the java.awt.Dialog class, while the Swing API would typically use the javax.swing.JDialog or the javax.swing.JOptionPane. The code example below shows how you might ask a user for input if an error occurred:

```
 7  private void showConfigErrorMessage(){
 8    String msg = "Unable to load user preferences file: create new file?";
 9    String title = "Application Error";
10    int result = JOptionPane.showConfirmDialog(null, msg, title,
11      JOptionPane.YES_NO_OPTION, JOptionPane.WARNING_MESSAGE);
12    if (result == JOptionPane.YES_OPTION){
13      // User wants to create a config file; call createNewConfigFile()
14      createNewConfigFile();
15    }
16    else{
17      // User wants to use defaults; call loadDefaultSettings()
18      loadDefaultSettings();
19    }
20  }
```

In this example, the showConfigErrorMessage method would be called if there was an error while reading the user's configuration information. The dialog box allows the user to specify whether they want to create a new file, or rely on default settings. In more complex situations, a dialog might allow users to perform some advanced action, such as specifying the configuation file location on their computer.

You don't always have to prompt a user for input. In more general terms, a method can query another part of the application, prompting it to supply information about an appropriate follow-on action.

3. Use Defaults or Alternate Data Values

Even if you encounter an exception when performing an operation, you can often continue to work if you use alternate or default values. In the case of our communication example, a suitable alternative might be a different server, or a different port on the same server. It's generally a good idea to include defaults in an application if there are any standard values you can identify. At the simplest level, you can make these values constants (static final values) within the application:

```
1  private static final String ALTERNATE_HOST = "denver";
2  private static final int ALTERNATE_PORT = 5280;
```

A slightly more involved option is to allow defaults to be stored within a configuration file and loaded into an application during runtime. The Properties class was introduced in JDK1.2 to provide a fairly easy way to do this.

```
1  private static final String ALTERNATE_HOST = "denver";
2  private static final String HOST_KEY = "client.app.host";
3
4  public void sendData(String host, int port,
5     Serializable information, String propertyFile){
6    if (communication == null){
7      communication = new ClientNetwork();
8    }
9    try{
10      communication.connect(host, port);
11      communication.sendData(information);
12    }
13    catch (IOException exc){
14      Properties serverProps = new Properties();
15      try{
16        FileInputStream input = new FileInputStream(propertyFile);
17        serverProps.load(input);
18        String serverName = serverProps.getProperty(HOST_KEY,
19          ALTERNATE_HOST);
20        sendData(serverName, port, information);
21      }
22      catch (IOException exc2){
23        exc.printStackTrace();
24      }
```

```
25     }
26   }
```

4. Forward control to another part of the application

Of course, you could argue that declaring an exception represents the ultimate form of delegation—the problem no longer belongs to your method and someone else has to deal with it. In the example below, saveOrderInfo calls the method handleFileSaveError if there's some problem saving file information. The handler method deals with the file I/O problems, if any occur:

```
 7   private void saveOrderInfo(OrderInfo info){
 8     try{
 9       OrderService.getInstance().saveOrderInfoToFile(info);
10     }
11     catch (IOException exc){
12       // Problem writing to a file; call handling method
13       handleFileSaveError(info);
14     }
15   }
```

There are less extreme ways to transfer exception handling responsibility to another part of a system, though—ways that don't involve total delegation from the exception-producing method. You can potentially develop an exception handling class and use it to centralize handling code for your application.

5. Convert the exception to some other form

Sometimes it makes sense to convert an exception into some other form. You'll usually do this to change the exception into a form that's more meaningful to the application—that provides better context on exactly what went wrong. Since you can wrapper the original exception inside another (starting with JDK1.4), you lose none of the context or data of the original exception. The example below shows an alternate way of dealing with the IOException that could be produced in the saveOrderInfo method. In this case, the catch block converts the exception into an OrderException that it throws to the method caller:

```
 9   private void saveOrderInfo(OrderInfo info) throws OrderException{
10     try{
11       OrderService.getInstance().saveOrderInfoToFile(info);
12     }
13     catch (java.io.IOException exc){
14       throw new OrderException("File I/O error when saving OrderInfo", exc);
```

```
15     }
16   }
```

6. Ignore the problem

Recognize that this approach can lead to severe problems in code if overused, and almost every programmer tends to overuse the silent handling option. Having said this, there are a few cases where an exception doesn't have any impact at all on the rest of the application. An example is the exception that can be produced when you call the close method of an I/O Stream. The method can throw an `IOException` that represents a problem, but there's generally nothing your application can do about it apart from logging the occurrence. What's more, such an exception will likely have no impact on your code or the resource, since you were in the process of trying to close the I/O stream in the first place. The code sample below is part of an application that echos a plain text file to standard output. During cleanup, you would call the close method for your file stream. If there's an IOException during shutdown, this code ignores the problem:

```
15      // Declare member variable sourceFile in the class
16      private FileReader sourceFile;
17      // ...
18         try{
19            sourceFile.close();
20         }
21         catch (java.io.IOException exc){
22            // IOException while closing sourceFile
23            //  Ignore, since it occurs during application shutdown
24         }
```

In this case, the application would have already handled and logged standard exceptions while reading from the file. For the remaining error case, it might be reasonable to ignore the error.[6]

7. Retry the action

In some cases, the best course of action is to retry an operation, after a wait period . Consider trying to establish a connection to a server or a database. In some cases, you may get an exception because the server has too much traffic. If that's the case, it may be entirely appropriate to wait for a period of time, then try to connect again.

---

6. It would also be acceptable if you still wanted to log the IOException during shutdown,

```
21   try{
22      clientNetwork.connect("www.talk-about-tech.com", 5280);
23   }
24   catch (java.io.IOException exc){
25      try{
26         Thread.sleep(10000);
27      }
28      catch (InterruptedException exc2){}
29      try{
30         clientNetwork.connect("www.talk-about-tech.com", 5280);
31      }
32      catch (java.io.IOException exc2){
33         // Retry failed; try an alternate strategy
34      }
```

8. Take an alternate or recovery action

In some cases, it's possible to compensate for a problem. If you're unable to connect to a server, for instance, you could cache data locally, with the understanding that you'll send it to the server at some later point in time. Ideally, a recovery action would allow an application to function normally. The following code sample shows how you might do this:

```
5          try{
6             // Try to connect to server for data transfer
7             svr.connect("www.talk-about-tech.com", 5280);
8          }
9          catch (IOException exc){
10            // Unable to connect to server; prepare to cache data locally
11            enableFileCache();
12         }
```

9. Prepare the system for shutdown

If an exception truly represents a critical error for the application, you may need to take steps to prepare the system for a shutdown. Basically, this means you should ensure that the application will not cause other parts of a system to fail, and it won't leave data in an inconsistent state. There are a few things that you might need to do to ensure this:

- If there are any files open, close them.
- If you have any connection-based resources, close them normally.
- If you have information that should be persisted, ensure that it's saved.

- If you need to notify applications, clients or subsystems that your application is about to end, do so.

Do's and Don'ts for Exception Handling

The previous discussion presented the major options that we have for dealing with exceptions. Now, let's discuss some fundamental do's and don'ts for exception handling. Like most best practices, there are potentially some times when it makes sense to bend or break a few of these rules. In general, though, these rules represent tried and true development practices. When implemented consistently, they lead to more effective handler code.

Exception Handling Do's

Most of the exception handling best practices focus on identifying specific error states and taking appropriate handling action. Generally, most of these rules boil down to basic common sense. You can deduce some or all of these by thinking about what exceptions were intended to accomplish in the Java language.

1. Do handle exceptions if you can

As we said at the beginning of this chapter, handle exceptions when you can, declare them when you must. You declare an exception for a specific reason—you are unable, for some reason, to handle it in your own code. It is a poor (and lazy) practice to simply declare that an exception is thrown because you don't want to address it in your own code.

2. Do handle specific exceptions specifically

Part of the benefit offered by exceptions is the capability to provide different handling actions for different types of problems. The key to effective exception handling lies in identifying specific failure scenarios and developing specific response behaviors that address the scenarios. To make the most of exception handling capabilities, you need to create specific handler blocks for specific types of problems.

3. Do log exceptions that can affect the runtime of an application

At a minimum, you should always record the exceptions that can disturb the operation of an application in some permanent way. The ideal, of course, would be to solve the underlying problem that caused the exception in the first place. It's almost always a good idea, though, to log a potentially critical problem with the application no matter what your intended handling action might be. Frequently, this simple action may mean the difference between being easily able to trace down the root of a complex problem within your application, and having to spend hours (or days) looking for the underlying cause.

4. Do convert exceptions to a business context if it makes sense to represent them that way

There's little cost involved in creating an exception, so it's usually worthwhile to convert an application into a different form if you need to signal an application-specific problem. Ultimately, it makes your code much more maintainable if you represent the exception with a business-specific state. With the enhancements to exceptions in J2SE 1.4, you can wrapper the original exception, so you lose none of the original context for the problem.

Some would say that any time you're planning to propagate an exception to a different context (that is, to another technology layer), it's reasonable to convert an exception into a form that makes sense to that context.

Exception Handling Don'ts

It's usually a lot easier to identify things which it's best to avoid; poor practices are usually much easier to isolate than best practices!

1. Don't ignore an exception, unless you're certain that it really is harmless to the system

One of the most dangerous things you can do in an exception handling block is to "silently" handle an exception. Here's an example of a silent handler block:

```
1   try{
2      Class.forName("business.domain.Customer");
3   }
4   catch (ClassNotFoundException exc){}
```

Looks innocent enough, huh? It's easy to do this in your code—way too easy, actually. It's tempting for someone who's coding and in a hurry to simply write an empty handler block, intending to fill it in with recovery code "later." Of course, we all know that "later" never comes. There's a lot of Java code out there today that looks like this.

All right, what's so bad about doing this? Well, if the exception really, truly has absolutely, positively no effect on the rest of an application, it's OK. Of course, that's often not the case. If your exception actually can disrupt the state of your application, this code block ignores the problem; it effectively sweeps it under the carpet and pretends the problem never existed.

It's difficult to predict what the effect of doing this will be in an application. If you're lucky, it may just lead to quirky behavior in an application—for instance, values that don't stay set in an application, or a GUI that won't behave. In more serious cases, it may cause major problems in application behavior, and without an exception to record the original point of failure, the problems often manifest in strange, hard to troubleshoot ways, such as repeated `NullPointerExceptions`.

The good news is that you don't *ever* have to encounter this problem if you at least log the exceptions that you catch. Basically, you should always log at a minimum, unless you can offer a compelling reason why the exception will have absolutely no impact on the rest of your code. Some people go a bit further and say, "Don't ever ignore an exception. There's too much risk it will cause unforeseen problems that will surface later in your code."

2. Don't use a blanket exception handling block

Another dangerous handling practice is the blanket handler. The basic structure of this code block is shown below:

```
1   try{
2     //...
3   }
4   catch (Exception e){
5     //...
6   }
```

Using a blanket exception handling block presupposes one of two things:

1. There is only one type of problem that can occur in your code.
   This may be true but, even if it is, there should be no harm in catching the more specific form of the exception, rather than using blanket handling.
2. There is a single recovery action that will always be appropriate.
   This is almost never true. It's a fairly rare method that can uniformly respond to

any problem that occurs, and even if you do have a method that responds uniformly to exception conditions, it's a poor policy to follow.

Consider what would happen if you wrote this in your code. As long as your method continued to throw the set of exceptions that you had predicted, all would be well. If, however, the method throws exceptions you haven't predicted, then you have no way to see what action has been taken. You will only see the results of your exception handling indirectly, when your blanket handler performs its uniform task with the new exception type. If your code has no print or logging statements, you may not see the results at all.

Worse still, if your code changes, the blanket handler would continue to be active for all new categories of exception . . . and it would handle *all* the categories the same way. Generally, this is unwise when modifying code—you want to consider the impact of your changes to a method, and structure your exception handling blocks accordingly.

3. Don't convert from a more specific to a more general exception, unless you preserve the original context of the exception

It's a poor practice to convert a specific exception into a more general form. Normally, the effect of this is to remove the context produced when the exception was originally thrown, making it harder to deal with the exception when it's propagated elsewhere in the system. Consider the following example:

```
1   try{
2      // Error-prone code
3   }
4   catch (IOException e){
5      String msg = "If you didn't have a problem before, you do now!";
6      throw new Exception(msg);
7   }
```

Without information from the original exception, there's really no way for a handler block to determine what went wrong, and by extension how to correct a problem. Worse still, the method must now declare that it throws Exception, which is virtually no help to anyone reading Java documentation about the method. What kind of recovery action do you perform for a method that throws a generic Exception object? In general, if you plan to re-throw an exception, you want to do so for three reasons:

1. To re-throw the same exception, when you want to take some action and then propagate the exception for further handling.
2. To wrapper or re-throw a more specific kind of exception, to narrow the type of problem for subsequent handlers.

3. To wrapper or re-throw a different kind of exception, converted to a context that makes sense to handlers in a different application subsystem. This is typically done when converting to a business exception.

4. Don't handle an exception that you could avoid in the first place

There's really no need to handle some types of exceptions. In general, you should stay true to the idea that you should use exceptions for unavoidable error scenarios. Although it's possible to deal with an amazing variety of problems using exceptions, that doesn't necessarily mean you should. When you handle or declare an exception, it does affect the efficiency with which your code runs. This means that it's often cheaper to avoid certain types of problems rather than using exceptions to represent them.

Usually, runtime exceptions fit into this category. It's possible to deal with problems like null pointers or array indices without resorting to exception handling. One reason that many of the RuntimeException subclasses are unhandled is that there's no reason you really ever have to handle them in the first place. For example, you never have to work with a `NullPointerException` in your code, because the following simple line of test code can assure that a reference is never null:

```
1   if (ref != null){
2     // code to work with the "ref" object reference
3   }
```

Advanced Exception Handling Concepts

Introduction

The last two chapters covered foundation concepts of using exceptions. They focused on the "hows" and "whys" of exception handling, showed how exceptions work and discussed how to deal with them in code. In this chapter, we move on to more advanced topics. Specifically, we discuss:

- How to create and use custom exceptions.
- Exception support for chaining and localization.
- How exceptions can be used in abstract classes and interfaces.
- Exception requirements for overridden methods.
- How exception handling code is represented in bytecodes.
- The efficiency of exception handling operations in an application.

These topics represent the more unusual tools in your exception handling toolbox. You probably won't need to use them in every single project, but you'll be glad to have them around for the more challenging programming jobs.

Custom Exceptions

So far, we've talked about how to handle exceptions when they're produced by calling methods in Java APIs. If you need to, Java also lets you create and use custom exceptions—classes of your own used to represent errors. You heard right. You can create brand new exceptions and use them within your applications.

Now that you know you *can* do this, a reasonable question is why would you want to? Why would you define new exception categories? *Would you do this for fun? Profit? Fame? Excitement?* Normally, you create a custom exception to represent some type of error within your application—to give a new, distinct meaning to one or more problems that can occur within your code. You may do this to show similarities between errors that exist in several places throughout your code, to differentiate one or more errors from similar problems that could occur as your code runs, or to give special meaning to a group of errors within your application.

As an example, think about any kind of server. Its basic job is to handle communication with clients. If you used standard Java APIs (classes in the `java.io` and `java.net` packages, for instance) to write your server, you would create code that could throw `IOExceptions` in a number of places. You could throw `IOExceptions` when setting up the server, while waiting for a client connection, and when you get streams for communication. You could also throw `IOExceptions` during communication and when trying to break the connection. In short, virtually everything a server does could cause an `IOException`.

Do these `IOExceptions` all mean the same thing to the server? Probably not. Although they're all represented by the same type of exception, there could be a different business meaning (and different reporting and recovery actions) associated with each exception. You might associate one set of exceptions with problems in server configuration and startup, another set with the actual act of communication with a client, and a third set with the tasks associated with server shutdown. Custom exceptions give you the freedom to represent errors in a way that's meaningful to your application.

It's fairly easy to create and use a custom exception. There are three basic steps that you need to follow.

1. Define the exception class

You typically represent a custom exception by defining a new class.[7] In many cases, all you need to do is to create a subclass of an existing exception class:

```
1  public class CustomerExistsException extends Exception{
2    public CustomerExistsException(){}
3    public CustomerExistsException(String message){
4      super(message);
5    }
6  }
```

At a minimum, you need to subclass Throwable or one of its subclasses. Often, you'll also define one or more constructors to store information like an error message

---

7. It's also possible to use an existing exception class if it meets your needs. Developers often like to use a new exception class, because they can subsequently check for the exception in a `try-catch` block.

in the object, as shown in lines 2-4. When you subclass any exception, you automatically inherit some standard features from the Throwable class, such as:

1. Error message
2. Stack trace
3. Exception wrappering

Of course, if you want to add additional information to your exception, you can add variables and methods to the class:

```
1   public class CustomerExistsException extends Exception{
2     private String customerName;
3     public CustomerExistsException(){}
4     public CustomerExistsException(String message){
5       super(message);
6     }
7     public CustomerExistsException(String message, String customer){
8       super(message);
9       customerName = customer;
10    }
11    public String getCustomerName(){
12      return customerName;
13    }
14  }
```

This example shows how you might modify the class `CustomerExistsException` to provide support for an additional property in the exception. In this case, you could associate a String called `customerName` with the exception—the name of the customer for the record that caused the exception.

2. Declare that your error-producing method throws your custom exception

This step is actually the same as the "declare" part of the "handle or declare" rule. In order to use a custom exception, you must show classes that call your code that they need to plan for this new type of exception. You do this by declaring that one or more of your methods throws the exception:

```
public void insertCustomer(Customer c) throws CustomerExistsException{
    // The method stores customer information in the database.
    // If the customer data already exists, the method creates
    // and throws the CustomerExistsException.
}
```

3. Find the point(s) of failure in your error-producing method, create the exception and dispatch it using the keyword "throw"

The third and final step is to actually create the object and propagate it through the system. To do this, you need to know where your code will fail in the method. Depending on the circumstances, you may decide to use some or all of the following conditions to indicate a failure point in your code:

External Problems

- Exceptions produced in the application
- Failure codes returned by other methods

Internal Problems

- Inconsistent application state
- Problems with processing in the application

In our example, we encounter a failure scenario when we are unable to create a new customer. As a result, we create an exception to represent the problem and throw it. You can see an example in the following sample method:

```
1   public void insertCustomer(Customer c)
2     throws CustomerExistsException, SQLException {
3     String selectSql =
4       "SELECT * FROM Customer WHERE first_name=? AND last_name=?";
5     String insertSql = "INSERT INTO Customer VALUES(?, ?)";
6     try{
7       Connection conn = dbmsConnectionFactory.getConnection();
8       PreparedStatement selStmt = conn.prepareStatement(selectSql);
9       selectStmt.setString(1, c.getFirstName());
10      selectStmt.setString(2, c.getLastName());
11      ResultSet rs = selStmt.executeQuery();
12      if (rs.next()){
13        // In this case, the failure condition is produced if you
14        //  can already locate a metching record in the database.
15        throw new CustomerExistsException("Customer exists:" + c, c);
16      }
17      else{
18        PreparedStatement insStmt = conn.prepareStatement(insertSql);
19        insStmt.setString(1, c.getFirstName());
20        insStmt.setString(2, c.getLastName());
21        int status = insStmt.executeUpdate();
22      }
23    }
24    catch (SQLException exc){
```

```
25          Logger.log(exc);
26          throw exc;
27      }
28  }
```

The Java keyword "throw" propagates the new exception object to this method's caller. Once you've followed these three steps, you've created a custom exception. Any objects that call this method will subsequently have to follow the handle or declare rule—unless, of course, you subclassed an unchecked exception class, such as RuntimeException or Error.

This raises an interesting point: What should you subclass when defining a custom exception? Well, you *must* subclass something in the Throwable class hierarchy, or you won't be able to propagate the exception in your application. Beyond that, you should never subclass Throwable directly. The Throwable class is intended to provide a behavioral base to the two main categories of problem—Exception and Error—and you shouldn't define new branches of the inheritance tree. It's also generally not a good idea to directly subclass Error or any of its subclasses, since custom exceptions don't usually fit the criteria for errors: "Serious problems that a reasonable application should not try to catch."

That leaves the Exception class hierarchy. You should generally define a custom exception as a subclass of whichever exception class that is a more general category of your own failure state. In our example, the `ServerConnectionException` subclasses `java.io.IOException`, since it represents a more specialized kind of that exception.

There's some question about whether it's good coding practice to define an exception that subclasses something in the RuntimeException tree. By doing this, you effectively circumvent the exception mechanism, since classes do not have to explicitly handle your exception even if you declare it.[8]

This example shows how to create a basic custom exception. In many cases, it will easily meet your needs. The custom exception class, and perhaps the message, are often the only things you need to use the exception in your application. Sometimes you may need to support more advanced features, though—and that usually means more code, right? There are two properties that you might want to use in some exceptions—chaining and localization.

---

8. There are a few Java APIs that use RuntimeException subclasses as a way to provide a flexible programming model—to ensure that the API can be expanded without forcing a developer to write an additional exception handling framework.

Chaining Exceptions

Starting with JDK1.4, the Throwable class introduced support for something called "exception chaining." Basically, chaining lets you set up an association between two exceptions. Prior to version 1.4, a few Java APIs used chaining as a way to group a set of related exceptions together. In JDBC, for example, `SQLException` objects can be chained so that it's possible to send back a variable number of exceptions associated with problems during the same database operation.

While you can certainly use chaining to set up groups of related exceptions in your code, a more common application is to set up a "root cause" association between exceptions. Suppose you catch an exception in code and want to throw a custom exception in response to the error. Normally, you'd lose all information from the original exception, or you'd have additional work to store additional information. If you use chaining, you can associate the original exception with your custom exception as the root cause of your problem. If you need any of the original information, you can get it by simply calling the method `getCause( )` on your custom exception.

There are two ways that you can set up a root cause for an exception: you can pass it in as a constructor argument, or you can set it after object creation by calling the `initCause(Throwable)` method. You can only set the root cause once, though. Once a value for the root cause has been set, the exception object you've created will hold onto that same root cause for the rest of its life. Setting the root cause of an exception in the constructor tends to be the more common way to establish it. It's quick, efficient, and leads to more compact code:

```
1   try{
2     // Lots of risky I/O operations!
3   }
4   catch (java.io.IOException rootCause){
5     throw new ConnectionException(rootCause);
6   }
```

Of course, you'd need to write a version of the constructor that would take Throwable as an argument and pass it to the superclass, in order to chain exceptions this way:

```
1   public class ConnectionException extends java.io.IOException{
2     public ConnectionException(Throwable cause){
3       initCause(cause);
4     }
5   }
```

The main reason you'd use the `initCause` method would be to chain a custom exception class that predates JDK1.4. If you were working with a legacy exception class, it might not have a constructor that supported exception chaining. Since `initCause` is defined at the Throwable class level, any exception can call it, and be able to save an associated exception after its creation:

```
1  try{
2     // Even more risky I/O operations!
3  }
4  catch (java.io.IOException rootCause){
5     throw new LegacyException("Old exception").initCause(rootCause);
6  }
```

As mentioned, you can use root causes to "chain" a bunch of exceptions together. When you have a series of errors in your code, you can feed each one into the next as a root cause, and so create a group of exceptions that are related to each other. Naturally, the hope is that you don't have many cases where you'd have to do something like this, but it's a handy ability to have for more complex systems. When processing chained exceptions, you can write handler code to "walk" a set of chained exceptions and use the data that each object contains:

```
1   try{
2      troublesomeObject.riskyMethod();
3   }
4   catch (ChainedException exc){
5      System.out.println("We're in trouble now!!!");
6      Throwable currentException = exc;
7      do{
8         System.out.println(currentException.toString());
9         currentException = currentException.getCause();
10     }
11     while (currentException != null);
12  }
```

Exception Localization and Internationalization

Starting with JDK1.1, Throwable defined the method `getLocalizedMessage()`. By default, this method returns the same value as that provided by calling `getMessage()`—it returns whatever message is associated with the Throwable object. If you choose to, you can redefine this method in a custom Exception class to support locale-specific error messages. This lets you set up exceptions that support localization (l10n) and internationalization (i18n) in your code. These two characteristics allow applications to be used in multiple nations or regions without forcing everybody in that region to learn English (or even American).

In many cases, there isn't a great need to support exception localization. Normally, applications only provide for i18n of GUIs or standard program output. Even if an application supports different languages, many products use one standard language for the exceptions, since software products frequently have technical support provided by a development team that is located in a single country.

For those cases where you need to localize the text associated with an exception, `getLocalizedMessage()` can be overridden in a custom exception class, so that you can load locale-specific exception messages.

Java supports l10n and i18n with classes in the `java.util` and `java.text` packages.[9] The two key classes (from our point of view, at least) are java.util.ReourceBundle and java.util.Locale. The ResourceBundle class is a localizable wrapper around a collection. It allows you to store a series of key-value pairs, and to associate these values with a standard ISO-based locale naming scheme.[10] The locale mapping allows you to define a region based on a combination of language and location codes. For instance:

Code	Language and Region
de	German
en-CA	Canadian English
en-GB	British English
en-US	American English
fr	French

The Locale class is Java's way of representing these codes. A Locale object maps to a specific language or region, and allows you to look up the "standard" preferences for that region. The following steps show how to create a custom exception class that uses a localized message.

1. Create a ResourceBundle subclass to hold your message

The ResourceBundle class is used as a holding place for your resources. If you're interested in storing exception messages, an easy way to hold them is to subclass `ListRe-sourceBundle`, a class that provides a base for managing arrays of elements.

---

9. The subclasses of `java.text.Format` are the key classes in the `java.text` package. They allow a developer to obtain locale-specific formatting for values such as numbers, dates, weights and measures and language syntax.

10. Actually, there's a good chance you have seen this kind of scheme if you've done work on the Web—the specification for language identification in HTML (RFC1766) is based on ISO639 (language abbreviations) and ISO3166 (country codes).

```
1  import java.util.ListResourceBundle;
2  public class ExceptionResourceBundle extends ListResourceBundle{
3     private static final Object [][] contents = {
4       {"criticalException", "A critical exception has occurred"}
5     };
6     public Object [][] getContents(){ return contents; }
7  }
```

2. Subclass the ResourceBundle for your different region(s)

The first ResourceBundle class you create will act as a default, the class to hold the messages that are used any time that Java cannot find a resource that is more suitable for the locale. To support other languages or regions, all you need to do is to create subclasses of the original ResourceBundle. When you do this, you're free to override some or all of the messages for the new language or region.

```
1  public class ExceptionResourceBundle_fr extends ExceptionResourceBundle{
2     private static final Object [][] contents = {
3       {"criticalException", "Il y'a quelque chose qui cloche!"}
4     };
5     public Object [][] getContents(){ return contents; }
6  }
```

3. Create a custom exception class that overrides `getLocalizedMessage` and uses the ResourceBundle to retrieve its message

The key modification for the custom exception class is to override the `getLocalizedMessage` method. If you plan to use localization, you need to call the static method `getBundle` from your ResourceBundle subclass. This method retrieves the appropriate `ResourceBundle` object based on the localization information used as input. Once that's done, you can call the method `getString` to retrieve a specific String stored in the bundle.

```
1  import java.util.Locale;
2  import java.util.ResourceBundle;
3  public class LocalizedException extends Exception{
4     public static final String DEFAULT_MSG_KEY = "criticalException";
5     private String localeMessageKey = DEFAULT_MSG_KEY ;
6     private String languageCode;
7     private String countryCode;
8     public LocalizedException(String message){
9       super(message);
10      }
```

```
11    public LocalizedException(Throwable cause, String  messageKey){
12      super(cause);
13      if (isValidString(messageKey)){
14        localeMessageKey = messageKey;
15      }
16    }
17    public LocalizedException(String defaultMessage, Throwable cause,
      String messageKey){
18      super(defaultMessage, cause);
19      if (isValidString(messageKey)){
20        localeMessageKey = messageKey;
21      }
22    }
23    public LocalizedException(String defaultMessage, String messageKey,
      String language, String country){
24      super(defaultMessage);
25      if (isValidString(messageKey)){
26        localeMessageKey = messageKey;
27      }
28      if (isValidString(country)){
29        countryCode = country;
30      }
31      if (isValidString(language)){
32        languageCode = language;
33      }
34    }
35    public void setLocaleMessageKey(String messageKey){
36      if (isValidString(messageKey)){
37        localeMessageKey = messageKey;
38      }
39    }
40    public String getLocaleMessageKey(){
41      return localeMessageKey;
42    }
43    public String getLocalizedMessage(){
44      ResourceBundle rb = null;
45      Locale loc = getLocale();
46      rb = ResourceBundle.getBundle("ExceptionResourceBundle", loc);
47      return rb.getString(localeMessageKey);
48    }
49    private Locale getLocale(){
50      Locale locale = Locale.getDefault();
51      if ((languageCode != null) && (countryCode != null)){
52        locale = new Locale(languageCode, countryCode);
53      }
54      else if (languageCode != null){
55        locale = new Locale(languageCode);
56      }
57      return locale;
58    }
```

```
59    private boolean isValidString(String input){
60       return (input != null) && (!input.equals(""));
61    }
62  }
```

When you do this, you've provided support for localization in an exception class. If you plan to use a number of localizable exception objects, it's probably worthwhile to define a localizable class that you can subclass for all of them. The best feature of the ResourceBundle is that it automatically defaults to the closest language/region match when you use any of the `getBundle` methods to perform a lookup. If we throw the following three `LocalizedException` objects

```
throw new LocalizedException("", "criticalException", "fr", "FR");
throw new LocalizedException("", "criticalException", "jp", "");
throw new LocalizedException("Internal application error");
```

and subsequently call the `getLocalizedMessage()` method in a handler block, we potentially get three different values for the exception message. In the first case, the call to getBundle uses the Locale object for French, and defaults to the closest match, `ExceptionResourceBundle_fr`. If we had defined `ExceptionResourceBundle_fr_FR`, it would have been used instead. In the second case, there is no Japanese version of the class,[11] so the class used defaults to the base resource bundle class, `ExceptionResourceBundle`. In the third example, the locale used is whatever is defined as the default for the system where the exception is created. If the application were run on a machine configured for a French speaker, the class returned would be `ExceptionResourceBundle_fr`. Otherwise, the base class `ExceptionResourceBundle` would be used.

Subclassing

When you create a subclass, you're free to redefine methods from the parent class, modifying the code. This is called overriding a method, and it gives you the freedom to modify how a method does its job so that it suits your needs for the subclass.

There are some fairly strict rules you have to observe when you override a method. You have to duplicate the method signature: the method's name, inputs and output have to match. You can never make the overriding method more private than its parent's method. You also must ensure that your method does not throw any exceptions other than those that are declared in your parent's method. This means that when you override a method, you can throw the same exceptions, or a subset of the exceptions,

---

11. Unfortunately, the author only knows enough Japanese to order sushi.

that were originally declared. You can *never* throw different exceptions without first defining them in your parent class method.

Think about why it's so important to throw the same exceptions that were declared in the parent class. Whenever a class defines a method, the exceptions declared in that method (apart from unchecked exceptions) represent the total set of things that can go wrong. When you write code that calls the method, you plan for that set of possibilities, structuring your handler code accordingly.

You can substitute a subclass for its parent. After all, the child class is a subclass of its parent, so you could potentially replace the parent with the child class anywhere in your code. If you call the overridden method, it will be the child's version of that method that is run.

Now, if the child's method can only produce a subset of its parent's exceptions, that's absolutely fine. If a calling method has a handler block for an exception that can never be produced, that isn't really a problem. You need to write some handling code for a problem that can never occur, but won't lead to application failure.

On the other hand, if a child class *could* override its parent's method and throw a different set of exceptions,[12] you could generate exceptions for which the handler code would be totally unprepared. Fundamentally, you'd be able to propagate errors that would have no recovery in your code, possibly halting your application and defeating the entire purpose of exception handling. For this reason, it's important that the compiler strictly enforce the "same or fewer" exception rule in overridden methods.

Exception Declaration for Interfaces and Abstract Classes

It's fairly obvious what an exception means when it's declared for a method of a class, but what does it mean when an exception is declared for an abstract method, or an interface? Keep in mind, after all, that an abstract method only provides a signature for a method; it can't actually define any code. And an interface is basically composed of nothing but abstract methods.

In cases like these, what does it mean to say that a specific exception can be thrown? Whenever you define an exception for such a method, you're basically setting an expectation of what could be expected to go wrong when the method is eventually implemented.

```
1   public interface CommunicationServer{
2     public void processClient() throws ServerConnectionException;
3     public void listen();
4   }
```

---

12. This could *never* happen in Java—it would result in a compiler error. For the sake of argument, let's imagine that it could be done, to see what the result would be.

If you create a class that implements `CommunicationServer`, you'll write your own version of the `processClient` method. Because the interface declares that the method can throw a `ServerConnectionException`, you're free to throw that exception in your code if you need to. More importantly, you know that if you decide to throw the exception, any other class that's using the `CommunicationServer` interface will have to handle or declare this exception. Even if you write an implementation of `CommunicationServer` many months after the interface was created, you can be certain that the classes using the interface are prepared to address the possible `ServerConnectionException`.

```
1   public class ServerManager{
2     private CommunicationServer commoServer = new CommunicationServerImpl();
3     private boolean shutdown;
4     public void handlerCycle(){
5       while (!shutdown){
6         commoServer.listen();
7         try{
8           commoServer.processClient();
9         }
10        catch (ServerConnectionException exc){
11          Logger.log("Client connection error", exc);
12        }
13      }
14    }
15  }
```

Exception Stack Traces

In object-oriented programming, most complex actions are performed as a series of method calls. This is a natural consequence of two programming goals: the desire to define reusable units of code, and the desire to progressively break complicated tasks into smaller, easier to manage subtasks. Combine this practice with the tendency to define a number of objects that work together to accomplish a programming task, and you have a programming model where a number of objects communicate with each other through a series of method calls to perform their work. It's normal for a chain of method calls, commonly referred to as a "call stack," to occur as an object-oriented application runs.

For a demonstration of this, think about a business task that a server might perform. For instance, how would the server handle a response to add a new customer record to a database? Although it would be possible for you to write the code for this entire behavior in a single method, the result would be *extremely* hard to understand, difficult to maintain, and probably impossible to reuse. Instead, it would be preferable to divide the work up among several objects. A Server would manage the overall server lifecycle, a Communication Delegate would handle communication with a client, a Business Delegate would interpret and act on client requests, a Customer Handler would hold the methods to handle any Customer business actions, and a `DataAccessObject` would communicate with the database. Table 3-1 shows a series of calls within a server as it processes a client's request to create a new customer account. The entries on the left show which class contains the method, and the ones on the right show the method call that has been made.

Table 3–1   **Call stack to create a new customer account**

Class	Method
Server	main
Server	configure
Server	connect
CommunicationDelegate	run
CommunicationWorkThread	run
CommunicationWorkThread	readInput
ShoppingService	processInput
CustomerAccountService	createCustomer
CustomerAccountService	isCustomerValid
CustomerAccountService	createAccount
AccountDAO	insertCustomer
AccountDAO	insertAddress
AccountDAO	insertPaymentInfo
ShoppingService	processOutput
CommunicationWorkThread	writeOutput

In this example, you can clearly see the series of method calls, as the main method runs the handler method, then receives a request from a client, then identifies it as a request to create a new customer. What happens when an exception occurs as a method in the call stack, such `insertCustomer`, is run? If the exception were handled in a `try-catch-finally` block of that method, nothing would happen. The `insertCustomer` method would handle the exception normally, and the code would continue to run.

If `insertCustomer` declared the exception, the situation would be quite a bit different. In that case, the exception would cause `insertCustomer` to stop execution, and the exception would be propagated to the method's caller, the method `createCustomer`. That method would have the same choice—to handle or declare the exception—and if it declared the exception, that method would halt, and the exception would be propagated further up the call stack.

As developers, we have the freedom to handle an exception at any point within a call stack that best suits our needs for an application. We can handle a problem in the method that produces an exception, or we can handle it at some remote point in the call sequence.

As an exception is propagated upward in a call chain,[13] it maintains a structure called a **"stack trace."** A stack trace is a record of every method that failed to handle the exception, as well as the line in code where the problem occurred. When an exception is propagated to the caller of a method, it adds a line to the stack trace indicating the failure point in that method. In the previous example, a stack trace might look something like this:

```
SQL Exception: The statement was aborted because it would have caused
   a duplicate key value in a unique or primary key constraint defined
   on 'CUSTOMER(LAST_NAME)'.
   at c8e.p.i._f1(Unknown Source)
   at c8e.p.q._b84(Unknown Source)
   at c8e.p.q.handleException(Unknown Source)
   at c8e.p.n.handleException(Unknown Source)
   at c8e.p.p.handleException(Unknown Source)
   at c8e.p.j.executeStatement(Unknown Source)
   at c8e.p.g.execute(Unknown Source)
   at c8e.p.g.executeUpdate(Unknown Source)
   at
RmiJdbc.RJPreparedStatementServer.executeUpdate(RJPreparedStatementServer.java:
74)
   at sun.reflect.NativeMethodAccessorImpl.invoke0(Native Method)
   at
sun.reflect.NativeMethodAccessorImpl.invoke(NativeMethodAccessorImpl.java:39)
   at
sun.reflect.DelegatingMethodAccessorImpl.invoke(DelegatingMethodAccessorImpl.ja
va:25)
   at java.lang.reflect.Method.invoke(Method.java:324)
   at sun.rmi.server.UnicastServerRef.dispatch(UnicastServerRef.java:261)
   at sun.rmi.transport.Transport$1.run(Transport.java:148)
   at java.security.AccessController.doPrivileged(Native Method)
   at sun.rmi.transport.Transport.serviceCall(Transport.java:144)
   at sun.rmi.transport.tcp.TCPTransport.handleMessages(TCPTransport.java:460)
   at
sun.rmi.transport.tcp.TCPTransport$ConnectionHandler.run(TCPTransport.java:701)
   at java.lang.Thread.run(Thread.java:534)
   at
sun.rmi.transport.StreamRemoteCall.exceptionReceivedFromServer(StreamRemoteCall
.java:247)
```

---

13. In this case, "up" means toward the method that was originally used to start the application.

```
    at sun.rmi.transport.StreamRemoteCall.executeCall(StreamRemoteCall.java:223)
    at sun.rmi.server.UnicastRef.invoke(UnicastRef.java:133)
    at RmiJdbc.RJPreparedStatementServer_Stub.executeUpdate(Unknown Source)
    at RmiJdbc.RJPreparedStatement.executeUpdate(RJPreparedStatement.java:80)
    at AccountDAO.insertCustomer(AccountDAO.java:69)
    at CustomerAccountService.createAccount(CustomerAccountService.java:13)
    at CustomerAccountService.createCustomer(CustomerAccountService.java:6)
    at ShoppingService.processInput(ShoppingService.java:6)
    at CommunicationWorkThread.run(CommunicationWorkThread.java:21)
    at java.lang.Thread.run(Thread.java:534)
```

Looks a little imposing, doesn't it? As promised, it holds a record of every point within the application where the execution stopped. Once you know the basic format of an exception stack trace, it's a lot easier to understand. The first few lines document the exception that was thrown—specifically, they show the exception class type and the detail message of the exception. Next, the stack trace documents the stopping points in your code. Each line in the stack trace shows a place where execution has halted in a called method. It indicates the class, the method name within the class, and the line in the file that corresponds to the failure point.[14] As the lines progress, they work from the innermost called method "upward" toward the starting point of the business action. In this case, the business action was performed by a thread, so the last entry is the thread's run method.

In a complex enterprise application, there can be many, many levels in a call stack. In this example, the business code in the example communicates with a database using a JDBC driver—an adapter that manages communications with the DBMS. Most of the entries in the call stack correspond to the internal code of the database driver. It isn't until you look at the bottom of the call stack that you can see the failure point in the application code: the `insertCustomer` method is the first method from the application code that has an error.

If you know how to interpret the information, a stack trace can be an exceptionally valuable tool when debugging code. For instance, if you look closely at the output from the earlier example, you can learn a few things about the problem. First, the exception was thrown because a database insert would have resulted in a duplicate primary key in the database—specifically, with the `last_name` field defined in the Customer table. Second, the point of origin in the application code was in the `insertCustomer` method. If you put these two facts together, you might think that the exception was thrown because of the customer entry for the account already existed.[15] You could subsequently develop a test for the theory and correct the problem in your code.

---

14. In some cases, the exact position within the source code may not be available; in that case, you will see the indicator Unknown Source if debug information is not available for the class file, or Native Method if the call corresponds to a method in native code.
15. And you would be right!

Low-Level Exception Handling

What exactly goes on in Java when you use exceptions? When you handle or declare an exception in your code, exactly what are you doing? To answer this question, you really have to look at the bytecodes that are produced when you compile a Java class. Java provides a utility called `javap`—a general purpose tool to *profile decompiled* class files—which can also interpret bytecodes when it's run with the correct switch. To get a good idea of what different exception handling choices mean in bytecode, we need to compare between three scenarios:

- A situation where no exception is produced
- A situation where an exception is declared
- A situation where an exception is handled

To ensure that we can see the differences in a uniform code example, we'll use an unchecked exception to demonstrate. This simple example takes an argument from standard input and tries to convert it into an integer by using the `Integer.parseInt` method. If you pass any non-integer value as an argument, the method will produce a `NumberFormatException`, which is a type of RuntimeException.

```
1 public class BytecodeExample{
2   public static void main(String [] args){
3     BytecodeExample app = new BytecodeExample();
4     if (args.length > 0){
5       app.readIntTryCatch(args[0]);
6       app.readIntDeclare(args[0]);
7         app.readInt(args[0]);
8     }
9   }
10
11  public int readInt(String input){
12    int returnValue = 0;
13    returnValue = Integer.parseInt(input);
14    return returnValue;
15  }
16
17  public int readIntTryCatch(String input){
18    int returnValue = 0;
19    try{
20      returnValue = Integer.parseInt(input);
21    }
22    catch(NumberFormatException exc){}
23    return returnValue;
24  }
25
```

```
26   public int readIntDeclare(String input) throws NumberFormatException{
27      int returnValue = 0;
28      returnValue = Integer.parseInt(input);
29      return returnValue;
30   }
31 }
```

After compiling this code, you can produce a text file with the interpreted byte-codes by executing the following command:

```
javap -c -verbose BytecodeExample > bytecodes.txt
```

This command runs the `javap` utility on `BytecodeExample.class` with byte-codes interpretation (`-c` switch) providing verbose output (`-verbose switch`) and saving the output into the file `bytecodes.txt`. When you run this command, you'll see the following result:

```
Compiled from BytecodeExample.java
public class BytecodeExample extends java.lang.Object {
    public BytecodeExample();
    /* Stack=1, Locals=1, Args_size=1 */
    public static void main(java.lang.String[]);
    /* Stack=3, Locals=2, Args_size=1 */
    public int readInt(java.lang.String);
    /* Stack=1, Locals=3, Args_size=2 */
    public int readIntTryCatch(java.lang.String);
    /* Stack=1, Locals=4, Args_size=2 */
    public int readIntDeclare(java.lang.String) throws
java.lang.NumberFormatException;
    /* Stack=1, Locals=3, Args_size=2 */
}


Method int readInt(java.lang.String)
    0 iconst_0
    1 istore_2
    2 aload_1
    3 invokestatic #7 <Method int parseInt(java.lang.String)>
    6 istore_2
    7 iload_2
    8 ireturn


Method int readIntTryCatch(java.lang.String)
    0 iconst_0
    1 istore_2
    2 aload_1
    3 invokestatic #7 <Method int parseInt(java.lang.String)>
    6 istore_2
```

```
   7 goto 14
  10 astore_3
  11 goto 14
  14 iload_2
  15 ireturn
Exception table:
   from   to   target type
      2    7     10    <Class java.lang.NumberFormatException>

Method int readIntDeclare(java.lang.String)
   0 iconst_0
   1 istore_2
   2 aload_1
   3 invokestatic #7 <Method int parseInt(java.lang.String)>
   6 istore_2
   7 iload_2
   8 ireturn
```

If you look at the listing, you'll notice a few interesting differences for the methods that work directly with the `NumberFormatException`. The `readIntDeclare` method has the same bytecodes produced as the standard `readInt` method, but the exception throw clause is declared in the method lookup table for the class. The handle example, `readIntTryCatch`, actually has several additional bytecode instructions and an "exception table" associated with the method. The exception table controls code routing if the exception is produced. In this case, the code silently handles the exception, so the method basically behaves the same as the other two methods.

By this time, I'll guarantee that a few people are wondering about how this affects performance. You've seen that handling or declaring an exception really **does** result in different bytecodes—so what's the cost in terms of runtime efficiency? It's a lot like taking a date to an expensive restaurant where they don't put the prices on the menu. At some point during the meal, you're bound to think, "This is all very nice, but what will it cost me?"

To get a general idea of the relative cost of using exceptions, we can run our `Byte-codeExample` using a homemade profiler. The profiler doesn't have to be very complicated—it just needs to be able to keep track of how long it takes to execute a method. The source code for a sample profiler is shown below:

```
1  import java.util.Date;
2  import java.text.SimpleDateFormat;
3  public class Profile{
4    private Runtime runtime;
5    private long startTime, stopTime, timeElapsed;
6    private SimpleDateFormat sdf = new SimpleDateFormat("mm:ss.SSSS");
```

```java
7     public Profile(){
8       runtime = Runtime.getRuntime();
9     }
10    public void startTimer(){
11      startTime = System.currentTimeMillis();
12    }
13    public void stopTimer(){
14      stopTime = System.currentTimeMillis();
15      timeElapsed += stopTime - startTime;
16    }
17    public void clearTimer(){
18      startTime = stopTime = timeElapsed = 0;
19    }
20    public long getStartTimeMillis(){
21      return startTime;
22    }
23    public long getStopTimeMillis(){
24      return stopTime;
25    }
26    public long getStartStopTimeMillis(){
27      return stopTime - startTime;
28    }
29    public long getTimeElapsedMillis(){
30      return timeElapsed;
31    }
32    public Date getStartTime(){
33      return new Date(startTime);
34    }
35    public Date getStopTime(){
36      return new Date(stopTime);
37    }
38    public Date getStartStopTime(){
39      return new Date(stopTime - startTime);
40    }
41    public Date getTimeElapsed(){
42      return new Date(stopTime);
43    }
44    public String getTimeElapsedAsString(){
45      StringBuffer buffer = new StringBuffer();
46      return sdf.format(new Date(timeElapsed));
47    }
48    public String getStartStopTimeAsString(){
49      StringBuffer buffer = new StringBuffer();
50      return sdf.format(new Date(stopTime - startTime));
51    }
```

```
52   }
```

To get a general idea of the relative cost of each exception handling option, we ran a profiler with each option 1,000,000 times, which produced the following results:

```
1,000,000 iterations, no exception produced
    Handle:         0.433 s total, 0.433 s/method call
    Declare:        0.411 s total, 0.411 s/method call
    No Handling:    0.414 s total, 0.414 s/method call

1,000,000 iterations, NumberFormatException produced
    Handle:         10.93 s total, 10.93 s/method call
    Declare:        10.52 s total, 10.52 s/method call
    No Handling:    10.49 s total, 10.49 s/method call
```

Based on the test results,[16] you can see that there really isn't a substantial performance difference between the different options. Even in situations where you execute the same code many, many times (keep in mind that the profiler ran the examples 1,000,000 times) there isn't a major performance gap between the three exception handling options. Naturally, you see a gap in application performance when you compare a situation where an exception is produced to one where no exception is generated, but that's to be expected.

The good news about all of this is that it essentially leaves you free to follow best programming practices; you aren't faced with unpleasant trade-offs between effective coding and performance. This means that our basic rule for working with exceptions can still stand. When working with exception-producing code,[17] the order of preference could still be the following:

1. Avoid throwing an exception if you can.
2. Handle an exception if you can.
3. Declare an exception if you must.

---

16. For detailed information about the test as well as complete code, refer to Appendix A.
17. Of course, this may not be the case when the exception has to be propagated across a network!

chapter 4

Exceptions and Threading

Introduction

No introduction to exception handling would be complete without a discussion of threading. Threading has been an important capability in Java since the language was first created. It allows an application to define multiple paths of action that can be performed, or appear to be performed, in parallel. Threading offers several important benefits to applications. First and foremost, it allows you to manage independent tasks unrestrained within a program. Beyond that, threading allows you to share memory in a running application, and can more efficiently use the available CPU resources within a computer.

Of course, in programming, every benefit has an associated price.[18] Threading allows you to share data, but that also means you have a much greater risk of data corruption. There are a host of problems associated with data collision and corruption, and you must deal with many of these by careful programming. Less well-recognized is the fact that you must carefully manage exceptions and exception handling within a multithreaded application. If you neglect problems in a single-threaded program, they will usually cause your application to crash. If you neglect exceptions in multithreaded code, your application may continue to run and problems may spread from thread to thread.

Before we get into a detailed discussion about how exception handling works in multithreaded systems, it's worthwhile to ask a more basic question:

When do you write threaded code?

A simple answer, and often the correct one, is "Only when you really have to." Under most circumstances, if you're writing code for production systems, you need to direct

---

18. This may come as a complete shock, but years of experience have taught me that there are **no** "silver bullet" solutions. Absolutely everything in software development has an associated price.

your development resources to solving the business problem. Frankly, cost and time to market are generally the most crucial considerations. Because of this, it's often not practical to develop a threaded business system unless it's actually required for the kind of problem you're trying to solve. The complexity of threaded systems, and the potential issues that you have to address because of threading, make it impractical to develop threaded code in many standard systems.[19]

If threading isn't used for most types of applications, which ones *are* appropriate for threading? The most obvious ones are servers. It's hard to imagine a commercially useful server that can't manage multiple client requests. Think about it—would you ever want to use a Web server that could only handle a single client request at a time? Other, more general, applications where threading is sometimes needed include:

- Systems that are based on producer-consumer models.

  Applications that produce data which must subsequently be processed, such as order processing systems, often require threading to do their work effectively. In these types of systems, the processing system usually has a variable or unpredictable workload which is most effectively serviced by threading.

  In some cases, some of an application's work may be performed by other programs. For example, one of the responsibilities of a Java application may be to periodically examine a directory on a system for files and "process" them in some way. If you don't want the rest of the system to halt while this task is being performed, you normally must create threads to perform the processing.

- Systems that naturally block when performing a task.

  Even standard systems may require limited threading so that they don't appear to "freeze" while waiting for an action to be performed.

  An example of such an application is one that has to pause to accept user input, or one that has to wait to read data from a network connection. One way to manage this activity is to delegate the task of waiting to an independent thread, so the rest of the application can run normally.

---

19. It's no accident that a lot of modern distributed protocols, and most of the distributed frameworks, handle threading for you. Multithreaded code tends to be so challenging to implement and difficult to perfect, that it's a prime "value add" for any kind of distributed API.

Exceptions in Multithreaded Systems

In a multithreaded Java application, every thread apart from the main application thread must fulfill two main requirements:

1. It must be managed by a Thread object that is used to keep track of the thread of execution in the application.
2. It must be associated with a class that implements the Runnable interface that represents the code to be run.

You can implement Runnable in two ways: by subclassing Thread, or by defining another class that implements Runnable. Regardless of the approach you choose, you must define the threaded code you intend to run in the run method. The signature of the method looks like this:

```
public void run()
```

Based on the method's signature, you can see that it's impossible to throw any checked exceptions from an independent thread. That narrows down the options in the code you write: you **must** handle all checked exceptions within the run method. That makes life a little harder for you, since you have to handle a larger set of exceptions within your code. At the same time, there are some benefits to knowing that Threads will never throw checked exceptions to the rest of an application; you can be certain that an exception won't shut down your currently running thread.

Of course, unchecked exceptions aren't subject to the handle or declare rule. What happens when a Thread's run method throws an unchecked exception? If the exception is a RuntimeException or Error, the Thread responsible for that specific path of execution will terminate. In other words, that thread will no longer be run within the application. Of course, if there are any other threads that are active, they can continue to run as though no problem had occurred.

Depending on your perspective, it's either very good or very bad that you don't stop the entire application when you throw an unchecked exception in a thread. On one hand, a problem within a single thread does not doom the entire application to failure. On the other, if you are not careful about how you handle exceptions, it's easy for a problem with a thread to have a "ripple through" effect, causing follow-on problems in other threads.

How do you respond to exceptions in a multithreaded system? If a catastrophic problem occurs in your application, you'll want to take steps to shut everything down. Although you could do this with a "brute force" solution (such as using `System.exit`), you often need to independently shut down all other threads to ensure that data isn't lost or corrupted.

If an exception only results in the termination of a single thread, you'll want to take steps to ensure that the remaining threads still have the resources they require to run normally. This may mean creating additional objects, or updating references used by the remaining threads in the system.

When you think about this, it basically means that you need to think carefully about how you handle exceptions, even unchecked exceptions, within code. In other words, multithreading requires you to be even more careful about how you respond to problems within code. Ideally, multithreaded systems should throw no exceptions, checked or unchecked, if the threads are interdependent. The risk of threaded activity causing corruption is too great.

A consequence of multithreading is that each thread has its own path of execution, and so has its own stack trace. If you need to examine the stack trace of a Thread, you can print it out to the standard error stream (`System.err`) by calling the method `dumpStack()` in the Thread class. If you do this when a thread is running normally (i.e., when no exceptions have been produced), the result is a print out of the Thread's current position in its call stack. If an exception was generated, the method prints a standard exception stack trace.

Exceptions in Synchronized Code Blocks

In threaded code, you sometimes need to protect a block so that only a single thread can execute a series of operations at a time. You do this by marking your method or code block with the keyword `synchronized`. The keyword makes the execution of the method or block contingent on obtaining a "lock flag" for the object referenced by the synchronized block. Basically, it ensures that only a single thread will be able to execute the method or code block at a time.

A natural question to ask is what exactly happens when a thread throws an exception as it executes synchronized code? First, a note of reassurance. There is no danger that throwing an exception from a synchronized block will endanger the lock flag. Java ensures that even if a thread leaves a synchronized block by throwing an exception, the lock flag will be returned to its object or class.

You may have another problem, though—an exception can cause you to prematurely exit your synchronized code block. If you exit a synchronized block early, there's a risk that you will compromise the state of the resource you were trying to protect. This means that you'll either want to avoid throwing an exception while in a synchronized code block, or ensure that your resource will remain in a stable state even if an exception is thrown.

A good practice is to ensure that you never throw exceptions that are propagated outside of a synchronized block—at least, unless you are certain that there will be no danger to the synchronized block. To get a perspective on the problem, look at the following code example:

```java
1    import java.util.*;
2    import java.util.logging.*;
3
4    public class BuggyTaskQueue{
5      private ArrayList scheduledTasks = new ArrayList();
6      private ArrayList completedTasks = new ArrayList();
7
8      public void addScheduledTask(Task t){
9        scheduledTasks.add(t);
10     }
11     public void addCompletedTask(Task t){
12       completedTasks.add(t);
13     }
14     public void performTask(){
15       Task taskToDo = null;
16       try{
17         synchronized (this){
18           if (hasTasks()){
19             taskToDo = getTask();
20             int result = taskToDo.runTask();
21             if (result == Status.SUCCESS){
22               addCompletedTask(taskToDo);
23             }
24             else if (result == Status.WAIT){
25               addScheduledTask(taskToDo);
26             }
27             else{
28               Logger.getLogger("default").warning(
29                     "There was a problem when performing " + taskToDo);
30             }
31           }
32         }
33       }
34       catch (RuntimeException exc){
35         Logger.getLogger("default").log(Level.SEVERE,
36               "Exception while performing " + taskToDo, exc);
37         System.out.println(scheduledTasks);
38         System.out.println(completedTasks);
39       }
40     }
41     public Task getTask(){
42       return (Task)scheduledTasks.remove(0);
43     }
44     public boolean hasTasks(){
45       return (scheduledTasks.size() > 0);
```

```
46    }
47  }
```

The class `BuggyTaskQueue` implements a queue that can hold Task objects—
actions to be performed by a system. There's one major problem with it—exceptions can
be propagated outside of the synchronized code block in the method `performTask`,
lines 14–40. If a thread calls this method and an exception occurs, the thread will prematurely exit the synchronized block, which can have major consequences for the `Task-`
`Queue`. For instance, if the method `runTask` on line 20 throws a RuntimeException, it's
possible that the Task will not be added to any of the `ArrayList` structures used to
hold scheduled and completed tasks. That's all right if you *want* the task to disappear, but
unacceptable if you want to reschedule it or place it in some collection that holds tasks
that require diagnosis or debugging. If you want to ensure that your synchronized
resources stay in a consistent state, the safest policy is to plan for the exceptions that
can be thrown in synchronized blocks, and to handle them within the synchronized
blocks as well.

Exception Risks Due to Threaded Activity

An additional use of synchronized blocks is to coordinate threaded activity based on
the state of a shared resource. This is accomplished using a series of wait/notify calls
within the synchronized blocks. Here's an example of how it works:

```
1   import java.util.*;
2   public class TaskQueue{
3     private List queue = new ArrayList();
4     public void pushTask(Task t){
5       synchronized(this){
6         queue.add(t);
7         notify();
8       }
9     }
10    public Task popTask(){
11      synchronized(this){
12        while (queue.isEmpty()){
13          System.out.println("Placing Thread in wait state");
14          try{
15            wait();
16          }
17          catch (InterruptedException exc){}
18        }
19        return (Task)queue.remove(0);
20      }
```

```
21    }
22  }
```

It isn't obvious, but you have to be careful about how you handle calls to wait/ notify. If you aren't, threads may continue to run before a resource is actually ready to be used. If this innocent-looking code used an "if" rather than a "while" test on line 12, a thread could continue to execute after an initial pause. If the wait/notify structure wasn't properly set up, the thread could try to use the `TaskQueue` before it was ready.

If this happened, there could be a number of consequences. If you didn't properly manage the wait/notify calls, your application could throw an `IllegalMonitorStateException`, for instance. Your code would throw this exception if you tried to coordinate with a shared object resource using wait/notify when you're not the owner of the object's lock flag.

The `IllegalMonitorStateException` potentially means that one or more of your resources is no longer in a consistent state, which means that you have big problems with your application. What's more, the `IllegalMonitorStateException` is a RuntimeException. This means it can potentially halt the thread that caused the exception, if you're not careful.

Of course, the `IllegalMonitorStateException` isn't the only problem that can result from incorrectly managing threaded activity associated with wait/notify. It's also possible to run into difficulties because you're trying to work with a resource that isn't ready for your thread's activity. Typically, this kind of problem manifests itself indirectly, as a `NullPointerException` or an exception produced due to inconsistent resource state.

Exceptions for Thread-based Communication

Based on what's been discussed, it's easy to get the impression that exceptions only present problems in threading. Actually, exceptions can also provide a very convenient communication mechanism between threads. Since threads are independently scheduled within an application, you generally can't predict when a specific thread will execute its code. As a result, it's often hard for one thread to signal to another thread that it has performed a task or requires a service.

Think about it: If a Thread finishes its work, how do you communicate the fact to a different Thread in an application? For instance, how would you signal a group of "consumer" threads when a "producer" thread is finished with some task? There are four ways to accomplish such an action:

1. Consumer threads can actively check the state of the producer.
2. Consumer threads can wait for the producer by calling the `join` method.
3. The producer thread can actively notify the consumers.

4. The producer thread can throw an `InterruptedException` to notify the consumer threads.

For the first option, consumer threads can check the runtime state of the producer by using the method `isAlive`, or by calling an API method on the producer thread. This scenario basically makes the consumers perform a "client pull" operation. Consumer threads will continue to run, and must spend some of their runtime checking the producer's state. What's more, the consumers will not be immediately notified when the producer thread is ready. Finally, consumer threads will not be able to poll if they are blocked for some reason.

In the second option, consumer threads call the method `join()` on the producer thread, waiting until the producer completes. This option still requires the consumers to be active in checking the producer thread's state. Unlike the previous approach, consumer threads could block while waiting for the producer thread, allowing more efficient use of runtime.

The third option resembles a conventional "server push" solution. The producer thread must have references for every thread it needs to notify, and must spend time signaling the consumer threads when producer resources are ready. The producer thread could use wait/notify to signal consumers indirectly, or could use a custom API for direct notification.

For the final option, the producer thread calls the `interrupt` method on the consumer threads. There are two ways that a consumer thread could learn about the interrupt. If the thread was running, it could call its method `interrupted`, which would return true if the thread had been the target of an `interrupt` call. If the thread was blocked during the call, the producer's `interrupt` call would cause an `InterruptedException` to be thrown for the consumer.[20]

The following table summarizes the main characteristics of each type of thread notification:

Option	Can threads be notified during blocking calls?	Easy to use for groups of threads?	Immediate notification?
1. Consumers poll using `isAlive` or Producer API	✗	✗	✗
2. Consumers wait on the Producer using `join`	✔	✗	✔
3. Producer notifies the consumers directly	✗	✗	✗
4. Producer calls `interrupt`	✔	✔	✔

---

20. The result of an interrupt call is a bit different for code written using the "new I/O" API. We talk more about how NIO handles interrupts in Chapter 8.

One of the main benefits of using the interrupt method is that it *can* wake up threads that would otherwise remain blocked. The `InterruptedException` works for all of the following blocking methods:

Thread class:

- `join()`, `join(long)` and `join(long, int)`
- `sleep(long)` and `sleep(long, int)`

Object class:

- `wait()`, `wait(long)`, and `wait(long, int)`

What's more, the interrupt method can be called on a single thread or a collection of threads if they are managed within a `ThreadGroup` object.[21] The following code example shows how this can be done:

```
 1   import java.util.*;
 2   public class ProducerThread implements Runnable{
 3     private ThreadGroup consumers;
 4     private Thread runner;
 5     private boolean shutdown;
 6     private ArrayList tasks;
 7     public ProducerThread(ThreadGroup msgConsumers){
 8       msgConsumers.checkAccess();
 9       consumers = msgConsumers;
10       tasks = new ArrayList();
11       runner = new Thread(this);
12       runner.start();
13     }
14     public void shutdown(){
15       shutdown = true;
16     }
17     public synchronized void addTask(Task t){
18       if (t != null){
19         tasks.add(t);
20       }
21     }
22     public synchronized Task removeTask(){
23       Task rtnTask = null;
24       if (!tasks.isEmpty()){
25         rtnTask = (Task)tasks.remove(0);
```

---

21. Every time you create a Thread, it becomes part of a ThreadGroup. By default, threads belong to a single "main" ThreadGroup. You can manage a set of threads as a unit by creating your own `ThreadGroup` object. You can subsequently register threads with the group using any constructor call that includes the ThreadGroup as an argument.

```
26           }
27        return rtnTask;
28      }
29      private boolean hasTasks(){
30        return tasks.isEmpty();
31      }
32      public void run(){
33        while (!shutdown){
34          if (hasTasks()){
35            consumers.interrupt();
36          }
37          try{
38            Thread.sleep(1000);
39          }
40          catch (InterruptedException exc){
41          }
42        }
43      }
44    }
```

The ThreadGroup offers one other important benefit to exception handling in threaded systems—it allows you to define a handler method for any uncaught exceptions in your threads. Here's how it works. Any time an unhandled exception is thrown from a Thread, the uncaughtException method on its ThreadGroup will be called.

```
public void uncaughtException (Thread t, Throwable e)
```

The default behavior for this method is to call the parent ThreadGroup's uncaughtException method if there is a parent. If there is no parent, the method will print the stack trace to the standard error stream, and the application will continue. Of course, you're free to override this method and define your own behavior that will be called when unhandled exceptions are thrown. This provides you with an ideal way to define global handling code for a group of threads, and to ensure that you take the necessary precautions to recover from critical errors.

```
1  public class HandlerThreadGroup extends ThreadGroup{
2    public HandlerThreadGroup(String name){
3      super(name);
4    }
5    public HandlerThreadGroup(ThreadGroup parent, String name){
6      super(parent, name);
7    }
8    public void uncaughtException(Thread t, Throwable e){
9      System.out.println("Thread " + t + " exception. Cause: " + e);
```

```
10        e.printStackTrace(System.err);
11    }
12  }
```

Deadlock

One further risk in threaded systems is the possibility of deadlock. Deadlock is a natural consequence of protecting data from threaded corruption.

When do you have a risk of data corruption? Any time you have a shared stateful resource, and you alter its state in a code block where multiple threads are active. If these conditions are met, multiple threads could potentially corrupt your resource state while they ran. Since threads are independently scheduled, there is no guarantee that they will run in a defined order, so resource corruption is always a danger. How do you solve the problem? Protect your data by making it private, and synchronize your code blocks.

Unfortunately, if you define synchronized code in your application, you run the risk of deadlock. Specifically, you may encounter deadlock when two threads that already have lock flags try to call synchronized code that is protected by the other's lock flag. If this ever occurs in your system, both threads will permanently become unable to run. What's more, any other threads that call methods that use the same lock flags will become deadlocked as well, unable to continue running. The problem is illustrated in Figure 4-1.

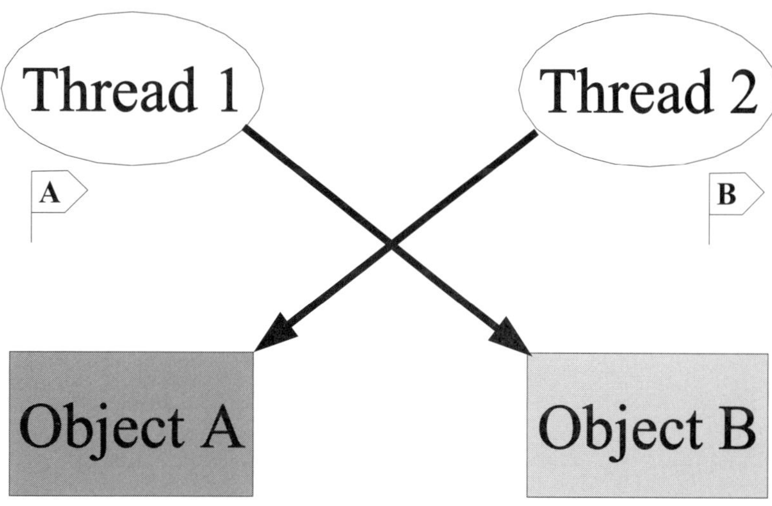

Figure 4–1
Thread deadlock scenario.

Unfortunately, there's no easy way to guard against the problem of deadlock. You could avoid synchronizing your code in the first place, but that would mean that your code wouldn't be protected against multithreaded activity and your data could be put into an inconsistent state. Since that usually isn't an option, you're faced with a number of other possible strategies that trade code efficiency for deadlock protection.

How do you protect against deadlock? As mentioned earlier, there's no API call you can make to eliminate the danger—deadlock is a natural consequence of synchronizing your code. There are, however, a few design options available.

1. Only use a single object for synchronization in your application.
2. Ensure that a thread never calls a synchronized method from within another synchronized method.
3. Acquire and release lock flags in a consistent order.
4. Consolidate lock flags; if you need two log flags to perform an operation, merge them into synchronized blocks that use a single lock flag.
5. Delegate the threaded operations to another class, which can ensure that it will be safely performed without deadlock.
6. Make a central lock flag manager object, which will allow you to acquire and release lock flags without the risk of deadlock.

Every one of these solutions requires careful design in your code. To some extent, each of these methods involves trading some runtime efficiency for safety from the risk of deadlock.

ThreadDeath

With any luck, you'll never have to deal with this exception in threaded code. It's been deprecated since JDK1.2, so it's unlikely you'll come across it anywhere but in very old legacy code.[22]

The error was defined for use with a set of thread control methods in the `Thread` and `ThreadGroup` classes called stop. The basic idea behind the stop methods was that they would enable an authorized caller to prematurely halt threads while they were running. This was accomplished by creating and throwing the `ThreadDeath` object, which would force a thread to halt its actions no matter where it happened to be in its runtime. The basic problem with the method was that it really *would* halt a thread absolutely anywhere in its execution. "Anywhere" could even include halting threads in the middle of executing synchronized code, which might have the unfortunate side effect of placing shared resources into an inconsistent state! For this reason,

---

22. The API was deprecated in 1998, which is basically infinity in programmer years.

it's really never advisable to call the stop method on a thread object. If you need to stop a thread, it's almost always better to use approaches like interrupt calls and stop variables.

chapter 5

Logging and Assertions

In JDK1.4, a couple of enhancements were made to Java that helped to improve the language's effectiveness when dealing with exceptions in code. One feature was the Logging API, designed to standardize the common task of writing output within an application and provide a more advanced logging framework for distributed applications. The other was a language feature called the assertion facility. Assertions provide you with a way to test for conditions that you feel should be true when running an application, making it easier for you to validate program logic and to identify misconceptions about the way an application should run. This chapter outlines the purpose, design and use of both of these new language features.

A quick caveat—this chapter is not intended to be a definitive work on either of these new features in Java. Since the main focus of the book is on effective exception handling within code, the chapter will present the highlights of each capability. It also describes how to use the new capabilities to support more effective coding and exception handling.

Introduction to the Logging API

Prior to JDK1.4, there wasn't a standardized way to manage logging in the language. Developers had to rely on simpler methods for providing output (such as `System.out`), use a third-party logging framework, or develop a custom API for a project.

The Logging API was introduced to provide improved logging support to the Java programming language. Looking more closely, there are two important objectives that the API satisfies. For simple applications, the API provides a simple, ready-to-use solution that's more powerful and configurable than what is already around. For larger, more complex applications such as distributed systems and frameworks, the API is flexible and extensible, to satisfy a variety of needs.

To provide a good perspective about what the Logging API provides, this section begins by discussing its high-level architectural model of the API. From there, the chapter describes the key classes in the API. Next, it presents standard configurations of the API for use in systems. Finally, it describes some standard tasks that you might perform.

When Should You Use the Logging API?

The Logging API provides considerable benefits for developers. It effectively realizes the goals of flexibility and configurability for logging functionality. It represents a coherent architecture that can be adapted for a variety of uses. Being a part of JDK1.4, it offers the additional value of providing an industry standard system to accomplish logging objectives.

There are two principal drawbacks for the API. Being a more recent addition to the JDK, it isn't available in earlier generation JVMs. Beyond that, there is an inherent amount of overhead required to use logging. Even simple uses of the API require the coordination of several objects. What's more, most of the important logging methods are synchronized. Naturally, this means that logging is thread-safe at the expense of some code performance.

Overview of the API

Fundamentally, there are three key parts of the API: Loggers, Handlers and Filters. Logger provide standard log methods, while Handlers work behind the scenes to perform the actual logging. Filters, if they are used, make decisions about what messages are logged. Figure 5-1 shows a sample configuration of a logging system.

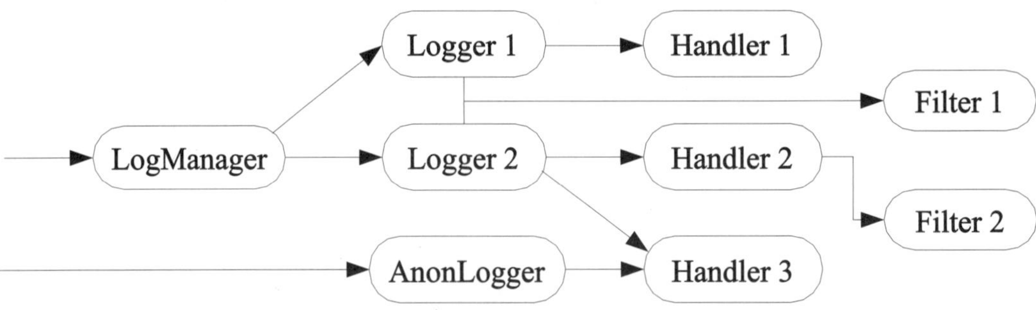

Figure 5–1
Sample configuration of the Logging API.

Notice that Loggers can be created for single use, or stored in a global object, the LogManager, for repeat calls. Also notice that the design of the Logging API promotes a fair amount of flexibility, allowing you to share Handler or Filter objects if it suits your needs. The use of the API in an application is fairly straightforward, based around four standard steps:

1. Create the Logger objects you will use in your application. If you plan to use a Logger many times, register it with the LogManager.
2. Create the Handler objects you will use, and associate one or more Handlers with each of your Loggers.
3. If you plan to filter your messages, create Filter classes and associate them with your Handlers or Loggers.
4. Each time you need to log a message, look up the appropriate logger and call one of its log methods.

Detailed API Use

To work with this API, you begin by creating one or more Logger objects. There are three ways to do this. For one-time logging in applications, you can create a logger using the following command:

```
Logger simpleLogger = Logger.getAnonymousLogger();
```

The anonymous logger is handy for use within a single method—you can easily use the API in your application with a minimal amount of overhead. Additionally, a default "global" logger is available for use in cases where you would like a reusable Logger without the work involved in creating and managing loggers yourself.:

```
Logger defaultLogObject = Logger.global;
```

For more complex systems, you can cache Logger objects for repeat use. There is a class called the LogManager that holds a collection of Loggers. The LogManager is a Singleton,[23] so it's easy to get the LogManager object for a JVM by calling the getLog-Manager method:

```
LogManager lm = LogManager.getLogManager();
Logger myLog = Logger.getLogger("app.log");
lm.addLogger(myLog);
```

---

23. The Singleton is a design pattern that is used to ensure there is one globally accessible instance of an object within a JVM. For details, see one of the design pattern books mentioned in the bibliography.

Once you register a Logger object, you can use the LogManager to look it up by its name. This following code sample shows how to perform a lookup if you wanted to use the same logger in some other method of the application:

```
LogManager lm = LogManager.getLogManager();

Logger myLog = lm.getLogger("app.log");
```

Although you can choose any name you want to identify a Logger, its name is intended to be a hierarchical, dot-separated string that's based on the package or class name of the component performing the logging. If you follow that naming convention, it will be easier to identify a Logger by its responsibility in your application.

What's more, if you represent Logger objects by progressive, dot-separated names, the LogManager will automatically associate them together in a parent-child relationship. For instance, a logger associated with the name "`domain.data.persistence`" would automatically become a child of one named "`domain.data`". The parent-child relationship between Loggers can be significant. If you call the method `setUseParentHandlers(true)` on a child, any logging calls that the child handles will automatically be passed on to the parent Logger as well. By managing sets of parent and child loggers, it's possible to establish a logging chain, where a log message will be forwarded to a series of Loggers for handling.

Once you've created or located a Logger, you can make calls to its logging methods. There are six main groups or categories of logging method based on the intended purpose of the API, as shown in Table 5-1.

Table 5–1   **Standard Logging Methods**

Method Type	Logging Purpose
log	General logging
logp	Messages with an associated source class and method
logrb	Messages with a designated ResourceBundle (used for localization)
entering exiting	Information associated with method entry and exit
config fine finer finest info severe warning	Logging messages with standard levels of severity
throwing	Logging a Throwable object generated within a method

At a minimum, you must pass a message string to every logging call. In addition, you may pass arguments to provide details about the exact nature of your logging message. The exact information you provide depends on your intended logging action. For instance, if you plan to log a method entry or exit, standard arguments include the class and method names. If you plan to log a problem in your application represented by a Throwable, you can pass the Throwable object that caused the error.

One of the most common additions to a log call is a logging level. If you pass a level with your message, your can flag a message with a specific level of urgency or severity. This allows a Logger to filter out log messages which do not have a minimum level of severity. The Level class represents the logging levels of the API, and defines the following constant values:

```
Level.SEVERE          Most severe
Level.WARNING
Level.INFO
Level.CONFIG                  ↑
Level.FINE
Level.FINER
Level.FINEST          Least severe
```

Notice that one group of the logging methods match the name of these standard levels; a method like config(String message) can be used to send a message that is preconfigured with a level of CONFIG. For any Logger, you can set the filter level for a message by using the `setLevel` method. For instance, to set a Logger to ignore all messages that have a level set below WARNING, you can call the following method:

```
myLog.setLevel(Level.WARNING);
```

There are two additional constants for logging level that can be useful. To set a Logger to accept all messages, you can pass the value `Level.ALL`. If you want to disable a Logger entirely, you can call `setLevel(Level.OFF)`, which would cause the logger to ignore every message passed to it. This can be useful if you need to selectively enable and disable loggers as your application runs.

Assuming that the level of the message is high enough to be logged, a Logger creates a LogRecord to hold the logging information. A LogRecord is used as an object wrapper around logging data, so that the data can be easily passed to multiple recipients. Since it's intended to communicate message information between a number of locations that potentially could be located on different machines, JVMs or class loaders, the class implements the Serializable interface. A LogRecord can hold quite a few pieces of information. It's hard to imagine a logging operation that would use all of its properties, but there are fields for just about any kind of message or exception-based data you can imagine:

- The "raw" (unlocalized, unformatted) log message
- The logging level associated with the message

- The Logger that created the LogRecord object
- The time of the event associated with the LogRecord
- An arbitrary number of Object parameters associated with the event
- A ResourceBundle for localization
- A "sequence number" for the message
- A source class and method that triggered or produced the event
- A Thread ID, if the event was generated in a running thread
- A Throwable object, if any is associated with the event

The main reason that a Logger creates a LogRecord is to make it easier to share the same logging data among multiple consumers. Specifically, the Logger will pass the LogRecord object to every one of its associated Handlers. The purpose of a Handler is to send LogRecords to some kind of destination—in a sense, you could say that each Handler routes logging messages to a specific logging location. Every Logger has at least one Handler object associated with it. You can add handlers to a Logger by calling the addHandler method of your Logger:

```
Logger myLog = Logger.getLogger("err.log");
my.addHandler(new ConsoleHandler());
```

Since there a quite a few conceivable kinds or destinations for logging messages, the API defines a number of standard Handler class types, as shown in Figure 5-2.

Every Handler uses a Formatter object to convert the LogRecord into a standard display format. Normally, a Handler uses one of two default formatters that are defined for its class type. A SimpleFormatter will print an output message in plain ASCII text, while an XMLFormatter will produce an XML version of the logging message.

Both Loggers and Handlers can determine whether to log a message. Both classes have an associated logging level that dictates the level of message that they will accept. Both classes define the method `setLevel`, which allows you to adjust the level of logging message that will be accepted, or to disable logging entirely. For more precise control over logging, both types of classes also let you use a Filter to determine whether a message should be logged. To associate a Filter with a given Logger or Handler, you call the `setFilter` method.

There are no standard Filter classes in the Logging API; Filter itself is actually an interface. It's straightforward to implement a filter, though—you need only write a class that implements Filter and, by extension, the method `isLoggable`. The following example shows a basic filter class that would only log messages associated with a Java error (a Throwable object):

```
1  import java.util.logging.*;
2  public class ExceptionFilter implements Filter{
3    public boolean isLoggable(LogRecord lr){
4      return lr.getThrown() != null ? true : false;
5    }
6  }
```

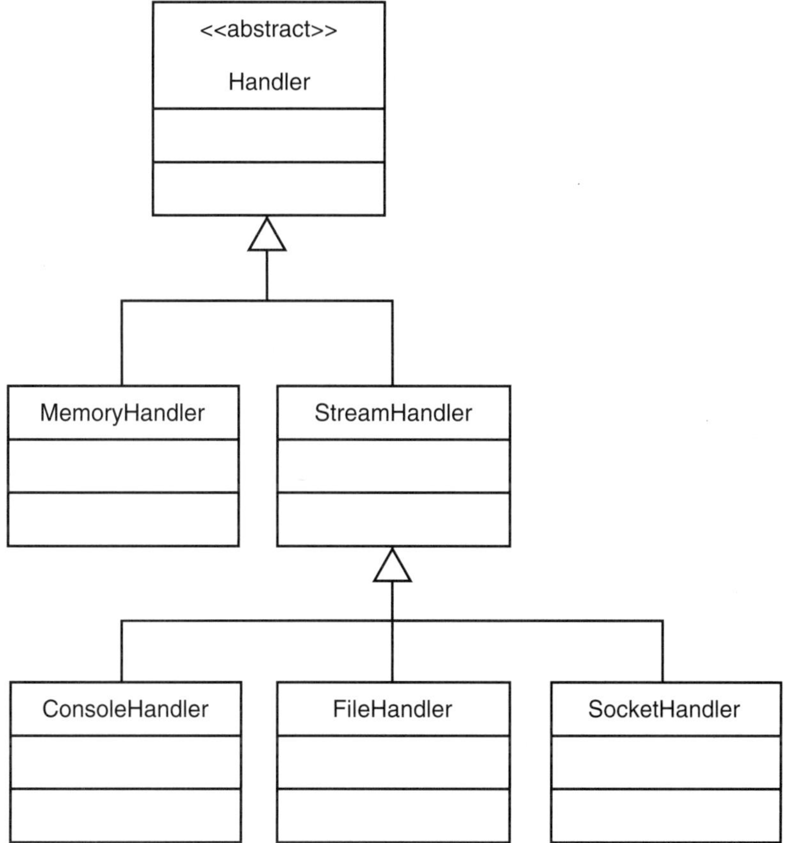

Figure 5–2
Handler class hierarchy.

To recap, here's what happens when you make a call on a Logger:

1. The Logger checks its internal log level to see if it should process the message.
   a. If the logger's level is set to `Level.OFF`, the logger will ignore all logging calls.
   b. If the message has a lower logging level than the logger's filtering log level, the Logger will ignore the message.
2. The Logger creates a LogRecord object, which holds all information relevant to the logging message.
3. If there is a Filter object associated with the Logger, the Logger calls the `isLoggable` method. If the returned value is `false`, the Logger ignores the input.
4. The Logger cycles through every Handler object and performs the following actions:

    a. The Logger calls the Handler's `publish` method

    b. The Handler decides if it will log the message, and how to log it

    c. If the logger is set to publish to its parent logger, get the handlers for the parent and repeat step 4.

There's one final class in the API to mention—the ErrorManager. An ErrorManager is associated with one or more Handler objects to provide recovery capability for any logging problems. If an error occurs with a Handler during logging, the associated ErrorManager will automatically forward the exception to its handler method, `error(String msg, Exception err, int code)`.

The rationale for this is that it's unlikely that you'll want to write handling code for every logging call in your application. The ErrorManager provides you with a suitable alternative—a central forwarding mechanism to a global handler. Notice that the error method provides an integer code for the call, providing a value to more accurately identify the source of the problem:

Error Code	Type of Error
`ErrorManager.CLOSE_FAILURE`	`Closing resource`
`ErrorManager.FLUSH_FAILURE`	`Flushing output stream`
`ErrorManager.FORMAT_FAILURE`	`Formatting output`
`ErrorManager.GENERIC_FAILURE`	`General errors`
`ErrorManager.OPEN_FAILURE`	`Opening a resource`
`ErrorManager.WRITE_FAILURE`	`Writing output`

Standard Logging Configurations

At this point, it's worthwhile to show a few complete code examples. This section presents three code examples, each of which represents a common use of the Logging API. These code examples probably won't cover everything you may want to do, but they should give you some starting ideas, especially when combined with the earlier discussion about API capabilities.

Example 1: Using the Simple, Default Logger

```
1   import java.util.logging.*;
2   import java.util.*;
3   public class SimpleDefaultLogger{
4     public static void main(String [] args){
5       SimpleDefaultLogger app = new SimpleDefaultLogger();
```

```
 6        app.printLoggers();
 7        app.logIt();
 8      }
 9    public void printLoggers(){
10      LogManager manager = LogManager.getLogManager();
11      Enumeration elems = manager.getLoggerNames();
12      System.out.println("Logger names:");
13      while (elems.hasMoreElements()){
14        System.out.println("\t" + elems.nextElement());
15      }
16      System.out.println();
17    }
18    public void logIt(){
19       Logger logger = Logger.global;
20       logger.severe("Stop me before I log again!");
21    }
22  }
```

This example uses the default Logger included the the API. The first method, print-Loggers, prints the name of the default Logger available for any JVM. The second method, logIt, shows an easy way to use the default Logger. By default, this logger prints messages out to standard output.

Example 2: Configuring and Using Multiple Loggers

```
 1    import java.util.logging.*;
 2    import java.io.*;
 3  public class MultiLogging{
 4    public static void main(String [] args){
 5      MultiLogging app = new MultiLogging();
 6      try{
 7        app.logTest();
 8      }
 9      catch (IOException exc){
10        exc.printStackTrace();
11      }
12    }
13    public void logTest() throws IOException{
14      LogManager manager = LogManager.getLogManager();
15      Logger standardLogger = Logger.getLogger("base.log");
16      Logger fileLogger = Logger.getLogger("base.log.file");
17      //  If the standard logger is set up as a parent for the file
18      //  logger, the parent will log all the messages passed on by
19      //  the child.
```

```
20          //
21          //  This is primarily useful for setting up forwarding chains,
22          //  to allow the same logging message to be directed to multiple
23          //  Loggers, and by extension, to multiple destinations
24          standardLogger.setLevel(Level.SEVERE);
25          fileLogger.addHandler(new FileHandler("ProblemLog.log", true));
26          fileLogger.setLevel(Level.INFO);
27          manager.addLogger(standardLogger);
28          manager.addLogger(fileLogger);
29          testLoggers(Level.INFO, "General-purpose info-message");
30          testLoggers(Level.SEVERE, "This is a very, very bad thing." +
31            "You may now begin to worry.");
32      }
33    public void testLoggers(Level level, String message){
34        LogManager manager = LogManager.getLogManager();
35        Logger specialLog = manager.getLogger("base.log.file");
36        specialLog.log(level, message);
37      }
38  }
```

This code example is a little more elaborate. The logTest method sets up two Loggers on lines 15 and 16, standardLogger and fileLogger. The logger names are associated in a parent-child relation, so that any logging message sent to the fileLogger will be passed on to standardLogger. On line 24, the call to standardLogger.setLevel makes the standardLogger ignore any messages that have a logging level below Level.SEVERE. The fileLogger is associated with a file handler on line 25, so it echos log messages to the ProblemLog.log file. Lines 27 and 28 associate the loggers with the LogManager, so they can be retrieved in other methods. Finally, lines 29 through 31 call the testLoggers method, which sends a message to both loggers.

Example 3: Simple Distributed Logging

```
1   import java.util.logging.*;
2   import java.io.*;
3   public class DistLoggingSender{
4     public static void main(String [] args){
5       DistLoggingSender app = new DistLoggingSender();
6       try{
7         app.logTest();
8       }
9       catch (IOException exc){
10        exc.printStackTrace();
11      }
12    }
```

```
13    public void logTest() throws IOException{
14      LogManager manager = LogManager.getLogManager();
15      Logger networkLogger = Logger.getLogger("netlog");
16      networkLogger.addHandler(new SocketHandler("localhost", 5280));
17      networkLogger.addHandler(new ConsoleHandler());
18      testLogger(Level.FINE, "Fine, go ahead and log. See if I care");
19      testLogger(Level.WARNING, "Global warning!");
20    }
21    public void testLogger(Level level, String message){
22      LogManager manager = LogManager.getLogManager();
23      Logger networkLog = manager.getLogger("netlog");
24      networkLog.log(level, message);
25    }
26  }
```

```
1   import java.io.*;
2   import java.net.*;
3   public class DistLoggingReceiver{
4     public static void main(String [] args){
5       try{
6         ServerSocket ss = new ServerSocket(5280);
7         System.out.println("Server started on port 5280...");
8         while (true){
9           Socket skt = ss.accept();
10          InputStream is = skt.getInputStream();
11          byte [] data = new byte[4192];
12          try{
13            is.read(data);
14          }
15          catch (IOException exc){
16            exc.printStackTrace();
17          }
18          String info = new String(data);
19          logToFile(info);
20          System.out.println(info.trim());
21          skt.close();
22        }
23      }
24      catch (IOException exc){
25        exc.printStackTrace();
26      }
27    }
28    public static void logToFile(String message){
29      try{
```

```
30         PrintWriter outp = new PrintWriter(new FileWriter("dl.log"));
31          outp.println(message.trim());
32          outp.close();
33      }
34      catch (IOException exc){
35          exc.printStackTrace();
36      }
37    }
38  }
```

The final code example shows how to use the logging API to send distributed messages. The class DistLoggingSender sends a logging message. The Logger networkLogger is associated with a SocketHandler on line 16, so logging output is directed across a socket connection. The class DistLoggingReceiver uses the standard java.net classes ServerSocket and Socket to receive and print logging messages.

Assertions

Assertions are a language features added to Java so that programmers could test assumptions about how their code should run. Assertions support a programming concept called invariants, where an "invariant" is a condition which must be true in order for an application to run properly.

Prior to this language feature, there was no standard way to support invariants in the language. A programmer could set up his or her own way to check coding assumptions, but would have to manually develop an API to perform the checking. Such a solution required a code framework (more maintenance) that tended to be harder to selectively enable and disable within a project (more runtime overhead).

Assertions, as a language feature, are supported by a new Java keyword called **assert**. There are two basic forms of an assertion that a programmer can use:

```
assert [logical condition];
assert [logical condition] : [expression] ;
```

In both cases, the logical condition will be evaluated if assertions are enabled in the code. If the condition is false, the JVM will throw an AssertionError. Since exceptions and errors record a stack trace, the AssertionError will contain the location in code where the execution stopped.

If you want to provide more detail than a stack trace, the second form of the assert structure lets you specify an expression which will be stored as a "detailed" error message within the AssertionError. The expression will be evaluated, converted to its String equivalent, and stored with the error object.

Using Assertions

Of course, you can't just add a new keyword to the Java language. You must also provide a way for the compiler to recognize it. Prior to JDK1.4, the assert keyword didn't exist—what if somebody had written a program using "assert" as the name for a variable or method? To safeguard against this possibility, a new compiler switch was added to the language. If you want to ensure that your code will recognize this new keyword, you must use the -source 1.4 option, as shown below:

```
javac -source 1.4 [file]
```

If you try to compile without this option, the compiler will assume that any occurrence of the word "assert" refers to an identifier.

After you compile a source file with assertions, you can selectively enable or disable them during runtime. Assertions are disabled by default, to avoid unneccessary runtime overhead in an application. The 1.4 JVM defines switches that allow you to enable and disable assertions on a local or global basis. To enable the use of assertions, you can run with the -enableassertions or -ea switches. To turn assertions off, you run -disableasssertions or -da.

When run without package or class names, these switches globally enable or disable assertions in the classes of your application. You can also use these flags to enable or disable assertion checking in specific classes or packages. Here are a few examples:

```
java -ea billing.domain.FinanceModel
java -ea order.process -da order.process.Billing order.OrderProcessor
```

The first example enables assertion checking for all of the application classes run while executing the `business.domain.FinanceModel` class. The second selectively enables assertion checking for all classes in the order.process package except for the `Billing` class.

There is an additional set of flags that can enable or disable assertion checking of the system classes. Enabling system assertions requires that you use the `-enablesystemassertions` or `-esa` flag, and disabling assertion checking (the default) uses the `-disablesystemassertions` or `-dsa` flag. If you want to enable assertion checking for system classes, you must do it independently of the assertion checks in your own application code.

Assertion Use in an Application

It's just as important to know when to avoid using assertions as it is to know when they're appropriate. The following are a few standard cases where assertions aren't a good idea:

1. You should not use assertions as a substitute for tests that must always be true in your code.

   Assertions can be selectively or globally disabled within code. Because of this, you can't really guarantee that assertions will always be used when your application is run. This in turn means you shouldn't use them to provide a permanent check on any critical invariants for your code. A better practice is to enforce such conditions directly, as checks in the application code itself.

2. You should not use assertions to test for trivial problems, or easily correctible error conditions.

   When they are enabled, assertions can cause your code to fail with an error. As such, they should usually only test for critical assumptions of a system—conditions that would cause problems with the application state of logic if invalidated.

3. You shouldn't use assertions to check the input arguments of public methods.

   By definition, public methods provide the calling interface of a class—the part of a class that describes its capabilities to the outside world. As a programmer, you don't have any direct control over how the public methods of a class are called, and so you should not make assumptions about whether the data will generally be valid. Since this is the case, you should explicitly check for invalid input in a method, rather than using an assertion to check for data validity.

Having said all this, here are some specific situations where assertions are probably called for. Assertions are helpful for test and validation of invariants, and specifically for the following types of invariants:

- Internal invariants
- Control-flow invariants
- Preconditions
- Lock status preconditions
- Postconditions
- Class invariants

An internal invariant describes an assumption about a test that is assumed to produce a specific outcome. According to the JDK1.4 documents, this type of assertion would be used in any part of the code where you would have normally written a comment to explain that you expect a certain result of a check or test. Standard cases where you'd use this type of assertion would be else blocks that should default to a known case and switch statements without a standard default behavior.

Control-flow invariants document locations in a control structure that you should not reach if your code is functioning properly. This kind of assertion will work only for a code block that logically could be reached—the compiler will give you an error if you try to write code in a block that will *actually* never be reached. If you use an assertion after an if statement that is always expected to trigger method termination, you're creating a control flow invariant.

Preconditions and postconditions are invariants that are associated with method entry and exit, respectively. Both are used to check for proper state of an object. In a precondition assertion check, you can check that the object is method ready, and if you have a non-private method, you can check for valid calling arguments.[24] A postcondition invariant might check that a resource was in a consistent state prior to exiting a method.

A specialized type of precondition check is a lock status precondition. The Thread class was updated with a new method to enforce this test:

```
public static boolean holdsLock(Object)
```

This method allows you to determine if a thread has acquired a given lock flag. When used with an assertion, it allows you to perform tests based on whether of not the currently running thread does or does not have a lock flag.

The final kind of invariant is the class invariant. This kind of invariant tests the state of an object to ensure that the object remains in a consistent state. The class invariant assumes that an object will remain in a consistent state, except for the case where it is in transition from one state to another. Normally, a class invariant would be used in multiple places in an application, during operations which result in a significant change of object state. To facilitate reuse, class invariants are often enforced by defining an internally-called method that will return a boolean value based on whether the object is in the correct state. You can subsequently call the method any time you need to perform an assertion check for the state of the object.

---

24. As mentioned earlier, it's generally not a good practice to use assertions to check the arguments of public methods.

part 2

EXCEPTION HANDLING AND DESIGN

chapter 6

Exception Handling and Design

Introduction

The previous section of this book concentrated on the core programming skills used to write effective exception handling code. These foundation skills are a necessity for any developer who wants to write error handling code within an application. At the same time, programming techniques aren't the only factors that determine whether an application effectively deals with exceptions. It's important to have an understanding of the "nuts and bolts" concepts of exception handling, but you should also know how to apply those principles in the code you write.

In other words, just being an effective coder doesn't guarantee that your application will be particularly robust. The focus of this chapter, and of Part 2 of this book, is on how to structure exception handling code in methods, between methods, and within software components. Its intent is to demonstrate how to apply the lessons from the first section to produce well-organized, maintainable code. In many ways, this section of the book represents a paradigm shift, a change in perspective from programming to software design.

The critical mistake that most programmers make is that they treat exception handling as an afterthought, addressing problems only when the compiler coughs up a few error messages that prevent them from running their code.[25] Developing code without considering the errors that might be produced is like trying to build a model airplane (or a sailboat, or a three-story condo) without reading the directions—you're trusting a lot to luck, and you can't really guarantee that the results will be satisfying.

In all fairness, the real weakness in software development lies in the fact that many traditional methodologies have neglected error handling. Is it any wonder that the products resulting from such methodologies are weak in their exception handling?

---

25. Sort of like hairballs from a cat.

Many methodologies have spent their energy on the question of how to create effective, reusable, object-oriented models for a problem. Don't get me wrong—there is great value in developing an effective OO model for a system. However, without a consideration of the possible causes of failure within an application, the software will be incomplete, and in a sense fundamentally flawed.

In this chapter, I hope to show you that the concepts of effective software design can be easily extended to factor in exception handling and the most likely causes of failure in an application. It doesn't require a huge amount of design overhead and, in the long run, you will be rewarded with more robust, maintainable code.

Principles of Effective OO Design

It's often been said that you should begin any new undertaking with the end in mind. Let's apply that concept to object-oriented software development: What are its key objectives and guiding principles? What should well-designed object-oriented code be like? At the most basic level, we'd like any code to accomplish its functional objectives and show acceptable performance characteristics. It should be clearly written and flexible, able to adapt to new requirements without a major rewrite, if possible. Ideally, it should be modular and reusable, so that it can easily be used in other projects without a lot of modification.[26]

Amazing, isn't it? Those goals all sound so reasonable when you write them down. Of course, it's a lot easier to express them than to actually make them a reality. Still, we all try as much as possible to accomplish these objectives, which means developing classes, components, systems, and frameworks[27] that exhibit certain desirable traits. The list of "desirable," object-oriented characteristics varies a bit depending on your source, but some of the most common are described below. To make the discussion easier, let's present these principles as they apply to a single class, bearing in mind that they apply to higher-level object-oriented components as well. A well-designed class is based around the following principles:

1. Abstraction: The class models a well-defined concept or entity. This principle also carries over to the state and behavior of an object created from a class.

   - Variables: Each variable models a specific concept or item that enables an object of the class type to accomplish its purpose, or that represents an object's internal state.

---

26. In addition, the code should be well-documented, on time and under budget. Also, you should be able to use your psychic powers to determine the end user requirements!

27. For the purposes of this discussion, consider components to be groups of classes that are specifically designed to work together as a unit. A well-designed component, system or framework tends to exhibit the same desirable, object-oriented characteristics as a well-designed class.

- Methods: Each method represents an operation that enables an object of the class type to accomplish its purpose, to retrieve or modify object state, or to perform standard life cycle or utility tasks.

2. Encapsulation: The variables and methods (also called members) of a class fall into two general categories.
   - Implementation: The variables maintained by an object of the class type, and the methods used to manage the data and maintain object state. The implementation represents the "inside" of an object, and cannot be accessed by the outside world.
   - Interface: The methods that enable an object of the class type to provide its services to other objects. The interface represents the way that an object can interact with the "outside." Some models further describe an object's interface as outbound. and inbound, associating the interface with presentation and control capabilities.

3. Cohesion: The class has a well-defined purpose or focus. As a part of this concept, the class has access to the basic resources required to accomplish its purpose.

4. Coupling: The class has only a limited amount of dependency on other classes in order to fulfill its purpose. A class that must constantly depend on other classes to do its job is usually poorly designed.[28]

When consistently applied, these design principles tend to produce a number of well-defined classes that are combined into more complex components, then systems, then an entire application. Likewise, the methods of the objects build in functionality, resulting in increasingly complex behavior.

Viewed from a higher-level perspective, an object-oriented application is comprised of a number of objects that work together to accomplish some common purpose. The way in which objects collaborate to achieve a common task is to communicate with each other through a series of method calls. If you combine this concept with the practice of providing focused, well-defined methods in code, it naturally tends to produce a hierarchical call chain in an application. Basic, low-level methods are called by higher-level methods, which are in turn called by other methods and so on. This kind of structure allows simple operations to be combined into behaviors of increasing complexity until you get business behaviors that represent application capabilities, business behaviors or use cases.[29]

Of course, all of the principles mentioned so far haven't really said anything about error handling. Where does exception handling fit in the practice of software design?

---

28. The pursuit of these and other desirable design characteristics have produced a sizable set of design heuristics. There's been quite a bit of work done on these topics that has resulted in some excellent literature on the subject. For design heuristics, there are a number of Web resources, notably the Wiki Web at http://c2.com/cgi/wiki?PrinciplesOfObjectOrientedDesign and the OOTips site at http://ootips.org/ood-principles.html

29. In procedural programming, the process of breaking down complex functionality into progressivley smaller operations was called functional decomposition. A similar process is performed in object-oriented development, with the added task of organizing behaviors into classes, which ultimately improves code flexibility, modularity and reuse.

Traditionally, that's been a problem when trying to develop a robust application. Many programming teams (and software methodologies) treat errors and exceptions as an afterthought. Handling problems in code is generally addressed during the final stages of software development, after the application's structure has already been established and is therefore difficult to change or modify. In this kind of situation, your development team becomes reactive, your design forcibly driven by problems as they surface in your code. Generally, there are three possible ways to address possible errors in an advanced stage of application design:

1. You can do your best to handle potential problems as you discover them in your methods. This has the least impact on your existing design, but it frequently results in a disjointed application, where problems may be silently "handled" even if other parts of the application need to be aware of what's gone wrong.

2. You can do limited redesign in an application, modifying the application structure to manage problems at a component level. This compromise doesn't normally involve substantial modification of code, but there are two major drawbacks to this approach. First, there is the danger that component-level code will be destabilized if there are too many modifications, requiring more extreme refactoring. Second, there is again the risk that exceptions will be silently handled at the component level and hidden from the rest of the application.

3. You can redesign the application. This action requires a substantial amount of commitment in a development project, since you are effectively returning to an earlier stage in the software development cycle. Additionally, there is a risk that a project may never complete its design phase if there are a series of problems that are successively discovered.

As you can see, none of these alternatives are particularly encouraging. This mirrors the fundamental weakness in dealing with potential problems late in a software development cycle. In a language like Java, errors have a communication infrastructure in an application, just like the normal business model does. The error communication model can be well-designed, promoting effective reporting and handling of problems as they occur. Or it can be disorderly, haphazard, unfocused—which tends to produce serious problems in testing, debugging, and maintainability.

To gain a perspective on how to design with exceptions in code, it's useful to establish best practices or desired principles, just like the ones used in object-oriented class design. The following nine principles describe characteristics and goals normally associated with effective exception handling code:

1. In an application, every sequence of business actions (every use case) can be described in terms of a set of likely failure scenarios. These failure scenarios can be defined in a natural hierarchy according to the probability that they will occur in a running application and their potential severity if they occur.

2. Effective object-oriented method design tends to naturally produce a set of focused behaviors with a small, well-defined set of potential failure points. As a use case or business action is refined into these behaviors and methods, the

failure points of a system tend to naturally become localized within specific methods or business actions.

3. There are two general approaches to address potential failure conditions: to develop code that will not allow the scenario to occur, or to develop handler code within the application. Handler code can be local, addressing the potential error within the method. It can also propagate exceptions within a business action, a component, a subsystem or an entire application.

4. Beyond a point, it's unproductive to try to design handler code for every possible failure condition, since doing so will substantially increase development time and will reduce code maintainability. It's generally better to specifically address likely, unavoidable problem scenarios, and errors that have major impact on the application.[30]

5. A method should advertise or broadcast only those error conditions that require more universal awareness within an application, or those that the method cannot address directly due to lack of context or resources.

6. A method should broadcast errors in a form that its consumers[31] can easily understand, based on the consumers' role and responsibilities.

7. A method should throw multiple exceptions only if:
   a. they are mutually exclusive (i.e., have different root causes).
   b. they potentially have different interest to consumers.
   c. it isn't appropriate to merge them into a single exception because they represent fundamentally different failure scenarios.

8. Exceptions or errors should be handled or reported as soon as possible after a problem has been detected in code—ideally in the same method that produced the problem. There is a substantial risk involved in waiting to address error conditions in code. In cases where you must defer reporting because of class or API design, there should be a well-defined method that can be used to obtain the exception or error.

9. In any software entity (a class, component, system, framework or API) exceptions should form a standard, explicit part of the entities' contract between itself and the outside world.

Of course, classes aren't the only programming structure in Java where you need to consider exceptions in application design. Java also lets you define interfaces to describe behavior related to a common purpose or capability.[32] Design guidelines for

---

30. For the remaining error scenarios, it's generally best to avoid the problems that can be avoided, and to develop local handler code (to log the problem, should it occur) for other problems.

31. The term "consumer" refers to any receiver of an exception message, whether human or machine. The idea of providing errors in a meaningful form is equally valid whether you're talking about a user, a class, or another system within your application.

32. The interface is sometimes compared to the concept of the "contract" in other programming languages. Interfaces provide major benefits to the Java programming language, since they allows developers to represent the concept of shared behavioral similarities without depending on the concept of class-based inheritance.

exception definition in interfaces are fairly straightforward, although they require even more foresight than what is required to develop ordinary methods in software components. If an interface has been designed to incorporate exceptions, it suggests that a developer has carefully considered the use of that interface within a code framework. Based on the requirements of the framework and the likely ways that others will implement an interface, the developer adds exceptions to the interface methods to represent what will become the possible failure points when the interface is used. Generally, well-defined exceptions in an interface observe the following two principles:

1. A well-designed interface will usually throw only a single exception type, unless there's a compelling reason for it to behave otherwise. Normally, an interface will represent or model a very specific capability if it is well-designed; in this case, it is generally better to define a single exception type to fit the interface capability.

2. Exceptions defined for an interface should directly relate to the capabilities described by the interface—they should be meaningful in the context of the action or ability that the interface describes. Often, this translates into defining interfaces with custom exceptions.

Interfaces tend to present a problem when establishing a flexible exception handling framework. By their very nature, they do not describe concrete behavior, and so a designer doesn't really have control over how implementations will eventually choose to use the exceptions which have been defined. If designers develop the framework that uses the interface, they can at least control how that framework responds to exceptions if they are produced. If they have limited control over both the framework and the interface implementation though, it is often difficult to handle exceptions properly in code.[33]

It's especially hard for an interface designer to enforce a level of genericity for exceptions produced by the interfaces, so that problems can be represented more flexibly. Typically, a developer has two choices when faced with this problem:

1. Develop the interface with a fixed set of interface-specific exceptions, and require implementors to throw those exceptions or subclasses to represent errors in code. This is typically the best option when dealing with interfaces that will be somewhat standardized in their implementation, or those that could generate errors of moderate to extreme severity.

2. Define the interface so that it throws no exceptions, forcing implementors of the interface to handle all exceptions internally. Generally, this option is required when the capability described by the interface is very general and it's impossible

---

33. Examples of this kind of problem occur in Java's connector-based APIs, such as JDBC. The design work has produced a set of interfaces to represent communication capability, but the interface designers could neither control their implementation (the JDBC drivers) nor the handling framework (developer-written JDBC code).

to predict exactly what code will be written, as in the Runnable interface used to define threaded behavior.

In either case, an implementor can always throw a RuntimeException or Error (accidentally or intentionally) for non-standard exceptions. Unchecked exceptions represent a problem for frameworks that use the interface; it's impossible to predict and, therefore, to address unchecked exceptions thrown by the implementor of an interface. For this reason, it's a good idea for handling frameworks to address unchecked exceptions as well as those defined by the interface, at least if they need to provide some guarantee of resiliency when working with an unpredictable implementation.

Integrating Exceptions into OOD—Design for Maintainability

Simply being aware of the principles for effective exception use in design can help you develop more robust code. Of course, it's also possible to directly incorporate these concepts into a software development process. If you combine the principles of effective object-oriented software design with the ones used to define effective exception handling in your code, the resulting practice might be called something like "design for maintainability."[34] There's really nothing revolutionary about this practice—at the foundation, it's just good object-oriented design, combined with consideration of the problems that could occur in your code. Including exceptions in your code design can go a long way towards making your application better managed and more maintainable in the long term.

You can apply the principles of design for maintainability no matter what process you use to develop software. The starting point is a behavioral model of a key business process within your system. You could define this model through a use case model, a walk-through of a business process—even through functional decomposition. Basically, the process of designing for exceptions in your code looks like what you see in Figure 6-1.[35]

Of course, the best way to appreciate the way that any process works is to demonstrate how it can be used. Let's discuss each of these phases using an example. As a common scenario, consider the situation where a customer wants to place an order online—a common activity that occurs in many business applications today. To make the problem more interesting, let's assume that there can be multiple order items and

---

34. The concept of Design for Maintainability naturally includes the principles of OOD. Think of it as a superset of the process you'd normally follow when trying to develop a good object-oriented model for your system, incorporating the principles of effective error handling and design for testability into a standard process of object-oriented software development.

35. Some experienced developers instinctively perform this sequence of actions, evaluating errors that can occur in code and building a handling strategy. It's rare to see the process applied consistently in an entire software development team, though.

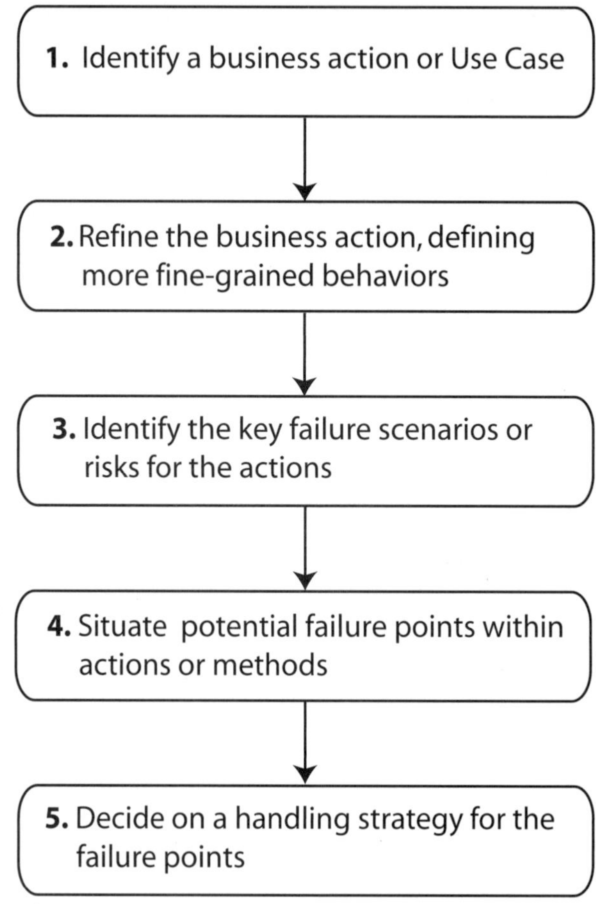

Figure 6–1
Process to incorporate exception handling into development.

multiple quantities for each item. We examine each step of the process in turn, describing what actions you would take, potential considerations, and possible deliverables.

1. Identify a business action or use case

To begin the process, you need to identify a specific use case or activity within your application. The business action in this example would be the processing that occurs in the application when a customer actually places the order—that is, the sequence of events that happen when a customer clicks the "check out" button on the Web browser. Of course, this operation assumes that the customer has performed a number of other activities (shopping, entering shipping and payment information) before the final order processing can occur. In a UML model, this is normally represented by using pre-conditions of a use case, or by relating the business action to other use cases associated with the system. The Use Case Diagram for a typical order fulfillment system might look like Figure 6-2.

2. Refine the business action, defining more fine-grained behaviors

During this stage, you define the actions associated with your use case. All that's really required in this step is an understanding of what major operations are to be performed, and what technologies will be used. Of course, it's also fine if you have greater detail on what occurs in a use case—such information contributes to a better understanding of failure modes in subsequent stages. A business activity normally needs to be described in terms of three things:

- Tasks performed within an application
- Tasks performed between applications
- Technologies or APIs that will be used

The products of this work can be effectively represented by quite a few UML artifacts: sequence diagrams and activity diagrams are particularly well-suited for the job.

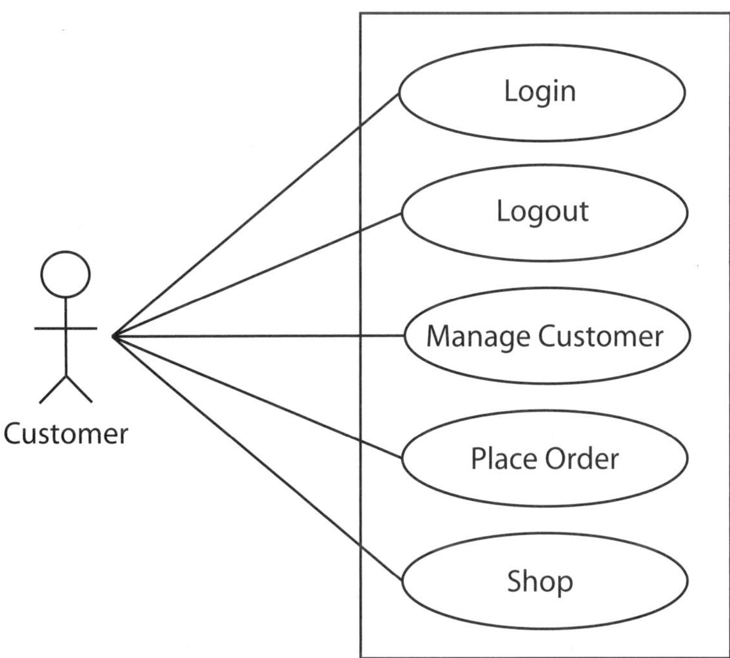

Figure 6–2
Use case diagram for an order management system.

At a basic level, you could simply describe the "place order" business action in terms of subtasks, such as those shown below:

Business Action: Place an Order[36]
>Verify the order information
>>1. Verify whether all order information is complete
>>2. Validate the customer's shipping information
>>3. Validate the customer's billing information
>
>Create and ship the order
>>4. Create the order, reserving items from inventory
>>5. Calculate the total order price
>>6. Finalize the order

Looking at the business model from a different perspective, you could identify the external systems that play a role in the business process:

- Inventory database (step 4, reserving items)
- Order database (step 4, creating the order)
- Credit processing service (steps 3 and 6, financial processing)
- Shipping service (step 6, finalizing the order)

Knowing about these systems helps you identify what technologies and communication protocols will likely be used in an application. This in turn provides detail on the possible failure modes for the use case. In this example, JDBC would probably be used to communicate with both of the databases. The API used to interact with the other external systems would depend on the way in which those systems made their services available—JMS would be the API of choice for messaging systems, JAXM or JAX-RPC for Web Services, and so on.

Figure 6-3 provides an activity diagram that describes the six basic subactions defined earlier. It provides a mid-level focus on the business process, such as you might find during the analysis phases of object-oriented development projects.

Notice that the first two phases of design for maintainability really represent tasks that most development teams would perform anyway, either as explicit steps of their design methodology, or as a natural part of the software development process. The third and subsequent steps apply the knowledge gained during these earlier phases to better understand and deal with possible errors within an application.

---

36. In this example, we assume that a certain level of validation will be required before placing the order. Depending on the system design, it's possible that some of these tasks would have already been performed as "early validation." For the sake of discussion, we perform late validation in this example.

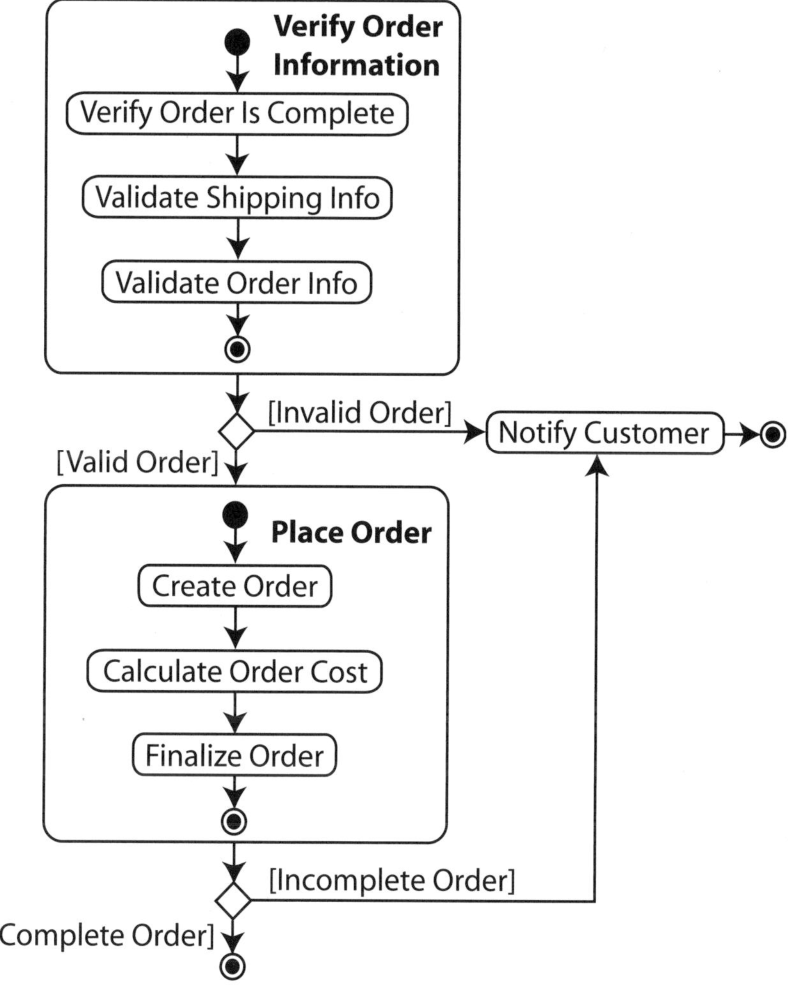

Figure 6–3
Activity diagram for the Place Order use case.

3. Identify failure scenarios or risks for the actions

Once you've established a picture of what will be done in a business process, you can identify the major failure modes for the business operations. As mentioned, the problems associated with a use case tend to flow naturally from the business process, systems and technologies associated with it. An understanding of what actions need to be performed helps designers to better identify potential risks. Once you know the risks, you can subsequently prioritize them and develop effective handling strategies for your application.

If you know what specific technologies or APIs you will use, you can be even more precise when predicting the possible failure modes of your system. Java is an excellent language for predicting trouble spots in an application, since it explicitly documents potential problems in its methods as exceptions or errors. An understanding of which Java API will be applied to solve a problem generally gives you a good perspective on the nature of potential problems, and lets you pinpoint their occurrence in specific methods.

Returning to the six major operations described in step 2, let's profile them and describe the probable sources of error.

1. **Verify whether all order information is complete**

   Operations: Internal validation of objects in the application

   Risks: Data corruption in the system

   Assessment: Low risk

   This operation involves checking an order for completeness—validating that the order has an associated customer, shopping cart, shipping and billing information. Since it doesn't involve complex API work and doesn't extend beyond a runtime boundary, this is a low-risk operation. The principal danger is that of data corruption. This type of risk indicates a need to validate that the business rules associated with the operation are properly enforced, which will likely require a testing strategy during the development cycle.

2. **Validate the customer's shipping information**

   Operations: Internal business rule validation

   Risks: Data corruption, incorrect business process flow

   Assessment: Low risk

   Again, this operation is internal to the system. Although the business rule validation is a bit more involved (checking the shipping method and verifying address information), the action doesn't run the risk of compromising order or system integrity. Like the previous action, this action primarily requires testing and rule validation.

3. **Validate the customer's billing information**

   Operations: Internal business validation, external verification

   Risks: Distributed communication, data corruption, incorrect business process flow

   Assessment: Moderate risk

   This operation is higher risk than the two previous actions. Since validation of billing information depends on an external system, there are risks associated with distributed communication as well as with business validation. Additionally, failure during this stage has possible side effects later in the order process. Still, a problem in this stage doesn't represent a threat to data in the system, and any problems will be effectively isolated to a single order. For these reasons, we classify this operation as moderate risk.

4. **Reserve items from the inventory**
   Operations: Business process, database interaction
   Risks: Distributed communication, transaction control, order and inventory data integrity
   Assessment: High risk

   This is one of the highest risk actions in this use case. The operation is database-intensive and involves transactional behavior that will potentially span many database interactions. In addition, there's the possibility that a number of users will perform operations on the same records, so there are potential concurrency issues as well. If a problem should occur during this action, there could be consequences to a customer's application, and to system data as a whole.

5. **Calculate the total order price**
   Operations: Internal business calculation
   Risks: Incorrect data for business process
   Assessment: Low risk

   This action involves using the information produced during the previous stage to generate a final order cost. This is an internally-performed action and represents a lower risk operation. As in the previous cases, it's important to establish a test strategy for this operation—especially since money is involved.

6. **Finalize the order**
   Operations: Business process, system-system coordination
   Risks: Distributed communication, transaction control, order and shipping data integrity
   Assessment: High risk

   The final action in the use case is also high risk. There is a high degree of coordination required between different distributed systems in this step in order to ensure that the order is finalized. A distributed transaction will likely be required to ensure that data integrity is maintained between the different enterprise systems. Ideally, we'll want to plan the actions in this phase to minimize the risk that a problem will harm data integrity across the coordinated systems.

In this example, the actions defined as part of the business process have helped to narrow the scope and nature of possible problems. You can also prioritize the possible failure points in your application, building a better understanding of the critical actions in an application. In this example, the highest risk operations are the business actions of creating and finalizing the order.

There are two general techniques used to identify failure modes in this example. You can more specifically pinpoint the areas of risk as you refine a use case into more specific business actions. Additionally, you can narrow the scope of possible problems when you know what technologies will be used for an application. Together, these approaches provide an accurate picture of the problems that can occur in code, and their relative severity.[37] A summary of the benefits of standard development activities is shown in Table 6-1.

Table 6–1   Benefits of standard development activities

Techniques/Focus Area	Result/Benefit
Define detailed operations in the use case	Pinpoint/localize failure modes
Identify key APIs (or technologies) used	Provide more detail on failure modes
Define the role of external systems	Highlight crucial coordination points and high-priority actions/operations

In a language like Java, potential failure points are explicitly described by the exceptions that an API or framework can produce. When you know which APIs you will use, you have a good idea about what can go wrong and why. Additionally, certain actions in an application are inherently risky; for instance, any form of distributed communication is subject to a number of potential problems. Activities that involve data sharing or coordination between systems, such as caching or transactions, represent a possible danger to application integrity.

Risks or failure modes can easily be described in more detail as you develop a picture of how the business action will be performed. The high-level view of a business action and its failure modes provide you with an idea of where and what the general problem areas might be. With every passing refinement to your functional model of the application, you can more explicitly describe potential trouble spots in your system.

4. Situate failure points within actions or methods

During this stage, you more specifically identify problems and pinpoint the location of trouble spots within your methods. Actually, this is a two-step process: you refine a general error condition into more specific causes, then you situate those causes within business methods. There are two ways to identify trouble spots within your code. You can let the ordinary OO process drive the method breakdown and identify where the failure modes occur. Alternately, you can design methods around failure modes, using error scenarios to help provide method demarcation. Either approach represents a valid design strategy, and can be used to develop robust object-oriented code.

---

37. We haven't talked much about exactly how you identify sources of error apart from the knowledge of an API. In more general terms, you can identify possible problems in an action or method by performing what-if scenarios on inputs and preconditions to the operation, and on the actions performed as part of the business action.

Let's demonstrate how you might identify failure modes during software development. We work with the Create Order action in the Place Order use case—a crucial operation for the business process. Figure 6-4 shows a fairly detailed sequence diagram for the operation.

If you combine the risks identified in step 3 with this diagram, you can build a picture of what objects and actions are associated with specific kinds of problems.

Risks associated with the Create Order action

1. Database operations for Inventory DAO:
   Connection management (create and destroy)
   Database operations (reserveItem)
2. Database resource management for the NamingDelegate:
   Lookup of the database connection pool
   Connection management (getConnection and release)
3. Concurrency for OrderProcessingService and InventoryService:
   Avoiding thread corruption issues (createOrder and reserveItems)
4. Transaction control in the OrderProcessingService:
   Transaction support for the createOrder method

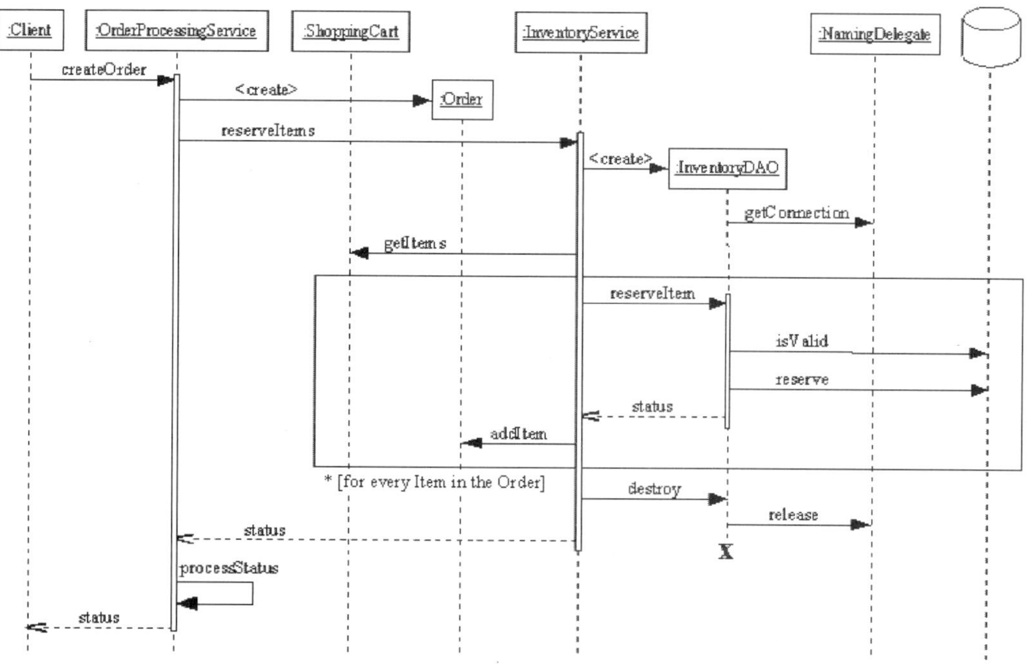

Figure 6–4
Sequence diagram for creating a customer order.

The second through the fourth stages of this process can easily be performed iteratively, establishing the basis to progressively build a better understanding of what can go wrong within an application.

5. Decide on a handling strategy for the failure points

In the final phase of the process, you plan a handling strategy for each of the failure modes of the application. The approach that you take can be high-level—for instance, a written description of the response to a failure scenario. Alternately, it can be very specific, detailing the code to be written or the logging output to be produced. You can plan a single-level handling strategy, or propagate errors through one or more layers of code. In the Create Order example, you might outline the following handling strategies:

Handling Strategies for Create Order example
Class: OrderProcessingService
Method: createOrder
    Risk: Transaction control
    Strategy: Catch exceptions in this method; for critical exceptions, roll back the transaction, log the problem, and restore application state (given the complexity of the operation, it may be worthwhile to split the transaction rollback into a separate method).
    Risk: Thread corruption
    Strategy: Avoid using shared stateful variables; if they are required, synchronize access to them during state-changing operations.

Class: InventoryService
Method: reserveItems
    Risk: Thread corruption
    Strategy: Avoid using shared stateful variables; if they are required, synchronize access to them during state-changing operations.

Class: InventoryDAO
Method: create
    Risk: Unable to obtain a database connection
    Strategy: Propagate the exception up the calling chain and abort the Create Order action (no rollback needed); consider storing the order for background processing.
Method: reserveItem
    Risk: Database errors while reserving items in inventory
    Strategy: Propagate the exception up the calling chain and abort the Create Order action (rollback required); consider storing the order for background processing.
Method: destroy
    Risk: Database problems while releasing connection resources

Strategy: Log the error, release the unhealthy connection; if possible, notify the connection pool that it may need to check the connection.

Class: NamingDelegate
Method: getConnection
    Risk: Problems with locating or accessing the database connection pool
    Strategy: Try to look up connection pool again; if the pool is not available, propagate the exception up the calling chain and abort the Create Order action (no rollback required); may send a notification requesting administrative intervention, or indicate order system unavailability.
Method: release
    Risk: Problems with releasing the connection
    Strategy: If pool is unavailable, send notification requesting administrative intervention or indicate order system unavailability.

Notice that we haven't spent much time talking about specific exceptions in this example. That's actually one of the strengths of this approach; it gives you flexibility in how you identify, and subsequently refine, the risks associated with your application. You could use the process to identify and plan for general risks in code, or you could plan all the way down to the level of specific exceptions. The concept of a "failure mode" can extend beyond a single, isolated exception. In fact, it's not unusual for a single failure mode to incorporate several Java exceptions. Depending on your level of comfort with the development process, you can refine the failure mode to specific exceptions, or make that a task for actual software development.

A principal advantage of design for maintainability is that it gives you greater ability to plan your error handling across a series of methods in an application. If you spend a little time studying the problems that can occur in your code, you're able to set up a much better thought out strategy for dealing with those problems. What's more, the approach tends to give you much better coverage of major problems than the typical, "handle as you code" approach to dealing with exceptions.

If you like, you can be more precise about how you respond to errors. Remember the list of handler options in Chapter 2? You could identify which of those options represent an acceptable response for a given failure mode.

Based on the perspective you've established during the previous steps of this process, you can develop a handling strategy that goes beyond a single method—one that spans several classes or components, if need be. What's more, the planning that you do can be incorporated at an application-wide level, resulting in a system that is able to react locally *and* globally to problems as they occur.

As you continue to expand and refine your design, you can include exception handling considerations in your application development plan and use it to build a stronger code infrastructure. Ultimately, making exception handling part of the standard design contract for an application is safer for a development team, since it clarifies coding responsibilities and increases collaboration when dealing with error conditions.

Design for Maintainability—Benefits and Drawbacks

At this point, we've talked about design for maintainability and how it works. Basically, it's a technique to help you identify and address key trouble spots within your code. It gives you a way to locate where a risk can occur, and subsequently make a global plan on how to address the problem. Best of all, it meshes neatly into standard development practices, so you don't need to radically modify your design process to accommodate the technique.

The technique is actually quite flexible. It's possible to perform this process at any time after you have clarity on the business actions you want to perform in a business sequence. You can potentially gain some benefit whether you only have a general concept of the behaviors to be performed or you have a fully articulated object-oriented model of the system.

In addition, you can use these considerations to help drive method design in object-oriented development. You can potentially use major failure points to help identify method boundaries in your code. If you approach the problem this way, you identify key actions in your system, derive failure points, and build a method around each sequence of actions that has an associated failure point.

Design for maintainability is general enough that you don't necessarily have to focus on specific exceptions until much later in the development process. If you like, you can use it as a technique to focus on the general problems associated with an application, and refine your handling strategy to incorporate exception handling during software development. It's also flexible enough to accommodate exception planning, if you have enough detail about specific Java technologies during software design.

Does design for maintainability cover every problem that could conceivably occur in your code? Probably not, and we could speculate that it really shouldn't factor in *every* problem—just the ones which are significant to your application. The technique is really intended to help identify key risk areas that have global impact. While you *could* potentially continue to identify and refine failure modes forever, such an act would significantly lengthen the design process, increasing the risk that your team would get stuck in "design gridlock." Like most design techniques, the effective use of design for maintainability depends on knowing how to apply the principles intelligently for the greatest payoff for your investment of time.

Finally, notice that this process is *not* described as a methodology, or as a perfect solution for exception handling in every development scenario. Any development principle has to be intelligently applied, rather than blindly followed. Consider these techniques as a suggestion, or an addition to your toolkit of design wisdom.

Failure Mode Analysis

To be successful, design for maintainability requires you to have an understanding of what problems can be expected in your code. You clearly need to understand what problems are likely to occur if you plan to address them during design. While the Java compiler can warn you about checked exceptions in methods that you've already written in code, it's of limited use when you're doing design work. The compiler is more helpful as a way to validate the design work that has been done, and the development work as it progresses.

Whether you plan to factor exception handling into software design or not, it's still a good idea to build a good understanding of the pitfalls associated with language features and APIs. The process of evaluating code—whether it be component, API or framework—for its risks and weaknesses could be called "failure mode analysis." Basically, it involves highlighting potential weaknesses in APIs or classes, and identifying reasonable approaches to address them. Failure mode analysis can give you perspective on how an API works and provide a clearer picture on what problems you should watch out for when you're using an API.

Summary

This chapter discussed the principles that form the foundation of developing robust code in a Java application. It described core concepts used to design an application with exceptions in mind, and presented a technique to use when developing an object-oriented application based on effective exception handling. In the chapters that follow, we perform failure mode analysis on many of the standard Java APIs and frameworks. The goal will be to build an understanding of how the APIs do their work, and specifically on what risks and error scenarios may exist. Table 6-2 summarizes the topics we'll cover in the rest of this section:

Table 6–2   Chapter topics for Part 2

Chapter	Topics (APIs or Frameworks)
7	**Core language**: primitives, arrays, common classes
8	**Commonly used APIs**: Collections, I/O, New I/O
9	**Distributed APIs**: RMI, JNDI, JDBC
10	**J2EE**: Servlet, JSP, EJB

For each chapter, we discuss an API's intended purpose and its standard risks and weaknesses. We identify major exceptions and failure modes in the API, and suggest possible strategies to address problems. Each section's focus on the intended purpose, and on standard problems encountered, helps you appreciate how to effectively use a given API. By reading the following chapters, you can build a better perspective on how to write robust code, how to analyze code on your own, and on how to identify and deal with problems if they occur.

chapter 7

Exceptions in the Java Core Language

Introduction

In this chapter, we discuss possible problems with the primitive data types, arrays, and some of the more commonly used classes in Java. The things we talk about are the workhorses of the language; they're the parts of Java that you tend to use on a day-to-day basis for general coding tasks. A lot of the problems described in this chapter fit into two categories: unchecked exceptions and issues addressed by the compiler. By definition, most of Java's core language features are fairly predictable in behavior; you can generally identify and fix most of these problems during development.

Since these data types and classes are so frequently used in Java programming, the exceptions outlined in this chapter represent some of the most commonly encountered in the Java language. In a sense, that's good news for you as a developer—it means that with a little effort, you can avoid many of the standard problems that surface in the Java language. Of course, it requires diligence to check for many of the problems—most of the core language features and classes throw RuntimeExceptions and are, therefore, hard to check.

Primitive data types, arrays and common objects are often used in other Java APIs to provide low-level data storage. For instance, the Collection Framework uses arrays to store elements in its collection objects. Because of this, the exceptions we talk about sometimes resurface as problems in other APIs. If you build a solid understanding of these language features and their behavior, it can help give you better perspective later on about underlying causes of problems in an application.

Primitive Data Types

Overview

Primitives in Java are basically like those in other programming languages—they hold simple units of data with a fixed amount of space, and they follow standard rules for data storage, retrieval and manipulation. Java defines eight primitive types in four general categories, as shown in Table 7-1.

Table 7-1   **Primitive Data Types, Storage and Range**

Type	Storage	Range
boolean	Logical value	true or false
char	Unicode character	16 bits
byte	Signed integer	8 bits (-2^7 to $2^7 - 1$)
short	Signed integer	16 bits (-2^{15} to $2^{15} - 1$)
int	Signed integer	32 bits (-2^{31} to $2^{31} - 1$)
long	Signed integer	64 bits (-2^{63} to $2^{63} - 1$)
float	Signed decimal value	32 bits
double	Signed decimal value	64 bits

Notes About Use

Normally, primitives are used when you need to store simple data and you don't want the overhead of an object. You often use primitives to store intermediate values in applications.

Primitives, especially Boolean values, are frequently used to enforce flow within a Java application. Standard looping and flow control structures such as `if`, `for`, `while`, and `do` are all based on Boolean values. In addition, standard arithmetic calculations are often performed using primitives, since most of the basic mathematical operations are defined for the integral and floating point types. Numeric primitives follow a natural order of promotion in the Java language, based on the storage capabilities of the data types:

$$\text{byte} \Rightarrow \text{short} \Rightarrow \text{int} \Rightarrow \text{long} \Rightarrow \text{float} \Rightarrow \text{double}^{[38]}$$

If you perform arithmetic operations, the resulting data type will be an integer if both the operands are smaller than or equal to an integer in storage size. If either

---

38. The `char` type can also be cast to a numeric value; it is treated as a 16-bit integral value.

operand is larger than an int, the result will be stored in a primitive that is the same size as the largest variable.

When performing arithmetic calculations, the base unit of storage is the integer. That means that no matter what the types of the operands, the resulting type will be an int. If you want it to be something smaller, you'll have to cast it. In practice, this isn't really an issue in many Java applications; using an int for data storage isn't generally a problem.

Potential Issues—General Overview

Normally, primitive data types don't represent much of a problem because they're so, well, primitive. Most of the problems are detected in advance by `javac`, reported as errors that you can fix during development. The few problems that cannot be caught by a compiler can be avoided with a little work.

1. Conversions between Boolean and numeric types are not allowed

In Java, Boolean variables cannot be converted to any other primitive data type. This means that you can't declare a method that returns an int and treat the result as a Boolean, a practice used in some C-language code. This doesn't really represent a problem or a risk—actually, it tends to avoid confusion in code that might otherwise be ambiguous due to free casting between the logical and numeric data types.

At the same time, it can be a problem for developers who are used to loosely-typed languages—those that allow integer-to-Boolean conversion, (such as the C dialects) or that perform automatic conversion between data types (such as Visual Basic). The solution to this problem is typically to design code based around this reality—to define methods that return boolean values only if they actually provide true-false results.

2. Data truncation with numeric data types

This problem surfaces in two ways: through narrowing conversions, and through arithmetic operations. Because primitive values have a fixed storage size, there's a chance that you may lose information if you don't check for storage.

Casting:
```
int i = 2048;
byte b = (byte)i;
```

When casting variables, the compiler prevents you from making a direct mistake; it will generate an error that will force you to cast your variable if you want to store it in a smaller data type. Of course, if you "fix" the problem, you may still introduce errors into your code, as you can see from the example. The integer has a value of 2048, but the byte will have a value of 0.

Arithmetic operations and casting can chop off the original result, and can yield unpredictable results if you aren't careful. Consider the following example:

```
int i, j, k;
i = 10000;
j = 400000;
k = i * j;
```

The correct value for k in this situation would be 4000000000. However, in this example the multiplication result will exceed the storage available in k, wrapping around and producing a value of -294967296.

The key risk in this case is that you'll get incorrect results from the arithmetic operations. Thanks to the acronym GIGO,[39] this could result in additional errors if the values were used in follow-on calculations.

There are two possible solutions to this problem. The first simply involves performing bounds checking on your values, and either reporting overruns or converting to larger data storage types. This effectively ensures that you don't have a danger of overrunning your storage space. If you expect to regularly encounter values that will exceed storage capacity, a better solution may be to use the BigInteger or BigDecimal classes. These classes provide methods for all of the arithmetic operations defined for the numeric primitive, but they don't have a danger of exceeding the available storage.

3. Loss of precision with numeric data types

This problem applies to floating point primitives—the float and double types. The root of the problem stems from the way the primitives represent floating point data— IEEE specification 754. IEEE754 provides a way to represent decimal quantities with varying amounts of precision. The fundamental problem is that there's only a finite amount of storage for the data, and you've got a tradeoff between the number's precision, its magnitude and its dynamic range. You can have a high precision number with limited range, or a broader range with reduced precision. Without an infinite amount of storage, there's no real way to have a precise value and a broad range for your data.

In Java, you see this problem in roundoff errors, or in direct assignment of extremely precise values. Arithmetic operations can cause small roundoff errors; even minor data conversions can cause the problem to manifest itself. The following example demonstrates how the problem can occur:

```
double c = 0.025;
double d = 21.003;
```

---

39. Garbage In, Garbage Out

```
double e = c * d;
System.out.println("c = " + c + ", d = " + d);
System.out.println("c * d = " + e);
```

In this case, the result of multiplying the two numbers is incorrectly reported as 0.5250750000000001. Granted, this is a *very* small error—about 1×10^{-16}. Still, it looks untidy, and it might conceivably be important to have absolute precision in some situations.

There are several possible solutions for this problem. If you want to have guaranteed exact precision when manipulating decimal values, you can always use the BigDecimal class. If you simply want to guarantee that your results are properly formatted for output, you can use classes in the `java.lang.format` package to handle rounding.

An additional risk for loss of precision comes when you convert from a large integral value to a floating-point value. Once again, the approach used to represent floating-point data can cause data values to be represented inaccurately when you convert from an integer or a long to a float. For example, if you try to cast 10000000001 (which can be represented as either an int or long) to a variable of type float, the result will be the value $1.0\ e^9$.

4. Arithmetic operations and the ArithmeticException

One of the standard runtime exceptions associated with the primitive types is java.lang.ArithmeticException. This exception is produced when there has been some problem performing an arithmetic operation. You'll typically see this exception in primitives when an operation would produce an infinite result. This can be produced in two cases—dividing by zero, and computing the modulo of zero. Clearly, these two situations result in some problems with the laws of reality when applied to computers.

The `ArithmeticException` is a RuntimeException, so you don't have to check for its occurrence. It's fairly typical of standard RuntimeExceptions since there's really no need for you to encounter it in your code, provided you do a little checking in advance. A simple check for a zero value when performing a division or modulo operation is all that's required to avoid the exception altogether.

General Recommendations

There's really no reason to encounter problems with primitives in your code. If you follow these simple rules of thumb, you can generally avoid any difficulties that may arise from using primitive types.

1. Know the data storage requirements for your application in advance, and plan accordingly. Options include:
   - Using BigDecimal or BigInteger.

- Selecting a storage type that is large and precise enough for your needs.
2. Check for 0 values in the operands when using the / or % operators.
3. When displaying values, use a strategy that is appropriate for your needs. Options include using:
   - Raw primitive types, for basic needs.
   - BigDecimal or BigInteger, for extended precision.
   - NumberFormat, for the greatest formatting control.

The Object Class and Objects in Java

Overview

Without a doubt, the Object class is vitally important in the Java language; it's the parent of all other classes, so all the code you write is based on its behavior. The issues associated with the Object class are at the heart of the language. In a sense, every class you work with deals with these issues.

Potential Issues—General Overview

Problems with the Object class represent issues encountered when creating and using subclasses. Problems are either associated with static or dynamic behavior.

There are two categories of failure points that we discuss in this section. The first describes potential issues with the Object class itself, issues that you need to be aware of when you create classes of your own. The second represents potential issues or error when using any object in code.

Static Behavior (Method Definitions)

The primary challenge with static behavior lies in the risks associated with writing generic code. The Object class has a few methods that potentially generate errors or cause varying results depending on their underlying implementation. Ideally, we'd like a base class to be defined in such a way that this can't happen—so that overriding methods does not run the risk of producing exceptions of ambiguous results.

1. *Cloning*

There have been several books that have described the problem with the `clone()` method in the Object class. Basically, the method exists to support copy operations for an object—it provides a standard place in Java to implement the design pattern called Prototype. The problem with this method stems from the fact that there's no standard implementation provided for the copy operation—if you call the `clone` method on an instance of Object, you get a `CloneNotSupportedException`. If a class supports the copy operation, it is supposed to implement the `java.lang.Cloneable` marker interface (an interface without methods) and override the `clone` method. A safe strategy would be to check for the `Cloneable` interface if you intend to use the standard clone functionality, and to handle the possible `CloneNotSupportedException` in your calling code.

An additional source of confusion lies in the fact that there is no way to clearly determine whether a given class supports a shallow or a deep copy. The distinction between a shallow copy, where the object itself is the only thing duplicated, and a deep copy, which copies underlying variables, may be an important one in your code. If this is important in the work you're doing, the `clone` method effectively requires that you understand in advance what kind of copy is being performed.

A potential fix for this is to define an interface of your own to use in place of the standard clone functionality:

```java
public interface Prototype{
    public Object shallowCopy();
    public Object deepCopy();
}
```

2. *Equality and equivalency—the `hashCode` and `equals` methods*

The Object class provides the `equals` method to allow developers to create a test for equivalency. Basically, equivalency allows you to determine if an object can be treated as another, *not* to determine if they are exactly equal. The `==` operator is intended to provide a test of strict equality, returning true only if two references point to the same object in memory.

What's more, you normally want to override the `hashCode` method in a class if you plan to redefine equals. The `hashCode` method is used by several classes in the Java Collections Framework to organize groups of objects. The `HashMap`, `HashSet` and `Hashtable` classes all use the `hashCode` method as a check for object equivalency for storage.[40] The basic rules for implementing the `hashCode` method are:

1. The `hashCode` method must consistently return the same value when called over time, provided that none of the underlying data used to produce the `hashCode` value has changed.
2. If two objects are equivalent (the `equals` method returns true), `hashCode` must return the same value.
3. If two objects are not equivalent (`equals` returns false), `hashCode` is not required to return different values—however, doing so may provide better performance for collections.

---

40. There are a number of other classes in the Java APIs that use these hashing collections internally, so the list is actually longer than this.

The collection classes use the `hashCode` and `equals` methods for an object to determine if the object already exists in a collection. For example, a `HashMap` will use the two methods to determine if a unique "key" for a key-value pair already exists in its storage.

The `hashCode` and `equals` methods can potentially cause some confusion if developers are not clear on the purpose of equality (or equivalency) tests within their code. Manifestations of the problem include difficulties in determining an object's identity, problems with validating unique object existence, and managing storage in collections. In extreme cases, problems in implementing the methods can lead to a collection disposing of objects that should be retained in a system.

3. Object finalization

Many object-oriented languages have the concept of destructors—methods that can be used to clean up after an object at the end of its life. In Java, this capability is available (sort of) in the standard Object method `finalize`. You can override this method for a class if you want a standard way to manage the behavior for object destruction and clean up.

Unfortunately, there are some fairly major issues with `finalize` method invocation. If any exception is thrown during the method call, the exception will be ignored and the `finalize` method will not complete. This means that you need to be careful to handle all exceptions if you want to ensure that your method runs completely.

Even more serious is that you really have no guarantee when—or if—the `finalize` method will be run in an application. The JVM will run the `finalize` method for an object when it determines that the object is no longer referenced by any other part of the application. This action is typically performed during garbage collection, and you don't really know when that will occur. JVMs run a separate thread that manages garbage collection, and the frequency and scope of object cleanup will depend on how the JVM is implemented. That means you will probably not see the `finalize` method called on an object immediately after you dereference it, and it could be quite some time before the method is invoked. It's even possible that the method will not be run at all—the only guarantee is that the JVM will make an effort to execute the method on any objects before the JVM terminates. If any error in the application leads to an improper shutdown, the `finalize` methods will probably not be called on many objects. You can call the method `runFinalization` from the System or Runtime classes as an attempt to ensure that any outstanding object finalizations are run. There's never a guarantee, however, it's still possible in a running application that some finalize methods will not be called.

If you need a guarantee that some sort of clean up behavior will be run, a better approach may be to create a custom method to handle the end of lifecycle actions and call it manually before you destroy the object.

Dynamic Behavior—Object Creation and Use

When using any object, there are a number of standard runtime exceptions you might encounter. For the most part, these are easily avoidable. With a little diligence, you have little risk of these problems in your code.

1. *NullPointerException*

If you write a substantial amount of Java code, you *will* see this exception at some point in your career. It's basically the "404 error" of the Java language. You will encounter this exception any time you try to use an object reference that has not yet been instantiated. The exception can occur with variables passed into a method, and with member variables. For a method declaration like the following one, there's really no effective way for a compiler to ensure that the value of Salary will be non-null under every condition, so you have to check for a null value yourself.

```
public void calculateTax(Salary s){
    // Calculate the amount of taxes required given a specific Salary
}
```

For local variables declared within methods or code blocks, the situation is much better. The compiler can determine when you may have a variable that is not initialized, and it will help you avoid the exception by producing the following error message:

```
ObjTest.java:4: variable s might not have been initialized
    if (s.equals("Q")){
       ^
1 error
```

The `NullPointerException` can cause cascading failures in an application, if the null value represents an object that is frequently used in the system. Luckily, this is one of the exceptions that you never need to encounter in code. You can always ensure that you have a valid object by performing a null check like this one:

```
if ((s != null) && s.equals("Q")){
```

2. *ClassNotFoundException*

Java throws a `ClassNotFoundException` when it cannot locate a class that it needs to load. This exception occurs as a natural consequence of the dynamic nature of the Java language. As a Java application runs, classes that are referenced will be loaded by a `ClassLoader` object. If the `ClassLoader` encounters a class that it cannot find, it will throw the `ClassNotFoundException`.

There are two reasons this problem occurs: either the class really doesn't exist in a location that's accessible to the JVM, or the loader cannot find it. You can usually avoid problems with class existence by packing all of your class files together for distribution. Many IDEs and build tools allow you to bundle a Java application into a JAR file, which helps ensure that you don't omit required classes from your application. In more demanding applications, there may be a post-install program to verify that all the required class files are accessible. In large corporate environments, this source of problem is sometimes resolved by storing class files on a network server and referencing them from client machines.

The second cause of the `ClassNotFoundException` is more common—there are many ways to "lose track" of files on a system. A JVM keeps track of all potential search points for classes using an environment variable called CLASSPATH. The variable specifies absolute or relative paths to directories or `.jar` files. The class loader will use the CLASSPATH values in sequence, searching for a subdirectory structure that matches the package in the class. Sometimes, programs may modify the value for CLASSPATH by using the `-cp` or `-classpath` switches for command-line utilities:

```
javac -classpath ./Resource.jar MyApp.java
java -cp ./Resource.jar MyApp
java -classpath ./Resource.jar MyApp
```

So if we had a CLASSPATH variable set to the following value:

```
CLASSPATH=.:/usr/java/jars/MyApp.jar       Unix
CLASSPATH=.;/usr/java/jars/MyApp.jar       Windows
```

and we tried to locate a class called `MyClass` in the `biz.app` package, the class loader would look first in the standard Java files, then in the current directory, then in the `MyApp.jar` file. In all cases, it would look for the biz/app directory structure, since that was specified as the package for the class.

3. *ClassCastException*

You'll see this exception any time you try to cast an object reference to an incompatible class type. Casting for objects is performed to "narrow" an object to a more specific type. Java, being a strongly typed language, depends on the reference types of its objects to determine what operations can and cannot be performed during compilation. There's only the risk of converting a reference to another object type if they are related by inheritance. If this is not the case, you'll see an error like this one during compilation:

```
Cast.java:4: inconvertible types
found   : Stranger
required: Parent
    Parent p = (Parent)s;
                      ^
1 error
```

There are two sources of errors: you can see this exception if you cast to an Interface type, or if you cast to an incorrect object type. Interestingly, the Interface is not checked during compile time, so you don't have the comfort of performing a compile check for interface compatibility.

There's a major risk for this exception when you working with collection classes. The classes internally store references as type Object, so there typically needs to be a conversion back to the original type in order to use the stored object once again. If you do programming work that makes use of polymorphism, you may also encounter this problem.

Once again, there's a fairly easy solution that allows you to avoid this potential problem. If you use the operator `instanceof`, you can determine whether an object reference can be cast to a particular class or interface type, and avoid the `Class-CastException`:

```
if (s instanceof Parent){
    Parent p = (Parent)s;
```

Common solutions to the problem also include defining methods that accept a given class or interface type as input. If you call the method

```
public void performTask(Worker w)
```

the compiler will ensure that the caller is the appropriate class type. If such is not the case, it will produce an error like the following:

```
Cast.java:6: doWork(Worker) in Cast cannot be applied to (Stranger)
    doWork(s);
    ^
1 error
```

4. *NoSuchFieldError* and *NoSuchMethodError*

These errors occur because of a version delta in your classes. They are thrown when running code which makes use of a field or method that does not exist in one of your classes. How is this possible? If a class were compiled using a version of another class, and subsequently used with a *different* version of the class during runtime, these errors can potentially be produced. Suppose we had the following two simple classes:

```
1   public class GenRefTest{
2     public static void main(String [] args){
3       try{
4         GenX myGen = new GenX();
5         System.out.println("Value is " + myGen.getValue());
6       }
7       catch (Throwable e){
```

```
 8            e.printStackTrace();
 9        }
10    }
11 }
```

```
1  public class GenX{
2     private int value = 42;
3     public String getValue(){
4        return "" + value;
5     }
6  }
```

Compiling and running the class `GenRefTest` would cause the message "`Value is 42`" to be displayed on the screen. Now, suppose you kept the compiled form of `GenRefTest`, but changed the `GenX` class to the following:

```
1  public class GenX{
2     private int value = 42;
3     public int getValue(){
4        return 42;
5     }
6  }
```

Running an example with the modified class will produce the following result:

```
java.lang.NoSuchMethodError: GenX.getValue()Ljava/lang/String;
    at GenRefTest.main(GenRefTest.java:5)
```

Note that this error can happen even if the type would not be "important" to the system. In this example, the integer value returned by `getValue` would be automatically converted to a String anyway, but you'll still get a `NoSuchMethodError` if you work with incompatible classes. After all, the compiler must assume that the difference between method signatures is significant, or you wouldn't have changed it in the first place. This is a consequence of working with a strongly typed language—even if the problem were a fairly minor one in your code, the fact remains that the class does not demonstrate its advertised behavior and could potentially cause problems in a running application.

Like the earlier `ClassNotFoundException`, this problem is usually best handled by performing a post-installation functions check, or by using a build or class distribution method that ensures the proper functionality exists in classes prior to their deployment.

Arrays

Arrays are the way that Java stores a group or collection of variables. Any time you are working with a group of primitives or object references in Java, you are using an array, either directly or behind the scenes. Java manages array space by allocating it as a unit or chunk of memory, then using a reference to point to the storage. Logically, there are three distinct operations related to array use:

1. Declaration: Create the reference used to represent or "track" the array:
   ```
   String [] names;
   ```
2. Creation: Allocate space on the heap for the elements of the array:
   ```
   names = new String[20];
   ```
3. Initialization: Set specific values for array elements:
   ```
   names[0] = "Emilio Lezardo";
   ```

Normally, arrays aren't used directly. Instead, many developers use the `Collection Framework` or similar classes that wrapper and extend array functionality. The main exceptions to this rule are cases where developers need a high efficiency implementation to store objects.

Dynamic array operations are the principal area of risk for arrays, since incorrect inputs can cause problems with array storage or access. There are three primary categories of problem with arrays: indexing, array storage management and object typing.

1. Indexing

There are several subissues dealing with array indexing. Fundamentally, they are all manifested by overstepping the array bounds. As mentioned earlier, Java has a fixed amount of storage space available—once you've allocated storage, there are only so many elements that you can hold.

Any time you overstep the bounds of your array, Java will throw an `ArrayIndexOutOfBoundsException` to reflect the problem. Like other exceptions in this chapter, this is a `RuntimeException`—which means that you can avoid this problem with proper development practices. The way to avoid the exception is to work within the relative bounds of the array—from 0 to one less than the size. Java is organized so that you can use a standard approach for collection traversal:

```
for (int i = 0; i < array.length; i++)
```

2. Array Storage Management

When you're dynamically allocating array storage, there's a risk that you will specify an array size that is negative. The `NegativeArraySizeException` is thrown any time when you try to create an array in a Java application with a negative storage size. This is also a fairly easy situation to avoid—you need only check to see if you are allocating a positive amount of storage:

```
if (arraySize > 0){
    Item [] orderItems = new Item[arraySize];
}
```

3. Object Typing

This kind of risk occurs when storing or retrieving elements in an array. Specific problems include trying to reference null values, and handling class types for an array. This represents the greatest risk when using arrays, since you access array elements frequently in an application, and it requires more work to check for this kind of problem.

The kinds of arrays that represent the greatest risk are arrays of object references. Arrays holding primitive data are easier to check and don't have the risk of null values, since the primitives are initialized to their zero-equivalent values. In the simplest cases, problems can occur because object arrays may not hold data, resulting in a `NullPointerException` being thrown. If you incorrectly typecast an object references that you've retrieved from an array, Java will throw a `ClassCastException`. If you incorrectly specify a class type when setting an array value, an `ArrayStoreException` will be thrown.

The Java compiler can perform a certain basic level of array type checking. Specifically, the compiler can verify that there is consistency between the values you want to store in an array and the array type; it can and will produce an error if the types don't match. For example, suppose you had the following class:

```
public class ArrayElem{
    private Elem[] elements;
    public void addElement(){
        if (elements != null){
            elements[0] = new Object();
        }
    }
}
```

If you try to compile it, you would see the following error:

```
ArrayElem.java:5: incompatible types
found   : java.lang.Object
required: Elem
        elements[0] = new Object();
1 error
```

Of course, the compiler cannot enforce any checking when the array is referenced by a more general variable during runtime. If you passed an array into a method that used a variable of type `Object[]` to reference the array, the compiler cannot perform any type checking and you'd have the danger of producing an `ArrayStoreException` while your application ran.

Interfaces in the `java.lang` Package

In addition to its classes, `java.lang` contains a number of standard interfaces that are used to identify common features among any Java class. These interfaces define a few basic exceptions that it's worthwhile to examine.

CharSequence

This interface was added to Java in JDK1.4 to describe standard operations performed on classes that used sequences of characters, such as the String and String-Buffer classes. It defines two exception-throwing methods, `charAt` and `subSequence`. Since both of these methods are based on accessing characters within a collection, they throw the `IndexOutOfBoundsException` in implementing classes.

Cloneable

This interface describes the clone capability in Java. Since it is a marker interface, it has no exception-generating potential. However, as mentioned in the Object class discussion, classes which do not support cloning will throw `CloneNotSupportedException` when their clone method is called.

Comparable

The `Comparable` interface contains a single method, `compareTo`. The method returns an integer result based on the compared object type:

result	compared value is
negative	less than the original
0	equal to the original
positive	greater than the original

If the method is called with a class type that cannot be compared to the base value, the method is expected to throw a `ClassCastException`.

Runnable

The `Runnable` interface describes threading capability in Java. Its single method, `run`, can act as the target for threaded execution. The method throws no exceptions, meaning that any checked exceptions must either be handled within the run method or wrapped in an unchecked exception.

String and StringBuffer

The String class is among the most fundamental and most commonly used of all the Java classes. StringBuffer is marginally less well-known, but is every bit as versatile as its counterpart. Both classes are used to implement the concept of strings in the Java language—sequences of characters that store or communicate information.

A natural question that often comes up is why do two classes exist to represent strings? Couldn't you just use a single class to do the job? Yes, but Java makes a distinction between mutable and immutable character sequences. String objects are immutable by nature—you can't change them without creating a new object. This makes them suitable for holding character sequences for repeat use, but less effective when performing a number of character operations, such as appends, inserts, and the like. The StringBuffer was created for this purpose, and tends to be more efficient when you perform character manipulation.

Both String and StringBuffer use character arrays to store their character data. Because of this, they're subject to the standard exceptions you'd expect to find for arrays. Specifically, sequencing operations or operations that allocate array size can throw the `StringIndexOutOfBoundsException`. The exceptions are reported as the parent class `IndexOutOfBoundsException`, but the source code actually throws the more specific exception type.

String Class

The String class has a number of standard exceptions it throws. Like many standard Java classes, a String may depend on initialization values—typically, an initial character sequence or character mapping. If the values are not provided, a `NullPointer-Exception` will be thrown.

String objects are sometimes used to handle translations to and from the Java runtime environment and native platform values. The String class handles translations something called a Charset—a mapping between a series of bytes and the 16-bit Unicode characters used in Java. Any methods which perform this translation will throw an `UnsupportedEncodingException` if called with an unrecognized charset name.

Typically, it's a good idea to compare for string equivalency rather than equality. String provides two methods, `equals` and `equalsIgnoreCase`, to perform the check. It can be misleading to compare Strings for true equality, since they are immutable by nature. In most programming circumstances, you want to compare the characters used to represent a String, so the comparison methods are more appropriate for your needs.

StringBuffer class

StringBuffer, like String, deals with an internal character array. Naturally, this means that operations like setting up an array size, adding characters or making character substitutions can all throw `StringIndexOutOfBoundsException`. Like the String class, any null initialization information will result in a `NullPointerException` being thrown. Additionally, since you can allocate space for a StringBuffer object without immediately populating it with character data, any array allocation can potentially throw the `NegativeArraySizeException` if called with a negative size for the internal character buffer.

BigDecimal and BigInteger

The `java.math.BigDecimal` and `java.math.BigInteger` classes were created to provide developers with the ability to perform arithmetic operations with unlimited precision and unlimited storage. They have methods that duplicate all of the standard operators defined for the Java language. For example, there are `add`, `subtract`, `multiply`, and `divide` methods.

Like String, both of these classes are immutable—which means that you're actually creating new objects when you perform arithmetic operations.

Both BigInteger and BigDecimal have constructors that allow initial values to be parsed into internal numeric storage. Any constructor that initializes the object based on a specific value throws a `NumberFormatException` when called with data that is null or is not a number. In addition, BigInteger has constructors that allow you to specify an initial random input value; both constructors will throw exceptions (`IllegalArgumentException` and `ArithmeticException`) when called with invalid lengths for the resulting BigInteger.

BigDecimal and BigInteger allow you to have total precision over the values produced by arithmetic operations, but they're still susceptible to the `ArithmeticException`. A number of operations in these classes cause the exception to be thrown. In the BigDecimal class, `divide` and `setScale` throw these exceptions. For BigInteger, the methods `probablePrime`, `divide`, `divideAndRemainder`, `remainder`, `pow`, `mod`, `modPow`, `modInverse`, `setBit`, `clearBit`, `flipBit`, and `testBit` all throw the exception.

BigDecimal and BigInteger can be converted into primitive values, but there's a risk for loss of precision. When converting to integral values, the lowest order bits will be returned in the number—which means you potentially have the same risk of loss of precision as before. When converting to floating point types, and values which are too large will be represented as the constants NEGATIVE_INFINITY and POSITIVE_INFINITY.

The Wrapper Classes

Wrapper objects are used for two main purposes. The first is to "wrapper" a primitive value in an object so that it can be used for some purpose—for instance, to store the primitive in a collection object, or to use it as a value in a Swing GUI component. The second is to manage parsing and conversion—between a String and a wrapper object, or between the wrapper object and a primitive value.

The primary issue associated with the wrapper objects lies in numeric conversion. Any of the integral wrapper classes will throw a `NumberFormatException` if they try to parse a string that does not represent an appropriate numeric value. This is a RuntimeException, so the compiler will not explicitly check to see if it's being handled.

The exception will be produced in every case when trying to parse a non-integer value. It will even produce the exception when called with an inappropriate numeric type. For instance, the integral types will throw the `NumberFormatException` when called with decimal values. Likewise, the exception will be thrown when the method is called on a value that is larger than the range of storage.

All of the numeric classes as well as the Character class implement the interface `java.lang.Comparable`, and so can be compared to one another. The single method of this interface, `compareTo`, throws a `ClassCastException` when used to compare dissimilar class types. In this case, the exception would be thrown if you used an argument other than the original class type of the wrapper object.

chapter 8

Collections and I/O

Introduction

In programming, there are certain tasks that are so common that they tend to surface in almost any application you write. Basic activities, such as managing a group of objects or reading from a file, are such a fundamental part of applications there's a good chance that any program will have them.

This chapter focuses on these higher-use APIs in Java. As you look at the APIs in this chapter, it's probably no surprise that you'll find more complex failure scenarios, more advanced considerations to bear in mind as you develop code. Three main APIs represent the focus of this chapter—the Collection Framework, I/O and New I/O APIs. Together, they provide vital services of collection management and communication within applications.

The Collection Framework

Overview

The Collection framework, a set of classes and interfaces in the `java.util` package, provides a way to store groups of objects in the Java language. While it's true that Java uses arrays at the foundation to manage groups of primitives and objects, most developers tend to prefer the Collection framework because of the rich feature set it provides.

The Collection framework is built in several layers. The basic behavior of collections is defined using a series of interfaces. At the foundation, the framework defines five general interfaces. Each interface represents certain general kinds of collection, and provides methods to model the associated concepts behind the collection type as shown in Table 8-1.

Table 8-1   The Collection framework interfaces

Interface	Purpose
Collection	The base interface that represent a group of objects; the interface defines standard features that any collection will have.
Set	A subinterface of Collection that does not allow duplicate objects to be stored and does not guarantee that ordering of elements will be preserved.
List	A subinterface of Collection that allows duplicate objects to be stored and guarantees that ordering will be preserved.
Map	An interface that represents a set of key-value pairs; maps require every object that represents a key to be unique, but allow the same object to be stored for multiple values; Maps do not guarantee ordering for keys or values.
Iterator	An interface that specifies a forward-navigable collection of objects; Iterators are produced from a collection and allow removal of elements from the underlying collection.

There are a few additional interfaces that are based on these foundation behaviors. `SortedMap` and `SortedSet` interfaces are subinterfaces of `Map` and `Set` that provide a guarantee of consistent ordering for the stored objects. `ListIterator` is a subinterface of `Iterator` that allows backward scrolling and the addition of elements to the underlying collection.[41]

Next, the Collection framework provides a layer of abstract classes that implement the interfaces. These classes define behavior that is common to all classes of a certain collection type. The `AbstractCollection`, `AbstractList`, `AbstractMap`, `AbstractSequentialList`, and `AbstractSet` classes implement for the base interface types. The final layer of the framework is represented by the concrete classes that provide a full implementation for a specific type of collection. Common classes in this layer are `ArrayList`, `HashSet` and `HashMap`.

Considerations and Issues with the Collections Framework

Before talking about specific exceptions produced by the Collections framework, it's worthwhile to spend a moment and cover some general issues associated with collections. These don't necessarily represent errors, but it's a good idea to be aware of them when you write code. We talk about thread safety, object storage and casting, and the relationship between the Collection framework and the older collection classes.

---

41. `Enumeration` is also a collection-based interface. Like the Iterator, it provides forward-only navigation through a collection of objects, but it does not support object removal.

1. Thread Safety

The classes of the Collection framework were designed to be lightweight. In other words, they're not thread-safe. While this provides greater runtime efficiency, it can cause problems if a collection class must be shared between threads. Collection objects are subject to the standard threading risks—if a collection object is shared between multiple threads, there's the danger that you may have corruption due to the threaded activity. If you aren't careful, you may see problems like value overwriting, inconsistent state and invalid data in your collection.

If you expect to use a collection object in code with a lot of threaded activity, it's probably worthwhile to create a thread-safe version of the collection. Luckily, there's an easy way to accomplish this if you use the Collections class. The class has methods which provide a thread-safe wrapper around each of the standard collection types: `synchronizedCollection`, `synchronizedList`, `synchronizedMap`, `synchronizedSet`, `synchronizedSortedMap` and `synchronizedSortedSet`. Each of these methods returns a class that synchronizes the key collection operations such as `add`, `remove`, `get` and `put`.

```
ArrayList aList = new ArrayList();
List threadSafeList = Collections.synchronizedList(aList);
```

This will guarantee thread safety—at least, at the single-method level. It will probably also cause your code to run more slowly—after all, any of the standard methods used to manage a List will be synchronized in the `threadSafeList` object. An alternative to this approach is to write code that directly synchronizes the crucial operations you need to perform. This requires you to have a good understanding of where the threading risks exist within your code, but it can provide greater runtime efficiency. It also allows you to synchronize behavior over several method calls for the collection.

Of course, there are some cases when you may not need to go as far as synchronizing the methods of a collection. In some situations, you only want to ensure that a collection doesn't change during a method. In situations like these, a good solution is to call the method `toArray`. Every Collection implementor has this method.[42] The method creates an array that holds the same objects as the original collection. You can subsequently use the array in place of the collection, and there's no risk that the elements can be changed. In addition, most of the collection classes implement the `clone` method for the Object class. This method allows you to produce a shallow copy of a collection object, ensuring that object order will be preserved as you use the collection.

---

42. For the `Map` interface, you need to call the method `values()` to obtain a Collection of values for the `Map`.

2. Casting

Collection classes store their elements internally using Object references. This allows a collection class to be used to store a wide range of objects; after all, any Java class will eventually subclass Object. However, it tends to make life harder when developers want to retrieve and subsequently use collection elements.

If you want to restore an object to its original form, the storage strategy used by the Collections Framework requires that you check for an object's identity (if you want to avoid casting problems) then cast the object back into its original class type. If we had an `ArrayList` called aList and wanted to cast the element referenced by an integer index idx, the code would look something like this:

```
Object o = aList.get(idx);
if (o instanceof Element){
    Element elem = (Element)o;
}
```

Of course, if you've consistently stored the same class type to the array, you could ignore the `instanceof` test and cast the object directly into the Element class. You could even cast an entire collection using the method `toArray`:

```
Element [] elems = (Element [])aList.toArray(new Element[1]);
```

This method automatically casts every element of the Collection to the type of the input argument and sizes the array as required to hold the elements. The method provides a convenient way to handle the conversion of an entire collection without having to write a loop to do the job.

No matter what you do, the process of converting back to original class types is bound to be inefficient. Any conversion strategy requires casting, which takes time and reduces runtime efficiency. If you also use the `instanceof` check, it takes even longer to perform the conversion, and if you don't there's a risk that you'll get a `ClassCastException`.

Historically, there's only been one fix for this problem—you had to create a collection class of your own to hold a specific class type. However, JDK1.5 introduced a new language feature that's very useful for this kind of problem—generic types. Generics, also called parameterized data types in some programming languages, allow you to define a class, method parameter or variable with a variable class type. In other words, you can create a class that accepts "plug in" classes when it is used. In order to identify a class to plug into a generic class placeholder, you wrap it in the characters < and >.

Generics have been used to redesign a few of the core Java APIs, including parts of the Collection framework. JSR-14 provides examples for a number of redesigned collection classes that use generics. With generic functionality, you could create a specific form of a collection, ready to work with your elements. There are two enormous benefits to working with a collection based on generics. The first is that code should become simpler and more robust, since you no longer have the additional work of testing objects and casting them back from a generic collection type. The second is that your code may run a bit faster, since you no longer have to store your objects in a generic `Object []` structure. The following code example shows how you could use generics with a common collection class, `ArrayList`.

```
1   import java.util.*;
2   public class GenericTest{
3     public static void main(String [] args){
4       ArrayList<Element> coll = new ArrayList<Element>();
5       for (int i = 0; i < 10; i++){
6         coll.add(new Element());
7       }
8       System.out.println(coll);
9       System.out.println("Item number for 3rd element is " +
10        coll.get(2).getItemNo());
11    }
12  }
```

```
1   public class Element{
2     private static int count;
3     private int itemNo = count++;
4     public int getItemNo(){
5       return itemNo;
6     }
7     public String toString(){
8       return "Element " + itemNo;
9     }
10  }
```

In this example, `ArrayList<Element>` creates a form of the `ArrayList` collection that stores Element objects. As a result of using generics, the compiler will automatically restrict the class of objects that you can store in this `ArrayList` to Element or its subclasses. An attempt to store an unrelated class, such as `java.lang.String`, would cause a compiler error. Likewise, you can retrieve and use the Element object without the need to test its class type using the `instanceof` operator, or cast it using (`Element`).

You can also use generic types in your own code. They can be used very effectively to create collection objects to meet your specific needs. The following example shows a basic form of custom collection called `SimpleList`. Note that the class is not based on the Collection framework; it is called a list only because it generally behaves like a list in that it uses a numeric index to keep track of its elements and permits duplicate elements in the collection:

```java
1   public class SimpleList<E> {
2     private static final int INIT_SIZE = 20;
3     private transient E[] items;
4     private transient int size;
5     public SimpleList(){
6       this(INIT_SIZE);
7     }
8     public SimpleList(int capacity){
9       if (capacity <= 0){
10        capacity = INIT_SIZE;
11      }
12      items = (E [])new Object[capacity];
13    }
14    public void add(E item){
15      if (size >= items.length){
16        growList();
17      }
18      items[size++] = item;
19    }
20    public E get(int idx){
21      if ((idx < 0) || (idx > items.length)){
22        throw new IndexOutOfBoundsException(idx +
23          " is not a valid index for this SimpleList");
24      }
25      else if (items[idx] == null){
26        throw new NullPointerException("Null element for SimpleList");
27      }
28      return items[idx];
29    }
30    public String toString(){
31      StringBuffer contents = new StringBuffer("[ ");
32      for (int i = 0; i < size; i++){
33        contents.append(items[i].toString());
34        contents.append(" ");
35      }
36      contents.append("]");
37      return contents.toString();
38    }
39    private void growList(){
40      E[] newItems = (E [])new Object[2 * items.length];
41      System.arraycopy(items, 0, newItems, 0, items.length);
42      items = newItems;
43    }
44  }
```

The generic tag on the end of the class declaration, `SimpleList<E>`, allows you
to use E anywhere you need to represent the generic class type. The compiler can ver-

ify the placeholder identifier E when creating `SimpleList.class`, and it can subsequently validate the compiled behavior for `SimpleList` when it is used with a plug-in class type.

Generics can provide some performance improvement over the current classes in the Collection framework. If you run the profiler class developed in Chapter 3 to compare the cost of creating and using a large collection, generic collections tend to be about three times faster when adding elements to an array.

3. Conversion between Legacy Code and the Collection Framework

Earlier versions of Java didn't have rich functionality available for collection management.[43] In JDK1.1 and earlier, there was only a small group of collection classes. Vector and Stack provided list storage, Dictionary and Hashtable supported map structures, and the Enumeration interface defined standard iterator behavior. When JDK1.2 was introduced, the older collection classes were merged into the new framework. This provided backward compatible implementations for collection capabilities while allowing the newer functionality to be used in future versions of the JDK.

Of course, there are still cases where you have to work with the older classes. The most common situations are those where you need to use the Vector class or the Enumeration interface. Quite a few other Java APIs have already been designed to work with these language features, and it didn't make sense to deprecate every API that used the older collection classes when the Collection framework came on the scene. In addition, there are situations where you may need to use the underlying object array in a Collection—perhaps to support legacy code.

You can obtain an Enumeration for any of the legacy collection classes by calling the `elements()` method. In addition, the Dictionary and Hashtable classes provide an Enumeration for the keys in the collection if you call the `keys()` method. There is also a method in the Collections class called `enumeration(Collection)` that will return an Enumeration for the newer Collection classes.

To convert a collection to a Vector, you need to use the constructor `Vector(Collection)`. Likewise, there is a convenience constructor for Hashtable that builds the Hashtable from a Map. To get elements from the legacy structures as a Collection, you can call the `values()` method for a Hashtable.

Conversion to object arrays is fairly straightforward. The Collection interface defines the methods `toArray()` and `toArray(Object)`. These methods convert a collection into an array of object references. The process for Map is a little more involved. First, you would obtain a Collection of elements, which you would then use to build an array.

---

43. And back when I was a developer, we had to pedal bicycles to generate power for our computers.

4. The hashcode method and object storage

A few collection classes use the `hashcode` method to determine how to store their elements. The `HashMap`, `HashSet`, `Hashtable`, `IdentityHashMap`, `LinkedHashMap` and `LinkedHashSet` all use object hashing as a way to determine object uniqueness. The way in which a collection uses `hashcode` to handle object storage varies depending on the management strategy used by a collection class. No matter what approach is used, it's important that you define the `hashcode` method so that it provides an accurate measure of object equivalence. If you don't define the `hashcode` method correctly for the objects you plan to store in a hash-based collection, the effects could range from slowing down storage to mistakenly overwriting object references in the collection.

Exceptions and Errors in the Collection Framework

In the technology overview, you saw that the Collection Framework is based on three layers: interfaces, abstract classes and concrete classes. These layers also help to define exception behavior for the framework. The interface layer defines the generic capabilities of collection—it also defines the basic exceptions that you should expect for the basic collection types. The abstract class layer defines the baseline implementation for a specific type of collection. This layer throws exceptions for unsupported features. Finally, the concrete layer provides the actual features and throws the actual exceptions for this specific collection type. Figure 8-1 illustrates the exception behavior for each layer in the framework.

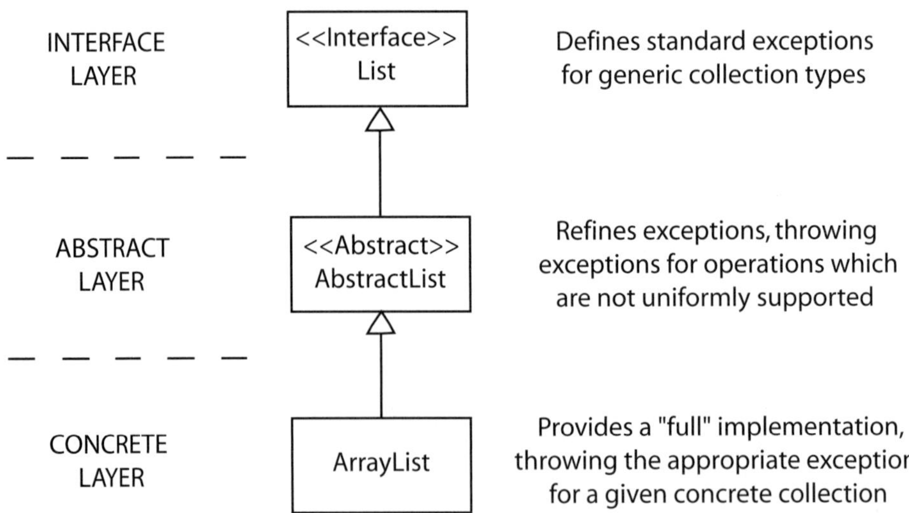

Figure 8–1
Exception behavior for the Collection framework.

Depending on how generic you want your code to be, you can write handler code based on the interface layer, the abstract classes or the concrete class subtypes.

The key to understanding the exceptions that can be thrown in the Collection framework lies in understanding how the classes are built. Fundamentally, every collection uses one or more lower-level storage arrays to do its job. The collection classes may provide more advanced management of the elements, but they're still just wrappers around arrays. Most of the key exceptions thrown by the framework are really based around problems in the managed storage. Bearing that in mind, take a moment to think about the operations provided by collection objects. There are a lot of classes in the framework, but their methods fall into some very simple categories, as shown in Table 8-2.

Table 8-2 Sample methods in the Collection framework

Behavior	Purpose	Sample Methods
Initialization	Initialize array storage	Collection constructors
Collection Management	Add, remove and access elements from storage	`add, remove, set, put, retain, clear`
Navigation and retrieval	Move within a collection and obtain elements	`previous, next, get`
Conversion	Create other collections based on this one	`iterator, subSet, toArray`
Information	Get data about a collection or its contents	`contains, size, isEmpty`

The exceptions thrown by collection objects are all RuntimeExceptions, so you need to explicitly plan for them if you want to handle the errors—the compiler will not check them for you. Luckily, the behavior of the classes is very consistent, so it is possible to anticipate standard kinds of problems. Specific exceptions occur for the categories of operation shown above, so you can plan handler code if you understand the risks associated with a certain kind of operation.

Initialization methods set up underlying array storage, and their exceptions represent problems with their input arguments. Normally, a constructor lets you do one of two things—you can specify the initial storage capacity of the collection, or you can pass an initial group of elements to the collection. The exceptions thrown for these methods are straightforward—constructors will throw an `IllegalArgumentException` if you specify a negative size for the storage capacity, and a `NullPointerException` if you pass in a null input collection. Both of these exceptions are easily avoidable if you validate your input prior to object creation.

Collection management methods deal with modifying the content of a collection once it's been created. Adding, removing or replacing elements are common activities associated with this category of methods. Exceptions produced from these methods depend on the specific type of operation being performed. As an example, take a look at Table 8-3, which summarizes the RuntimeExceptions for remove methods in the API.

Table 8–3   RuntimeExceptions for **remove** methods in the API

Type	Condition	Exception
remove(int)	Beyond collection boundaries	IndexOutOfBoundsException
remove(Object)	Null input	NullPointerException
	Incompatible class type	ClassCastException
remove(Collection)	Null input - for the collection, or elements if nulls are not allowed	NullPointerException
	Incompatible class type	ClassCastException
remove()	Invalid current position (Iterators)	IllegalStateException

Generally, an operation (add, remove, set, put) that accepts a single Object input will throw NullPointerException if there is null input, a ClassCastException if the data type is not compatible with the collection, and an IllegalArgumentException if there is some general problem with the element which prevents it from being added to the collection. Any indexed operations additionally throw an IndexOutOfBoundsException if they go beyond the range of the collection storage. Multi-element operations (addAll, removeAll, retainAll) may throw NullPointerException in two situations: if the Collection itself is null, or if there are elements in the collection that are null and the collection does not allow null values to be stored.

Methods that deal with navigation and retrieval allow you to move within a collection and retrieve individual objects. You typically use Iterators and ListIterators for navigation and retrieval, although other collection types such as Enumeration, LinkedList, SortedMap, SortedSet also provide standard navigation methods. Navigational methods throw the RuntimeException NoSuchElementException if you attempt to access a collection element that does not exist. You can easily avoid this exception by ensuring that you perform a standard test for element existence. The following code sample shows a standard iteration block that avoids the danger of accessing a nonexistent array element:

```
Iterator elems = coll.iterator();
while (elems.hasNext()){
    System.out.println(elems.next());
}
```

In addition, getter methods that take an integer position throw an IndexOutOfBoundsException if you exceed the array boundaries. This is also a RuntimeException and can be avoided if you perform bounds checking before accessing a collection element.

Conversion methods create another collection that contains some or all of elements from the original. Some of these methods build a different type of collection object, while others create a subset of the collection. The risks of calling these methods depend on the type of collection you want to produce. The `iterator` and `list-Iterator` methods throw no Exceptions, creating a navigational wrapper object around the underlying collection storage. The method `toArray` creates an array from the collection elements. If you use the form of this method that accepts an input array, the method will attempt to cast the collection elements to the array's specified storage type. Consequently, the method throws an `ArrayStoreException` for a class type mismatch and a `NullPointerException` if the input array is null.

Another type of conversion method produces a subset of the collection type. Example methods include `subSet` (`SortedSet` implementors), `headMap`, `tailMap`, `headSet` and `tailSet`. Conversion methods accept an argument that specifies a starting index for the subcollection. There are three kinds of RuntimeExceptions produced from these methods: `ClassCastException`, `IllegalArgumentException` and `NullPointerException`. The `ClassCastException` is thrown when the input class type is incompatible with the class type used to organize the collection, the `NullPointerException` is thrown if the selector used to define the subset is null, and the `IllegalArgumentException` is thrown if the key doesn't represent a value that is within the navigation range of the collection.

Information methods retrieve various pieces of information about a collection object, or elements stored in the collection. Since these methods only provide data, they have no exception-producing behavior.

The I/O API

I/O is one of the most fundamental needs of any application, and the `java.io` package was the original one developed to meet these needs. The API designers wanted to make it flexible, suitable for a variety of applications to use for both low- and high-level data transfer. Of course, simplicity, ease of use and cross-platform compatibility were also goals, and the balance of these objectives probably had a lot to do with the end result.

The I/O API is built around the concept of streams, as it is in many programming languages. Basically, a stream is a programming structure that can be used to manage data transfer in an application. In Java, all the original communication endpoints were based around streams—whether they transferred data over sockets, wrote data to files, or sent output to a terminal window.

The key to understanding the `java.io` package lies in understanding how streams work in Java. There are a number of subcategories in streams. Specifically, streams have the following concepts to set them apart:

Direction: Streams are associated with input or output.
Level: Streams are high-level (character-based) or low-level (byte-based).
Connectivity: Some streams attach to endpoints (node), while others are attached to other streams (filter).

These properties define the core of the I/O model, as well as how it can be extended. All I/O behavior is based around four abstract classes, as shown in Table 8-4.

Table 8–4   I/O Behavior Classes

	Input	Output
Byte level	InputStream	OutputStream
Character level	Reader	Writer

Typically, developers "build" a stream object in several stages. First, they create a node stream to connect to a specific destination. The node stream is the actual communication endpoint—it is the stream which ultimately commits bytes or characters to some destination. Table 8-5 shows a few common node streams.

Table 8–5   Common Node Streams

Purpose	Stream type
File-based I/O	FileInputStream, FileOutputStream, FileReader, FileWriter, RandomAccessFile
Standard I/O Streams	System.in, System.out, System.err
Sockets	java.net.Socket methods getInputStream( ), getOutputStream( )
Java variables	ByteArrayInputStream, ByteArrayOutputStream, CharArrayReader, CharArrayWriter, StringReader, StringWriter
Threads	PipedInputStream, PipedOutputStream, PipedReader, PipedWriter

Next, developers attach one or more filter streams to the node. Filter streams are specialized kinds of streams that can be attached to other streams through their constructors. A filter stream modifies the data from its associated stream in some way. Filter streams allow you to progressively modify I/O until it suits your needs. Commonly used filter streams are shown in Table 8-6.

Table 8–6 Common Filter Streams

Purpose	Stream type
Buffering	BufferedInputStream, BufferedOutputStream, BufferedReader, BufferedWriter
Conversion between bytes and characters	InputStreamReader, OutputStreamWriter
Read/Write Java data types	DataInputStream, DataOutputStream, ObjectInputStream, ObjectOutputStream
Printing	PrintStream, PrintWriter
Line Number	LineNumberReader
Pushback Reads	PushbackInputStream, PushbackReader

Using this stream model, you can create a wide variety of stream objects to meet your needs with a fairly small number of base classes.

Exceptions and Errors in the I/O API

I/O is based around the concept of wrappering. Typically, any I/O operation is performed using a chain of streams, with one connected to the next until you reach a node stream. An I/O problem that occurs at the node stream or at one of the intermediate filter streams will be propagated through the other filters until it reaches the end stream—the stream that was originally used to trigger the read or write operation.

When you write code that uses the `java.io` package, get used to seeing the `IOException`—nearly every standard I/O method throws this exception. There's a good reason that `IOException` is such a major part of the exception class hierarchy—I/O is one of the riskier operations in any language. Any time you try to route information to someplace else, you have to account for the possibility that things can go wrong. The `IOException` class is refined for more specific types of I/O problems—as of JDK1.5, there are 25 direct subclasses in J2SE.

`IOException` is a checked exception, so you will have to handle it at some point in your code. You have some flexibility in how you work with specific kinds of I/O problems, though. Since most of the exceptions thrown in the `java.io` package subclass `IOException`, blanket handling is an option in your code—you can write a try-catch block that intercepts the `IOException` and use it to handle a variety of I/O problems. The API also gives you the flexibility to check for more specific exception types, if that approach is better suited to the needs of your application.

Most of the I/O problems you have to deal with are based around the core behavior defined in InputStream, OutputStream, Reader and Writer—the four basic classes used to define stream behavior. As you might expect, these classes define standard methods which have common, predictable issues. Each of the input-based streams can perform a number of read operations and have methods that allow you to perform multi-pass reads, if the underlying stream supports them. The output streams have a set of write methods and a method to flush the output stream. The following sections discuss issues with these basic methods.

1. Reads and Blocking

Input-based streams respond differently to read operations. Depending on its class type, an input stream may:

1. Return a -1 when the end of input has been reached.
2. Throw an `IOException` for invalid reads.
3. Block indefinitely until input is available.

Node streams that are attached to a static data source (such as `ByteArrayInputStream` or `StringReader`) return -1 for end of stream reads, and don't throw the `IOException` at all. Node classes that attach to dynamic destinations—STDIN, Socket streams, piped streams—tend to perform blocking reads and tend to throw an `IOException` if there are problems with reads. Filter streams propagate their read operations to the next level stream—they also propagate the exception thrown by their underlying node stream.

For blocking input streams, you need to do some design work if you don't want an application to "freeze up." Any input-based stream that depends on output from a remote host, a different JVM, or a different thread, can block during its reads. If you plan to perform reads with these types of streams, and especially if the read sequence is important to your application flow, you'll probably want to consider running the read operations in a separate thread. This allows you to have greater control over your reads, and lets you avoid having your application appear to halt during reads.

2. Writes and Buffering

It's common for output streams to buffer their data. In other words, output is normally collected in an array, and directed to its destination only when the buffer is full. The motive for buffering output is to increase the efficiency of write operations, which tend to be among the more inefficient actions in an application. Of course, the downside to buffering is that you can't predict when—or if—output data will be sent to its destination.

For some types of applications, it's important that output reach its destination at the time a write occurs. This is especially important for coordinated communication between two processes, where there's a risk that one or both participants will lock up if communication doesn't occur in a set sequence. Fortunately, there's a simple solution to this problem. Every output stream in Java has a method called `flush()`. This method will ensure that any data in the output stream will be sent to its destination, regardless of whether the buffer is full or not.

3. Streams and Thread Safety

This is a more general issue with streams that pertains to any stream object. The only stream-based classes that provide any guarantee of thread safety are the classes PipedInputStream, PipedOutputStream, PipedReader and PipedWriter. What's more, these classes will only ensure that the data sent between a pair of piped streams is protected—there is no threading protection for the streams themselves. For cases where streams need to be shared between multiple threads, you need to carefully manage the threaded interaction. Individual reads and writes are thread-safe, but there's a danger of corruption if you perform multiple read-write operations. Of course, the risk is even greater for streams than for most other objects, since you risk compromising the state of the stream and its payload—the data you want to read or write.

4. General Exceptions

For the InputStream and Reader classes, read methods which accept a byte array throw a `NullPointerException` if the array is null. Any indexed reads such as `read(byte[], int, int)` throw `IndexOutOfBoundsException` if you overstep the boundaries of the array. In addition, OutputStream and Writer throw a `NullPointerException` if any arrays passed into write operations are null.

For any input streams or readers which support pushback operations for reads, the mark method will throw an `IllegalArgumentException` if the integer read-ahead value is less than zero. If you move past the end of the mark you specified, the mark will be reset. Any attempt to call reset on the stream once you have moved beyond the end of the mark will cause the stream to throw the `IOException`.

Exceptions and Errors for I/O Subclasses

General Problems

1. Buffering and Buffer Size

A lot of the I/O classes allow you to use an internal buffer for incoming or outgoing data. The following streams fit into this category:

BufferedInputStream	ByteArrayInputStream	PushbackInputStream
BufferedOutputStream	ByteArrayOutputStream	PushbackReader
BufferedReader	CharArrayReader	StringReader
BufferedWriter	CharArrayWriter	StringWriter

For most of these classes, there is one form of the constructor that specifies the size for the array. If the buffer size is less than zero, the constructor will throw an `IllegalArgumentException`.

The only exceptions to this rule are the input streams that connect to Java objects—ByteArrayInputStream, CharArrayReader, and StringReader. Since constructors for these stream types accept their data array directly, they don't take a size argument and will not throw the `IllegalArgumentException`. Instead, they'll throw a `NullPointerException` if called with a null data array. Consequently, you should check for null values during object creation for these streams.

2. Character Encoding and Conversion

Some stream types support character set conversion; they allow you to translate characters using character encoding. The best-known examples are the InputStream-Reader and OutputStreamWriter, which allow you to convert between bytes and characters. PrintStream, with its ability to print out a variety of data types, is another stream with this capability. For these streams, constructors let you specify an encoding type that manages how data conversion is performed. If you call the constructor with an unknown or unavailable encoding type, it will throw an `UnsupportedEncodingException`. A related problem occurs in the `readUTF` methods for the DataInputStream, ObjectInputStream and RandomAccessFile. The `readUTF` method can throw a `UTFDataFormatException`, indicating that the bytes don't represent a valid UTF-8 encoded character string.

3. Reading and Writing Primitives and other Data Types

Five stream classes—DataInputStream, DataOutputStream, ObjectInputStream, ObjectOutputStream and RandomAccessFile—can read and write a variety of data types besides bytes. These input streams have special versions of the read method for primitive data types, to read UTF streams, and to read the entire contents of a stream into a buffer. Likewise, the output streams have `write` methods for primitive types and UTF streams. RandomAccessFile, which models a file with read-write capabilities, has both read and write methods. In addition to the `IOException`, the `read` and `write` methods of these classes throw the EOFException, indicating that the end of the stream was reached before the required data type had been fully read.

Problems with Specific Stream Types

1. Piped Streams and Threading

The piped stream classes let you transfer data between two threads. Piped streams give you the ability to communicate more directly than other approaches to thread communication. With these streams, one thread sends output that can be directly read by the other thread as input.

The downside to piped streams is that you usually have to invest a lot of effort to make these streams work properly. To connect two piped streams, you have to attach one stream to the other. A piped stream can only be connected to one other stream—if you call the constructor or connect method on a stream when already connected, you'll get an `IOException`. The following code example shows how you might attach a PipedReader to a PipedWriter:

```
PipedReader pipeIn = new PipedReader();
PipedWriter pipeOut = new PipedWriter(pipeIn);
new SendThread(pipeOut);
new ReceiveThread(pipeIn);
```

You have to be careful about how you manage the read-write sequence between piped streams. If you don't sequence the data transfer correctly, there's a chance that a PipedInputStream or PipedReader will miss the output and block forever. One final word of caution—you should never, ever use a matched pair of piped streams to transfer data within the same thread. Piped streams were designed for transfer between two threads and you risk deadlock if you use them in the same thread.

2. Print Streams and Delayed Exception Reporting

If you look at the PrintStream and PrintWriter classes, you'll notice something unusual—none of the `print` or `println` methods throw the `IOException`. The reason for this change from the other output streams is to make it easier for classes to handle basic output, releasing you from the responsibility of writing a handler block every time you write a call to the `System.out.println` methods. The print stream classes cache any I/O problems internally. If you need to check the state of your stream, you can simply call the `checkError` method. A value of `true` tells you that there's been a problem during your I/O operation.

3. Files and File I/O

An important part of the I/O API allows you to open and manipulate files. These features are primarily based around six classes. The File class represents a file or directory, and allows you to perform basic file test and manipulation operations. Notice that the File class doesn't actually let you read or write to a file. Six stream classes—FileInputStream, FileOutputStream, FileReader, FileWriter and RandomAccessFile—provide the actual read or write capabilities for a file.

File Class

The File class represents a file or directory, and allows you to perform basic file test and manipulation operations. File objects let you do things like listing a directory's contents, creating a file, and renaming a file. Since Java was designed to be a platform and OS-neutral language, there's a potential issue with file and directory naming. The File class (and all of the File streams, for that matter) can accept a String in the constructor as a file name. If you specify an incorrectly formatted path to a file or directory, the constructor will fail. This is hardly surprising, since an incorrect path divider—such as switching the '\' and '/' characters—is enough to make an entire path invalid.

Assuming that you specify a valid file or directory, there's another issue to consider —permissions and security. Quite a few of the methods in File throw the Security exception. If you try to perform one of these operations, such as renaming a file, the JVM will check with the SecurityManager to see if the action is approved. The Security-Manager is free to veto the operation, throwing a SecurityException to the caller. There are two reasons why a JVM might throw this exception: either the OS itself will not permit the operation for the specified directory or file, or the security policy of the JVM will not allow the operation on **any** file or directory. Operations that can throw the SecurityException include:

- Get operations for an absolute path, (`getAbsoluteFile`, `getAbsolutePath`)
- File attribute checks (`canRead`, `canWrite`, `isDirectory`, `isFile`, `lastModified`, `length`)
- File system queries (`exists`, `list`, `listFiles`)
- File system commands (`createNewFile`, `delete`, `mkdir`, `createTempFile`, `renameTo`)
- File attribute changes (`setLastModified`, `setReadOnly`)

File methods throw a few additional exceptions in addition to these standard issues. Any input-sensitive operations throw an `IllegalArgumentException` for invalid input data. Methods which can produce this exception are the `setLastModified`, `createTempFile` and the File constructor which accepts a URI argument. Any of the `get` operations that specify a canonical file or path can also throw an `IOException` if the query of the file subsystem fails. Any constructors throw an `IOException` if the create fails. Finally, constructors with arguments throw a `NullPointerException` for null input values.

The File Stream Classes

FileInputStream, FileOutputStream, FileReader and FileWriter handle file-based input and output. Their constructors open a link to a file, and subsequently allow you to perform I/O. Since the constructors actually attempt to connect you to a file, they are fail-fast—they'll throw an exception if you don't specify a valid file. Any constructor will throw a `NullPointerException` if the input arguments are null. In addition, all constructors can throw the `FileNotFoundException` for various conditions. FileInputStream and FileReader objects will throw this exception if the specified file doesn't exist, is not a valid path to a file, (a directory, for instance) or doesn't have read permission. FileOutputStream and FileWriter throw the exception if the argument is not a valid path to a file or doesn't allow write operations. As with the File object, constructors for any of these objects throw the SecurityException if the SecurityManager doesn't allow a connection to be made to the file for input or output.

The RandomAccessFile class combines file input and output in a single object, providing read and write capability for a file. Depending on the constructor arguments, you can open the file in one of four standard modes:

- r   read-only
- rw   read-write
- rws   read-write, with synchronous update to underlying storage for file content or metadata
- rwd   read-write, with synchronous update to underlying storage for file content

If you don't specify one of these combinations when creating a RandomAccessFile, the constructor will throw the IllegalArgumentException. As with other file-based streams, the constructor also throws the FileNotFoundException, NullPointerException and SecurityException.

Once you create a file stream object, subsequent I/O operations are fairly straightforward. The classes throw the standard `IOException` for reads or writes—just like all of the standard stream classes. The only caveat to this rule is the RandomAccessFile. Its higher-order methods like `readInt` and `writeDouble` throw the EOFException in addition to the standard `IOException`.

4. Object Serialization

The JDK1.1 API introduced object serialization to provide an easy way to send object data directly across a stream. The approach is simple enough—a developer flags a class as being serializable by implementing the marker interface `java.io.Serializable`.[44] This makes it possible to use the ObjectInputStream and ObjectOutputStream classes to transfer the object. When you call the `writeObject` method of the ObjectOutputStream, any non-static variables will be sent to the location indicated by the stream. The `readObject` method of the ObjectInputStream can subsequently read the data from a stream and re-create an object with the same values for its variables.

The `readObject` and `writeObject` methods will transfer primitive variables and any other object that implements Serializable. If you want to avoid serializing a variable in your class, you need only use the `transient` modifier for the variable. The Employee class shown below is an example of a class that can be serialized.

```
1    public class Employee implements java.io.Serializable{
2        // These variables will be serialized
3        private String firstName;
4        private String lastName;
5        private double salary;
```

---

44. A marker interface is one that defines no methods. You implement a marker interface to indicate that your class has some capability that doesn't require a specific method.

```
 6
 7    // Transient variable - will not be serialized
 8    private transient Thread freeWill;
 9
10    public Employee(){}
11    // ... rest of the class ...
12  }
```

Probably the most import thing to realize is that you have to enforce the requirements for object serialization yourself—the compiler won't check to see if your objects
can be transferred through a stream. If you try to write an object that is not serializable
—because the object or one of its variables fails to implement the Serializable or
Externalizable interfaces—the write operation will throw an exception.

It's also important to recognize that serialization is a deep copy operation. When
you make a call to `writeObject`, you actually serialize all of the object's data. If your
object contains other complex objects, all of their data will be serialized, too. Clearly,
you need to carefully plan for the data you want to transfer to avoid slowing down serialization. This is especially important when you're sending the object to a remote destination—sending an object across a network, for instance.

ObjectInputStream and ObjectOutputStream Constructors

The ObjectInputStream and ObjectOutputStream are filter streams, so their constructors wrapper other streams. As you might expect, both constructors throw
`NullPointerException` if the wrappered stream is null. Both classes will throw an
`IOException` if some general I/O problem prevents object instantiation. In addition,
the ObjectInputStream constructor will throw a `StreamCorruptedException` if the
serialization data associated with the stream doesn't register as valid.

Write Operations

The ObjectOutputStream has a number of methods to serialize an object, but the
most commonly used one is the `writeObject` method. As with other writes, the
method will throw an `IOException` if there are general problems with the write operation. It is your responsibility to ensure that the object you pass to this method implements the Serializable or Externalizable interfaces. If the object you want to write does
not implement these interfaces, the `writeObject` method will throw a `NotSerial-
izableException`. A useful workaround for this problem is to wrapper the write
method so that it checks that the object is in fact serializable. The following method
shows how this might be done:

```
public void writeObj(ObjectOutputStream oos, Serialiable obj2Write){
  try{
    oos.writeObject(obj2Write);
  }
  catch (IOException exc){
```

```
      exc.printStackTrace();
  }
}
```

If the object to be serialized contains any non-static variables, they must be primitives, implement Serializable (or Externalizable) or be marked as transient. If your variables don't meet these conditions, `writeObject` will again throw a `NotSerializableException`.

Read Operations

You deserialize an object using the `readObject` method of the ObjectInputStream. In order for this method to succeed, the JVM must be able to find a class that matches the one that was used to serialize the object. If there's no matching class, the `readObject` method will throw a `ClassNotFoundException`. It's worth spending a minute to explain what a "matching" class is. The JVM considers a class as a match if it has the same class type as the one used to serialize the object, and if it has the same value for a computed number that represents the serialization version for the class.

Any class that implements Serializable will automatically be associated with a long value called the serialVersionUID. This ID is written to the stream along with an object's serialized data. When read by the `readObject` method, the ID will be compared to the value present in the class.[45] If the version ID for the object read from the ObjectInputStream is different than that of the class in the VM, the method will throw an `InvalidClassException`.

If you plan to perform multi-generational releases of your software, you can hard-code the serialVersionUID variable to avoid problems with the generation of your serialized objects:

```
private static final long serialVersionUID = 42L;
```

Of course, you have to be very careful about how you use this. When you define a static version ID for your class, you're overriding the JVM's internal consistency check for serialization. Think about what would happen if you had serialized data from an older version of your class. If your new class had additional variables, they would be initialized to a zero or null values by default! For this reason, you generally want to ensure that any class with a static version ID has initialization code for all of its variables in the no-argument constructor.[46]

Deserialization

When you deserialize an object using the `readObject` method of the ObjectInputStream, you have to create a new object. The JVM must create an empty object for you, then fill in values from the serialization stream. How exactly does this occur? The

---

45. The value of the serialization ID will change if there's a change to the source code of the class.
46. Actually, this is a good general recommendation for Serializable classes.

JVM needs to have some way to perform default initialization for the serializable object.

This translates into one additional requirement for object serialization—the need for object initialization. Classes that implement the `Externalizable` interface must have a no-argument constructor. Classes that implement `Serializable` must have a no-argument constructor for their first non-Serializable parent class.[47] There's only one problem: there's no way for the compiler to enforce this requirement. No interface can specify a requirement for constructors. This can lead to some interesting problems if your aren't careful.

If you forget to satisfy the coding requirements for constructors, your code will still compile! Consider this simple example of an Externalizable class:

```
1   import java.io.*;
2   public class Ext implements Externalizable{
3      private byte bVal;
4      public Ext(byte b){
5         bVal = b;
6      }
7      public void readExternal(ObjectInput in)  throws IOException{
8         bVal = (byte)in.read();
9      }
10     public void writeExternal(ObjectOutput out)  throws IOException{
11        out.write(bVal);
12     }
13  }
```

You could compile and even serialize an Ext object. However, when you tried to deserialize it, your code would throw an InvalidClassException and you would see something like this:

```
java.io.InvalidClassException: Ext; no valid constructor
    at java.io.ObjectStreamClass.<init>(ObjectStreamClass.java:379)
    at java.io.ObjectStreamClass.lookup(ObjectStreamClass.java:253)
    at
java.io.ObjectOutputStream.writeObject0(ObjectOutputStream.java:1010)
    at
java.io.ObjectOutputStream.writeObject(ObjectOutputStream.java:278)
    at SSerTest.serialize(SSerTest.java:15)
    at SSerTest.main(SSerTest.java:6)
```

---

47. The reason that an Externalizable class must provide a no-argument constructor is that it directly performs low-level reads and writes itself. Serializable classes benefit from a substantial amount of automation that handles Serializable object initialization, among other things.

The situation is a little trickier with Serializable classes. Take a look at the following example:

```
1   public class Parent{
2     private String id;
3     public Parent(String initId){
4       id = initId;
5     }
6     public String toString(){
7       return id;
8     }
9   }
```

```
 1   import java.io.*;
 2   public class SerChild extends Parent implements Serializable{
 3     private int sequence;
 4     public SerChild(String initId){
 5       super(initId);
 6     }
 7     public String toString(){
 8       return sequence + " " + super.toString();
 9     }
10   }
```

SerChild fulfills all the requirements for a Serializable class. However, its non-Serializable parent class, Parent, doesn't have the required no-argument constructor. If you tried to deserialize an instance of SerChild, you'd get an InvalidClassException again:

```
java.io.InvalidClassException: SerChild; no valid constructor
    at java.io.ObjectStreamClass.<init>(ObjectStreamClass.java:379)
    at java.io.ObjectStreamClass.lookup(ObjectStreamClass.java:253)
    at
java.io.ObjectOutputStream.writeObject0(ObjectOutputStream.java:1010)
    at
java.io.ObjectOutputStream.writeObject(ObjectOutputStream.java:278)
    at SerTest.serialize(SerTest.java:13)
    at SerTest.main(SerTest.java:6)
```

Notice that there's no mention of the parent class in the stack trace, even though it's the cause of the deserialization problem! Clearly, this issue can be hard to track down if you aren't aware of the requirements for Serializable objects.

The New I/O API-NIO

While `java.io` provides a good core model for data transfer, it has a few notable shortcomings. Specifically, there isn't much support for threaded coordination of multiple I/O objects, especially if they're connected to different threads or applications. It isn't easy to send the same data to a number of different destinations—since most remote streams are built in pairs, you have to manually set up and coordinate the transfer of any shared data. Finally, character set conversions are fairly basic, mostly limited to mapping locale-specific characters to 16-bit Unicode. To address these needs, and to improve the basic efficiency of I/O, JDK1.4 introduced a new API called, appropriately enough, NIO.

NIO is a little more complex than the original I/O API. The basic I/O API was built around a single concept—streams—and nothing else. NIO is built around four central ideas: buffers, channels, charsets and selectors. In the API, Buffers provide flexible storage for data. There are a number of Buffer subclasses, each of which handles a certain kind of object storage. A Channel represents a connection to an I/O destination. Depending on its class type, a channel may be able to send data, receive data, or to handle both input and output. Table 8-7 shows standard buffer and channel classes.

Table 8–7   **NIO Buffer and Channel Classes**

NIO Category	Classes
Buffers	ByteBuffer, CharBuffer, DoubleBuffer, FloatBuffer, IntBuffer, LongBuffer, ShortBuffer
Channels	DatagramChannel, FileChannel, Pipe.SinkChannel, Pipe.SourceChannel, ServerSocketChannel, SocketChannel

Selectors allow you to send I/O to multiple destinations with greater threading control than was previously possible, and to multiplex your I/O. Finally, Charsets handle character translation, enabling you to encode and decode data.

It's fairly straightforward to use NIO, once you get used to the standard coding model. You usually begin by creating a Channel object to connect to a specific destination. Next, you create a Buffer to hold your data. If you need to perform character conversions, you create a Charset, and if you need to manage a set of Channels—for threaded or socket-based communications—you create a Selector. The following code sample shows how you could use Channels and Buffers. In this example, the application reads a file and prints it to the standard output stream:

```
1   import java.io.*;
2   import java.nio.*;
3   import java.nio.channels.*;
4   public class ReadFile{
```

```java
5      private FileChannel inFileChannel;
6      private WritableByteChannel stdOutChannel;
7      private ByteBuffer inBuffer;
8      public static void main(String [] args){
9        if (args.length > 0){
10         ReadFile app = new ReadFile();
11         app.openFileIn(args[0]);
12       }
13     }
14     public void openFileIn(String fileName){
15       try{
16         inFileChannel = new FileInputStream(fileName).getChannel();
17         stdOutChannel = Channels.newChannel(System.out);
18         inBuffer = ByteBuffer.allocate((int)inFileChannel.size());
19         inFileChannel.read(inBuffer);
20         inBuffer.rewind();
21         stdOutChannel.write(inBuffer);
22         stdOutChannel.close();
23         inFileChannel.close();
24       }
25       catch(IOException exc){
26         exc.printStackTrace();
27       }
28     }
29   }
```

Most of the NIO API is built around abstract classes. The API defines a series of interfaces and abstract classes, then uses plug-in classes that are collectively called a service provider interface that manages the actual I/O.

There are quite a few Java APIs that use the concept of the service provider interface. The idea is simple enough: an API is defined as a set of interfaces or abstract classes. Vendors subsequently write classes that implement the functionality of the API. It's possible to dynamically plug in an implementation into a Java application while it runs, and you can use the API as a placeholder for the full implementation. This model has enormous benefits for developers, since they can write application code using the generic capabilities described by API. There's no need to rely on vendor-specific implementation details—the interfaces or abstract classes define the core behavior that can subsequently be refined to meet the needs of a specific environment or technology.

Exceptions in the NIO API

Most of the heavy lifting in NIO is performed by the Channel classes. Channels are the objects that actually handle data transfer and manage operations like connection management. This means that a lot of the significant exception-producing behavior centers around the creation and use of channels. In the rest of this section, we describe the basic issues associated with the other parts of NIO—buffers and charsets. We move on from there to the main event—discussing issues associated with the use of channels and selectors.

Buffers

Buffer Creation

As with buffered streams in java.io, Buffers allow you to specify the size of their underlying array. You can set up Buffer storage in one of three ways:

- Call the static method `allocate`, creating a basic buffer
- Call the static method `allocateDirect`, which creates a direct buffer[48]
- Calling the `FileChannel` method map, mapping part of a file directly into a Buffer

It probably comes as no surprise to you that these methods will throw an `IllegalArgumentException` if the buffer size specified is less than zero. Once allocated, the space associated with the buffer is a hard limit. In fact, if you look at the API, you'll notice that there aren't any methods to expand the size of an existing buffer. If you need to grow a buffer, you have to re-allocate the space for it. Some buffers are read-only. In fact, most of the buffer classes have a method `asReadOnlyBuffer` that produces a read-only copy of the buffer contents. Unfortunately, there's no direct way to determine whether a buffer is read-only or not. If you try to write to such a buffer using the put methods, they will throw a `ReadOnlyBufferException`.

When you use a buffer, you read and write by calling the methods `get` and `put`. Buffers let you perform gets and puts with absolute or relative positioning. Either approach has its dangers. For absolute operations, the `get` and `put` methods will throw an `IndexOutOfBoundsException` if you exceed the storage associated with the buffer. A `get` operation with relative positioning will throw a `BufferUnderflowException` if the get tries to read beyond the end of the Buffer. A put operation with relative positioning will throw a `BufferOverflowException` if you try to write beyond the end of the buffer. If your code throws either of these exceptions, no data will be transferred.

Buffers are not thread-safe, so it's possible to corrupt a buffer's contents if you write to it using more than one thread. Read-write operations can also pose a threat when performed by two threads, since changing the buffer's current position can again cause the buffer's contents to be corrupted during a write.

---

48. A direct buffer may be more efficient than an regular buffer. The JVM will attempt to perform any I/O operations directly on a direct buffer, without using any intermediate buffers.

In addition to a value indicating its current position, every buffer also has a mark. The mark value indicates the position in the buffer to which the position will be reset if the reset method is called. The value of the mark must always be between zero and the current position counter in the buffer. If you call reset before the mark value has been defined, the `InvalidMarkException` will be thrown.

Charsets

Charset objects manage character translations. Examples of the kind of work performed by charsets include UTF mappings, locale-based character translations, or conversions to character representations used in different operating systems. You set up a charset by calling a constructor that specifies the character mapping you want to use. An invalid name will cause the charset to throw the `IllegalCharsetNameException`. The static methods that check for the existence of a named character mapping, such as `isSupported` and `forName` will also throw this exception. In addition, `forName`, will throw the `UnsupportedCharsetException` if the name is valid but is not available for the currently running JVM.

Once created, a charset has the ability to create CharsetDecoder and CharsetEncoder objects. These classes are the ones that are used to perform the actual encoding and decoding of text. As their name suggests, the classes have methods that allow you to decode and encode character content. There are two forms for the methods: one produces a Buffer, and one provides an object called a CoderResult. These forms are shown in Table 8-8.

Table 8–8 Charset objects

Class	Method
CharsetDecoder	CharBuffer decode(ByteBuffer in)
	CoderResult decode(ByteBuffer in, CharBuffer out, boolean endOfIn)
CharsetEncoder	ByteBuffer encode(CharBuffer in)
	CoderResult encode(CharBuffer in, ByteBuffer out, boolean endOfIn)

Methods that return the Buffer are fail-fast—if there's a problem with encoding or decoding, they will immediately throw an exception. The methods throw the `IllegalStateException` if there is threaded corruption during the operation, `MalformedInputException` if the data isn't valid input for the charset, `UnmappableCharacterException` if the input is legal but doesn't map to a specific charset, and `CharacterCodingException` if a more general error occurs.

Methods that return a CoderResult use deferred error reporting for some cases. The methods throw only two exceptions—`IllegalStateException` for threaded corruption, and the `CoderMalfunctionError` if there has been a problem with the encoder or decoder. All other error states are returned as part of the CoderResult object. CoderResult has a method called `isError`. The method will return true if the input was malformed or unmappable. Additionally, other methods can provide you with greater detail about problems if they occur—isMalformed, `isOverflow`, `isUnderflow` and `isUnmappable`. If you want to convert the result to an actual thrown exception, you can call the `throwException` method, which will convert the result to an appropriate exception type.

If you want to specify how decoders and encoders respond to standard errors, you can use a standard CodingErrorAction. This class defines three basic responses: `CodingErrorAction.IGNORE`, `CodingErrorAction.REPLACE`, and `CodingErrorAction.REPORT`. You can use these constants to set the reporting strategy for encoders and decoders using the methods `onMalformedInput` and `onUnmappableCharacter`.

Channels

Channels are where the data transfer is actually performed for NIO; consequently, they're the place where you tend to see most of the potential problems when using the API. Channel classes are either open or closed. Only open channels are capable of performing I/O, and once a channel is closed it cannot be re-opened. Some channels can be configured for blocking. A blocking channel blocks the currently running thread when performing a read or write, while a non-blocking channel returns immediately, whether or not there is data. Some channels can be associated with a Selector, allowing them to be multiplexed for I/O. Table 8-9 shows the standard channels and their capabilities.

Table 8–9   NIO Channel Capabilities

Channel Class	Input Capable	Output Capable	Blocking/ Non-blocking	Selector Registration
DatagramChannel	✓	✓	✓	✓
FileChannel	✓	✓		
Pipe.SinkChannel		✓	✓	✓
Pipe.SourceChannel	✓		✓	✓
ServerSocketChannel			✓	✓
SocketChannel	✓	✓	✓	✓
ReadableByteChannel*	✓			
WritableByteChannel*		✓		

* The Channels class can produce implementors of these interfaces through the `newChannel` method.

Opening and Closing a Channel

There are three ways to open a channel. The first way is to use the Channels class; this class has static methods that accept stream objects and return channels. This approach lets you build a channel if you already have a basic InputStream or Output Stream. The second approach is to use I/O-based classes to get a channel; you do this by calling the `getChannel` method on the FileInputStream, FileOutputStream, or RandomAccessFile classes. This lets you open a NIO channel if you have a file or source. A third way is to directly open the channel itself. You can do this by calling the static open method. This lets you build a channel directly, without using other classes at all. The code below demonstrates how to use each approach:

```
WritableByteChannel writeCh = Channels.newChannel(System.out);

FileChannel fileCh = new FileInputStream("Order.txt").getChannel();

SocketChannel sktCh = SocketChannel.open();
```

The `newChannel` method doesn't throw any checked exceptions, though it will throw the standard `NullPointerException` if called with a stream that is null. The `getChannel` methods do not throw exceptions, since you must already be connected to a data location before you can create the channel. The socket-based classes DatagramSocket, ServerSocket and Socket also have the `getChannel` method, but they cannot be used to obtain a new channel. The methods can only be called once a channel has already been set up by calling the open method. If you create a socket object and then call `getChannel`, the method will return a null value. The open methods throw the `IOException` if there has been some problem establishing the channel.

Channels don't work until they have been opened. If you try to perform I/O on a channel before it has been opened, the channel will throw a `NotYetConnectedException`. An open channel allows data transfer until the `close` method is called. Like open, the `close` method throws an `IOException` if there is some problem closing the channel object. Once a channel is closed, it cannot be re-opened; the channel must be recreated. Even if you call the open method again, the channel will remain closed and its `isOpen` method will return false. Furthermore, any reads or writes that you try to perform on a closed channel will throw the `ClosedChannelException`.

Basic Data Transfer

The methods used by channels to transfer data are the `read` and `write` methods. The core behavior model for these methods is defined by a set of interfaces. `ReadableByteChannel` and `WritableByteChannel` define basic reads and writes. NIO also supports multi-source I/O, reads and writes that work with multiple Buffers. This behavior is specified by the GatheringByteChannel and ScatteringByteChannel interfaces. The core exception behavior defined in the interfaces is subsequently overridden by the basic Channel classes. Table 8-10 shows the core exceptions for each interface:

Table 8–10 **Standard Exceptions for Channel Interfaces**

Method	Interface	Exceptions
read	ReadableByteChannel	NonReadableChannelException, ClosedChannelException, AsynchronousCloseException, ClosedByInterruptException, IOException
	ScatteringByteChannel	Sub-interface of ReadableByteChannel; in addition to the exceptions above, read with an index can throw IndexOutOfBoundsException
write	WritableByteChannel	NonWritableChannelException, ClosedChannelException, AsynchronousCloseException, ClosedByInterruptException, IOException
	GatheringByteChannel	Sub-interface of WritableByteChannel; in addition to the exceptions above, write with an index can throw IndexOutOfBoundsException

The exception names provide a good indication of the errors that the classes represent. A channel that was not opened in read mode will throw the `RuntimeException` `NonReadableChannelException`, and a non-writable channel will throw the `RuntimeException` `NonWritableChannelException`. Any I/O performed on a closed channel will throw the `ClosedChannelException`. If some other thread closes a channel while it's blocked in I/O, an `AsynchronousCloseException` will be thrown. If a thread is interrupted by another thread when performing a blocking read or write, a `ClosedByInterruptException` will be thrown.

DatagramChannel, FileChannel, and SocketChannel implement both the ScatteringByteChannel and GatheringByteChannel interfaces, and by extension ReadableByteChannel and WritableByteChannel. Since the Pipe class has separate objects for its input and output channels—Pipe.SinkChannel and Pipe.SourceChannel—they implement the inbound and outbound interfaces separately.

SocketChannel and DatagramChannel

In addition to the open method, both of these channels have a `connect` method. This method is separate and distinct from open, since it represents the ability to connect to a socket address. The connect methods throw the following exceptions:

Unchecked exceptions

`AlreadyConnectedException`—the socket is already connected

`ConnectionPendingException`—the socket is currently waiting for a connection

    `SecurityException`—Socket connect operations are not permitted by the JVM's
        SecurityManager

    `UnresolvedAddressException`—the address cannot be resolved

    `UnsupportedAddressTypeException`—the address type is not supported

Checked exceptions (IOException subclasses)

    `ClosedChannelException`—the channel is not open

    `AsynchronousCloseException`—the channel has been closed by another
        thread while waiting for the connection

    `ClosedByInterruptException`—the thread waiting for the connection has
        been interrupted by another thread, stopping the connect operation

    `IOException`—A general I/O problem has occurred

Both channels also have methods to disconnect the socket. The DatagramChannel has a disconnect method, while the SocketChannel's method is `finishConnect`. Both methods throw the `ClosedChannelException`, `AsynchronousCloseException`, `ClosedByInterruptException` and the more general `IOException`. In addition, the SocketChannel throws the exception `NoConnectionPendingException` if the channel is not connected and there are no pending connection requests.

Locking FileChannels

If you plan to use a FileChannel in a multithreaded application, you may want to lock all or part of the file to protect it against threaded corruption. You can lock a file by calling the one of the `lock` or `tryLock` methods of the FileChannel. If successful, these methods will return a FileLock object that represents the lock on the file or file region. The difference between the two methods is that `lock` will block while `tryLock` will not. If `tryLock` cannot obtain the requested file lock, it will return a null value.

The `lock` method will throw exceptions if the channel has already been closed (`ClosedChannelException`, `AsynchronousCloseException`) and if there are problems obtaining the file lock while in blocking mode. (`FileLockInterruptionException`, `OverlappingFileLockException`) The method will throw `NonReadableChannelException` for unreadable FileChannels if the lock indicates the file should be shared for reading. Likewise, the method will throw `NonWritableChannelException` if the channel has not been shared and the file channel is non-writable. The `tryLock` method throws `ClosedChannelException` and `OverlappingFileLockException`. Both methods will throw the `IOException` for more general I/O problems.

Selectors

The Selector class is used to manage multiple Channel objects. Typically, this kind of capability is used for servers, which usually have to handle the I/O needs of many different clients. A Selector object keeps track of any Channels you register with it, and keeps track of when the Channels are ready to perform I/O-related activities.

You can register a DatagramChannel, Pipe.SinkChannel, Pipe.SourceChannel, ServerSocketChannel or a SocketChannel with a Selector. However, when you register a Channel with a Selector, you indicate what I/O operations are meaningful for that Channel. There are four in all:

Accept—Accept an incoming connection
Connect—Initiate a connection
Read—Receive data
Write—Send data

The Selector will keep track of the Channel, and any others you register, in a group of three sets. The Selector has a general set containing all the Channels associated with the Selector, a set of selected keys (currently ready to perform some operation) and a set of canceled keys. When you request the set of selected keys, the Selector will check its Channels and see if any are ready based on the I/O operations you've specified. If any are ready, the Selector moves them into the set of selected keys, and returns the set to you.

Creating a Selector and adding Channels

You can create a Selector by calling the static `open` method on the class—this method potentially throws an `IOException`, but this rarely happens and would probably indicate bigger problems in your application. Once you have an active Selector, you can register Channel objects by calling one of several `register` methods defined for Channels. Every `register` method throws the checked exception `ClosedChannelException`, which indicates that the channel cannot be registered with the Selector because it has been closed. Additionally, register methods throw the following unchecked exceptions:

`IllegalArgumentException`—The `register` method doesn't specify valid operations, ones that match the capabilities of the channel.

`IllegalBlockingModeException`—Channels must not be in blocking mode when they use a Selector.

`IllegalSelectorException`—There is a mismatch between service providers used to create the Selector and the Channel.

`CancelledKeyException`—The Channel has already been registered with the Selector, and its key has been canceled.

Registering with a Selector enables the selector to keep track of a channel—it associates the channel with a SelectionKey and places the key in the selector's managed sets. You can obtain the group of keys that are ready for I/O operations by calling one of the select methods. There are three different `select` methods, with different behavior based on an application's blocking needs:

```
select()            Blocks until a channel is ready for I/O
select(long)        Blocks until a channel is ready or the timeout value expires
selectNow()         Returns immediately, whether channels are ready or not
```

Each of the methods throws two standard exceptions: the `IOException` and the `ClosedSelectorException`. In addition, `select(long)` throws an `IllegalArgumentException` if the specified timeout value is negative.

These methods return the number of currently available channels. If you want to get the channels, you subsequently call the method `selectedKeys`, which returns a Set containing all of the keys referencing channels which are ready for I/O. You can call methods on the SelectionKey objects of the Set to determine exactly what a given Channel is ready for: `isAcceptable`, `isConnectable`, `isReadable`, `isWritable` and `readyOps` all provide a way to determine what actions a channel can perform.

It's important to recognize that the Set returned by the `selectedKeys` method is *not* guaranteed to be thread-safe, nor are its Channels. Translated, that means that additional Channels can be added to the available keys while you use the Set. More importantly, it means that a key identified as "ready" may actually have been cancelled prior to your use. Any of the information methods for the SelectionKey can throw a CanceledKeyException if it the key has been canceled and is no longer managed by this Selector. If you prefer to call a method that does not throw an exception, `isValid` will return `true` if a given key can be used for channel operations.

Once you have obtained a Set from a Selector, you cannot directly modify it; the `selectedKeys` method is intended only to return keys for the purpose of iterating through the collection of Channels that are ready for I/O. If you attempt to directly modify the Set of a Selector, its methods will throw an `UnsupportedOperationException`. This means that you should get the Iterator from the Set and use it in a single thread to avoid problems with threaded interaction.

When you're done with a Channel in a Selector, you need to cancel its key to remove it from the Selector's check queue. There are three ways to do this: you can call the `cancel` method directly on a SelectionKey, if you only need to unregister a single channel but still keep it open. You can close the channel associated with the key, if you want to shut down the channel and remove it from the Selector's channel set. Finally, you can call `close` on the Selector itself, which will shut down the Selector and remove all of its registered channels.[49]

---

49. I know what you're thinking now—why oh why didn't I take the blue pill? NIO is definitely one of the more complex of the Java APIs, and its exception model is also fairly detailed.

chapter 9

Distributed Java APIs

Introduction

Java has been associated with distributed communication from the beginning. Over a few short years following its creation, the language developed an incredibly rich and diverse set of APIs to work with nearly every standardized distributed technology. Today, Java has APIs that allow developers to communicate with enterprise systems such as databases, messaging systems, e-mail servers, and a variety of Web-based services.

Distributed communication also represents one of the riskiest actions that can be performed in an application. If you consider the sum total of things that can go wrong from the moment you make a request to the moment you get a reply, it's amazing that applications can exchange data at all. This chapter describes the errors and exception model for some of the key distributed technologies. First, we discuss the basic principles of distributed communication. Next, we show how Java manages remote communication—the basic model and the potential pitfalls. Finally, we focus on a few specific APIs:

- Remote Method Invocation (RMI)
- Java Naming and Directory Interface (JNDI)
- The Java Database Connectivity API, JDBC

It probably comes as no surprise that there's a reason for choosing these specific technologies—there are actually three reasons. First, they're a good representative sample of Java distributed APIs. Second, there are a lot of Java applications that use these specific APIs. And finally, they're important for Java 2, Enterprise Edition (J2EE).

Though J2EE uses many distributed technologies in its own right, each of these APIs have special significance for J2EE. RMI provides the basic communication model for J2EE business components, Enterprise JavaBeans.[50] JDBC manages communica-

---

50. RMI-IIOP has been the required protocol for EJBs since the EJB2.0 / J2EE1.3 specification, in order to promote standardization among J2EE containers, as well as interoperability between J2EE and CORBA-based systems.

tion with the most commonly used enterprise system, databases. Finally, JNDI provides registry services for a J2EE application.[51]

Distributed Communication Fundamentals

Distributed communication is based on the concept of standardized protocols. A **protocol** is basically a network language, a communication standard that ensures participants can have a meaningful exchange of data even if they're running on different hardware or operating systems—even if they're written in entirely different programming languages.

Equally important is the concept of **protocol layering**—building more advanced forms of communication on top of lower-level protocols. Layering makes it possible to set up communication for an application without spending months developing the infrastructure you need for data transfer. These days, every distributed communication technology owes its existence to the time-honored principle of layering. A distributed system, such as a database application, will build a layer of functionality over an existing transport layer protocol. The higher-level database protocol provides vital services for the database client, such as connection management and SQL communication. Meanwhile, the underlying protocol layers deal with other practical matters, like finding a target machine and managing reliable data transfer.

The great thing about protocol layering is that developers can enjoy the capabilities of the lower-level protocols without actually having to develop and test them in an application. For example, TCP/IP provides a guarantee of reliable communication, and you can safely assume that any protocol you build on top of TCP/IP will have those abilities as well. That's an enormously powerful concept—the idea of layering makes the Web possible, among other things. The next time you're developing a Web application for users around the world, take a moment to be thankful for the concept of protocol layering. Without layering, you'd have to build and manage your own wide area network.

In many ways, we owe the substantial flexibility of distributed communication to TCP/IP. Originally developed as a monolithic communication channel, its designers subsequently refined the technology, defining a series of protocols that provided successive capabilities. Over time, the model became generalized to the OSI 7-Layer communications model, as shown in Figure 9-1. Of course, programmers rarely have to deal with the detailed requirements of the OSI model today—it's usually acceptable to take a standard protocol stack and build a new distributed protocol on top of it.

---

51.   Specifically, JNDI is used to store the location of Enterprise JavaBeans and "factory" resources—classes that can connect to things like databases and messaging services.

Layer 7	Application	
Layer 6	Presentation	
Layer 5	Session	
Layer 4	Transport	Transmission Control Protocol (TCP)
Layer 3	Network	Internet Protocol (IP)
Layer 2	Data Link	Ethernet
Layer 1	Physical	Fiber Optic Channel
	Layer Name	**TCP/IP Stack Example**

Figure 9–1
The Open Systems Interconnect Communication Model.

Although there's no formal requirement, almost all of Java's distributed technologies use TCP/IP. The Java language has always had interoperability and platform-neutrality as key design goals, so it's easy to see why TCP/IP is a good protocol choice. When you bring these language objectives into the realm of distributed communication, it's sensible to base your APIs around a widely-used protocol so that they can be used in many different computing environments. Thanks to its long-term standing as an open standard, as well as the tremendous success of the Web, TCP/IP is the most widely-used protocol around. Any computer that's Internet-capable has a TCP/IP implementation. It's natural that Java distributed technologies should be built to run on such a network protocol.

In programming, it's common to base communications on an API that supports a specific kind of distributed communication—a certain kind of technology or type of system. As long as the supported technology or system is fairly generic, the API can remain generic, too. Unfortunately, there's a tendency for protocols to become more product-specific (or even proprietary) as they become more complex. This means there's a real danger of vendor lock-in if you aren't careful about your choice of technology. Early DBMS products provide a good example of this problem. Early generation DBMS vendors would develop their own distributed API to support their proprietary communication protocol and product-specific features. Every RDBMS used

SQL for database communication,[52] but every vendor had a different approach to support SQL communication with its database. As a result, development teams often had to rewrite applications if the database changed.

Clearly, this isn't an ideal scenario for software developers, since they have to change business applications based on changes in the enterprise technology. In a perfect world, you'd prefer that changes in the business software be based around one thing only—changes to the business model. Luckily, there's a solution to this type of problem. You build a generic API that supports distributed communications with a type of server, then let the vendors implement the API for their systems. Clearly, this requires a lot of cooperation within the software industry, but it ultimately makes life much easier for developers. Rather than writing applications to a vendor's database-specific API, developers can use a generic API such as JDBC and "plug into" a vendor's implementation. The vendors win, since they can support a wider variety of applications with their products. Developers also win, since they can work with a generic API and don't need to constantly rewrite software as products and features change in the marketplace.

Java's Distributed Communication Models

All of Java's distributed APIs use these foundation principles to some degree. Java APIs build on top of lower-level protocols to provide advanced communication capabilities. Distributed APIs abstract communication functionality: they provide a product-neutral, technology-focused solution to developers that can be associated with a variety of products. Broadly speaking, there are four kinds of distributed APIs in Java:

1. **Low-level APIs** provide a layer of abstraction around basic communication protocols. Examples include the Socket and Datagram classes in the java.net package, which support TCP/IP and UDP, respectively.
2. **Generic object APIs** enable a model for distributed method calls. CORBA and RMI are examples of this type of API.
3. **Content-based APIs** use lower-level protocols, but focus instead on providing a generic model for data transfer. Web Service APIs fall into this category.
4. **Technology-specific APIs** provide communication capabilities for a specific type of enterprise system. This is the most numerous group of APIs in Java, and includes JDBC, JNDI and JMS.

Java has a special advantage where distributed APIs are concerned. Since the Java language has the concept of the interface, it's possible to build a distributed API as a

---

52. Of course, vendors did (and do) provide various degrees of SQL compliancy. This tends to present less of a problem to developers than the communication API itself—it's often possible to modify the SQL without changing the basic structure of the application. You usually don't have this guarantee when working with a different vendor's distributed communication model.

series of interfaces rather than using concrete classes. Why would you want to do this? An interface defines a behavior without tying you to a specific implementation, which is helpful if you want to define an API that can subsequently be dynamically matched with a concrete implementation. That's exactly what many of the Java distributed APIs do. You write your code to a set of interfaces, then load a product-specific implementation of the interfaces during runtime. The implementations of a distributed API are usually called drivers or communication adapters. A driver provides an implementation of the interfaces in the API; it can be associated with a Java application during runtime, thanks to the principle of dynamic class loading.

Issues with Distributed Java APIs

Many of Java's distributed APIs are based on a group of interfaces, which are subsequently implemented by vendors. This means that the actual behavior of an implementation is a little unpredictable. After all, interfaces can't actually mandate *any* behavior—all they can do is require an implementor of the interface to write code for all of the methods. There's no way that the compiler can actually verify that an implementation of an interface performs the correct actions—in fact, there's really no way that you could specify exactly what a "correct action" might be.[53]

From your point of view, this means that interface-based standards can only do two things—guarantee that an API has standard methods, and define checked exceptions that should be dealt with in the code that uses the interface. For instance, if you're using JDBC, the interfaces will show that you'll need to handle or declare the `java.sql.SQLException` in most of the methods of the API. It won't actually tell you what a given driver will do during runtime.

If most distributed APIs can't define specific behavior, how do you know that a given driver implementation is actually doing its job? There are a couple of ways. First, the specification of many distributed APIs includes a set of rules that a service provider must follow when developing an implementation. If the service provider follows those rules, you're safe. Second, it's common for the more popular distributed APIs and frameworks to have a compatibility test suite. JDBC, for example, has an online document that details what an implementor must do to create a compliant JDBC driver, and the Sun Web site provides a searchable database of JDBC-compliant implementations.[54]

---

53. The concept of the interface doesn't encompass the specific actions required of its methods. In order to implement an interface, software developers must understand the intended behavior of the methods. In distributed APIs, developers must also understand how client invocation of a method should affect the underlying framework, and write their code accordingly.

54. As another example, J2EE has a very thorough compatibility test suite. If the vendor of a J2EE server passes the compatibility tests, customers can be comfortable that the implementation follows the "rules" required for the J2EE architectural model to work properly.

Of course, an implementation is only as perfect as the specification upon which it is based. It's difficult to anticipate all of the issues and technology-specific variations for a distributed technology. If there are gray areas in a specification, an API might have slightly different implementations. It's possible that a communication adapter might have some vendor-specific quirks—the product might follow the API specification, but have variations in its implementation. It's always prudent to stay up to date on driver documentation, so that you remain aware of any special coding requirements for a vendor's product.

Finally, recognize that a communications API cannot control unchecked exceptions at all. Runtime exceptions and errors are a possibility when using a communication adapter. When developing distributed applications, it's prudent to plan for handling unchecked exceptions as well as those mandated by the API specification.

Java Exception Model

As mentioned, the world of distributed APIs is a complex one. There's a lot that can go wrong. If you think about the standard flow of communication for a standard Java's API, there are a lot of failure points, as seen in Figure 9-2.

Take a look at this diagram and use it for a simple "what-if" scenario. What could go wrong during a single distributed call? There could be a problem with the driver, with the distributed communication channel, or with the receiving enterprise system. There could be additional layers of technology, and additional failure points, depending on the architecture of the remote system. Finally, the communication channel itself is based on a number of layers, so there could be multiple failure points due to

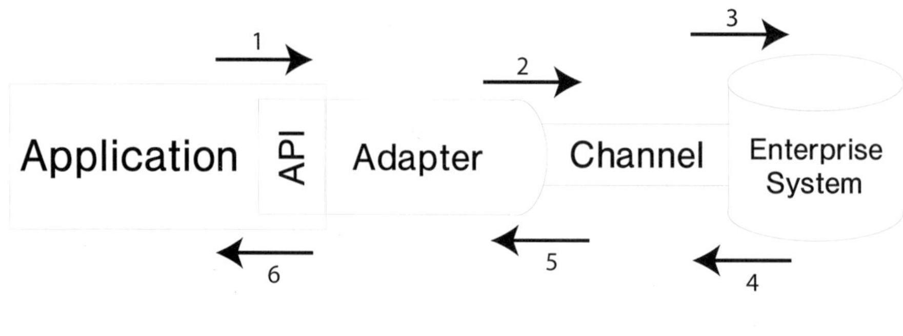

Outbound Communication

1. Application to Adapter
2. Adapter to Channel
3. Channel to Enterprise System

Inbound Communication

4. Enterprise System to Channel
5. Channel to Adapter
6. Adapter to Application

Figure 9–2
Standard Java Distributed Communication Model.

various problems in the protocol stack. Once again, it's amazing that you can transfer data at all.

Practically speaking, how does Java represent all of these possible failure points in a distributed API? How do you represent problems when there could be as many as six or seven distinct places for errors to occur? Most distributed APIs base their exception model around one generic exception class. There are a lot of things that can go wrong when you make a distributed method call, but you often don't need to know the cause of the problem in excruciating detail.

Distributed APIs usually provide greater detail about the cause of a problem in the exception itself, or they define subclasses to represent more specific types of problems. This gives you the freedom to drill down to the root cause of a problem or to address it using a generic handler block—the choice is yours. An example: in JDBC, the `SQLException` indicates a problem when trying to communicate with a database. If you want, you can look at the message—or at another piece of data, the SQL error code—to get a better picture of what has occurred.

Distributed Communication Model and Standard Issues

Whatever API-specific exceptions there are for a distributed Java technology, there are a few common issues that you should address. Specifically, there are two categories of problems that you'll almost always encounter—in some form—simply because you're working with a distributed system. The first set relates to server limitations, and the second to limitations with the network.

All servers have practical limitations on their processing and communication capabilities. Since many clients tend to use the services of a single server, the server usually has a client load that varies dynamically over time. In many distributed systems, the peak client load is more than the server can handle.[55] That's all right in some business cases—provided you're realistic and you provide a safe way for a server to tell clients when it is saturated. After all, if you exceed the amount of traffic that a server can comfortably handle, it *will* fail. You have the ability to make a server failure more or less graceful. This means you should design your system so that problems in server load won't cause the server to crash, and won't trigger follow-on errors in other clients.

The other standard set of problems lies in the communication channel itself. Though it's comforting to believe otherwise, networks aren't perfect, and you should design your system with that reality in mind. The sources of network problems are varied—network latency, signal corruption, and dropped connections are among some of

---

55. Often, the cost of providing servers that can comfortably handle peak loading is prohibitively expensive for a company—especially since peak client use often occurs during very narrow time windows. It's usually important to plan for transient usage "spikes" in your distributed systems, since client load over time can be hard to predict.

the more universal issues. Whatever the source, developing a robust distributed system means that you need to plan for communication problems in your application.

Every API defines distinct interfaces, with standard methods that you use to manage a certain type of distributed communication. That isn't surprising—part of the reason for using a specific API in the first place is that the communication model is different from the other distributed APIs in Java. Having said this, there are some standard tasks that you can reasonably expect to perform in any API simply because you're working with a distributed programming model. When you use most of the APIs in this chapter, you usually perform the following actions:

1. Find a server
2. Connect to the server
3. Prepare a request
4. Send a request
5. Receive a response
6. Interpret the response
7. Disconnect from the server

There are standard, predictable problems that can occur when performing these basic operations. What's more, distributed APIs typically follow these basic steps in a fairly consistent way—after all, the steps describe a generic request model for remote communication. By understanding an API and associating its operations with a basic model, you're able to develop more robust code for distributed communication. You're better able to anticipate and plan for problems, and this benefits your applications as a whole.

Remote Method Invocation–RMI

RMI provided Java's earliest technology to support remote method calls. RMI runs on a TCP/IP backbone by default, and adds a protocol layer to support distributed method calls. Originally, it used a protocol called the Java Remote Method Protocol, or JRMP. Since JRMP was developed specifically for RMI, the API had some practical limitations—you could only use it for Java-to-Java communication. In JDK1.2, RMI was modified so that you could use a more universal protocol than JRMP—the Internet Inter-ORB Protocol, IIOP. This protocol was developed as part of the CORBA specification, and is supported by a wide number of programming languages. The use of IIOP as a channel protocol effectively allows RMI-based applications to interoperate with CORBA.

Basic RMI Communication Model

There are three basic parts to an RMI communication model—a client, a server and a registry. Both the client and server share an interface called the **remote interface**. This interface defines the methods that a client can call—the remote services available on the server through RMI. The remote interface acts as a foundation for a communication proxy.[56] On the client side, a proxy called the **stub** handles remote communication. The client treats the stub as the local representative of the distributed object, making method calls to it. The stub translates the local method call into a remote request using either JRMP or IIOP and sends requests to the server.

The server is responsible for creating and managing **remote objects**. A remote object receives method calls from a client and performs server-side processing. The server advertises the availability of its remote objects by storing entries for them in a **registry**. Specifically, an RMI server stores a stub in the registry that is configured with the server's location. The entry in the registry associates the stub with a String—some commonly understood name for the remote service. When a client wants to call a method on the server, it contacts the registry and looks up the remote object using its name. The registry in turn provides the stub, enabling the client to proceed with distributed communication.[57] Figure 9-3 provides a simple picture of how RMI works:

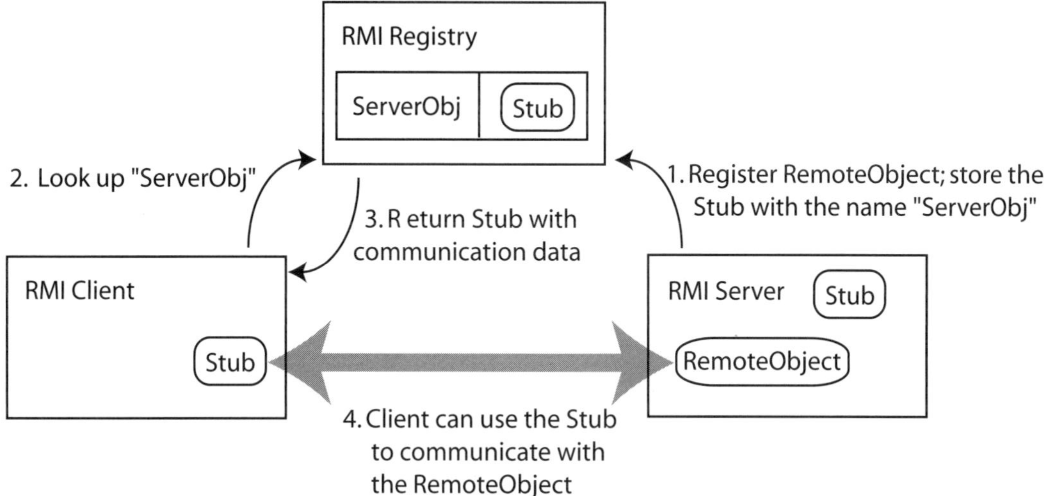

Figure 9–3
RMI Communication Model.

---

56. The Proxy is a useful design pattern for distributed communications. Many distributed frameworks allow the auto-generation of remote communication proxies, so that client and server developers don't have to iimplement their own protocol.

57. In earlier versions of RMI, the server-side object had a communication proxy called the skeleton. As of JDK1.2, the skeleton was no longer required, since the server object handled its own communication needs internally. The classes `java.rmi.server.UnicastRemoteObject` and `java.rmi.activation.Activatable` implement the server-side communication model for RMI.

General Issues with RMI

It's useful to profile the major issues associated with RMI before talking about specific problems and exceptions.

1. Protocol Selection—JRMP or IIOP?

As mentioned, RMI can communicate using one of two protocols—JRMP or IIOP. For many applications, the distinction isn't all that important. However, it is always useful to have a perspective on the respective strengths of the protocols for cases where you have to make an informed decision between the alternatives.

IIOP is a more universally supported protocol than JRMP. Since the protocol is based around a long-standing, established communication technology, it can support a broader group of callers than JRMP. In addition, IIOP has a better chance of being able to interoperate with a technology infrastructure such as the Web without major configuration changes. Of course, that flexibility has a price—any data sent using this protocol must be converted to a language-neutral format called the Interface Definition Language, or IDL. That conversion takes time and effort, reducing the communications efficiency for greater universality.

JRMP, on the other hand, is directly associated with Java technology, and has a few capabilities that IIOP doesn't. Specifically, JRMP can be set up to pass an entire serialized class across a network connection. Since IIOP has to work with a number of systems, it can only pass the data associated with a class, not the class itself. In some applications, it is desirable to have the capability to dynamically add class files to a server as it runs; JRMP would be a desirable protocol for this situation.[58]

2. Code Location

The class files for RMI must be placed on the right systems for the technology to work properly. That sounds basic, but the structure for an RMI application is somewhat complex, involving a large number of classes and interfaces. In addition, there are three locations where you need to place the code—registry, server and client. Table 9-1 shows file locations for a general RMI system:

---

58. The ability to dynamically download code requires some additional configuration of the RMI system. You can find further details on dynamic downloading at http://java.sun.com/j2se/1.4.2/docs/guide/rmi/codebase.html.

Table 9–1 Classes and Interface Location for RMI

Class or Interface	Client	Registry	Server
Remote interface	Yes	-	Yes
Remote object	-	-	Yes
Server	-	-	Yes
Stub*	Yes	Yes	Yes
Classes for value objects passed as parameters for method calls†	Yes	Yes*	Yes
Client class	Yes	-	-

* Stubs don't have to be stored on the client if the system is configured for dynamic code downloading.
† Likewise, value classes don't have to reside on a client that uses dynamic code downloading.

At a minimum, the RMI registry must hold the stub—the object that allows a client to communicate with an RMI server. Additionally, a registry can be configured to dynamically provide the classes passed in remote method calls.

If you don't place the classes in the correct location on each of the systems, your RMI application will have problems. The RMI server will fail during object creation and registration without the remote interface, remote object class and stub. The RMI client will fail when it tries to locate the RMI server if it lacks the remote interface and cannot obtain the stub. The registry will likewise fail to register a remote object if the registry does not have access to the stub. In addition to these issues, you can potentially see problems during communication if the classes used to pass data between client and server are not on the required systems. Typically, such problems are manifested as `RemoteException` subclasses with root cause exceptions such as `ClassNotFoundException` or `NoClassDefException`. For instance, if a client did not have a stub when it tried to connect to an RMI server, you could expect to see the following stack trace:

```
java.rmi.UnmarshalException: error unmarshalling return; nested exception is:
    java.lang.ClassNotFoundException: RmtSvcImpl_Stub (no security manager: RMI
class loader disabled)
    at sun.rmi.registry.RegistryImpl_Stub.lookup(Unknown Source)
    at java.rmi.Naming.lookup(Naming.java:84)
    at RMIClient.lookupSvc(RMIClient.java:30)
    at RMIClient.main(RMIClient.java:18)
Caused by: java.lang.ClassNotFoundException: RmtSvcImpl_Stub (no security
manager: RMI class loader disabled)
    at sun.rmi.server.LoaderHandler.loadClass(LoaderHandler.java:371)
    at sun.rmi.server.LoaderHandler.loadClass(LoaderHandler.java:165)
    at java.rmi.server.RMIClassLoader$2.loadClass(RMIClassLoader.java:631)
    at java.rmi.server.RMIClassLoader.loadClass(RMIClassLoader.java:257)
    at sun.rmi.server.MarshalInputStream.resolveClass(MarshalInputStream.java:200)
```

```
at java.io.ObjectInputStream.readNonProxyDesc(ObjectInputStream.java:1513)
at java.io.ObjectInputStream.readClassDesc(ObjectInputStream.java:1435)
at java.io.ObjectInputStream.readOrdinaryObject(ObjectInputStream.java:1626)
at java.io.ObjectInputStream.readObject0(ObjectInputStream.java:1274)
at java.io.ObjectInputStream.readObject(ObjectInputStream.java:324)
... 4 more
```

3. Data Problems

Data is often passed between an RMI client and server. The exact vehicle for data transfer depends on the wire protocol being used—object serialization is used for data transfer with JRMP, while IIOP involves converting object data into IDL. Regardless of the technology used, there are a few issues associated with data transfer. First, any form of data transfer has a risk of a code delta,[59] so you need to ensure that you keep careful track of the class versions used on both the clients and servers. Second, data transfer means that there's the risk of improperly initialized objects—objects that have only some of the data they require.[60] When sending data between RMI client and server, you should be careful to ensure that *all* the variables are properly initialized. Failure to do so usually causes runtime exceptions, such as the `NullPointerExcep-tion`, to occur while your code runs. Finally, data exchange between systems implies a risk of data synchronization problems, and requires you to manage data across a distributed system. You need to carefully design the RMI system so that data doesn't get out of sync in your application.

4. Server Limitations

RMI servers have a limit to the number of incoming connection requests they can service at a given time. Actually, this limitation has nothing to do with RMI itself—a server can only handle so much traffic at a given instant. In addition, TCP/IP sockets have a limited connection "backlog." If the number of incoming requests exceeds the backlog, subsequent client connection attempts will fail. If a client tries to connect to an RMI server when the server is saturated with communication requests, the client will fail with a `java.rmi.ConnectException`, like the one shown in the sample stack trace below:

```
java.rmi.ConnectException: Connection refused to host: localhost; nested
exception is:
    java.net.ConnectException: Connection refused: connect
    at sun.rmi.transport.tcp.TCPEndpoint.newSocket(TCPEndpoint.java:567)
    at sun.rmi.transport.tcp.TCPChannel.createConnection(TCPChannel.java:185)
```

---

59. Of course, this is also a risk for the basic RMI classes—the remote object class and its communication stub.

60. This risk is most obvious for object serialization. You can explicitly choose *not* to serialize some of an object's variables. If you do you must explicitly initialize the variables on the "receiver," or they will remain at their default "zero" values.

```
    at sun.rmi.transport.tcp.TCPChannel.newConnection(TCPChannel.java:171)
    at sun.rmi.server.UnicastRef.newCall(UnicastRef.java:313)
    at sun.rmi.registry.RegistryImpl_Stub.lookup(Unknown Source)
    at java.rmi.Naming.lookup(Naming.java:84)
    at ThreadedRMI$CliThread.run(ThreadedRMI.java:42)
Caused by: java.net.ConnectException: Connection refused: connect
    at java.net.PlainSocketImpl.socketConnect(Native Method)
    at java.net.PlainSocketImpl.doConnect(PlainSocketImpl.java:305)
    at java.net.PlainSocketImpl.connectToAddress(PlainSocketImpl.java:171)
    at java.net.PlainSocketImpl.connect(PlainSocketImpl.java:158)
    at java.net.Socket.connect(Socket.java:452)
    at java.net.Socket.connect(Socket.java:402)
    at java.net.Socket.<init>(Socket.java:309)
    at java.net.Socket.<init>(Socket.java:124)
    at
sun.rmi.transport.proxy.RMIDirectSocketFactory.createSocket(RMIDirectSocketF
actory.java:22)
    at
sun.rmi.transport.proxy.RMIMasterSocketFactory.createSocket(RMIMasterSocketF
actory.java:128)
    at sun.rmi.transport.tcp.TCPEndpoint.newSocket(TCPEndpoint.java:562)
    ... 6 more
```

Naturally, the continued well-being of an RMI session depends on the health of its server. The good news is that you don't need the RMI registry throughout an RMI communication session. Once the client has successfully located its server host from the RMI registry, it uses the same server throughout its session. Once a connection has been established, a client will establish a network link to the server only for the duration of a method call. That makes it a bit easier for the server to handle ongoing traffic—in most cases, the server only has to manage a subset of the total client load at any given point in time.

Exception Model for RMI

Now that you've had a chance to see general issues associated with RMI, we focus on specific errors within an RMI system. We examine each part of a full RMI implementation, highlighting special considerations and failure points associated with each part. We talk about coding requirements and responsibilities, which provides a good perspective about what you'd need to do when developing an RMI system.

1. The Remote Interface

The remote interface represents the shared contract between client and server, defining any behavior that is remotely callable. The interface must implement `java.rmi.Remote`, and each of its methods must at a minimum declare the `java.rmi.RemoteException`. The `RemoteException` is the generic exception sent to a client when an error occurs in RMI communication. It represents any problem associated with the remote object, or the communication channel. In addition, you can add checked exceptions to your RMI methods if you wish.

Unfortunately, there's no way for Java to enforce the requirement that you must declare the `RemoteException` for every method in your interface. If you forget to declare the exception, your code *will* compile. However, you will not be able to subsequently generate a communication stub using the RMI compiler, **rmic**. When you execute `rmic`, the compiler will produce the following message:

```
error: DateService is not a valid remote interface:
    method java.util.Date getDate() must throw java.rmi.RemoteException.
1 error
```

2. Remote Object

You can create two kinds of server-side remote objects. The first, based on the class `UnicastRemoteObject`, is designed to be run over time on the server. The second is based around the `Activatable` class. `Activatable` objects can be created on the server on an as-needed basis.

Your server-side remote object must implement the remote interface that you defined. Additionally, it must be able to receive, process and respond to client communication requests. Remote objects delegate the actual work of remote communication to one of the following classes: `java.rmi.server.UnicastRemoteObject` or `java.rmi.activation.Activatable`. `UnicastRemoteObject` provides a server model for a single-instance remote object that must be run as part of a server. `Activatable` provides support for server-side RMI objects that can be created as required by the server.

If you don't implement the remote interface, you'll encounter similar problems to those you had if you forgot to declare a `RemoteException` for your methods. The rmic utility will produce the following error message:

```
error: Stubs are only needed for classes that directly implement an
interface that extends java.rmi.Remote; class DateServiceImpl does not
directly implement a remote interface.
1 error
```

You'll encounter a more serious problem if you don't use the `UnicastRemoteObject` or `Activatable` classes in your remote object. In this case, the class will compile with both `javac` and `rmic`, but will fail when you subsequently try to run it. Specifically, it will produce a runtime exception that looks something like this:

```
java.rmi.MarshalException: error marshalling arguments; nested exception is:
    java.io.NotSerializableException: DateServiceImpl
    at sun.rmi.registry.RegistryImpl_Stub.rebind(Unknown Source)
```

```
    at java.rmi.Naming.rebind(Naming.java:160)
    at DateSvr.main(DateSvr.java:10)
Caused by: java.io.NotSerializableException: DateServiceImpl
    at java.io.ObjectOutputStream.writeObject0(ObjectOutputStream.java:1054)
    at java.io.ObjectOutputStream.writeObject(ObjectOutputStream.java:278)
    ... 3 more
```

Whether you use the `UnicastRemoteObject` or `Activatable` classes, you have two choices for how to set up your remote object. You can either subclass one of the classes, or you can create an object and delegate remote handling to it within the constructor. In either case, the RMI class will manage communication for the remote object, acting as a server-side proxy. It's really up to you which approach you use to manage remote communication—either works perfectly well. Subclassing is recommended by some, since the parent class can handle the mechanics of equality across a network boundary. In other words, it will take care of resolving equality using a distributed version of the `equals` and `hashCode` methods.[61]

Regardless of the approach you use to set up your remote object, you'll need to handle or declare the `RemoteException` that can be thrown during object creation. Both UnicastRemoteObject and Activatable can throw this exception during object creation, which means you'll have to address the exception when you set up your remote object. You don't need to pass any special information to the `UnicastRemoteObject` constructor, so you can create any constructor that you wish for the remote object. Classes that use `Activatable` are a bit more stringent in their requirements—they must have two arguments passed into the constructor. The first, `java.rmi.activation.ActivationID`, holds important information used to "activate" a remote object. The second argument, `java.rmi.MarshalledObject`, holds initialization data (if any) passed to the object during its creation. If you omit these required arguments in the constructor, the remote object will trigger an `ActivateFailedException` that wrappers an underlying `NoSuchMethodException`. Basically, this exception signals that you must provide the expected constructor in order to properly activate the remote object.

```
java.rmi.activation.ActivateFailedException: failed to activate object; nested
exception is:
    java.rmi.activation.ActivationException: Activatable object must provide an
activation constructor; nested exception is:
    java.lang.NoSuchMethodException:
ActTestImpl.<init>(java.rmi.activation.ActivationID, java.rmi.MarshalledObject)
    at sun.rmi.server.ActivatableRef.activate(ActivatableRef.java:256)
    at sun.rmi.server.ActivatableRef.invoke(ActivatableRef.java:106)
    at ActTestImpl_Stub.getDate(Unknown Source)
```

---

61. If you plan to use `UnicastRemoteObject` or `Activatable` within the constructor, you will need to set up your own approach to handle remote equality in your class—the ability to determine whether two objects on different JVMs should be considered the same.

```
    at ClientAct$ActCliThread.run(ClientAct.java:41)
Caused by: java.rmi.activation.ActivationException: Activatable object must
provide an activation constructor; nested exception is:
    java.lang.NoSuchMethodException:
ActTestImpl.<init>(java.rmi.activation.ActivationID, java.rmi.MarshalledObject)
    at
sun.rmi.server.ActivationGroupImpl.newInstance(ActivationGroupImpl.java:273)
    at sun.reflect.NativeMethodAccessorImpl.invoke0(Native Method)
    at
sun.reflect.NativeMethodAccessorImpl.invoke(NativeMethodAccessorImpl.java:39)
    at
sun.reflect.DelegatingMethodAccessorImpl.invoke(DelegatingMethodAccessorImpl.jav
a:25)
    at java.lang.reflect.Method.invoke(Method.java:324)
    at sun.rmi.server.UnicastServerRef.dispatch(UnicastServerRef.java:261)
    at sun.rmi.transport.Transport$1.run(Transport.java:148)
    at java.security.AccessController.doPrivileged(Native Method)
    at sun.rmi.transport.Transport.serviceCall(Transport.java:144)
    at sun.rmi.transport.tcp.TCPTransport.handleMessages(TCPTransport.java:460)
    at
sun.rmi.transport.tcp.TCPTransport$ConnectionHandler.run(TCPTransport.java:701)
    at java.lang.Thread.run(Thread.java:534)
    at
sun.rmi.transport.StreamRemoteCall.exceptionReceivedFromServer(StreamRemoteCall.
java:247)
    at sun.rmi.transport.StreamRemoteCall.executeCall(StreamRemoteCall.java:223)
    at sun.rmi.server.UnicastRef.invoke(UnicastRef.java:133)
    at java.rmi.activation.ActivationGroup_Stub.newInstance(Unknown Source)
    at sun.rmi.server.Activation$ObjectEntry.activate(Activation.java:1481)
    at sun.rmi.server.Activation$GroupEntry.activate(Activation.java:1132)
    at sun.rmi.server.Activation$ActivatorImpl.activate(Activation.java:262)
    at sun.reflect.NativeMethodAccessorImpl.invoke0(Native Method)
    at
sun.reflect.NativeMethodAccessorImpl.invoke(NativeMethodAccessorImpl.java:39)
    at
sun.reflect.DelegatingMethodAccessorImpl.invoke(DelegatingMethodAccessorImpl.jav
a:25)
    at java.lang.reflect.Method.invoke(Method.java:324)
    at sun.rmi.server.UnicastServerRef.dispatch(UnicastServerRef.java:261)
    at sun.rmi.transport.Transport$1.run(Transport.java:148)
    at java.security.AccessController.doPrivileged(Native Method)
    at sun.rmi.transport.Transport.serviceCall(Transport.java:144)
    at sun.rmi.transport.tcp.TCPTransport.handleMessages(TCPTransport.java:460)
    at
sun.rmi.transport.tcp.TCPTransport$ConnectionHandler.run(TCPTransport.java:701)
    at java.lang.Thread.run(Thread.java:534)
    at
sun.rmi.transport.StreamRemoteCall.exceptionReceivedFromServer(StreamRemoteCall.
java:247)
    at sun.rmi.transport.StreamRemoteCall.executeCall(StreamRemoteCall.java:223)
```

```
    at sun.rmi.server.UnicastRef.invoke(UnicastRef.java:133)
    at sun.rmi.server.Activation$ActivatorImpl_Stub.activate(Unknown Source)
    at java.rmi.activation.ActivationID.activate(ActivationID.java:90)
    at sun.rmi.server.ActivatableRef.activate(ActivatableRef.java:246)
    ... 3 more
Caused by: java.lang.NoSuchMethodException:
ActTestImpl.<init>(java.rmi.activation.ActivationID, java.rmi.MarshalledObject)
    at java.lang.Class.getConstructor0(Class.java:1929)
    at java.lang.Class.getDeclaredConstructor(Class.java:1293)
    at sun.rmi.server.ActivationGroupImpl$1.run(ActivationGroupImpl.java:228)
    at java.security.AccessController.doPrivileged(Native Method)
    at
sun.rmi.server.ActivationGroupImpl.newInstance(ActivationGroupImpl.java:222)
    at sun.reflect.NativeMethodAccessorImpl.invoke0(Native Method)
    at
sun.reflect.NativeMethodAccessorImpl.invoke(NativeMethodAccessorImpl.java:39)
    at
sun.reflect.DelegatingMethodAccessorImpl.invoke(DelegatingMethodAccessorImpl.jav
a:25)
    at java.lang.reflect.Method.invoke(Method.java:324)
    at sun.rmi.server.UnicastServerRef.dispatch(UnicastServerRef.java:261)
    at sun.rmi.transport.Transport$1.run(Transport.java:148)
    at java.security.AccessController.doPrivileged(Native Method)
    at sun.rmi.transport.Transport.serviceCall(Transport.java:144)
    at sun.rmi.transport.tcp.TCPTransport.handleMessages(TCPTransport.java:460)
    at
sun.rmi.transport.tcp.TCPTransport$ConnectionHandler.run(TCPTransport.java:701)
    at java.lang.Thread.run(Thread.java:534)
```

Once you've satisfied the requirements for the constructor, you can concentrate on the server-side logic for your methods. Your methods don't need to throw the `RemoteException`—they will be automatically produced, if required, by the classes that manage the remote communication channel.

As a best practice, you should convert any problems that occur within the remote object to business exceptions if you intend to throw them to a client. It is undesirable, as well as quite risky, to use `RemoteException` or its subclasses to represent problems within your code. After all, `RemoteException` and its subclasses were designed to represent communication problems. They were *not* designed to signal problems within the business code of the remote object. If you use the `RemoteException` this way, it's misleading and confusing to other developers, and could lead to an inconsistent handling strategy within the RMI system.

3. RMI Server

If you're working with a `UnicastRemoteObject`, your server needs to create the object, then register the instance. The reference implementation in the Java language provides a basic registry called the RMI Registry, which can be accessed by using the `java.rmi.Naming` class.[62] Typically, the server object calls the bind or rebind methods to register the remote object, associating them with a String name. Interacting with a registry has a few exception risks. The `bind` method can throw the following exceptions:

AccessException—the application does not have permission to bind a name to the registry

AlreadyBoundException—the name is already in use by another remote object

MalformedURLException—the URL used to bind the server object to the naming server and is incorrectly formatted

RemoteException—some general problem with RMI has occurred

The `AccessException` and `AlreadyBoundException` are subclasses of `RemoteException`, since you often only need to determine if there has been some RMI-based problem when using the Naming class. The rebind method will first unbind any remotely registered object, so it will not throw the `AlreadyBoundException`.

4. Client Code

The client must use the registry to locate the remote object, then make distributed method calls on the object. Assuming that the server used the Naming class to store a key-value pair, the client calls the Naming method `lookup` to find the remote object. Like `bind` and `rebind`, the `lookup` method can throw the `AccessException`, `MalformedURLException` and `RemoteException`. In addition, the method will throw the `NotBoundException` if there is no remote object stub associated with the lookup name.[63]

Since the `lookup` method returns an Object, the client must cast the result to the remote interface type before using it. For JRMP-based RMI, you can perform a simple class cast. This operation has the risk of throwing a runtime exception, the `ClassCastException`. If you use RMI-IIOP as a wire protocol, you must call the following method:

```
javax.rmi.PortableRemoteObject.narrow(Object narrowFrom, Class narrowTo)
```

The narrow method converts an object to a Java class before you perform the actual class cast in your code. This method will throw a `ClassCastException` if the `Class` passed to the method is incompatible with the Object. Both approaches throw the runtime exception `ClassNotFoundException` if the casting class cannot be found on the client. This is a fairly common problem in RMI, since the client code actually needs the stub generated from the server-side code with the RMI compiler.

---

62. JNDI also provides an RMI registry implementation. We talk about how to use JNDI in the next section.
63. `java.rmi.NotBoundException` is a direct subclass of `Exception`, so you have to handle it separately from the `RemoteExceptions` in your code.

Once the client converts the remote object to the appropriate type, it can call the server's remote methods.

A second way that the client can obtain a reference to a remote object is by calling a remote method that returns a stub. It is possible for a remote object to return an RMI stub directly to a client, bypassing the registry completely. In some ways, this option greatly reduces the number of potential failure points. The client doesn't have to make a method call to Naming, the client no longer has to use a String-based lookup, and the client doesn't have to cast the remote object. Of course, the client would first have to look up at least *one* remote object in order to use this option, but the server-side object could potentially be used as a way to access other server-side services, if desired.

The base exceptions for a remote call are defined by the remote interface—any method can throw the `RemoteException`, and methods can also throw other exception types if they have been declared for a method. When a declared exception is thrown from the server to the client, RMI preserves the server-side stack trace as well as that of the client code.[64] The server-side stack trace can be a big help when performing remote debugging. In cases where you'd prefer to suppress the server-side error information, you can set the system property `sun.rmi.server.suppressStack-Traces` to true. This will cause RMI to purge all server-side stack traces prior to returning an exception to a client.

What about unchecked exceptions and errors? If the remote object throws a `RuntimeException`, the exception will be propagated to the client with the same class type. This makes things a little complex for exception handling—you potentially have to handle the `RuntimeException` class itself to be certain you've handled all of the potential errors from the server.

The situation is a little different for errors. If the remote object produces an Error, it will be wrapped inside of the class `java.rmi.ServerError` as a base cause. The name `ServerError` is a bit misleading, since the class is actually a subclass of `RemoteException` and, therefore, not an Error at all. Why was this done? One reason may have been to avoid any danger of an Error on the server being "sent back" to the client and destabilizing the client JVM. By making the original Error the root cause of an exception, the distributed model avoids any risk of inadvertently crashing a client application. As a consequence of this design, you should consider trapping runtime exceptions separately in your code, so that you can retrieve server-side Errors if required.

The Java Naming and Directory Interface, JNDI

In the previous section, a central part of the system was the RMI registry. Registry technologies are frequently used in distributed systems—they help to decouple the client

---

64. This has been a feature of RMI since JDK1.4

from the server. Specifically, they help make client code more generic, since they allow the server's location to be changed without having to modify client code. Registries also allow you to dynamically route your clients to one of several servers, making things like load balancing and failover possible. Registries have become so established in distributed systems over the past few years that Java introduced an API—the Java Naming and Directory Interface. JNDI was introduced to provide a flexible model to support two key capabilities provided by registries:

- **Naming Services**: the ability to store a name and associate it with some object
- **Directory Services**: the ability to store names in a hierarchy, tree or directory-like structure

It probably comes as no surprise that RMI is only one of many supported technologies in JNDI—there are actually quite a few naming and directory servers that you can use out of the box. The base JNDI implementation in J2SE can support service providers based on LDAP, COS naming (the naming service for CORBA), RMI Registry, and DNS.[65] Like most distributed APIs, JNDI is built around a layer of generic interfaces, so you can add additional service providers to a running system.

At the foundation, JNDI is based around the idea of a **context**. A context is basically a location on a naming server which can hold entries (objects associated with names) and subcontexts. A subcontext is like a subdirectory—in other words, it is a context organized "under" another context that can hold naming entries and subcontexts of its own. The common tasks performed using a naming and directory service—navigation, storage and retrieval—use contexts as a way to interact with the registry.

If you wrote a client application to use JNDI, you'd start by connecting to the server at some initial context, some starting location. If required, you would navigate to a subcontext. When you got to the context in the registry where you expected to find your entry, you would retrieve the object using its name for a lookup. Finally, you would convert the object into your desired class type, (using casting or an operation called narrowing) and then use the object. There are a few other operations that you might perform using JNDI, but the basic list of capabilities is still fairly simple. Basically, a JNDI server lets you perform the following operations:

1. Locate and connect to the server (the service provider)
2. List the contents of a context
3. Navigate to the subcontext
4. Manage contexts, creating and deleting them
5. Store objects in a context, associating them with a String
6. Retrieve objects from a context
7. Shutdown, disconnecting from a JNDI service

---

65. Lightweight Directory Access Protocol, Common Object Service and Domain Name Service. The list of JNDI service providers reads like a "who's who" of acronyms.

General Issues with JNDI

1. Server Communication

As with any server model, JNDI servers have limits in terms of how many clients they can service at any one time. Of course, it's much less resource-intensive to use a JNDI resource than a "standard" server. After all, you typically only use JNDI for a short time, long enough to look up the resources you actually need for your application. This means that for normal use a JDNI server can handle greater throughput on average than most other kinds of servers. Once a client has located a resource using JNDI, it no longer requires the JNDI server. For things such as RMI servers and resource factories,[66] you can use the servers directly once you have performed the JNDI look up. An important exception to this rule is the case where you plan to use JNDI for ongoing data storage and retrieval. In a situation like this one, you would have the standard constraints associated with server communication.

2. Caching JNDI Lookup Results

Many clients cache JNDI values once they have been retrieved from a server. This is generally a good idea for distributed systems, since a JNDI lookup can be a fairly expensive operation for a client. Of course, cached values may become invalid on a client. The risk is particularly great when JNDI is used to manage remote communication with another server. In this case, it is prudent to write recovery logic into your client, performing another JNDI lookup of your resource if the object you have cached becomes invalid.

3. Issues with Name Storage and Retrieval

Since the basic operations associated with the JNDI are so uniform, the exception model for the API is fairly straightforward. Most issues with JNDI revolve around naming conflicts. For "write" operations, such as context creation and binding a name to an object, this problem manifests itself as either an invalid name or a conflict in names. "Read" operations typically fail due to invalid naming or being unable to locate a name on a JNDI server. Another key risk associated with naming lookup operations is type conversion. Like all generic APIs, JNDI lookups return an Object, which must usually be converted to a different class type. This carries some standard risks, such as the `ClassCastException` and `ClassNotFoundException`. It is also possible to have a delta between the local class type and that returned by the JNDI lookup.

---

66. Standard examples include `javax.sql.DataSource` and `javax.jms.ConnectionFactory`, which provide connections to databases and messaging servers, respectively.

Exception Model for Common JNDI Operations

1. Locating the JNDI Service

In order to use JNDI, you must first establish a link to a JNDI server. You do this by creating an `InitialContext` object. The constructor for `InitialContext`, if successful, establishes a link with a JNDI server. Of course, you need to pass information into the constructor to find the server in the first place. At a minimum, `InitialContext` needs two key pieces of information—the factory class it will use to connect to a specific naming server, and a URL to the server. On some systems, such as J2EE servers, this information is internally provided in a property file. Other applications require explicit configuration of the values. This is normally done by passing a Hashtable to the `InitialContext` constructor that has the following values:

```
java.naming.factory.initial
```

This is the class used to connect to the JNDI server. This class must be based on the underlying technology used by the JNDI server you want to use.

```
java.naming.provider.url
```

The URL of the JNDI server; represents the server's location.

If you don't have these values properly configured, you won't be able to locate or connect to the JNDI server. A `NamingException` thrown by the constructor indicates a problem in locating or establishing a connection to the naming server.

2. Listing the Contents of a Context

One of the standard operations of a Context is listing—providing an iterator-like structure called a `NamingEnumeration`. The methods `list` and `listBindings` return a `NamingEnumeration` that lists the contents of a specific Context. `NamingEnumeration` is actually a subinterface of `Enumeration`, the J2SE interface that defines operations for list traversal. Its purpose is to make it possible for the `NamingException` to be thrown while traversing the elements of the enumeration.

If any exception is thrown while using a `NamingEnumeration`, the enumeration will become invalid, and cannot be subsequently used. It's extremely risky to continue using a `NamingEnumeration` once it has thrown an exception, since the specification states that subsequent method invocations will yield undefined results.

The methods `list` and `listBindings` are deferred return methods. In other words, they do not complete until the `NamingEnumeration` has been used. This means that there's a potentially great threading risk when using the enumeration. What's more, the `NamingEnumeration` itself is not thread-safe and does not have synchronized operations. This means you have to carefully plan its use if you have more than a single thread that uses the enumeration.

When you use a method such as `list` or `listBindings`, the list operation could potentially produce an exception based on a problem with the listing criteria. An example would be the exception encountered when you have only a partial set of results returned, the `PartialResultException`. Rather than immediately invalidating the enumeration, the method will throw a `NamingException` after the enumeration is fully used. At that point, a developer can call the method hasMore to retrieve the more specific "root cause" exception produced by the system.

3. Managing Contexts

You can use the methods `destroySubcontext` and `createSubcontext` to manage context objects within a "parent" context. The `createSubcontext` method can produce the `NamingException` and the more specific exceptions, `InvalidAttributesException` and `NameAlreadyBoundException`. The `InvalidAttributesException` is produced if you must specify specific attributes in order to successfully create a new context. Some JNDI implementations require specific data in order to successfully create a context, and the server would throw this exception if it didn't have all of the required data. The exception `NameAlreadyBoundException` indicates that the context cannot be created due to a naming conflict with some entry in the current context.

The `destroySubcontext` method declares three exceptions in addition to the `NamingException`: `ContextNotEmptyException`, `NameNotFoundException`, and `NotContextException`. These exceptions are largely self-explanatory—the `ContextNotEmptyException` indicates that there are entries in the context, which prevent the context from being deleted. The `NameNotFoundException` means that the server cannot find the requested name, and the `NotContextException` means that the entry was located but is not a context.

4. Managing Entries in a Context

A series of methods allow a developer to store String-Object entries in a context. The methods `bind`, `rebind`, `unbind` and `rename` are all associated with the management of named entries that are not contexts. The exceptions produced by the methods, shown in Table 9-2, are fairly predictable.

Table 9-2

Method	Purpose	Exceptions
bind	Binds an object with a designated name; the method does **not** attempt to replace an entry that is already bound	InvalidAttributesException NameAlreadyBoundException NamingException
rebind	Binds an object with a designated name, replacing an existing entry if required	InvalidAttributesException NamingException
rename	Changes the name associated with an object	NameAlreadyBoundException NamingException
unbind	Removes the specified name-value entry	NameNotFoundException NamingException

5. Retrieving Entries from a Context

The `lookup` method allows you to retrieve an entry associated with a name. This method can be used for subcontexts as well as standard JNDI entries. Like every method in the Context interface, lookup declares a `NamingException`, which is thrown if there's some problem with the lookup.

The `lookup` method takes a name as input (either as a String or an implementor of the Name interface) and returns an Object associated with the name. Since the method has several different uses, the object returned could be a number of different class types. If the name represents a context, the value returned will implement the Context interface. If the name represents a stored value, the return value will be the object associated with the name. If the name represents a "link" to a stored object, the object associated with the link will be returned.

6. Shutting Down

To disconnect from a JNDI server, you can call the method `close`. This method declares a `NamingException`, which would be produced if there were a problem during the shutdown. It is generally a good idea to call the `close` method explicitly at the end of JNDI use. Although JNDI will automatically release the context when the Context is garbage collected by the virtual machine, the fact that garbage collection is not guaranteed to occur on a set schedule argues in favor of manually calling the close method for more efficient connection management.

JDBC, The Java Database Connectivity API

In many ways, JDBC is one of the best examples of a "typical" distributed API. It was created to provide a generic bridging technology for databases, allowing Java developers to communicate with DBMS systems using SQL. JDBC is based around a series of interfaces in the `java.sql` and `javax.sql` packages, which are subsequently paired with a set of classes collectively called a JDBC driver. The driver manages communication with databases, and handles common tasks such as connection management and communication.

In most applications, a developer using JDBC follows six basic steps. As with many distributed APIs, the exact way in which the steps are performed within an application may vary somewhat, but the model is a good starting point for a lot of API development:

1. Locate a class that can connect to the DBMS
2. Acquire a `Connection`
3. Create a `Statement`
4. Execute the `Statement`
5. Process the results
6. Close down resources, release a `Connection`

Exceptions in JDBC

JDBC is consistent in its exception model: nearly every method you call can throw a checked exception called the `SQLException`. The name "`SQLException`" is a little misleading, since it represents a substantially larger set of possible problems than those related to SQL execution. The `SQLException` represents actual errors with SQL execution in the database, but it also indicates communication problems with the DBMS, unsupported features, and even problems with the lifecycle of the driver resource. It's debatable whether it's actually a good thing to represent *every* exception as a `SQLException`. There are some problems, such as invalid arguments in a JDBC method call, that are not really related to the DBMS at all.

In some ways, the generic nature of `SQLException` makes robust exception handling more difficult in JDBC. Because `SQLException` is so general, you often have to determine the cause of an error based on the method that threw the exception. Developers work with the JDBC exception model in one of two ways. They may make generic handler blocks, treating any problem with JDBC as a general database error. This strategy can cause in problems in some production systems, since it involves a "one size fits all" approach to a much more complex distributed model. Alternately, developers may handle exceptions in specific units based on JDBC lifecycle and often grouped around methods. This approach provides greater flexibility in handling, but increases the overall complexity of an application.

The `SQLException` provides additional detail on the source of an error by defining a few additional properties within the exception. In addition to the standard String value used to specify an error message, the `SQLException` has several other properties—the SQL state and error code. The SQL State, provided by the `getSQLState` method, is a String that represents a standard error state. Depending on the driver, the values can use values from either the XOPEN or the SQL 99 conventions. Another value is the error code. This is a vendor-specific integer provided by the method getErrorCode.[67]

A `SQLException` can be used to reference a series of chained `SQLException` objects. In some cases, operations in JDBC can produce a series of errors. A JDBC driver associates these errors together so that the client can process some or all of them. When you handle a `SQLException`, the method `getNextException` will retrieve the next exception, if any, in the chain.

There are three subclasses of `SQLException`: `BatchUpdateException`, `DataTruncation` and `SQLWarning`. These exceptions are produced under certain specific circumstances, so it's easy to predict when they can occur. The `BatchUpdateException` is thrown if an error occurs during batching operations. In other words, this exception is only thrown when executing a batched series of SQL commands in a `Statement`, `PreparedStatement` or `CallableStatement`. The method `executeBatch`, used to trigger batch execution, will throw this exception if an error occurs in one or more of the SQL commands. By definition, no batch-processed command in JDBC can return a `ResultSet`, so this exception will also be thrown if a command executes successfully but returns a `ResultSet`.

The `DataTruncation` exception is fairly self-explanatory—it is thrown if data is unexpectedly truncated during a database read operation. Additional properties of `DataTruncation` include a Boolean value that indicates whether a column or parameter has been truncated, an index of the truncated value, a Boolean value that specifies whether the operation was a read or a write, the size of the target field, and the actual number of bytes transferred. If you want to avoid the `DataTruncation` exception, you can call the method `setMaxFieldSize` on your `Connection`. If you set a maximum size, any reads or writes that exceed the size will not cause a `DataTruncation` exception to be thrown.

`SQLWarning` is produced if database warnings occur. Since a DBMS warning isn't considered to be a critical failure, a `SQLWarning` is never thrown by JDBC code. Instead, any warnings are associated with the object that produced the warning in the first place—a `Connection`, `Statement` or `ResultSet`. If you want to work with `SQLWarning` objects, you must call the `getWarnings` method in the appropriate interface. Like `SQLException`, `SQLWarning` objects can be chained, so it's possible to retrieve a series of these exceptions using the `getNextWarning` method in the `SQLWarning` class.

---

67. Often, this value is passed directly to the driver from the DBMS if a SQL-related error occurs.

Universal Issues with Database Communication Technologies

Most of the common problems encountered when using JDBC are really manifestations of broader issues centered around database use. Any kind of shared data repository will likely have data sharing and synchronization considerations. Any distributed system will probably have issues associated with server communication, and any API that involves data transfer between dissimilar systems will have issues with data translation. JDBC only provides a generic communication channel with a SQL-based system. It does not and cannot "solve" any of these standard problems. Ultimately, you must evaluate the risks to your application and design a system that properly meets your specific needs.

1. Data Volatility and Transactions

Most database applications have a medium to high degree of data sharing among clients. As a result, there's a risk that one client will try to change data that is being used by another client. Historically, databases have prevented this kind of problem through transactions. When you define a transaction for a database, you specify a series of database operations that should be treated as a single, logical operation. Once you have defined your transaction, it will succeed or fail as a unit. Either your operations will all succeed and "commit" the changes to the database, or an operation will fail and the database will "rollback" or reverse any operations that were defined as a part of the transaction. It's common for modern databases to lock records that are known to be part of a transaction, allowing only one caller to modify data until the transaction completes.[68] This means that transactions can effectively prevent many write-write conflicts.

Of course, most solutions in technology create other problems. Because you can define multiple database operations as part of a transaction, there can also be data corruption if one client reads data being modified by another. There are three common problems related to read-write conflicts in a transaction:

Dirty read: Transaction A can read the uncommitted changes of another transaction B. This makes it possible for transaction A to see "dirty" data—data that isn't guaranteed to be permanently written to the DBMS.

Nonrepeatable read: Transaction A reads a row of data. Transaction B changes the row of data as part of a transaction. Transaction A rereads the row and gets different data—data that isn't guaranteed to be written to the DBMS until transaction B completes successfully.

Phantom read: Transaction A retrieves a bunch of rows that satisfy a WHERE clause in SQL. (a SELECT query, for instance) Transaction B inserts one or more

---

68. Earlier generation databases locked entire database tables during transactions, which had a significant performance impact on applications.

additional rows of data that happen to satisfy the conditions of the WHERE clause. Transaction A "rereads" the rows and gets the new rows. Once again, the rows aren't guaranteed to be valid until transaction B completes successfully.

You can avoid these problems in a transaction if you're willing to lock your data for various types of reads as well as writes. You can do this by specifying what's commonly called a "transaction isolation level." The higher the isolation level, the more aggressive the lockdown on your data. This usually causes a database to run more slowly, so you may have to make a tradeoff between data security and database efficiency.

In JDBC, you can request that a database provide a certain transaction isolation level to your application code by calling the method setTransactionIsolation in Connection. This method takes an integer constant defined in Connection:

TRANSACTION_NONE	Transactions are not supported in this JDBC driver
TRANSACTION_READ_UNCOMMITTED	No read-locks: dirty, non-repeatable and phantom reads can occur
TRANSACTION_READ_COMMITTED	Prevents dirty reads
TRANSACTION_REPEATABLE_READ	Prevents dirty and non-repeatable reads
TRANSACTION_SERIALIZABLE	Prevents dirty, non-repeatable and phantom reads

You can get the current level by calling the getIsolationLevel method. Realize that these methods do not guarantee that the database will satisfy your request. Remember—it's ultimately the database that enforces transaction isolation levels, so it's up to the database whether or not to provide the level of protection you request.

2. Data Conversion

SQL defines a standard model to interact with a DBMS. Since the data representation isn't the same as that used in the Java language, you often have to plan for conversion between SQL and Java. One difference between data models relates to indexing used for data values. The column indexes in a JDBC ResultSet begin with an index of one, rather than the zero index that is standard for Java arrays and Lists. As a result, you have to adjust your coding style if you plan to use numeric indexes to access data.

Another difference relates to data representation itself. ResultSet getter methods allow you to retrieve SQL values as standard Java data types, and the Statement and its subinterfaces let you pass Java data to the database. However, there isn't an exact one-to-one correspondence with SQL data types. It's important to ensure that you've properly mapped your data types between the two systems so that you avoid problems like conversion and retrieval errors. Since SQL3 introduced advanced storage types that allow a more natural mapping between databases and object-oriented languages, data conversion has become easier for some Java applications.[69]

3. Server and Driver Limitations

The SQL standard defines a large set of operations; in fact, there are far more operations defined in SQL than most database vendors support. As a result, SQL defines various levels of compliance, and allows vendors to support a subset of the complete standard. This philosophy is quite reasonable, since databases tend to vary dramatically in the capabilities they provide. JDBC follows this model as well; it allows driver vendors to support a varied set of features beyond a certain baseline level of functionality. Every JDBC-compliant driver must support the following features:

- Entry-level SQL92 command set
- The DROP TABLE command
- Escape syntax
- Transactions

Beyond this core set of requirements, a driver may implement additional JDBC operations and SQL commands. Of course, drivers must indicate which features are supported and which are not. They do this through the methods of the `DatabaseMetaData` interface. If you plan to use JDBC features that are somewhat out of the ordinary, it is always a good idea to verify that the features are supported by the driver, either through the vendor documentation or the `DatabaseMetaData` interface.

There are also some practical limits of the DBMS itself that are relayed to clients through JDBC. Specifically, some JDBC drivers limit the number of open connections and active statements for each connection. Drivers don't provide an explicit way to determine the available server resources; instead, you will get a `SQLException` if you're unable to obtain a `Connection` or `Statement`.

4. SQL Checking

JDBC is fundamentally a transport technology—it passes SQL commands to a DBMS, and retrieves results for a Java client. For flexibility, the API accepts SQL arguments as String values. While this is a sensible approach given the purpose of the API, it means there is a practical limit to what you can do with the compiler. You can verify that a `Statement` is associated with a String, but you cannot verify the contents of that String. In other words, JDBC cannot validate your SQL commands. You can't tell until execution whether your String is SQL and has properly formatted values. For this reason, it's prudent to check your SQL commands in advance, and to provide the ability to log your SQL commands during runtime.

---

69. Support for extended SQL storage types, such as BLOBs, CLOBs, arrays, and references, was introduced in JDBC2.0.

Standard JDBC Lifecycle

1. Locate a class that can connect to the DBMS

Before you can connect to a DBMS, you need to load a driver into your JVM—the set of classes that will ultimately let you communicate with a specific DBMS. There are two ways to load a driver into your system. The first way is to load a specific class that implements `java.sql.Driver` into your application. You can use any of the following three techniques to load the Driver class:

1. Explicitly create a Driver:
   ```
   Driver drv = new vendor.specific.DbDriver();
   ```
2. Use `Class.forName`:
   ```
   Class.forName("vendor.specific.DbDriver");
   ```
3. Command-line loading:
   ```
   java -Djdbc.drivers=vendor.specific.DbDriver JDBCExample
   ```

There are drawbacks to each approach. As a developer, you must always explicitly specify the full package and class name of your driver. In two of the cases, you even have to hard code the Driver class, which would require you to modify code if your JDBC driver ever changed. What's more, `Class.forName` has a risk of throwing a `ClassNotFoundException` if the Driver cannot be found during compile time or runtime. Because of these drawbacks, JDBC2.0 introduced an alternate approach for Driver loading. Rather than manually loading your class, you can use JNDI to look up a `DataSource`. The `javax.sql.DataSource` acts as the loading point for a driver, so you no longer need to know the details about the driver you want to use:

```
Context ctx = new InitialContext();
DataSource dataSce = (DataSource)ctx.lookup("jdbc/myDBMS");
```

Rather than having to hard-code the class name of a driver, you can pass a standard name to a JNDI server. The server can subsequently be configured to point to a specific vendor's driver. If the DBMS ever changes, you can simply change the driver associated with the standard name. Of course, there are failure modes associated with the JNDI lookup. Specifically, you'd need to configure your application for a JNDI lookup and handle the standard `NamingException` and `ClassCastException` that could be thrown as a result of the lookup.

2. Acquire a Connection

Once you've loaded a driver, you need to obtain a database connection. Once again, there are two ways you could connect to a DBMS. If you manually loaded your driver, you would typically connect by using one of the `getConnection` methods of the `DriverManager` class.[70] Manually loaded Driver classes self-register with the DriverManager, so you can use the class to connect to one of several drivers loaded in your system. A sample `connect` call might look something like this:

```
Connection conn = DriverManager.getConnection(
    "jdbc:drv://localhost/myDb", "username", "password"
);
```

The `DriverManager` would work down its collection of registered Drivers, calling the `connect` method on each Driver in turn. A Driver returns a null value if the URL String (in this case "`jdbc:drv://localhost/myDb`") is not correct for the specific type of Driver. If the URL String *is* correct but the Driver cannot connect, it will throw a `SQLException` to the `DriverManager`. The `DriverManager` ultimately returns a `Connection`, or throws a `SQLException` if no connection could be made.

If you use a `DataSource` to access JDBC, you obtain a connection by calling one of its `getConnection` methods:

```
Connection conn = dataSce.getConnection("username", "password");
```

It's fairly common to pre-configure a pool of live database connections and associate them with a `DataSource`. In that case, the `getConnection` method doesn't typically require a username or password, since the `getConnection` method returns an existing `Connection` from the pool. In this situation, you normally want to authenticate clients earlier in your application, long before they request a database connection. There are obviously potential security risks involved in using a pool of ready connections which are normally associated with a generic user and already have an established set of permissions. If you plan to use pooled connections, you should factor security considerations into your application and use early authentication.

3. Create a Statement

There are three different interfaces in JDBC that let you process a SQL command: `Statement`, `PreparedStatement` and `CallableStatement`. A `Statement` is an object that can execute standard dynamic SQL commands. A `PreparedStatement` is a set SQL statement that can accept variable SQL input over time. A `CallableStatement` represents a database stored procedure; as such, it can accept dynamic input and supply output in its variables. The statement interfaces are arranged in a hierarchy: `CallableStatement` is a subinterface of `PreparedStatement`, which is a subinterface of `Statement`.

---

70. It's also possible to connect using the Driver method `connect`. This method, like most of the methods in JDBC, will throw a `SQLException` if you have problems connecting to your database.

The interface hierarchy can cause problems due to incompatible methods. Not all of the methods defined in `Statement` apply to the other two interfaces. In cases where you call a method that doesn't apply to your statement type, JDBC will throw a `SQLException`. You can see this in the `Statement`'s execute methods—every method takes a String argument that specifies the command to run on the DBMS. That's fine for a `Statement`, but `PreparedStatement` and `CallableStatement` objects require that you specify the SQL command when you create the statement. If you were to use a `PreparedStatement` but call the execute method inherited from the `Statement` interface, your code would compile but throw a `SQLException` during runtime.

4. Execute the Statement

Once you've created a statement, you can use it to send SQL commands to a database. There are two ways to execute a SQL command in JDBC. You can either execute a single command, or you can run in batch mode, running a number of commands together.

If you execute a single command, you call one of these methods: `execute`, `executeQuery`, or `executeUpdate`. The `executeQuery` method returns a `ResultSet` and can be used to execute SQL SELECT commands. `executeUpdate` is used to run INSERT, UPDATE, or DELETE commands, or any other SQL command that isn't expected to return a result. Finally, `execute` can be used to execute any SQL command on the database. Batch operations are performed by calling the method `executeBatch`. For drivers that allow batching, you can configure a SQL command then call `addBatch` to add it to your list of commands for execution.

The execute methods provide a good example of JDBC's limitations on input validation. The API cannot verify that the input to any of the methods is correct, so it throws a `SQLException` if you try to execute an incompatible or illegal SQL command. A few examples are:

- Calling the `executeUpdate` method with a SQL SELECT statement
- Calling `executeQuery` with a statement that doesn't return a single `ResultSet`
- Calling the `executeBatch` method with a driver that doesn't support batching
- Calling the `Statement`'s `execute(String)` methods from a `CallableStatement` or `PreparedStatement`

In addition to the basic execution commands, the `Statement` interface defines a number of setter methods that allow you to configure some properties of your `Statement`. A few examples include `setFetchDirection`, `setFetchSize`, `setMaxFieldSize`, `setMaxRows` and `setQueryTimeout`. These methods all throw `SQLException` for general DBMS errors, but also for invalid inputs.[71] For example, the method `setFetchSize`, which suggests the number of rows that can be retrieved from the DBMS during a fetch operation, will throw `SQLException` if the input is less than zero or greater than the value `getMaxRows`.

5. Process the Results

After you've executed a SQL command, you process the results returned from the database. Most of the standard SQL operations return status codes, and are represented by the integer return value of methods like `execute` and `executeUpdate`. The SELECT statement, on the other hand, returns a `ResultSet`, which represents a cursor into a data set. A `ResultSet` allows you to retrieve data by using one of a number of getter methods. Since these methods convert information from the DBMS into Java variables, it's important to properly manage your type mappings so you avoid problems such as data truncation.[72]

You can navigate within a `ResultSet` by using the method `next`, which advances the cursor by one "row" and returns true if it points to data. A `ResultSet` initially points to the location before the first row of real data, so it's easy to use a loop to iterate through select results. With JDBC2.0, a number of other methods were introduced that allowed extended navigation within a `ResultSet`. Examples include the methods `absolute(int)`, `relative(int)`, `first()`, and `last()`. These methods support both absolute and relative positioning, so you can choose nearly any strategy you want to navigate within the results of a select query. Naturally, the navigation methods will throw a `SQLException` if you call a method that is not supported by the driver, call a method that is not supported by your type of `ResultSet`,[73] or overstep the bounds of your data set.

In general, a `Connection` does not allow you to have multiple active `Result-Sets` associated with a single `Statement`. If you try to obtain a second `ResultSet`, you typically find that the original reference now points to a new data set. If you need to cache data from an earlier SELECT operation, you can manually cache data or use a worker object such as a `RowSet`.

6. Close Down Resources and Release a Connection

When you're finished with JDBC resources, you can formally release them by calling the `close` method. The `close` method exists for the `ResultSet`, `Statement` and `Connection` interfaces. After you call the `close` method, you can no longer use the object associated with the method. For example, if you called any method on a

---

71. In JDBC, you must trap `SQLException` for invalid input, rather than the `IllegalArgumentException` that is used in many other Java APIs.

72. The same is true of values you send to the DBMS through the `Statement` and the setter methods used in the `PreparedStatement` and `CallableStatement` interfaces.

73. ResultSet navigability can be set in both the `Statement` and `ResultSet` interfaces. If you try to perform an operation that's incompatible with your `ResultSet`'s navigation capability, the driver will throw the `SQLException`.

`Connection` after calling the `close` method, the method would throw a `SQLException`. What's more, the `close` method has a cascading effect. If you call `close` on a `Statement`, the method also closes the `ResultSet` associated with the `Statement`.

It's always a good idea to explicitly close resources when you're done with them. In JDBC, it's especially vital to close `Connection` objects. Some drivers will keep database connections open if you fail to call this method. These "phantom connections" will reduce the runtime efficiency of your database, and can ultimately cause your database to crash. Even if you have a DBMS that will eventually release the connection resources on its own, you have no way to ensure that they will be released in a timely manner. If you don't explicitly call `close`, you must wait until the `Connection` is garbage collected for a chance of connection release, and you don't know exactly when that will occur. Ultimately, you're much safer if you define some standard shutdown behavior for database connections and run it when you are finished with your connection. The following method shows how you can close database elements in a manageable way within your code:[74]

```
1   public void shutdown(Connection c, Statement s, ResultSet r){
2     if (r != null){
3       try{
4           r.close();
5       }
6       catch (SQLException e){}
7     }
8     if (s != null){
9       try{
10          s.close();
11      }
12      catch (SQLException e){}
13    }
14    if (c != null){
15      try{
16          c.close();
17      }
18      catch (SQLException e){}
19    }
20  }
```

Conclusion

You've probably noticed a change in the API discussions of this chapter. It's evident that there's a definite design impact on an application based around the risks and

---

74. This useful coding technique was originally suggested by a peer of mine at Sun Education, Evan Troyka.

standard exceptions associated with each API. This is in part due to the fact that distributed APIs are no longer based around classes and interfaces operating in isolation. These APIs are really groups of codependent classes and technologies used to solve a common problem. This trend will become even more evident in the next chapter as we talk about J2EE.

As you move away from the "single class" API model into frameworks, there are a couple of natural tendencies of failure modes.[75] First, they tend to become based around a standard lifecycle model defined by the framework. Second, they tend to become associated with risks that are a natural part of the framework, or common errors within the framework.

This makes it especially important to understand the exception model for systems based around the more complex APIs. By studying the exception model and failure modes of a framework API, you can avoid common problems, but you also gain insight into how to more effectively use the API as a whole. You can more effectively use the API as a unit, a tool whose use results in more robust application code.

---

75. For a well-designed framework, anyway.

chapter 10

J2EE

Introduction

When it was created, the Java 2 Enterprise Edition (J2EE) provided a revolutionary approach to enterprise computing. Based around a flexible, component-based architectural model, J2EE opened up whole new vistas for distributed applications. Among other things, it unified many of the desirable features from earlier enterprise computing models. For instance, it incorporated the flexibility of "built-from-scratch" enterprise applications, while preserving the modularity common to many of the Enterprise Resource Planning (ERP) frameworks. In addition, its focus on platform-independent containers and container-provided services has been crucial in establishing a new era for servers—one where it's actually possible to deploy an application on different platforms *and* vendor products. Since J2EE is a generic specification, you can install an application on any J2EE-compliant server without major modifications to your code.[76]

J2EE is probably the best example of the difference you can make by understanding a little about how exceptions work. Without a perspective about the exception models of the key J2EE APIs, your code tends to be haphazard and disjointed. You may create a multi-tier enterprise application, but your exception handling infrastructure will still be localized at its foundation. As a result, your applications will be limited, unable to take full advantage of the benefits of J2EE.

In J2EE, exception handling is based at its foundation on communication with the J2EE containers. It's ultimately the containers that intercept the exceptions thrown by a component, and they decide how to respond to a specific problem. A container is responsible for managing its components after all, and that responsibility includes exception handling—even to the point of destroying a component and creating a new one, if need be. That's a big adjustment for many developers—most of us have spent

---

76. Of course, the act of migration or porting—moving a fully configured J2EE application from one server to another—may be more difficult. Developers may have to convert server-specific configuration information, and possibly modify code, to meet the requirements of the new server.

our careers propagating exceptions to a client or writing handling code on a server. The J2EE model requires that we adjust our thinking a little.

We begin the chapter by providing a high-level introduction to the key concepts behind J2EE. Next, we describe how exceptions work in key J2EE technologies. Since J2EE is more than just a collection of independent APIs, we also discuss exceptions in an application-wide context. We present key issues for J2EE design, and look at key considerations involved in working with exceptions within and between the tiers of an enterprise system. As a result, you'll gain valuable insight into how exception processing and erros handling works in a distributed multi-tier computing environment.

The Basic J2EE Application Model

At its heart, J2EE is based around three fairly simple concepts: Components, Containers and Connectors. Figure 10-1 shows the relationship between these parts of a J2EE system.[77]

Components provide business functionality in J2EE. A component wrappers or encapsulates code for your enterprise application. Developing an application as a series of components promotes code reuse and tends to increase an application's maintainability and flexibility. In addition, components reduce some of the dangers associated with monolithic code, such as brittleness and code complexity. When you

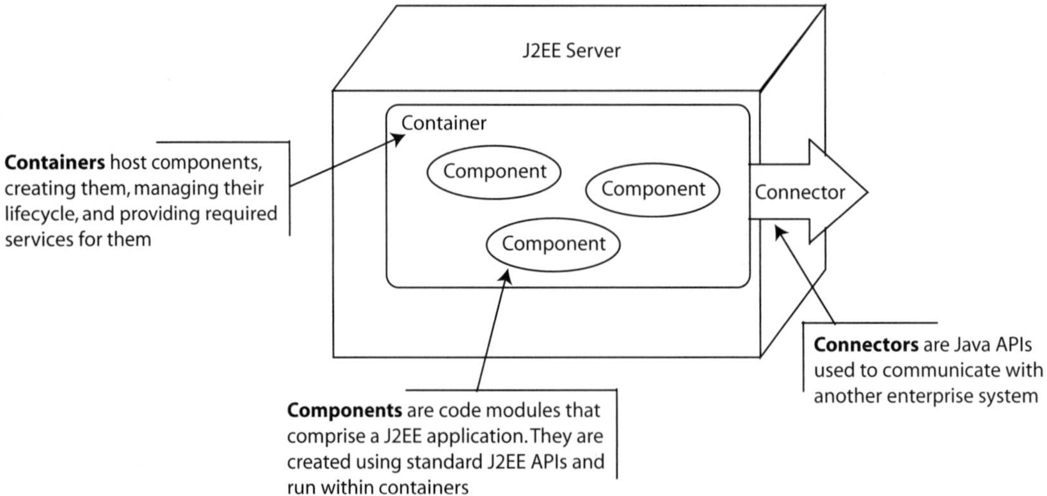

Figure 10-1

Components, Containers and Connectors.

---

77.   As is often the case with programming technology, the simplest principles are also the most profound.

write a J2EE application, you're usually writing a group of components that work together to form an enterprise application.

Unlike earlier distributed programming models, J2EE components focus almost exclusively on business programming. As a developer, you write components that perform business logic, manage application flow, or display data to your users. You don't write code that implements a communication protocol. You don't develop server threads to manage interaction with multiple clients. You don't even create or manage the component objects on your server. Naturally, this raises a question: if *you* don't write the code to support these services yourself, how are they provided in J2EE?

Containers provide these crucial services. A container is a process that runs as part of a server, managing components and providing them with services. The container provides a runtime environment for one or more types of J2EE components and manages them within the server. Containers also provide standard J2SE and J2EE APIs to their components, and enable components to communicate with other enterprise systems. Figure 10-2 shows some of the standard services provided by containers in J2EE.

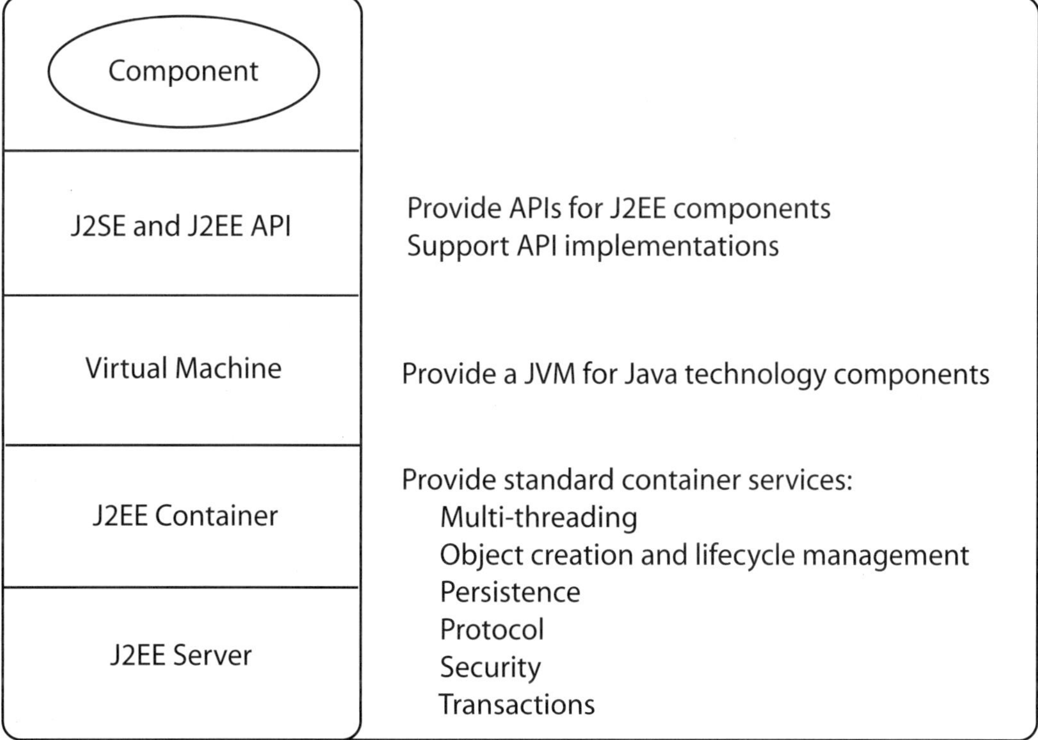

Figure 10–2
Layered Container Services.

In J2EE, you configure container-provided services with an XML file called a **deployment descriptor**. The deployment descriptor lets you configure the use of a container's services without actually having to write code for them in your components. For example, you can use the deployment descriptor to specify the transactional behavior of EJBs. The container manages transactions for your methods, giving you the flexibility to reconfigure EJBs to use transactions differently in the future without having to rewrite all of your code.

Because all J2EE-compliant servers use a common specification for their containers, their core services are the same no matter what server or operating system you use. This means that you can actually deploy the same components on different servers and use standard services without code modifications. Of course, it's possible for server vendors to provide additional services on their containers, and those services are generally not portable. However, since vendor services are separately managed and configured, it's easier to migrate an application from one environment to another than it has been for other distributed architectures in the past.

The third concept—**Connectors**—represent another key service provided by containers. Containers use connectors to make it possible to communicate with other enterprise systems. As with the other parts of the J2EE model, there's a lot of value in making this process as generic and vendor-neutral as possible. To support this goal, J2EE uses distributed APIs like the ones we talked about in the previous chapter. An adapter-based API such as JDBC allows you to write generic code that is vendor-neutral and portable across many platforms.

A J2EE container manages connector implementations, making them available to components. Typically, a J2EE system allows an administrator to pre-configure a connector for a specific enterprise resource, such as a database or messaging system. The administrator uses a naming server to store connection factories to an enterprise resource, and developers can use JNDI to access the named resource. What's more, many J2EE implementations use techniques such as connection pooling to make connectors more efficient. These services are also managed by containers, so components can benefit from performance-enhancing technologies without changing their coding models.

The J2EE Application Model

The J2EE architectural model is based on a series of standard **tiers**—software modules that play a common role in an enterprise system. Some tiers are directly associated with specific J2EE component technologies, and therefore have a standard container. Typically, a J2EE application is based around the tiers shown in Table 10-1.

Table 10–1 **Summary of J2EE Tiers**

Tier	Example	Purpose
Client	GUI, Web Browser	Allows human users to interact with the J2EE system
Web	Web Server	Provides Web-based capabilities for the J2EE system; this tier is associated with a Web container, and hosts Servlet and JSP components
Enterprise JavaBeans (EJB)	Application Server	Provides application server functions for the enterprise system, and hosts EJB components
Enterprise Information System (EIS)	DBMS	Represents other enterprise systems

Since a J2EE application is comprised of a bunch of components, there should be some relatively easy way to bundle them together for installation. After all, if you had to perform a piecemeal installation of components across tiers and servers, the process would be difficult, time-consuming and error-prone. To simplify the job, J2EE uses the Java Archive (jar) utility to combine the parts of an application into one convenient file. Typically, a J2EE application is deployed as a JAR file called the Enterprise Archive (EAR) file. The EAR file in turn holds EJB-JAR files with EJB components, and Web Archive (WAR) files with Web components. Each archive contains the resources required for installation on a specific tier. For example, a WAR file contains the deployment descriptor for the Web tier, Servlets and JSPs, and any other Web resources, such as HTML files and images.

Exceptions in J2EE

Now that we've discussed the foundation concepts of J2EE, let's talk about potential issues for the framework. Because J2EE is so strongly associated with the concept of tiers, it makes sense to start the discussion with potential problems that can occur for each of the tiers. Once we've talked about specific capabilities for each of the tiers, we'll be in a good position to talk about the exception handling model of J2EE as a whole.

First, recognize that components and containers ultimately define the exception model for J2EE. Since components represent the code modules at each tier used to service client requests, it follows that the exception handling model must be based on the behavior of its key components. The exceptions that can be propagated between tiers, and the way that containers respond to exceptions is ultimately defined by the specifications for Servlets, JSPs, and EJBs.

All exceptions are **not** treated equally in the component APIs. The component specifications tend to divide exceptions into two broad categories: those that are propagated to clients, and those that are used internally by a J2EE container. Any nonstandard exceptions produced by your components must either be handled or converted to one of these two types of exception.

In addition, there are two types of methods that are important for a component API—business methods and lifecycle methods. Business methods are invoked by clients, and are therefore directly associated with satisfying a client's request. Lifecycle methods, on the other hand, are container-called. The lifecycle methods of a component are used by the container to manage the component, performing tasks such as initialization and shutdown.

The key to understanding how to effectively deal with exceptions in J2EE lies in understanding the exception model for each tier. This means you need to understand the foundations of the component model associated with that tier. Specifically, you need to understand:

- The lifecycle of a component, and how it is managed by a container.
- Exceptions associated with a component, and what they mean.
- The impact of a specific exception on the component, container and client.
- How, when and by whom exceptions can be produced.
- How an exception fits into the larger J2EE application.

Having said this, let's look at the exception model of the client tier.

The Client Tier

The client tier allows users to interact with a J2EE application. In a sense, this tier is one of the hardest to generalize in J2EE. One reason for this is that there are so many options available when developing client tier applications—Java or non-Java, XML or HTML-based, and so on. Another reason is that many client tier applications are developed from scratch, and so it's notoriously hard to provide meaningful generalizations. We pick out the few that we can, then progress to client-specific factors.

In most enterprise systems, servers don't keep track of individual clients. Even if they do, there are usually many more clients than servers—that's one of the incentives for using a server in the first place. The upshot of this fact is that there's a fairly high overhead for servers to communicate with clients.[78] What's more, many of the problems that occur within servers are either not relevant to a specific client or can be observed in a much more dramatic way.[79] Practically speaking, most enterprise applications should report problems to a client only if they relate directly to the client's own use of the application.[80]

---

78. This is one of the reasons why client pull is generally preferred to server push, unless near real-time response is crucially important.

79. Such as loss of service, or one's computer bursting into flames.

80. You could argue that global, catastrophic failures should be reported to a client. However, you could also contend that such a problem is meaningful to a user only if it's directly relevant to her or his own use of the application.

Client tier software doesn't usually propagate errors back to a server for similar reasons—many client tier problems are not relevant to the server. If you're developing software for the client tier, you normally want to internally handle errors if possible. If a catastrophic error occurs, you typically want to report the problem in a meaningful way, and suggest a suitable follow-on action to the user. You frequently try to store the user's data and application state, if possible. It can also be helpful to store information about the error itself, so that it can be sent to developers at a later time. Normally, exceptions produced in the client tier shouldn't be propagated to a server unless there's a compelling reason. Unless properly managed, exceptions or errors sent to a server from a client have the potential to degrade performance, or even to produce a cascading failure in the enterprise system.

If you send errors from a server to the client tier, it's very important to present them in a form that's meaningful to the user. In most applications, users haven't been involved in the development of the software. Even if they have a background in programming, they won't necessarily understand the implications of an error message presented in its "raw" form. You should convert exceptions to a form that makes sense to a business user, and represent them in a standard, intuitive way in the user interface.

Normally, errors or exceptions in this tier serve two major purposes. They notify the user about some error that has occurred, and explain what action has been taken to correct or compensate for the problem. Sometimes they also request a decision: they ask users which of several actions they want to take in response to a failure within the application.

There are quite a few different kinds of clients that can exist for a J2EE application, and it's possible for one application to have several different client-tier applications. There are four general categories that are typically used to differentiate clients.[81]

'Simple" Web clients

Clients that use HTTP to communicate with J2EE, and have little to no dynamic execution capabilities.

'Rich" Web clients

Clients that use some dynamic technology in addition to HTML, such as Applets or client-side scripting languages (e.g., Java Script).

Java clients

Java GUIs, whether statically installed or dynamically downloaded using Java Web-Start.

Non-Java clients

GUIs that use a technology other than Java.

---

81.   In recent years, another type of client has appeared—one that accesses a J2EE application using Web services.

The type of client used for a J2EE application has a major impact on the kind of error information that the tier can process. A simple Web client can only process HTML information, so any errors that should be sent to the client *must* be converted to HTML pages or HTTP error codes. Rich Web clients can process HTML/HTTP errors, and may be able to use Java exception information, depending on the client's capabilities. Java clients naturally have the ability to process Java exceptions, and *may* be able to interpret HTTP-based errors, depending on how they interact with the J2EE system.[82] Finally, non-Java applications typically use a data structure to represent an exception, so they must convert the data structure into a format meaningful to the application before they present it to the user.

The Web Tier

The Web tier is host to the Servlet and JSP component technologies. Part of the challenge for the Web tier in J2EE lies in determining how to represent errors to clients. A Web tier actually works with two error models—HTTP errors associated with the Web server, and exceptions associated with Java technology. HTTP errors are sent to the client as a technology-neutral status code used to communicate problems related to a client's Web request. Exceptions, on the other hand, are used internally within the Web tier. Components use exceptions to provide information to the container about problems which occur as they run. HTTP status codes, including error values, are defined in RFC 2616,[83] and are based around five broad categories, as shown in Table 10-2.

Table 10–2   **HTTP Status Codes**

Status Code Range	Meaning		Examples
100-199	Information	100	Client may continue its request
200-299	Success	200	Client request successful
300-399	Redirection	303	Request at different URL
400-499	Error with client request	404	Resource not found
500-599	Server error	500	Internal server error

---

82. Most Java and non-Java GUIs interact directly with the EJB tier. If they do this, they use IIOP as a wire protocol, so they cannot normally process HTTP-based error messages.
83. This RFC defines the HTTP1.1 protocol. An earlier version of the status codes was defined in RFC 1945, for the HTTP 1.0 protocol.

Any exception or error that is sent to a Web container *will* be converted to an HTTP error for the client. Any exception thrown by a Web component is ultimately sent to a client as an HTTP 500 error, which indicates a general problem with the server.

Because the normal output displayed for most HTTP errors isn't terribly easy to interpret, many Web applications send their own error pages to clients instead. This has a number of advantages, including giving the developer more control over an application's look and feel, and making it possible to generate error output that is more user-friendly.

Declarative Error Handling

Consistency is often a priority in Web applications, just as it is in standalone GUIs. It's often desirable to define standard HTML error pages in a Java Web application, so that you can guarantee that a certain problem will always be routed to a given URL. J2EE lets you specify a URL mapping for errors declaratively, using the deployment descriptor.

It's possible to use the Web tier deployment descriptor to define a blanket "handling policy" for a specific type of exception or HTTP error code. You can also define a standard error page for logins, if your J2EE application uses form-based authentication. When you do this, you configure the container so that it consistently routes to a given location any time a certain kind of problem occurs. The format is fairly straightforward, and looks like this:

```
 1   <?xml version="1.0" encoding="ISO-8859-1"?>
 2   <!DOCTYPE web-app
 3       PUBLIC "-//Sun Microsystems, Inc.//DTD Web Application 2.3//EN"
 4        "http://java.sun.com/dtd/web-app_2_3.dtd">
 5   <web-app>
 6
 7     <error-page>
 8       <error-code>404</error-code>
 9       <location>/errors/404Handler.html</location>
10     </error-page>
11
12     <error-page>
13       <exception-type>java.io.IOException</exception-type>
14       <location>/errors/ioPage.jsp</location>
15     </error-page>
16
17     <login-config>
18       <auth-method>FORM</auth-method>
19       <form-login-config>
20         <form-login-page>/forms/login.jsp</form-login-page>
21         <form-error-page>/errors/loginErr.jsp</form-error-page>
```

```
22          </form-login-config>
23        </login-config>
24    </web-app>
```

The error-page entry on lines 7 through 10 causes all 404 errors to be routed to the URL `/errors/404Handler.html`, while the one on lines 12 through 15 forwards all `IOExceptions` to `/errors/ioPage.jsp` in the Web application. Line 21 causes any errors in the login form to route to the `/errors/loginErr.jsp`.

Declarative error handling guarantees consistency in your application. It's also easy to set up, and it doesn't require you to manually route to error pages in your Servlets or JSPs. Of course, the declarative model also implies a few tradeoffs that have to be made. It doesn't provide flexibility in routing—by definition, you *always* have to route a given error to a given location.[84] Another potential drawback for this model is that you have to set up a mapping for each error code or exception type that you use. If you specify a routing for the IOException, the container will *not* route to the specified URL if you throw a subclass of `IOException`, such as a `FileNotFoundException`.

Components in the Web Tier

There are three key considerations that relate to how the Web tier technologies work with exceptions and errors. The first is the way that a component technology produces HTTP-based errors—the way a component sends an error to clients, in other words. The second is the exception model for components, the failure points for the component and how the container responds to those errors. The third relates to the common issues associated with the technologies, specific problems or risk areas associated with the technology.

As you read about Servlets and JSPs, keep in mind that their exception model is designed so containers can properly manage the exceptions that can occur in a component. Though the programming model may seem restrictive, it enables developers to write code that will run on many different Web containers and platforms—even if there are problems in the Servlets or JSPs.

The key exceptions in the Web tier are based around the lifecycle methods. The lifecycle model is essentially the same for all of the Web component technologies. Whether you're dealing with Servlets, Filters or JSPs, the container still has essentially the same kinds of basic methods that it calls to initialize a component, run the component as part of a request, and destroy a component at the end of its life. Table 10-3 shows the lifecycle methods for each type of Web components.

---

84. Of course, the location could be a Servlet or a Filter. You could write a Web component to provide variable output, if that's a requirement for your application.

Table 10-3 Lifecycle Methods for Web Components

Method Type	Http Servlet	Filter	JSP
Initialize	init() init(ServletConfig)	init(FilterConfig)	_jspInit()
Business	service(HttpServletRequest, HttpServletResponse) do______()*	doFilter(ServletRequest, ServletResponse, FilterChain)	_jspService(HttpServletRequest, HttpServletResponse)
Destroy	destroy()	destroy()	_jspDestroy()

*   The Servlet API defines "do" methods for each of the standard HTTP operations: `doGet`, `doPost`, `doHead`, `doPut`, `doDelete`, `doTrace` and `doOptions`. Each of these methods takes two arguments—an object that implements `HttpServletRequest` and one that implements `HttpServletResponse`.

Exception Model for Servlets and Filters: Programmatic Error Handling

Servlets and Filters allow you to handle HTTP error routing using methods in the `javax.servlet.http.HttpServletResponse` interface. Specifically, the following methods send an HTTP Error code to the container:

```
sendError(int status)
sendError(int status, String message)
```

It's also possible to forward to a specific Web resource[85] with a `RequestDispatcher`. You obtain a `RequestDispatcher` for a given URL by calling one of three methods:

```
javax.servlet.ServletRequest.getRequestDispatcher(String url)
javax.servlet.ServletContext.getRequestDispatcher(String url)
javax.servlet.ServletContext.getNamedDispatcher(String url)[86]
```

After you obtain a `RequestDispatcher`, you can call the `forward` method to transfer control to the new URL. You can use this method if you want some flexibility

---

85. In the context of the J2EE Web Tier, a "Web resource" is a Servlet, Filter, JSP, or HTML page.
86. The `getRequestDispatcher` method in `ServletRequest` works only with resources located in the same Web application. The methods in `ServletContext` will work within the current Web context, but you can also call `getContext` to retrieve a different `ServletContext` on the server. In addition, `getNamedDispatcher` will allow you to get a dispatcher given the internal name for a Servlet or a JSP, instead of requiring a mapping to an external URL.

in your error forwarding, since it lets you dynamically route to *any* Web resource you want, rather than using a static URL mapping configured in the deployment descriptor.

```
RequestDispatcher
    forward(ServletRequest req, ServletResponse rsp)
        throws IOException, ServletException
```

It's worth mentioning that Filters always forward to other resources. By definition, a Filter object is intended to perform processing before or after some other Web resource is executed. What's more, the API allows Filters to be chained together, so you can perform a sequence of Filter-defined operations. When you're ready to run the next Web resource, you call the `FilterChain`'s `doFilter` method from within your own `doFilter` method:

```
FilterChain
    doFilter(ServletRequest, ServletResponse)
        throws IOException, ServletException
```

As you can see, this method declares two exceptions. These exceptions can be propagated back to the Filter from any other Web resource up the chain. Clearly, this represents a risk to a Web application—if you don't properly handle exceptions within a chain, it's possible for an exception to halt all filter processing in a chain. For this reason, it's often prudent to wrap your `doFilter` method in a try-catch block to avoid any problems as you run.

The Servlet and Filter Exception Model

Since Web components have a standardized calling model, it's fairly easy to identify their key exception-producing methods. Servlets and Filters fundamentally have the three crucial method types identified in Table 10-3: the `initialize`, business and `destroy` methods. Two of these categories declare exceptions—the initialization and business methods. Specifically, the `init` methods declare the `javax.servlet.ServletException`, and the service methods declare `javax.servlet.ServletException` and `java.io.IOException`.

Of course, you can still throw subclasses of `RuntimeException` and `Error`, but it isn't recommended. The core exception model is based around using the `ServletException` to represent errors in a Web component. You must ultimately do one of two things for your checked exceptions—handle them within a Servlet's method, or convert them to a declared exception by throwing a `ServletException`. The `ServletException` has a constructor that accepts a Throwable "root cause" so you can preserve the original cause of the problem.

The `ServletException` has a subclass called the `UnavailableException`. This exception indicates temporary or permanent unavailability of a Servlet or Filter. If you specify a "wait time" value with this exception, you indicate temporary unavailability to the container. If no value is specified, you're indicating that the component is permanently unavailable. Depending on the type of problem you encounter in a Servlet or Filter, you can throw one of these exceptions to tell the container which action to take.

1. The `init` Method

You throw exceptions in the `init` method to indicate that a Servlet or Filter cannot be properly initialized. If you throw a ServletException, the container will release the instance, effectively destroying the object. The container is subsequently free to create a new instance and re-initialize the Web component. If you throw an `UnavailableException`, the container will also release the object. If you have specified a wait time for the `UnavailableException`, the container *must* wait until the specified time has elapsed before it attempts to re-create the component. The container will not call the destroy method if an exception has been thrown, since the component didn't complete its initialization properly. To prevent problems due to inconsistent state within your application, you should normally call any cleanup code *before* you throw a `ServletException` or `UnavailableException`.

2. The `service` Method

If you throw an exception during the service method, you're telling the container that there has been some problem with processing a request, or that a component cannot process requests in general. An `IOException` indicates an I/O problem with a specific request. The container will terminate the request, sending an HTTP 500 error (server error) to the client. The container will continue to use the component and it will still use the object to process other requests. This exception is normally produced indirectly, as a result of a problem with the component's `PrintWriter` or `Output-Stream`. You can also throw a `ServletException` to signal that there are problems with a specific client request. Like the `IOException`, the container will terminate the client's request and return a 500 error code.

The container's behavior is much different for an `UnavailableException`. This exception signals to the container that this component cannot process *any* client requests. If you don't specify a wait time, you are signaling permanent unavailability for the component; the container will call the `destroy` method and remove the component. Any client requests for the Servlet will result in a 404 error (resource not found) by the container. If a Filter throws this exception, it will halt processing down a filter chain, effectively preventing a set of related filters from being run.

If you specify temporary unavailability by using a wait time in the exception, the container has a choice. It can either wait for the specified time, returning an HTTP 503 error code (service unavailable) to clients, along with the HTTP header field Retry-After to indicate when it is acceptable to try again. Alternately, the container can treat temporary unavailability in the same way as permanent unavailability. In that case, the container will call the destroy method, remove the instance from the container and send an HTTP 404 error to clients.

3. The `destroy` Method

Unlike the other lifecycle methods, `destroy` doesn't throw any exceptions. There are two potential reasons for this. First, you could argue that it isn't necessary to notify the Web container if there is a problem shutting down a Servlet or Filter. After all, the container calls a Servlet's destroy method when it plans to destroy the object anyway. The container can't really do anything to recover from a problem, so you basically have to handle any problems in the shutdown yourself. In addition, you put code in the destroy method to clean up after the Servlet before shutdown. In many cases, cleanup code has a limited opportunity to fail, at least in principle.

Common Issues and Risks with Servlet Components

Because you have much more direct, low-level API control when developing a Servlet or a Filter, there are a number of issues that present a greater risk than they would for technologies such as JSPs.[87]

1. Managing Content in a Servlet or Filter

One of the greatest drawbacks cited for Servlets is that it's difficult to manage the content generated by a component. After all, Servlets and Filters use a `ServletOutputStream` to send binary data or a `PrintWriter` to send textual information. The data to be sent is divided up into a series of print statements, making it harder to verify, validate, test and manage. In addition, text output suffers from a common problem associated with API calls that abstract input arguments—it's impossible for the Java compiler to check whether the String input actually represents valid output. For this reason, it's a good idea to limit the amount of I/O performed by Servlets and Filters, delegating primary I/O responsibility to JSPs or to static pages.

2. Mixing I/O and Content Types within a Request

Another I/O risk of the Servlet API is that of mixing data. HTTP is set up to return a single content type for a query. The API provides calls that let you set up character *or* byte I/O. The API lets you identify the return data type in the HTTP response header through the `setContentType` method. However, a Servlet or Filter can only generate *one* type of content per client request—and of course, a client "request" can be forwarded to other Servlets, Filters or JSPs. The API can only enforce the "one content

---

87. "With great power comes great responsibility."

type" requirement indirectly, by throwing exceptions if you try to change the I/O type or content type while processing a client's request.

If you try to "mix and match" I/O, a Servlet or Filter will throw an `IllegalStateException`. The `ServletResponse` methods `getOutputStream` and `getWriter` throw this exception if you call both methods while processing the same client request. Likewise, the `ServletRequest` methods `getInputStream` and `getReader` throw an `IllegalStateException` if you call both methods during the same request.[88]

You can chain your calls to satisfy a client's request, so the `RequestDispatcher` also has the similar risks for mixing I/O. If you call the `forward` method after *any* I/O has been sent to a client (that is, if any data from the buffer of your output stream has been flushed), the method will throw the `IllegalStateException`. This happens because the forward method is intended to be used for a progressive processing model, allowing you to divide the work you do on a client request between a number of Web components. Additionally, any uncommitted output will automatically be purged from the `ServletResponse` stream when you forward to another component, so you need to store any data in memory when forwarding.

The `RequestDispatcher`'s `include` method does not throw an `IllegalStateException`, but does prevent another Servlet or Filter from changing any HTTP response headers that could change the response itself. This means that you can't call the following methods:

```
ServletResponse          setContentLength
                         setContentType
                         setLocale
HttpServletResponse      setDateHeader
                         setHeader
                         setIntHeader
                         setStatus
```

This reflects the purpose of the `include` method—to allow a component to include another component's output as it runs. When you call another Web component using this method, any `ServletResponse` methods that would modify header fields are ignored.

3. Concurrency Management

Java Web components are run in a multithreaded environment. Usually, this means that the container maintains a pool of worker threads and uses them to execute the service methods of Servlets, Filters and JSPs for multiple clients over time. Of course, this model means that it's entirely possible for several worker threads to run

---

88. A request in the Web tier can involve multiple Web components, so the `IllegalStateException` can be thrown if you try to change the level of the streams in a series of components used to satisfy a client's request.

the same service method of a Web component at the same time—which means that Web components have threading risks. Specifically, a Web component is a threading risk if you use shared, stateful resources in your Web component, and their state is changed during a client's request.

The Servlet API provides a lot of places where you can store data, with different scopes and risks for thread corruption. Table 10-4 summarizes the different types of variable storage.

Table 10–4 Threading Risks for Variable Storage in the Servlet API

Type	How to define and use the variable	Potential threading risk?
Instance	Member variable	Yes; unpredictable behavior depending on how a container manages Web components
Class	Static member variable	Yes
Local	Local variable	No, each worker thread has its own local variables
Request	ServletRequest methods setAttribute, getAttribute, removeAttribute	No, each worker thread has its own ServletRequest and ServletResponse
Session	HttpSession methods setAttribute, getAttribute, removeAttribute	Yes, if a client of a Web application uses multiple browser windows to access the application
Context	ServletContext methods setAttribute, getAttribute, removeAttribute	Yes, if any components in a Web application on the same Web server access the ServletContext object

Even though Request-scoped variables are not shared between threads, it's important to realize that none of the methods in the `ServletRequest` and `ServletResponse` interfaces are synchronized. This means if you ever store a ServletRequest or ServletResponse object in a Session object that could be accessed by multiple threads in the Web tier, you give up any guarantees of thread safety. If you want to ensure thread safety of request scoped variables, you should pass them using thread safe technologies: the Servlet API RequestDispatcher or the JSP include or forward tags.

4. Session Management

In many Web applications, you need the ability to cache information over a number of calls by a client. Unfortunately, HTTP was designed to be stateless, so there is no native caching capability in the protocol.[89] As a result, dynamic Web technologies had to develop state caching mechanisms that were independent of HTTP. Like many modern Web technologies, Java Web components have two main options to preserve state. They can cache data on the client or server, using the `javax.serv-`

let.http.Cookie class or the javax.servlet.http.HttpSession interface, respectively.[90]

Neither approach is perfect. Cookies free the server from the responsibilities of managing state, but they limit the size and type of data that can be stored. Since cookies are stored on a client, they make it easier to perform some server activities such as load balancing. Cookies increase the bandwidth of an application, since they must be sent by the client to the server with each request. Since cookies are stored on a client's system, the server loses control of the data—it is possible for data to be compromised or corrupted. This means that cookies also represent a security risk for an application, since they are exposed on a network during multiple HTTP requests. Finally, some clients cannot or will not allow cookies to be stored by the browser.

An HttpSession provides a server with more direct control over data, since the object is stored in the Web container. Since the data never leaves the server, there is reduced bandwidth required and better security for the data. Additionally, the session object has no storage limitations—an HttpSession can hold any object and any volume of data. Of course, there's a price for everything. Server-side caching increases the processing load on a server, and managing a lot of complex data can impact server performance. Another issue is the challenge of associating the cache with a specific client. By definition, cookies are always associated with the browser that sends them. You need some way to associate a session with a given Web client. In J2EE, a session ID variable identifies a client, and there are two standard ways to track the session ID. The first involves setting a single cookie on the client with the session ID. The second involves appending the session ID to the return URL for any hyperlinks and form submission controls—the process called URL rewriting.

Once you have established the session, there are some additional challenges to session use. As mentioned in the previous section, the HttpSession can present a threading risk. In addition, you have to be careful when deciding how to remove an HttpSession. While it's possible to purge a session from a container using the HttpSession method invalidate, the fact that an HttpSession can be used by multiple threads makes this a risky operation. If you try to use a session object after invalidation, one of two things will happen. If you want to retrieve the session, you will get a new object without any previously cached data. If you try to use a cached HttpSession object after it has been invalidated, you will see exceptions in your code. Specifically, any calls to attribute management methods (getAttribute, getAttributeNames, removeAttribute, setAttribute) will throw an IllegalStateException. Because of these risks, it's prudent to carefully control how

---

89. The lack of state in the HTTP model is a direct result of the design goals when Web servers were first developed. Web servers were traditionally focused on optimizing client throughput, which tends to discourage servers from caching client state. In addition, servers historically had no need to cache client state, since they were used to send static content to distributed clients.

90. A third option is to pass the state between client and server without any form of caching. This is a useful solution for some caching problems, such as dynamic navigation.

sessions can be destroyed, perhaps even requiring an explicit logout process in the Web application.

Exception Model for JSPs

In many ways, the exception model for JSPs is more straightforward than the one used for Servlets. After all, most of the complex I/O work for a JSP is handled by the container, as part of the process of converting a JSP to a Servlet-like class. Of course, it's still possible for a JSP to make direct Servlet API calls, but that's generally discouraged. If you make low-level API calls from the JSP, you have to deal with the same issues mentioned in the previous section, *and* you have the added challenge of managing Java code within a JSP. It's much harder to understand, maintain, test and debug API code from within a scripted page, so most developers avoid writing Java code inside a JSP if possible. One of the main reasons for using JSPs, after all, is to simplify the process of creating a Web component, automating most of the complex work that you'd normally have to code by hand.

Direct Error Forwarding in JSPs

JSPs provide action tags that allow you to programmatically forward to other Web components or static pages using a `RequestDispatcher`. In general, they're a little easier to work with than the Servlet API.

```
<jsp:include url="errors/MyError.jsp" />
<jsp:forward url="errors/Handler.html" />
```

In addition, you can specify a Web resource as a general "exception handling page" for your JSP. You can do this by writing a page directive with an `errorPage` attribute. In the JSP 2.0 specification, there are two equivalent formats that you can use. Both are shown below:

```
<%@ page errorPage="errors/errorHandler.jsp">
<jsp:directive.page errorPage="errors/errPage.html" />
```

When you use the `errorPage` attribute, the service method of your JSP is wrapped in a try-catch block. If an exception is produced, the exception will automatically be forwarded to the target URL identified in the `errorPage` attribute. Any time an exception is forwarded to an error handler page, the container will set up a standard attribute in the `ServletRequest` object. The name of the attribute is "`javax.serv-let.jsp.jspException`" and its value is a Throwable object, the error that was thrown by the forwarding JSP. In addition, if the receiving JSP is set to be an error handler using the `isErrorPage` attribute of the page directive, the JSP can use the implicit object "exception" to represent the Throwable object.

```
<%@ page isErrorPage="true">
<jsp:directive.page isErrorPage="true" />

    An error has occurred: <%= exception %>
```

The "exception" variable is set to the value of the `HttpServletRequest` attribute `javax.servlet.error.exception`. If the attribute is not present, the exception will be stored in the attribute used by earlier versions the JSP specification, the attribute `javax.servlet.jsp.jspException`.

There's another way that you can access information about an exception—you can use a class called `javax.servlet.jsp.ErrorData`. JSP2.0 introduced this class to extend the JSP error page handling mechanism. An `ErrorData` object is a wrapper around exception data produced by a Servlet, Filter or JSP page. The container will automatically create an `ErrorData` object for any JSP which has a page directive with the `isErrorPage` attribute set to `true`. You can get the object by calling the `Page-Context` method `getErrorData`. The `ErrorData` object has the following standard methods:

```
getRequestURI, getStatusCode, getServletName, getThrowable
```

You can use either the request attribute or the `ErrorData` object in an error handling JSP, depending on the information you need to represent.

The JSP Exception Model

Unlike the Servlet model, the JSP initialization method `jspInit` doesn't throw any exceptions. It's fairly uncommon to implement `jspInit` and `jspDestroy` in a JSP; if you want to write any code, you have to define these methods in a JSP declaration. The equivalent of the service method, `_jspService`, throws the same exceptions as the Servlet API: `java.io.IOException` and `javax.servlet.ServletException`.

The JSP service method provides a base level of exception handling by default. During JSP page translation, the Web container will automatically generate a handling block around the converted JSP. The following sample shows a standard code block produced by the reference implementation of the Web container, Apache Tomcat.

```
try {
    // *****************************************
    //    Converted JSP page would be placed here
    // *****************************************
} catch (Throwable t) {
```

```
  if (!(t instanceof javax.servlet.jsp.SkipPageException)){
    out = _jspx_out;
    if (out != null && out.getBufferSize() != 0)
      out.clearBuffer();
    if (pageContext != null) pageContext.handlePageException(t);
  }
} finally {
  if (_jspxFactory != null)
    _jspxFactory.releasePageContext(pageContext);
}
```

As you can see, any exception produced within a JSP (apart from the `SkipPage-Exception`) is guaranteed to be forwarded to a standard handling method in the `PageContext`, `handlePageException`.

Translation and Runtime Errors of a JSP

A JSP must be converted into a class file before execution. If there's a problem that prevents conversion or compilation of the JSP resource, the container will not be able to provide access to the JSP. The exception that is logged by the container is implementation dependent, varying based on the way that the container converts the JSP into a class.[91] The response to clients *will* be consistent, however. If a client tries to access a JSP that cannot be converted to a class, the Web container will return an HTTP status of 500, indicating a server error.

For exceptions that occur while a JSP is running, there's a hierarchy of handling behavior. Any unhandled exceptions will first be forwarded to the JSP's error page, if one is specified. If there is no error page, the exception will be handled using the default destination specified in the Web application's deployment descriptor. Finally, if there is no formal handling strategy defined for the specific exception thrown by a JSP, the exception will be forwarded to the `PageContext` method `handlePageException`. By default, this exception will return an HTTP 500 error code to the client. Any time that the container handles an exception for a JSP, it will log the exception's stack trace, and return the stack trace to the caller by default.

Custom Tag Libraries

JSPs allow you to use **custom tag libraries** to further extend the capabilities available to a JSP through scripting language syntax. A tag library consists of one or more standard Java classes called **tag handlers**. You use a tag library descriptor file (TLD) to

---

91. In   recent   versions   of   Tomcat,   a   JSP   page   conversion   error   is   represented   by   a
     `org.apache.jasper.JasperException`, for example.

map a tag handler into XML syntax. Page authors write JSPs that use the XML tags. During page translation, the container converts the XML tags into method calls on the tag handlers. The primary purpose of custom tag libraries is to hold reusable code that can easily be incorporated into a JSP without having to write raw Java code.

There are four basic kinds of tag handlers, based around standard interfaces and classes defined in the `javax.servlet.jsp.tagext` package—`SimpleTag`, `Tag`, `IterationTag` and `BodyTag`. Each tag handler has certain standard methods that are called as part of the execution lifecycle of the JSP. The simplest handler is defined by `SimpleTag`, which has a single worker method called `doTag`. Slightly more complex is `Tag`, which has the `doStartTag` and `doEndTag` methods. The `IterationTag` extends the `Tag` by adding the method `doAfterBody`. Finally, the `BodyTag` interface extends `IterationTag` and adds the method `doInitBody`. The model for tag handlers guarantee a standardized calling sequence for these methods, so they will always be consistently executed as a JSP runs.[92]

The use of tag handlers has little impact on the exception model of a JSP. All of the business methods defined for a tag handler declare a standard exception, the `javax.servlet.jsp.JspException`. This exception will be caught and handled within the default JSP page handler block. There are two subclasses of `JspException`, `JspTagException` and `SkipPageException`. Both are used for communication between a tag handler and the JSP page. The `JspTagException` is thrown by a tag handler if there is some error during its business methods; if it is thrown, the `_jspService` method of the JSP page will catch the exception and forward to an error handler JSP if one is specified, or to the `PageContext` for default error handling.

The `SkipPageException` is thrown by a tag handler to signal that the rest of the JSP page should not be processed.[93] The JSP page will catch this exception and exit the `_jspService` method normally, bypassing the rest of the page in the process. It's debatable whether it's really good form to use an exception like the `SkipPageException`. After all, it's really being used to communicate between the tag handler and its JSP page, and not to communicate an exception or error. The reason that the `SkipPageException` is used is that it can provide an effective means to halt page evaluation at any point during JSP page processing. Since there's really no simple way to bypass the execution of the body of a method, the `SkipPageException` was used as a convenient way to halt method execution.

A helpful capability of tag handlers is their ability to define a standard exception handling mechanism. If desired, a tag handler can implement the `TryCatchFinally` interface. If a tag handler implements this interface, the entire tag invocation is wrapped in a try-catch-finally code block in a JSP. The method `doCatch(Throwable)` will be run within the catch block, and the `doFinally()` method will be run regard-

---

92.   For further details on custom tag libraries, consider a book like Core Servlets and JSP Pages.

93.   The SkipPageException was introduced to support the new "simple" tag handlers defined in the JSP 2.0 specification.

less of the outcome of the tag handler's execution. The `doCatch` method declares a Throwable exception, so it's possible to handle an exception and still propagate it to the enclosing JSP.

The EJB Tier

When people first start to develop Enterprise JavaBeans, they're often overwhelmed by the complexity of the exception model. That's understandable—there are a *lot* of exceptions defined in the EJB API. In part, the exception model reflects the complexity of business components in general. It's difficult to develop an effective API for business components that covers all of the issues associated with distributed object middleware.

What's more, the standard services provided by the EJB container—security, transactions, cache management (both for EJBs and the data they hold) and concurrency control—are among the most difficult services to manage in an enterprise system. As a result, the exception model used to communicate errors to the container and client is detailed and complex, since it has to address a wide variety of problems.

Standard EJB Methods

In order to understand the EJB exception model, it's important to know the standard methods defined for each type of EJB. As of the EJB2.1 specification, there are three types of EJB with two subcategories:

Session Bean	Components that define business services
Stateful	Components that can preserve conversational state with a client over a series of method calls
Stateless	Components that do not retain state between method calls
Entity Bean	Components that define business entities mapped to persistent data storage
Message-Driven Bean	Components that define "asynchronous message receivers", components that will be called upon receipt of a message

Starting with EJB2.1, EJBs could optionally implement the `TimedObject` interface, allowing an EJB to be triggered automatically through an `ejbTimeout` method. This allows you to perform an action with an EJB at a set time or with a configurable frequency. Since the `ejbTimeout` method declares no exceptions, it can only throw runtime exceptions and errors. Since the `ejbTimeout` is called by the container, any exceptions or errors will be logged but not propagated to a caller.[94]

Tables 10-5, 10-6, 10-7 and 10-8 summarize the methods of each component, including how they are called and by whom.

Table 10–5   **Standard Methods for a Stateless Session Bean**

Method Type	Method Name	Called on	Who Calls?
Create	ejbCreate [exactly one method]	Bean	Container
Lifecycle management	setSessionContext	Bean	Container
Business	*Developer defined*	Component interface	Client
Destroy	ejbRemove	Home or component interface (remove method)	Container

Table 10–6   **Standard Methods for a Stateful Session Bean**

Method Type	Method Name	Called on	Who Calls?
Create	ejbCreate [one or more methods]	Home interface (create method)	Client
Lifecycle management	setSessionContext ejbActivate ejbPassivate	Bean	Container Container Container
Business	*Developer defined*	Component interface	Client
Destroy	ejbRemove	Home or component interface (remove method)	Client
Transaction Support (for a CMT bean that implements SessionSynchronization)	afterBegin afterCompletion beforeCompletion	Bean Bean Bean	Container Container Container

---

94.   After all, the only "caller" in this case was the container, which has already responded to the error in the EJB.

Table 10–7 **Standard Methods for an Entity Bean**

Method Type	Method Name	Called on	Who Calls?
Create	ejbCreate, ejbPostCreate [0 or more paired methods]	Home interface (create method)	Client
Lifecycle management	setEntityContext unsetEntityContext ejbActivate ejbPassivate	Bean	Container Container Container Container
Business	*Developer defined*	Component interface	Client
State management	ejbLoad ejbStore	Bean	Container Container
Search	ejbFindByPrimaryKey ejbFindBy______ select______	Home interface Home interface Bean	Client Client Code*
Home	ejbHome______	Home interface	Client
Destroy	ejbRemove	Home or component interface (remove method)	Client

* Only CMP Entity Beans have these methods

Table 10–8 **Standard Methods for a Message-Driven Bean**

Method Type	Method Name	Called on	Who Calls?
Create	ejbCreate	Bean	Container
Lifecycle management	setMessageDrivenContext	Bean	Container
Business	onMessage	Bean	Container
Destroy	ejbRemove	Bean	Container

General/Common Issues with EJBs

1. Validation

One of the most difficult things for developers to adjust to in the EJB component model is the fact that it is not compiler-enforced. There are a lot of rules that you must follow to create a valid EJB component. Unlike other Java classes, you can't rely on the compiler to be sure that you've followed all the steps required to make an EJB. For instance, an externally called Stateless Session Bean requires you to do the following:

1. Create a Home interface which extends `javax.ejb.EJBHome` and defines the following method:

   ```
   public <ComponentInterface> create() throws
           javax.ejb.CreateException,
           java.rmi.RemoteException
   ```

2. Create a `Component` interface which extends `javax.ejb.EJBObject` and defines any business methods. All business methods must declare `java.rmi.RemoteException` in addition to any application-specific exceptions.

3. Create the bean class, which implements `javax.ejb.SessionBean`, and which must define methods to match the business methods of the `Component` interface, and a method to match the create method:

   ```
   public void ejbCreate()
   ```

4. Create an XML deployment descriptor with the EJB name, type, class and interfaces.

Naturally, you still have to verify that an EJB follows these rules—but the Java compiler can't verify an XML file or check that an interface method has a given signature. Instead, you must check to see if an EJB is properly set up during a special validation stage for the component, or when you deploy it to a container.

2. Local versus Remote EJBs

In the original EJB specification, there was only one way to access Session and Entity Beans—remotely, using an RMI-based calling model. EJB2.0 introduced the ability to define local as well as remote interfaces for beans. The rationale for this new model is easy enough to understand—a local calling model for an EJB is often more efficient than remote invocation, since it avoids network calls and passes arguments by reference rather than object serialization.

However, the decision to use a local rather than a distributed calling model is complicated—it involves more than a simple question of runtime efficiency. If you define your EJB with local interfaces, you effectively rule out location independence, since the bean must be colocated with its caller. That ultimately limits the horizontal scalability of your EJB tier. If you define a bean with both local and remote interfaces, its business model is different depending on how a client accesses the bean. In particular, EJBs have fundamentally different exception propagation models depending on whether they are locally or remotely called.

Defining a Session or Entity Bean with remote interfaces implies the following tradeoffs:

- You will have the overhead of network calls when you use the bean.

- You can have location independence, and have more flexibility in how you deploy the bean.
- You have looser coupling between the bean and its clients.
- Any calling parameters must be Serializable, and you will have to manage copies of the same parameters across multiple systems.
- Any methods must declare the `RemoteException`, and have the possibility to fail due to communication problems.

On the other hand, locally accessed EJBs have a different set of tradeoffs:

- You access the bean through local calls.
- You must colocate the bean and its client, implying that they are tightly coupled.
- You lose the flexibility of independent deployment.
- The exception model is simpler, since there is no risk associated with distributed communication.
- Data is passed by reference, which has lower overhead but implies that you have to be discerning about how you change data, since data is effectively shared between the client and bean.

Which model should you use? Ultimately, it depends on your goals. General recommendations are to define remote interfaces for loosely-coupled, coarse-grained business services. Examples include Session Beans, especially those used as a façade to access the EJB tier. You typically define a local calling model for fine-grained calls and explicitly dependent relationships. Examples include Entity Beans, especially when their use is coordinated through a Session Bean or when they are part of a container-managed relationship, managed as a reference from a Container-Managed Persistence Entity Bean.[95]

Bean-Specific Issues

1. Issues with Stateful Session Beans

Stateful session beans can store data over multiple method calls for a client. Unfortunately, this means that there's no way for a container to effectively "share" the beans between clients. By definition, every client must have access to its own personal data storage. This means that a container really can't manage bean instances as effectively as it could for other bean types.

The only option available for a container to make a limited number of beans available to a larger number of clients is passivation. The container can persist a bean's

---

95. The rules and guidelines for this section reference the EJB component specification, Chapter 5. This is an incredibly valuable resource for all who want an in-depth understanding of the foundation principles and rules behind EJB behavior.

state to secondary storage,[96] and make the bean instance temporarily available to another client. When the original client calls a method on the bean, the container restores the state to a bean instance and runs the method. This solution works well for short-term spikes of client activity and for a fairly infrequent call model—one where clients do not call bean methods that often.

If there are many more clients than stateful session bean instances and the clients call the EJB methods frequently, this approach doesn't work as well. The server will have to spend time and effort activating and passivating stateful session bean instances to service client requests. In extreme cases, it is even possible for server thrashing to occur. The EJB container will be forced to spend so much time swapping beans in and out of its pool that it will starve the application server, resulting in substantial performance degradation. The best remedy for this problem is to avoid it, monitoring server performance and adjusting the bean's pool size (or distributing load among multiple containers) as required.

Because stateful session beans store a client's state, a special risk exists when using the remove method. Like most data caching mechanisms, the container has the ability to purge a stateful session bean that has been unused for a container-configured period of time.[97] If this should occur, a client will receive an exception if it continues to make method calls on the bean. Specifically, the component interface will throw a `java.rmi.NoSuchObjectException` for a remotely accessed EJB, and a `javax.ejb.NoSuchObjectLocalException` for a locally accessed EJB.

One final risk exists with a stateful session bean. Under one specific circumstance, its remove method will not be called. When a stateful session bean is passivated, the remove method will not be called if the bean is not used before its timeout occurs.[98] For this reason, it is prudent to execute any required removal code in `ejbPassivate` as well as `ejbRemove`.

2. Issues with Entity Beans

An entity bean must be matched with data in the database. The container uses a primary key object to match the bean with data, and to represent the bean's identity as a database entity. If data is shared between many clients, it's likely that a container will use multiple entity bean instances to represent the same data. Since multiple entity bean instances can be used to represent the same data from the DBMS, it's important that their primary key objects properly indicate that the beans are equal. Specifically, primary key objects should implement the `equals` and `hashCode` methods so that they show equivalency if the same data is stored in two different EJBs. This requirement isn't usually a problem for single-table mappings, since you usually store the

---

96. Usually a file system.
97. This is a practical requirement for server-side caching—if client data was never purged, it could overwhelm a server that hosts many clients.
98. In other words, the container will not activate a bean simply to destroy it.

table's primary key in a Java object such as a String or Integer. It's when you need to handle compound primary keys or multi-table mappings that you usually need to create a custom class to represent your primary key. In these cases, you need to be careful to manage object equality.

Although entity beans can synchronize their state to a DBMS, it's important to remember that they don't have any special ability to dynamically detect changes to a database. If a process, client or component other than the entity bean is making changes to the underlying data, it is possible that the EJB container will not be able to synchronize data changes to the entity beans. In cases where there's a chance that your entity bean could contain stale data, it's a good idea to refresh your bean's state around transactional boundaries.

Entity beans, by their nature, keep data synchronized with a data source. This implies periodic updates with the database—the container will invoke the `ejbLoad` and `ejbStore` methods across transaction boundaries and as required to keep the entity bean up to date. This implies that there is overhead with using entity beans, and that they are not ideal for some types of database access. Entity beans are ideal for managing data that is limited in volume, highly shared, and highly volatile. In such cases, you are making the best possible use of your container management. In other situations, you have to evaluate the performance tradeoff, and compare entity bean technologies to other methods of data access.[99]

3. Issues with Message-Driven Beans

Depending on how it's coded, a message-driven bean can potentially have issues with message acknowledgement. It's possible to configure a messaging server for guaranteed delivery. In other words, the server will send a message to a destination until it receives confirmation that the message has been properly received. If a message-driven bean is configured for transactional behavior and the transaction rolls back, the server will retransmit the message. This means you have to be careful about how you code the worker method of the message-driven bean—if you experience a recurring problem and rollback a transaction, it's possible for the server to saturate the server with message traffic. In such cases, it's usually better to send an acknowledgement to the messaging server and handle the problem locally.[100]

---

99. Some developers prefer to moderate the transactional overhead associated with entity beans by implementing only the `ejbLoad` and `finder` methods. These "read-only" entity beans are useful for some enterprise applications. As of the EJB2.1 release, the API developers have expressed interest in developing a read-only CMP entity bean in a future version of the specification.

100. This problem has been well-documented in a number of excellent works, including Bitter EJB. I first heard about the problem from the trainer and author, Kathy Sierra.

The EJB Exception Model

The EJB specification formally divides exceptions into application and non-application exceptions. An **application exception** represents a business exception in the EJB tier—it is ultimately intended to be sent to a client, whether the client is another EJB or some other caller. An application exception is defined to be any exception apart from the RemoteException that an EJB declares in any of its interface methods. The following represent application exceptions for EJB:

- Business exceptions
- CreateException and its subclasses
- RemoveException
- FinderException and its subclasses

Generally speaking, application exceptions are intended to represent problems in business logic, so you should normally throw this type of exception for business-related problems you encounter in your code. Clients are often able to recover from, or at least respond to, application exceptions. Any custom business exception you define must subclass Exception and must not subclass either the RuntimeException or RemoteException classes.

Any other exception is classified as a **non-application** exception. These exceptions represent broader problems with an EJB, errors which normally require action by the container. A client may or may not be able to recover from non-application exceptions in an EJB. The following classes define major categories of non-application exception:

- RemoteException and its subclasses
- RuntimeException and its subclasses
- EJBException and its subclasses[101]

The EJB specification specifies that all remotely-called EJB methods throw the RemoteException, and all locally-called methods can throw EJBException. This provides a way for non-application exceptions to be propagated back to a caller as required. Table 10-9 provides a basic summary of the exceptions used for EJBs, including a summary of where they are thrown or when they are produced.

---

101. EJBException is actually a subclass of RuntimeException, but it's such an important exception category in the EJB specification that it deserves special mention.

Table 10–9 Summary of EJB Exceptions

Exception	Type	How is it declared or thrown?
javax.ejb.CreateException	Application	create<Method> ejbCreate, ejbPostCreate
javax.ejb.DuplicateKeyException	Application	Entity Bean create<Method> ejbCreate, ejbPostCreate
javax.ejb.RemoveException	Application	ejbRemove
javax.ejb.FinderException	Application	findBy<Method>, select<Method>
javax.ejb.ObjectNotFoundException	Application	findBy<Method>, select<Method>
javax.ejb.EJBException	System	RuntimeException: Base class used to represent EJB exceptions. Can be thrown by business methods or callback methods
javax.ejb.AccessLocalException	System, Security	EJBException: Thrown to indicate a client does not have permission to call a local business method
java.rmi.AccessException	System, Security	RemoteException: Thrown to indicate a client does not have permission to call a remote business method. A container can also throw the RemoteException
javax.ejb.NoSuchEntityException	System	EJBException (**Entity Bean**): Thrown when you call a method on an entity bean after the underlying entity has been removed from the DBMS
java.rmi.NoSuchObjectException	System	RemoteException: Thrown when you try to call a method on a remote bean instance that no longer exists
javax.ejb.NoSuchObjectLocalException	System	EJBException: Thrown when you try to call a method on a local bean instance that no longer exists
javax.ejb.TransactionRequiredLocalException	System, Transactions	EJBException: Thrown when you call a local method that requires transactions from a non-transactional context
javax.transaction.TransactionRequiredException	System, Transactions	RemoteException: Thrown when you call a remote method that requires transactions from a non-transactional context
javax.ejb.TransactionRolledbackLocalException	System, Transactions	EJBException: Thrown to a client to indicate that a transaction has been marked for rollback on a local call
javax.transaction.TransactionRolledbackException	System, Transactions	RemoteException: Thrown to a client to indicate that a transaction has been marked for rollback on a remote call

Though it's difficult to define any hard and fast rules for how you should use exceptions in your EJB code, the specification suggests the following general rules of thumb. You should throw application exceptions to signal problems with business processing or problems in the standard lifecycle methods. For system exceptions, you should generally propagate `RuntimeExceptions` to the container in unaltered form, and wrap any checked exceptions in an `EJBException`.

Lifecycle Management
Client-Called Methods

The client-called methods include the create, finder, business and remove methods. These methods are called by a client on a session or entity bean. Since there are two models for client communication, there are two types of access for these methods. The remote call model requires the bean to implement `EJBHome` for the home interface and `EJBObject` for the component interface. If a bean uses this model, all of its client-called methods declare the `java.rmi.RemoteException` in addition to its standard exceptions. Locally called beans must implement `EJBLocalHome` and `EJBLocalObject`, respectively. The client-called methods of a local EJB declare the `javax.ejb.EJBException` in addition to the standard exceptions. Recognize that the message-driven bean doesn't have any methods that are client invoked. Since it was designed to be triggered for incoming messages, all of its methods are called by the container.

1. Creation: the `create<Method>`

All EJBs can have at least one `create` method. The purpose of the method depends on the type of bean. For session and message-driven beans, the method makes a bean instance available to the caller.[102] The entity bean's `create` methods, if there are any, perform a SQL INSERT.

Any `create` method must declare `javax.ejb.CreateException`. You would throw this exception from the `ejbCreate` method in your bean to indicate that there has been a problem creating a bean. For session and entity beans, the `CreateException` is sent on to the client by the container.

Create behavior is a bit more complex for entity beans. First, there are two methods in a bean for a single create method—`ejbCreate` and `ejbPostCreate`. Both methods can throw the `CreateException`. Second, the meaning of the `CreateException` is a bit more complex for an entity bean. Since the create method inserts data into a DBMS, a client cannot be certain whether a DBMS insert has, in fact, occurred when this exception is thrown. It's generally a good idea to include some

---

102. Depending on how the EJB container is configured and when a client calls the `create` method, it may or may not create a new EJB object. Once created, it's common for EJB containers to pool EJBs to improve performance.

data in the exception to indicate the state of the DBMS for the client's benefit. The entity bean can also throw a subclass of the `CreateException`, `javax.ejb.DuplicateKeyException`. This exception signals a more specific error to a client—the DB insert could not be performed because a record already exists with the same primary key.

2. Location: the `find<Method>` and `select<Method>`

The finder methods can be defined for entity beans only, and provide a way to run a SQL SELECT. All entity beans have a `findByPrimaryKey` method, and may declare single or multi-entity finder methods.

Finder methods are intended to be called by clients to "look up" database entries for entity beans. The finder methods throw the `javax.ejb.FinderException`, which indicates some problem in running the finder behavior. A subclass of `Finder-Exception` is `javax.ejb.ObjectNotFoundException`, which indicates that a DB entry with the matching primary key could not be found.

Single-entity finder methods should throw the `FinderException` if there are multiple results returned that match the SELECT criteria, or if there are problems running the SELECT on the DB.[103] The method should throw the `ObjectNotFoundEx-ception` if there are no values returned that satisfy the SELECT query.

Multi-element finders throw the `FinderException` if there is some problem executing the SELECT. The method never throws the `ObjectNotFoundException`, since it is considered acceptable for a multi-element finder to return an empty collection of results. In addition, duplicates are permitted in multi-element finders: if there is no DISTINCT clause in the SELECT, it is acceptable for the results to contain duplicate database entries.[104]

CMP entity beans can also define internally used finder methods that are called `ejbSelect` methods. `ejbSelect` methods can perform a broader set of SELECT behavior for an EJB. In addition to performing a SELECT on the entity primary keys, `ejbSelect` methods can search for any CMP or CMR-mapped field. In other words, the methods can return references to beans, bean data fields, or other entity beans.

Like the finder methods, `ejbSelect` methods can return a single element or multiple elements. Single element select methods throw a `FinderException` if the query returns multiple values, or if there is some problem executing the finder method. They throw an `ObjectNotFoundException` if no values are returned. Multi-element select methods throw a `FinderException` if there are problems with the SELECT behavior.

---

103. A BMT entity bean is not required to throw a `FinderException` if there are more than one primary key matches, but the exception *will* be thrown for CMT entity beans should this occur.

104. Of course, the implication of this behavior is that you may have non-unique primary keys in your DBMS, which could represent another problem in your application!

3. Business Methods

Session and entity beans can define any number of business methods. These methods can throw any type of application-specific exception to indicate a problem with the execution of the method.

4. Home Methods

Entity beans can declare home methods, which are business methods that don't implement entity-specific logic. Since home methods don't require a database entity, they can be invoked from the bean's home interface. Like ordinary business methods, the home methods can declare application exceptions that are meaningful to the business environment.

5. Removal: The `remove` Method

Beans use the `ejbRemove` method to prepare the bean for removal by the container. The calling model differs for this method depending on the type of bean:

Stateful Session Bean	Client or container called
Stateless Session Bean	Container called
Entity Bean	Client called
Message-Driven Bean	Container called

All remove methods declare the `javax.ejb.RemoveException`; you would throw this exception to indicate a problem removing the bean from service. Specifically, the exception indicates that the bean or container will not allow the bean to be removed for some reason. You cannot guarantee that the `ejbRemove` method will be called if there's a major problem within the EJB tier, such as a container crash. For this reason, some applications run dedicated recovery code in the case of a catastrophic failure. Finally, recognize that the remove method in an entity bean corresponds to a SQL DELETE operation, and is not called to remove a bean object from service.

Any attempt by a client to access an EJB after removal would cause an exception to be thrown. Specifically, the container would throw the `NoSuchObjectException` for remotely accessed EJBs, and the `NoSuchObjectLocalException` for locally-called EJBs. Since removal corresponds to a delete for Entity Beans, the container would throw `NoSuchEntityException` to indicate that the underlying database entry no longer existed.

Container Callback Methods

Container callback methods are automatically run by a container as part of an EJB's lifecycle. Callback methods are standardized for each types of EJB, and are defined in an interface that a bean must implement:

Session beans	`javax.ejb.SessionBean`
Entity beans	`javax.ejb.EntityBean`
Message-driven beans	`javax.ejb.MessageDrivenBean`

All of an EJB's container-called methods declare two standard exceptions—the `java.rmi.RemoteException` and `javax.ejb.EJBException`. The 1.0 and 1.1 versions of the EJB specification used the RemoteException to signify a problem during the container-called methods. Today, the exception is still declared for backward compatibility. However, any EJB coded to a 2.0 or later specification must only throw the `EJBException` to indicate a problem during a container-invoked method.[105]

1. Context management: set_____Context, unsetEntityContext

Every bean type has a standard method to set the bean's context object. The context represents the way that the bean can access container services. Basic services available for EJBs include security and transaction control. In addition, entity beans define the method `unsetEntityContext`, which is called before an entity bean object is destroyed.[106]

2. Passivation and Activation: ejbActivate and ejbPassivate

Both session and entity beans define these methods. For stateful session beans, the container calls `ejbPassivate` method to store a client's state so that it can reuse the bean instance for another client. The container calls `ejbActivate` to restore the client state to a bean instance prior to running a method on the bean. For entity beans, the container calls the methods for a completely different reason. It calls `ejbActivate` when it removes an entity bean from the pool, prior to populating it with data. The container calls `ejbPassivate` before it places a bean back into the pool. In both EJB models, these methods provide the developer with a chance to take action before a major change in bean state occurs.

3. Load/Store Behavior: ejbLoad and ejbStore

Entity beans define these methods to perform SQL SELECT and UPDATE operations, respectively. The `ejbLoad` method is called to refresh a bean instance with data from the DBMS; the container will call it when the bean is first loaded, at the beginning of a transaction, and when the container determines it's necessary to refresh the bean instance with data. The `ejbStore` method is called to update the DBMS with

---

105. Since the `EJBException` is a subclass of `RuntimeException`, it's possible that it may not be declared in your EJB source code, especially if your EJBs have been auto-generated by an IDE tool.
106. Entity beans require this method, since their ejbRemove method is not called to destroy an EJB, but to perform a SQL DELETE operation instead.

data from the entity bean. The container will call this method when a transaction commits for the associated EJB.

Container View of Exceptions

The container has a lot of responsibility for exceptions generated by an EJB. After all, a J2EE container is ultimately responsible for managing components. For EJBs, that responsibility often extends to managing a pool of bean instances, so the action taken by a container can ultimately affect many clients.[107] Key parts of a container's response to an exception thrown by an EJB include object management, transaction behavior, exception logging, exception conversion and exception propagation to a client.

Container management of bean instances is very consistent. For non-application exceptions, including runtime exceptions and errors, the container will always discard the bean instance. This is true no matter what type of EJB you use and no matter which method has been called. When the container discards the bean instance, it will call no more methods on the bean. It's important to emphasize that non-application exceptions always cause a bean instance to be discarded by the container. Any subsequent calls on an EJB by a client will therefore cause a `NoSuchObjectException` or `NoSuchObjectLocalException` to be thrown to the client. For non-application exceptions, the container will also log the exception or error, so that an administrator will be able to review the problem. After all, this category of errors is considered to represent a critical error or unexpected failure scenario with the bean.

Application exceptions are considered to be non-critical or business-related errors. As such, they will not be logged, and the container will not discard the bean instance. If an application exception is thrown by a bean method, the container will always propagate the exception to the caller. If the caller is a remote client or local EJB, the client will receive the exception and handle (or declare) it normally. For message-driven beans, the exception will be propagated to the resource adapter that sent the message to the bean.

Transactions in J2EE and EJBs

One of the services provided in J2EE deserves special treatment in a discussion about exceptions—transaction management. Because they often involve many different components and enterprise systems, transactions tend to be complex and difficult to manage in enterprise applications.

It's possible to use a distributed API such as JDBC, JMS or the Connector Architecture to manage transactions in J2EE, but it's generally recommended that you use the

---

107. EJB containers manage stateless session beans, entity beans, and message-driven beans in a pool. Although there is no formal requirement that stateful session beans be pooled, containers sometimes pool them to further improve server performance.

more global APIs, the **Java Transaction API (JTA)** and **Java Transaction Service (JTS)**. Together, these two APIs define the contract used to communicate with a transaction server, which in turn can coordinate transactions between many enterprise systems. Since these APIs allow you to enforce transactions that involve many systems, they also enable a distributed two-phase commit model in J2EE.

It is possible for you to use JTA from any of the tiers,[108] but it's commonly considered a best practice to only use EJBs for transaction management if possible. After all, EJBs run within an application server, which means they are "close" to the enterprise systems that require state management as part of a transaction. EJBs are also used to model business logic and business entities, which typically require transactional behavior.

The JTA `UserTransaction` object has standard methods that you can use to coordinate transactions from any of the J2EE tiers. The following code sample shows how a transaction might be managed for an EJB with an EJBContext implementor called "context."

```
20 public void doTransaction(EJBContext context){
21   javax.transaction.UserTransaction trans = context.getUserTransaction();
22   try{
23     trans.begin();
24    // Perform business processing which could fail with an EJBException
25     trans.commit();
26   }
27   catch (EJBException exc){
28     //  Roll back the EJB state, if required
29     rollbackTransaction(trans);
30   }
31   catch (javax.transaction.RollbackException exc){
32     //  Roll back the EJB state, if required
33     rollbackTransaction(trans);
34   }
35   catch (javax.transaction.HeuristicMixedException exc){
36     //  Roll back the EJB state, if required
37     rollbackTransaction(trans);
38   }
39   catch (javax.transaction.SystemException exc){
40     // General system exceptions that occur due to an
41     //  unexpected error condition; the prudent thing
42     //  to do would be to rollback or retry
43     //  Roll back the EJB state, if required
44     rollbackTransaction(trans);
45   }
46   catch (javax.transaction.NotSupportedException exc){
```

---

108. The `UserTransaction`, an object that can be used to manage transactions in JTA, is stored in JNDI with the standard lookup `java:comp/UserTransaction`. Servlets, JSPs and clients can look up this object and use it to manage transactions if required.

```
47        // Unable to perform a transaction; thrown by the
48        //  begin method if the enterprise system doesn't
49        //  support transactions
50     }
51     catch (javax.transaction.HeuristicRollbackException exc){
52        // The transaction was rolled back;
53        //  Roll back the EJB state, if required
54     }
55  }
56  public void rollbackTransaction(UserTransaction trans){
57     try{
58        trans.rollback();
59     }
60     catch (javax.transaction.SystemException exc){}
61  }
```

EJBs allow you to obtain a `UserTransaction` object by calling the method `getUserTransaction` in the `EJBContext`. Other J2EE components, such as Servlets, can also access the `UserTransaction` through a JNDI lookup. The J2EE specification guarantees that the `UserTransaction` will be stored on JNDI servers under the location `java:comp/UserTransaction`.

In addition, EJBs have the option of delegating transaction management to their container. **Container-managed transactions**, or CMT, associate EJB methods with one of six standard transactional attributes. The container uses the attribute to determine how it will manage transactions when the method is called. Like any service that is container-managed, CMT is configured in the EJB's deployment descriptor—each EJB method is associated with a transactional attribute, which in turn controls how the method is run. Table 10-10 summarizes the transactional attributes and their behaviors.

Table 10–10   Transaction Attributes for EJBs

Attribute	Transaction in progress	No Transaction in progess
Required	Run within the existing transaction	Start a new transaction
RequiresNew	Suspend the existing transaction; start a new transaction	Start a new transaction
Supports	Run within the existing transaction	Execute normally
NotSupported	Suspend the existing transaction	Execute normally
Mandatory	Run within the existing transaction	Throw RemoteException or EJBException
Never	Throw TransactionRequiredException or TransactionRequiredLocalException	Execute normally

As mentioned, transactions are often difficult to coordinate in an enterprise application. The exception model of EJBs becomes much more complex when you factor transactions into the equation. The container must determine whether to rollback a transaction or mark it for rollback. Additionally, a container may convert an exception into a form that more clearly indicates to a caller that there's been a transaction-related problem. Tables 10-11 and 10-12 summarize container behavior for various exception scenarios involving EJBs and transactions.

Table 10–11 Rollback Behavior During Transactions

	Mark transaction for rollback	Rollback Transaction
Session Bean or Entity Bean, CMT, non-application exception		
Caller's transaction	Y	N
Own transaction	N	Y
Unspecified transaction*	N	N
Session Bean, BMT, business method, non-application exception	Y	N
Message-Driven Bean		
CMT	N	Y
BMT	Y	N
ejbTimeout( ), system exception		
CMT	N	Y
BMT	Y	N
Container-invoked callback, run within a transaction	Y	N

* An "unspecified transaction context" is a case for which the EJB architecture does not fully define transaction semantics. The specific cases where this applies are defined in the specification in 17.6.5. Generally speaking, EJB developers should follow a "conservative" strategy when dealing with problems that occur during such methods, since they cannot predict what strategy will be used by an EJB container implementor to recover from errors. Typically, this means performing a check and recovery of resource managers and key EJB data.

Table 10–12 Exception Behavior During Transactions*

	Exception Thrown	Caller Response
Session Bean or Entity Bean, CMT, non-application exception		
Caller's transaction	TransactionRolledBackException or TransactionRolledBackLocalException	It is pointless to continue the transaction
Own transaction	RemoteException or EJBException	Client's transaction (if any) may or may not be rolled back
Unspecified transaction	RemoteException or EJBException	Client's transaction (if any) may or may not be rolled back

Table 10–12   Exception Behavior During Transactions* *(continued)*

	Exception Thrown	**Caller Response**
Session Bean, BMT, business method, non-application exception	RemoteException or EJBException	
Message-Driven Bean		
CMT	EJBException (thrown to container)	Container discards bean
BMT	EJBException (thrown to container)	Container discards bean
ejbTimeout( ), system exception		
CMT	NONE (no conversion; log exception)	Container discards bean
BMT	NONE (no conversion; log exception)	Container discards bean
Container-invoked callback		
Own transaction	RemoteException or EJBException	Client's transaction (if any) may or may not be rolled back
Caller's transaction	TransactionRolledBackException or TransactionRolledBackLocalException	It is pointless to continue the transaction

*   Some containers can transparently retry a failed transaction. In that case, the exceptions defined in the table would be thrown only after a designated number of container retries.

You may have noticed that application exceptions aren't mentioned in either of the tables. The reason for this is simple—application exceptions don't automatically mark a transaction for rollback. This means that you must make a decision when you receive an application exception from an EJB:

1. Continue the transaction; in this case, you should ensure that a commit attempt won't compromise data integrity.
2. Explicitly mark the transaction for rollback by calling the method `setRollbackOnly` on the `UserTransaction` (BMT) or `EJBContext` (CMT).

J2EE and Exception Handling–Global Considerations

At this stage, we're ready for a big-picture discussion of exceptions in J2EE. As you've seen, each of the tiers is optimized to perform certain tasks, to solve specific problems. As a result, the component technologies tend to do certain things well, but they also have standard problems. That's right—the J2EE technologies inherit both the strengths and weaknesses of their associated tier. Table 10-13 shows the standard challenges for each of the Java-based tiers.

Table 10–13 **Standard Challenges for J2EE Tiers**

Tier	Standard Challenges
Web	Content management, navigation, sessions, security, threading, caching
EJB	Cache management, persistence management, transactions
EIS Integration	Connection management, data collisions, transactions

A consequence of the J2EE enterprise model is that there are natural changes in protocol and exception handling model as you traverse the tiers. Figure 10-3 shows the full exception model for a standard 4-tier J2EE application.

As you can see, there's a change in the exception processing model that matches the transition from tier to tier. The EIS tier is accessed by one or more distributed APIs that convert vendor-specific errors into standard API-based exceptions, such as the `SQLException`. The EJB tier can propagate a few types of exception forward: the `RemoteException`, `EJBException`, and application exceptions. The Web tier must ultimately convert its exceptions to HTTP errors or standard pages for client use.

The difference in exception model between the tiers tells you a little about your responsibilities for the tiers. You must ultimately convert exceptions that you choose to

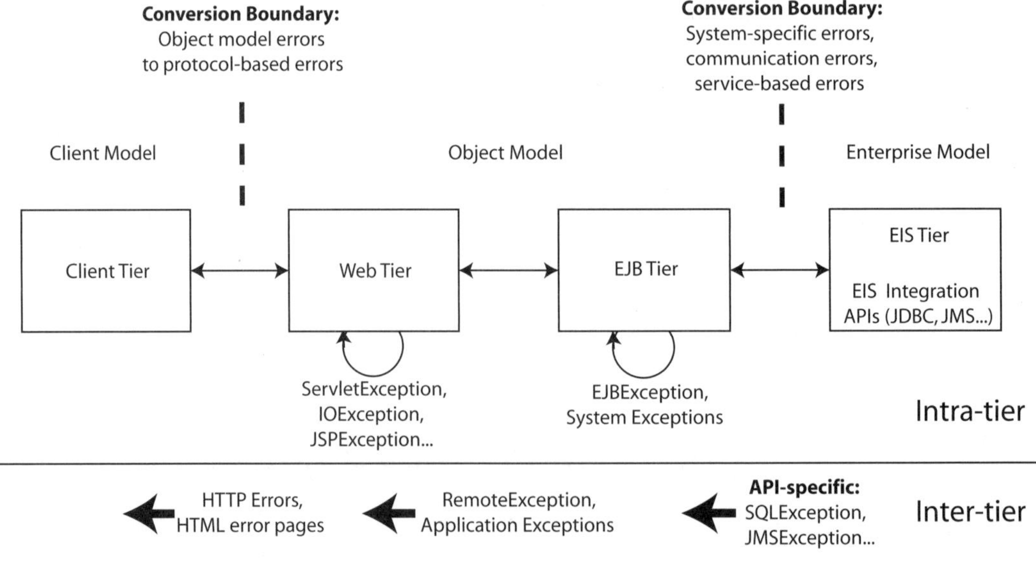

Figure 10–3
The J2EE Exception Model.

propagate forward in the enterprise system, or declare them as business exceptions in the EJB tier. The "best practices" for exception propagation are generally to throw application exceptions for the EJB tier, or to return HTTP errors or error pages for the Web tier.

For internal processing of exceptions by the container, you throw a different set of exceptions. The container uses these exceptions to manage its components, which may include temporarily removing a component from service or even destroying it. For the EJB tier, you typically throw the `EJBException` or one of its subclasses, and for the Web tier the `IOException` or `ServletException`.

The different handling models used for the J2EE technologies suggest that a slightly different approach may be required for exception processing than the one we discussed in earlier chapters. Instead of a basic "handle or declare" decision, you now need to consider the impact on the container, and determine whether to propagate an exception in its raw form or convert it to a new form.

A general exception handling model for J2EE might work like this. If one of your components threw an exception, you would first handle the exception internally if possible. If you were unable to handle the exception, you would next determine if the exception represented a global problem that would require the component's removal. If so, you'd propagate an appropriate exception to your container. If not, you would then convert the exception to an appropriate business exception and propagate it to the client.

Factors to Consider for J2EE Exception Handling

In a perfect world, you could use these basic rules and best practices to dictate all of your error handling in a J2EE application. However, as you're probably aware, the realm of enterprise computing is *far* from a "perfect world" scenario. There are a number of considerations that may require you to modify your exception handling strategy, including logging, network latency and the overhead associated with wrapping exception objects.

Logging

Logging is a fairly high overhead operation for many servers—so much so that a number of J2EE-compliant servers give you the ability to filter the output according to the severity of the message. Applying this consideration to exceptions, you have to ask how you want to log exceptions in your application. Depending on the volume of exceptions encountered, it may be impractical to log all of them, or to log a full exception stack trace every time an error occurs for a component. It's also important to realize that some exceptions will naturally be logged by a J2EE server. For example, the EJB container will automatically log all non-application exceptions thrown by your EJBs, and the Web container will log declared exceptions from the service method of Web resources.

Exception Overhead

A standard exception is a fairly small object, but exceptions propagated from a J2EE tier often have a larger than normal stack trace. Since a component's exception is propagated *through* the container before it reaches a handler layer, it's possible for an exception to pick up a sizable stack trace before it's finally handled by a server. What's more, it's possible for even more overhead to be added if the exception is propagated across tiers. The following example demonstrates this principle. The foundation exception was a `SQLException` with a minimal amount of associated data. However, by the time it was finally received by the Web tier, the total serialized size of the exception object was over 4kB.

```
java.sql.SQLException: Invalid table name "TEST" specified at position 14.
    at com.pointbase.net.netJDBCPrimitives.handleResponse(DashOB3242)
    at com.pointbase.net.netJDBCPrimitives.handleJDBCObjectResponse(DashOB3242)
    at com.pointbase.net.netJDBCStatement.executeQuery(DashOB3242)
    at ejb.ExcDAO.getData(ExcDAO.java:36)
    at ejb.ErrBeanBean.getDataRawExc(ErrBeanBean.java:71)
    at ejb.ErrBeanBean_EJBObjectImpl.getDataRawExc(ErrBeanBean_EJBObjectImpl.java:57)
    at ejb._ErrBeanBean_EJBObjectImpl_Tie._invoke(Unknown Source)
    at com.sun.corba.ee.internal.POA.GenericPOAServerSC.dispatchToServant
(GenericPOAServerSC.java:569)
    at com.sun.corba.ee.internal.POA.GenericPOAServerSC.internalDispatch
(GenericPOAServerSC.java:211)
    at com.sun.corba.ee.internal.POA.GenericPOAServerSC.dispatch
(GenericPOAServerSC.java:113)
    at com.sun.corba.ee.internal.iiop.ORB.process(ORB.java:275)
    at com.sun.corba.ee.internal.iiop.LocalClientRequestImpl.invoke
(LocalClientRequestImpl.java:96)
    at com.sun.corba.ee.internal.corba.ClientDelegate.invoke(ClientDelegate.java:237)
    at com.sun.corba.ee.internal.POA.GenericPOAClientSC.invoke
(GenericPOAClientSC.java:97)
    at org.omg.CORBA.portable.ObjectImpl._invoke(ObjectImpl.java:457)
    at ejb._ErrBean_Stub.getDataRawExc(Unknown Source)
    at ejb._ErrBean_Stub.getDataRawExc(Unknown Source)
    at exc.EJBDelegate.getDataRawExc(EJBDelegate.java:68)
    at exc.ExcServlet.process(ExcServlet.java:36)
    at exc.ExcServlet.doPost(ExcServlet.java:24)
    at javax.servlet.http.HttpServlet.service(HttpServlet.java:760)
    at javax.servlet.http.HttpServlet.service(HttpServlet.java:853)
    at org.apache.catalina.core.ApplicationFilterChain.internalDoFilter
(ApplicationFilterChain.java:247)
    at org.apache.catalina.core.ApplicationFilterChain.access$000
(ApplicationFilterChain.java:98)
    at org.apache.catalina.core.ApplicationFilterChain$1.run
(ApplicationFilterChain.java:176)
    at java.security.AccessController.doPrivileged(Native Method)
    at org.apache.catalina.core.ApplicationFilterChain.doFilter
(ApplicationFilterChain.java:172)
```

```
    at exc.ErrEvalFilter.doFilter(ErrEvalFilter.java:35)
    at org.apache.catalina.core.ApplicationFilterChain.internalDoFilter
(ApplicationFilterChain.java:213)
    at org.apache.catalina.core.ApplicationFilterChain.access$000
(ApplicationFilterChain.java:98)
    at org.apache.catalina.core.ApplicationFilterChain$1.run
(ApplicationFilterChain.java:176)
    at java.security.AccessController.doPrivileged(Native Method)
    at org.apache.catalina.core.ApplicationFilterChain.doFilter
(ApplicationFilterChain.java:172)
    at org.apache.catalina.core.StandardWrapperValve.invoke
(StandardWrapperValve.java:265)
    at org.apache.catalina.core.StandardPipeline.invoke(StandardPipeline.java:505)
    at org.apache.catalina.core.StandardContextValve.invoke
(StandardContextValve.java:212)
    at org.apache.catalina.core.StandardPipeline.invoke(StandardPipeline.java:505)
    at org.apache.catalina.core.StandardHostValve.invoke(StandardHostValve.java:203)
    at org.apache.catalina.core.StandardPipeline.invoke(StandardPipeline.java:505)
    at com.iplanet.ias.web.connector.nsapi.NSAPIProcessor.process
(NSAPIProcessor.java:157)
    at com.iplanet.ias.web.WebContainer.service(WebContainer.java:598)
```

Individually, 4kB may not seem like a great amount of data, but imagine the overhead for your servers if an exception occurs hundreds of times every hour. Depending on the exception model for your servers, you may not want to use a root cause exception for every exception you propagate, or you may want to wrap only a limited set of the total exception data.

Latency of the Network Layers

In a local application, there's relatively little cost to "sending" an exception object from one part of a system to another. After all, a single JVM passes references to objects—it doesn't send a full copy of the object. For a distributed system, such as a J2EE application, the situation is often much different. Any exception that is propagated between the tiers will likely be serialized across a network connection. Any network has a finite amount of bandwidth, so it will take time to send the exception from one server to another. What's more, exception propagation will affect a server's performance to some degree. Individually, there may not be a substantial impact, but working with a large number of large exception objects could have a measurable effect on a server's runtime efficiency. Because of these considerations, you may want to consider local communication for some of your J2EE resources[109] (or at least co-located servers) as a strategy to moderate the overhead of tier-tier communication.

---

109. Another option is to co-locate servers on the same physical machine. In this case, you often gain a slight performance improvement over remote communication, since your servers make local network calls to manage their communication.

Additional Best Practices for J2EE Systems

It's generally considered a good practice to validate data as early as possible in the J2EE communication process. One reason for this is that it improves application performance if you avoid propagation of unnecessary data. However, an equally compelling reason to validate data early is to save enterprise resources from the overhead of late validation, and the subsequent need to propagate exceptions back to the caller to indicate invalid data.

For EIS integration, it's often a good idea to monitor resource availability from the tier using the API. You generally want to check for your EIS resource after a period of prolonged inactivity. Normally, any problems with availability at this level should be converted into a more global unavailability exception within the J2EE application. If data integrity is important to you, you may want to consider secondary caching during periods of resource unavailability. To minimize the amount of handling code, it's often useful to access the EIS through a dedicated handling layer. The Data Access Object[110] design pattern is a good example of how this may be applied in the realm of EIS integration. In addition, it may be worthwhile considering other patterns such as the Decorator[111] or DecoratingFilter[112] to selectively roll in general exception handling for resource access.

EJB-related problems often have different preferred handling strategies depending on the type of problem encountered. For resource-based problems or communication errors, an often-used strategy is to attempt to reestablish communication and report resource unavailability of the problems persist. If the EJBs hold information that was intended for long-term storage, it's often a good idea to cache the data so there is less risk of data loss. For problems in EJB lifecycle, you should generally try to reinitialize EJBs if possible, re-establishing references. From a client's perspective, it's often a good practice to check for EJB resource availability after periods of prolonged inactivity.

---

110.   You can find details on this pattern in *Core J2EE Patterns*.
111.   A classic pattern from GoF, *Design Patterns*.
112.   Also a Core J2EE Pattern.

part 3

EFFECTIVE USE OF EXCEPTIONS, ERRORS, AND HANDLING

chapter 11

Architecture, Design and the Exception Model

Introduction

In recent years, a new job role has appeared in the field of software development—the architect. There are many different perspectives about the role of a software architects, but many agree that they have at least two key responsibilities:

- Architects identify the non-functional requirements of a system, also called systemic qualities or architectural capabilities.

  Examples of non-functional requirements include availability and performance. Although these goals are not based around business functionality, the long-term success of modern applications often depends on them.

- Architects guide high-level technical decisions, evaluate tradeoffs in a system, make recommendations and set policy for applications so that architectural capabilities are satisfied.

The role of the software architect has evolved in the industry as a result of a number of changing needs in technology. In the early years of software engineering, you could argue that there was less need for the job role. After all, many systems in those days serviced small numbers of local users. There were usually a very small number of servers in a system, and a server was often dedicated to supporting a single application. Vendor and technology selections were limited, so there was less need for comparative evaluation of technologies. Most organizations had little existing IT infrastructure, so legacy system integration requirements were fairly modest.

Over the course of a few decades, the progression of technology changed most of these rules. Today, software projects[113] often need an architect because of the following factors:

---

113. At least, software projects with a reasonable amount of complexity.

Complexity: Software systems today are much more complicated than they used to be. Over the decades, the expectations of end users and business sponsors have become more advanced. The computer systems and infrastructure used to host applications have become much larger and diverse. The same computing resources now host many different systems, meaning that an application may well have to share common resources. In addition, applications today are expected to support a diverse user population with different needs and capabilities—and users can potentially be located anywhere in the world.

Technology choices: There are many different alternatives available for applications today, with a vast number of technologies associated with system infrastructure, hardware, software and servers. The decisions about which technologies are most suitable to use are often fairly complicated. Metrics such as total cost of ownership (TCO) and return on investment (ROI) tend to be difficult to assess without a high-level technical expert.

Integration needs: Many applications must now interact with other systems, whether they are legacy applications within a business or enterprise systems from other companies. The needs of B-B or legacy systems integration can greatly increase the complexity of enterprise applications.

Increased demands on applications: Modern applications are required to support higher availability, and a larger user base, than ever before. These needs naturally tend to drive development teams to provide the expertise required to make the correct choices for an application to meet its needs.

An architect guides high-level hardware and software decisions to ensure that applications can effectively meet user requirements for reliability, availability, performance, usability, maintainability and the like. The architect identifies key requirements for a system, evaluates technology alternatives, profiles system behavior, and communicates decisions through documents, application models and architectural diagrams.

Why Should Architects Care About Exceptions and Errors?

To date, there hasn't been much discussion devoted to an architect's focus on exceptions in a software system. Part of the reason is probably the fact that the field of software architecture is so new. Another reason is that exception handling has traditionally been a lower-level concern, the realm of the software developers and designers. This isn't surprising—many of the choices associated with developing a manageable error handling infrastructure fall into the zone between architecture and design.

Is it appropriate to consider exceptions at a high-level as well as a low-level view? Is it actually a good idea for an architect to consider potential problems and failure modes in an application? Clearly, I'm going to tell you yes. Writing a complex application that is robust demands the sort of high-level, "big picture" perspective that architects possess. In many cases, you need an architect role to help guide the policy decisions based around problems within your code, so that you can avoid larger-scale problems with application integrity and performance. Here are some additional details.

The Cost of Failure

What are the potential implications of a disjointed, ad hoc strategy for handling problems in an application? For many years, we haven't looked that closely at the global impact of our low-level error handling decisions—custom and habit have steered us away from that practice. But let's talk about it now: what are the risks when you have localized, uncoordinated exception handling? The following list is probably not comprehensive—no person has enough experience to see all the implications of this issue—but it's a good start.

Poor extensibility and maintainability: The system will almost certainly be harder to modify if it doesn't have a standardized handling model.

Cascading failures: Without any global, directing vision for errors, there's a chance that an error in one part of a system could spread throughout an application. It could even cause a server or series of servers to crash, lowering an application's availability.

Handling inconsistencies: If exceptions are handled without a broad organizing model, developers will probably make decisions that conflict with others of their development team. This tends to lower the overall usability and manageability of the system.

Lower system performance: Improper handling can lead to unnecessary method calls or wasteful data transfer, which in turn will lower the overall performance of a system.

Data loss, corruption or compromise: A side effect of localized exception handling is often a failure to coordinate with the other parts of an application. This increases the risk that problems, even minor ones, can compromise the business model and threaten the integrity of business data.

Looking at these factors, it seems that you can make a reasonable case for addressing exceptions and trouble spots as part of the architect's role. What are these risks based around? If you scan the list, you'll notice direct impact on standard architectural capabilities. Based on the issues above, the exception handling decisions in an application have an impact on a system's extensibility, maintainability, manageability, performance, availability, usability, and reliability.

In other words, the way you deal with exceptions has a direct, bottom-line impact on the value of your applications to end users. When you look at the problem that way, it seems reasonable to involve architects in establishing an application-wide strategy for dealing with problems in code. It makes sense for them to develop a high-level model that can subsequently be refined during system development.

The Price of Success

If you accept the idea that architects may want or need to make global decisions to guide error handling in applications, you'll probably want some perspective on the kinds of decisions they might need to make. Broadly speaking, a software system needs to have an error handling and propagation strategy. It needs some uniformity in its exception representation and reporting. In addition, it's normally important to factor in standard services that impact overall system resiliency and reliability, such as support for recovery, logging, testing and debugging. These requirements can be condensed into the following general responsibilities:

1. Establish the high-level error handling requirements for a system.
2. Define a model that enables effective handling and propagation for exceptions and errors.
3. Determine a system's global response to various problem scenarios.
4. Designate the types of exceptions and errors that can be produced.
5. Establish rules for when and how error information is conveyed through the system.
6. Provide guidelines to communicate error information between parts of a system.
7. Define guiding standards and best practices for using exceptions and errors in code.

At first, the list seems a little daunting. Realize that you can rely on standard architectural tools, although your decisions don't have to be made in a vacuum. Practices such as benchmarking, prototyping, best practices and patterns can all contribute to making better, more informed decisions about the error handling model. Better still, these practices tend to be used as a standard part of the architectural role anyway. If you factor in error handling as part of your system study, you'll be rewarded with a more maintainable, predictable, resilient and robust application.

Architecture, Design, and Development

Based on the previous discussion, a natural follow-up question is this: What's the impact of these architectural decisions on the design process? This is a notoriously difficult question to answer. The difference between an architect and a designer is a line in the sand, and there's no simple way to mandate where the line should be drawn. The answer depends on the needs of the company, development team, methodology, and software system. It is possible to define general responsibilities, of course, so that's as reasonable a starting point as any.

Architect and Designer: The Thin Line in the Sand

We talked a bit about architect responsibilities at the beginning of the chapter. Generally speaking, an architect defines high-level policy, evaluates requirements for a system, sets up a core model for a software product, evaluates system performance and adjusts the model accordingly. Depending on the needs associated with a software project, an architect may also profile and even develop a prototype for a system. The architect may use high-level design patterns and best practices as an aid when developing the overall view of the software. As an example, an architect might identify the need for global logging in a distributed application, and define the high-level component to allow any part of the application to log problems. The architect might even prototype the logging function, to ensure that it doesn't compromise other system characteristics such as performance.

The designer, on the other hand, defines specific technologies that will be used to accomplish the global objectives for the software system. An architect is associated with strategy, while a designer's focus is on high-level tactics. Designers flesh out the core model established by the architect, providing further detail on the technologies, approach and structure of a system. The designer ultimately translates the high-level model or architectural prototype into detailed systems and subsystems that can be made into a real product. Following the earlier example, a designer might use the earlier guidelines for logging to identify a suitable API for logging within the application, such as log4j[114] or the logging API. What's more, the designer might identify a design pattern for the logger, a pattern that would enable global communication with the logging component.

Developers: The Front Line

It would be natural for you to wonder what role the developers play in all of this. With the responsibilities of the architects and designers for managing errors in a system, what do the developers need to do? Ultimately, they must carry out the high-level vision established by architects and refined by designers into detailed requirements. In the context of exception and error management, that means a developer must write code that:

- follows the global model for error and exception management within the system defined by the architect.

---

114. log4j is one of the APIs developed by the Apache Jakarta project. It provides powerful logging capabilities within an application, and can be effectively used with products that predate the JDK1.4 release.

- uses the technologies, frameworks and services established by the designer.
- performs as expected with a component and between components in a system.

You can't overstate the importance of developers in realizing the vision of a software system. Ultimately, they're the ones who have to actually deliver on the promise of the system's architecture and design. In the context of exception and error management, that means they need to understand and follow the guiding principles set down in a project. Developers are responsible for using best practices and patterns in their code that will promote effective exception handling and propagation within the system.

Regardless of the software development methodology, the effectiveness of a system's error handling model ultimately depends on how well the development team works together. When these three roles—developer, designer and architect—effectively combine their efforts, the end result is a much more robust and maintainable software system. In the long term, the system will be easier to extend and manage, because it is based around a consistent model.

Key Architectural Decisions for the Exception Model

At this point, it's productive to talk about the specific kinds of decisions a development team might make when developing a handling model. What do you need to work out to effectively define your system's exception and error model? Naturally, some decisions fall squarely into the realm of architecture, while some fall somewhere between architecture and high-level design. We talk about both, and about specific tradeoffs you might make as you develop your system.

Partly, the key to understanding how to make appropriate architectural decisions lies in understanding the special requirements and priorities associated with your system. I've deliberately avoided the term "application" in much of this chapter because you may develop Java software that is *not* an application in the classic sense of the word. Different types of software projects tend to have different architectural requirements. They tend to have different tradeoffs, different priorities, and different fundamental types of risk. These days, there are a number of standard kinds of systems developed:

Application Programming Interfaces (APIs): Libraries of related classes designed to be reused when developing other software systems.

Frameworks: APIs associated with, and used in the context of, an application model. A framework is a software system that has been designed to be reused, extended with a limited amount of additional programming.

Components: A software module intended for use as part of a larger system. A component may consist of a single class or a group of related classes. A component is similar to both APIs and frameworks in some ways, but is often more generic in its purpose and use.

Applications: Software intended to be used by clients or other applications. Depending on the requirements of the software project, application extensibility and reuse may or may not be a priority.

Distributed Applications: A specialized type of application, this software is inherently based on locating different parts of a system in a networked computing environment. Distributed applications may be built from scratch, or designed to run on existing servers.

Distributed Services: A software module intended to be hosted in a distributed environment. It could be independently used, or invoked in combination with other services. You could contend that distributed services represent the concept of the component brought into the network world. In some ways, they combine some of the goals associated with both components and distributed application software.

Key Priorities and Architectural Characteristics

No matter what kind of software you plan to develop, all systems tend to share certain basic objectives for addressing problems in code. Any project tends to have these as a baseline, whether you're developing a simple component or a complex application. One such requirement is **consistency in the codebase**, similar exception behavior throughout the system. You want to set up your system so there won't be any surprises, so that software can be used and extended without major restructuring in different parts of the system. A second priority is **standardization of the exception model**. The same type of problem should result in the same type of exception anywhere in the system. A third requirement is **failure scenario predictability**. The system should behave consistently for repeat success and failure scenarios.

These core priorities tend to drive a systematized exception model—one that's established and managed on a global scale within a project. In other words, they tend to argue in favor of a system based on a global strategy defined by the architect and designer. Beyond this base set of goals, an architect often factors an extended set of requirements and priorities into the development of a system. Table 11-1 provides a list of other standard architectural capabilities and how they relate to the exception model of a system. Unlike the previous priorities, this set usually involves a few architectural tradeoffs. The architect will probably attach different levels of importance to these goals based on the key objectives of the system and the priorities of the business sponsors.

Table 11-1   Architectural characteristics related to the exception model

Capability	Meaning in the Exception Handling Context
Extensibility	Support for the extension of the exception model; the ability to modify system behavior with a minimum amount of reengineering of the exception model
Manageability	The ability to use the system and its exception model without major administrative impact
Performance	The ability for the exception model to be used with a minimum impact on a system's performance
Recoverability	The system's ability to return to an operational state despite critical errors
Resiliency	The ability to have the system continue to perform even if there are problems
Scalability	The ability of the exception model to be used under conditions of increased load and still maintain quality of service
Security	Propagation of errors and exceptions without compromising potentially sensitive information
Testability	The ability of the system to support test configurations, both during development and after deployment
Usability	The system can communicate problems in a clear, understandable way

Unlike some other architectural characteristics, most of these goals are not mutually exclusive. You can design a system with good behavior for most of these characteristics—if you're willing to spend the time to factor them into your high-level model. Of course, certain software projects tend naturally to be associated with some of these capabilities. For instance, any user-facing system tends to have usability as one of its priorities. Systems that transfer business information, especially if they send data across a network, generally have security as a priority.

Architectural Decisions for the Exception Model

What constitutes the exception model? Stated another way, what are common considerations for a system? In this section, let's talk about the high-level decisions you generally want to make when defining an exception handling strategy for your system. There are three general considerations that collectively form the exception model within a system. You typically end up factoring all of these into your system in some form:

- Handling and propagation strategies
- The Exception and Error class model
- Pervasive services, such as reporting and recovery

In the sections that follow, we talk about each of these topics in turn. We examine common options and tradeoffs associated with each of these considerations, so that you have a good perspective on why you might make certain choices in an application architecture.

Handling and Propagation Strategies

This is basically the architect's version of "handle or declare." These two considerations link directly with Chapter 6, Exception Handling and Design. Decisions you make at the architectural level about handling and propagation provide important guidance to the design process. In fact, the decisions you make here define your exception communication infrastructure within a system. After all, an effective exception communication infrastructure ultimately depends on having a standardized model, a well-defined set of problems that will be propagated to callers.

At the architectural level, you provide explicit guidance for which sort of problems must be handled, and which must be propagated to callers. You can either adapt risk assessment results to make this decision,[115] or you can apply the failure mode analysis techniques explained in Chapter 6 to guide your decision. Naturally, this decision tends to be a high-level one. As an architect, you are less concerned about specific component and method behavior, and more focused on dealing with broad categories of a problem. As such, you tend to define handling and propagation based on use case scenarios, general API use, or technologies.

Handling Strategy

Handling represents the system's behavior with respect to problems that can be addressed locally within the code. When you decide to handle certain kinds of problem within a system, you elect not to propagate exceptions or errors to users of the component. Generally, a handling strategy involves dealing with a problem as the point where it occurs within code.[116]

One of the most important decisions you will make for a handling strategy is where to address an error within your system. One option is to handle the problem locally, at the point where it occurs in code.[117] This solution has the advantage of keeping your code fairly self-sufficient. Localized handler code also tends to be easier to understand, since the handler is more directly associated with the cause of a problem. Of course, localized handling may not always be an option, especially in cases where you need to take action within a component or subsystem to address a problem. In such

---

115. Risk assessment is a standard part of an architect's job, and can be effectively used to define a global handling and propagation policy.
116. Of course, it's also possible to defer handling until some later point in system processing. In some more complex business operations, it may be reasonable to delay handling until a later stage.
117. Depending on your design, the local handler may a class, or part of a component.

cases, you might develop a handling layer within your code and propagate this type of exception or error through the call stack to the handling layer. This option allows you to consolidate your handler code.[118] This approach tends to be useful for systems that naturally use layering themselves, such as distributed multi-tier systems. Of course, there may be a performance impact of the handling layer, so it's worthwhile to evaluate the impact of this approach. For systems that require greater flexibility when forwarding to a handler, a third alternative is to create a handler delegate and forward to the delegate for this exception or error. If you have a suitable strategy for creating a global delegate,[119] this approach gives you a great deal of flexibility for global handling with less overhead than a separate code layer. Of course, both global handler alternatives have one key drawback—it is difficult to return to the point in code that produced the exception in the first place.

Another key choice for handling is whether to send out a more global notification for the problem within your system. Some failure scenarios mandate a global handling strategy, so they require broader notification within a software system. Global notification in a system can be active or passive. Active notification typically requires an event notification system if the exception must be sent to receivers in different parts of the system. Passive notification allows subsystems to determine that an error has occurred if and when they require the information. Typically, this approach either involves using layering in the system or holding a globally accessed object to represent system errors.

It may also be a priority in some systems to be able to dynamically configure your handling strategy. Such a decision gives you flexibility to substitute different actions when the system is used or extended. Such a system could even be used to allow you to select between handling and propagation for a given category of exception. In such cases, it's generally worthwhile to at least define a default strategy to be used in the system, to ensure that problems do not go unhandled in your code.

Propagation Strategy

Propagation refers to communication of internally occurring problems outside the system boundaries. The exceptions and errors that you choose to propagate to callers ultimately represent your contract with the outside world, your way to communicate the type of problems that can be expected to occur. Clearly, the decision to propagate needs to be carefully made, for the right reasons. If you simply propagate all exceptions to your callers, you lose all coherency for your exception model—and exception communication becomes devalued within your system.

There are a number of reasons why you might choose to propagate a certain type of exception or error in your system. You might propagate if you encounter a problem

---

118. The Proxy design pattern can be used effectively to support a handling layer in code. In some systems, a proxy is standardized into a type of component called a filter (as in the Web tier of J2EE).
119. For instance, creating a static class resource or using the Singleton design pattern.

with global impact, one that extends beyond your system boundaries. You might choose to propagate because there are several possible response strategies to a problem, and you don't have enough context to decide on the "correct" approach. Finally, you might propagate because a problem prevents your system from functioning properly, and you must notify callers of that fact. An equally important decision is when to propagate errors or exception for your systems. There are three common techniques that are often used in systems.

Fail-fast: This approach involves propagating an exception or error as close to the root cause of the problem as possible. This model is often useful for performance-sensitive systems, since it provides early notification to callers of problems that might affect their use of the system. In addition, the fail-fast approach tends to make it easier to isolate the root cause of problems in code, since there's a definite cause-effect relationship between a problem and the exception.

Action-Based Reporting: This approach associates an exception or error with a more coarse-grained operation, or even sequence of operations. This approach is often used for complex, many-layered systems. It provides a reasonable way for problems to be communicated to a user with a meaningful context. This technique may also be useful for non-critical reporting, cases where problems can safely be deferred until an operation is complete.

Report on Request: With this approach, you notify the caller of problems only when specifically requested. Typically, this approach involves holding exceptions or errors in a collection, and providing the contents only when a `getErrors` method is called. Report on request tends to be useful for non-critical problems where the caller has some handling discretion within the exception model. It may also be used when the caller can reasonably ignore some problems, as with the JDBC `SQLWarning` class.

When you propagate an exception or error, you need to consider include how to represent additional information. You typically need to communicate a general level of severity of a problem. Depending on your business model, you may also need to convert the root cause exception or error into a different class. In this case, you must decide on how much of the original root cause exception you want to keep.[120]

As with the handling strategy, you may need to be able to dynamically swap your propagation strategies. The motivation for doing this is to provide flexibility in a system. Systems which allow you to reconfigure propagation strategies typically give you control over the reporting technique, (fail-fast, action-based reporting, report on request) and possibly control over the level of detail of information that you will retain. Finally, some systems might require you to propagate an exception or error internally as well as externally. The motivation for this would typically be that a given

---

120. As we saw in Chapter 10, holding the original root cause exception also means preserving its stack trace, which can add a substantial amount of overhead if you need to propagate an exception across a network connection.

failure scenario had global impact, potentially impacting other subsystems and causing other business operations to fail.

Exception and Error Class Model

The classes and properties within classes that are used to communicate information about a problem through the system. The decisions for classes involve establishing a clear, consistent representation for your error data in the system. Remember that exceptions and errors ultimately represent the message you send between parts of a system, or propagate outside the system.

Depending on your needs, you may have to develop exception classes for your system. In some cases you may even need to create a class hierarchy to meet your communication needs. The class model you use to represent exceptions and errors has a fine balance to maintain. It's often desirable for a system to use a simple core exception model, so that handling is straightforward. Since handler blocks in Java effectively use an `instanceof` test for handling, this tends to steer you towards a single base class type for the exception model. On the other hand, it's useful in some systems (especially those with greater complexity) to have diversity in the model, so that you can manage a finer-grained handling strategy if required. This tends to guide you towards multiple class types.

Depending on your specific application requirements, you could use existing classes if they meet your needs. You could also develop a single custom exception or error class, a series of classes, or even a full class hierarchy, as we've seen with distributed APIs such as JMS. As a general rule, you want to designate an exception or error class to control high-level filtering for a specific category of problem. If you define a custom class, you can add additional properties to hold information. Typically, you add properties if you want to send data that contributes to logging or recovery within your system.

In Chapter 3, we talked about general choices when defining custom exceptions. At this stage, let's refine the model a bit for architectural considerations. You typically subclass `Exception` to communicate standard problems which should be explicitly declared in your system, and must be acknowledged and acted upon in some way by the caller. This covers the majority of development cases—in most situations, you want to explicitly communicate a problem because you require some kind of recovery action by the caller.

You subclass `RuntimeException` to communicate problems of mild to moderate severity that can occur in an unpredictable way from the user's point of view. You should also use this type of exception to represent "avoidable" problems—exceptions that you never have to see if you use the component, subsystem or system properly. Finally, you subclass `Error` only if you have a serious or unrecoverable problem that should halt your system in some cases, and that may occur in an unpredictable way. This last scenario is rare for many kinds of system.

As mentioned, you can effectively use some exception classes, saving you from having to create and manage a custom exception class yourself. An added benefit that comes from reusing existing Java exception and error class is that they have a more universal meaning within the developer community. It's common to use the sub-classes of RuntimeException in a software system. The core Java APIs define a number of standard runtime exceptions that have universal meaning. Table 11-2 provides a summary of some of the most commonly used classes.

Table 11-2   Standard RuntimeException subclasses and their meaning[*]

Exception	Meaning
IllegalStateException	A method is not in an appropriate state to perform the operation
IllegalArgumentException	A method was called with an illegal or inappropriate argument
IndexOutOfBoundsException	A method has overstepped the limits of a collection
NullPointerException	An object used by the system has not been instantiated
SecurityException	The caller is not allowed to perform the requested operation

[*]   Other more specialized RuntimeException subclasses include the `BufferOverflowException`, `BufferUnderflowException`, `CannotRedoException`, `CannotUndoException`, `Concurrent-ModificationException`, and `IllegalMonitorStateException`.

Since many of the runtime exceptions have universal meaning, it's often useful to propagate them directly if they occur within your system. This means you only have to document them, and not explicitly throw them within code. It may also be worthwhile to declare that your method can throw a specific type of `RuntimeException`. This will *not* cause the system to enforce handling of the exception, but it *will* show up within Java documentation for the class.[121]

Bending (and Breaking) the Rules for Unchecked Exceptions

In addition to the best practices discussed above, you can use unchecked excep-tions for a few other purposes. It's worth emphasizing that these are far from best prac-tices—and you should think very carefully before using them. These practices involve using Java's exception model in an *extremely* nonstandard way. In general, I'd recom-mend against using them, but it's realistic to acknowledge their existence. Since the risk is so high with these practices, you might effectively consider them to be anti-pat-terns unless they are managed very carefully.

---

121. This is a somewhat controversial practice. Though it's useful to be aware of the explicit exceptions that can be thrown in code, you could also contend that the principal purpose of Java documentation is to define the checked exceptions for your APIs.

Unchecked exceptions are sometimes used to provide flexible communication within your system—to enable you to jump to a designated point in your system's code. Some APIs, such as Tag Libraries used in JSPs, use this technique as a way to redirect execution within the component during runtime. A simple JSP Tag Handler will throw a `SkipPageException` to halt execution of the JSP that called it—in other words, to finish the JSP and return any output to the user. If you use this technique in your code, be very careful to use it internally within your system, and to ensure that you have an ironclad handling mechanism. The only reason the approach works for JSPs is that the compiler ensures that the calling JSP will always handle the exception within its `_jspService` method.

Unchecked exceptions can also be used to design a system with extreme calling flexibility in the exception model. This practice has been used in some of the component APIs, such as EJBs. Typically, the purpose of this practice was to define a convenient blanket handling model for the container—in other words, for a part of the system that would intercept and act on any problems that occurred. Without an intercepting handler layer to protect you and your code, this practice could easily spiral out of control and cause substantial handling problems in a software project.

Options for Exception Representation

As mentioned earlier, you may need to decide whether to propagate an exception in its original "raw" form or to convert it into another exception object. If you convert it, you have the added question about whether you should wrap the original exception as the "root cause" of the original problem. Typically, the main reason to omit the root cause exception is a desire to conserve system memory or bandwidth. In these cases, it's usually desirable to log the root cause exception so that it isn't lost when you propagate the new exception. Another option may be to store the root cause as a different type of property, such as a String. This allows you to hold information about the cause of code failure without the overhead of a full stack trace within your system.

Many systems define standard exceptions based on a type of method. It's true that certain categories of method often tend to have the same core set of problems. Of course, the decision about what specific exceptions to throw for given method categories can be more accurately said to be a design focus rather than an architectural consideration. A few common method categories with common exception types are listed below.

Creation or initialization: These methods often throw exceptions that involve invalid or incomplete configuration information. These methods basically enforce the global setup rules, or preconditions, for a part of your system. As you might expect, exceptions in these methods often represent problems with enforcing the preconditions.

Destruction or finalization: The complement of the creation methods. This category may throw exceptions if the developer is unable to release resources or if there's been a problem in cleaning up an object or component. These methods, and their exceptions, may represent problems with global postconditions in your code.

Variable, link, or collection maintenance: These methods manage resources of an object or component. Typically, they may throw standard runtime exceptions if the resource hasn't been initialized or if there is an indexing problem. In addition, the methods may throw exceptions to represent illegal attempts to access the elements.[122]

Business: This is one of the hardest categories to characterize. Business methods tend by their nature to be associated with the underlying problem domain. In addition to exceptions representing business rule violations, these methods may throw exceptions that center around problems with the method sequence, threading problems, or problems with method-level preconditions or postconditions.

Pervasive Services

It's often said that in architecture there are no absolutes, only tradeoffs. That saying is especially evident when working with pervasive services in the exception model. There a number of services that you may want to develop to accommodate specific functional requirements, and nearly every one of your decisions has implied tradeoffs in terms of architectural capabilities. Common services that you might use in your applications include:

- **Logging**: the ability to store information about exceptions and errors which have occurred in the system.
- **Recovery**: the ability of a system to return to stability after a major failure.
- **Data Persistence**: the ability to store data in the event of a system failure.
- **Testing and Debug Support**: the ability to check your system, evaluating its functions after deployment.
- **Management Options/Support**: the ability to have global evaluation and control over your system's runtime characteristics.

Logging represents the most commonly implemented of the services. There are a vast number of tradeoffs for logging in a system. For instance, part of your logging strategy might include providing filtering capabilities, or choices for the amount and format of exception data. As we've seen, these abilities are fairly easy to accommodate with log4j or the Java logging API. Beyond these basic decisions, you may want to consider working with a global log file instead of multiple distributed log files. This decision tends to be especially important in multi-server environments, especially if they have redundancy at the tiered level. Logging capabilities are central to both testing

---

122. Common examples include trying to use a resource at an inappropriate time, or attempts to concurrently modify a resource that only supports single-threaded use.

and debugging in applications. Without a record of system errors, you're essentially guessing whether a system is "normal" (whatever that means) or not. Unfortunately, logging also impacts the performance of a system. The detailed output used to diagnose a complex problem often causes an application to run noticeably slower.

Support for recovery involves designing a system so that the individual parts can easily re-establish themselves as part of a working whole even if there are system failures. Typically, that involves developing your system to manage transient failures throughout the system, typically manifesting as a loss in communication or invalid references. Recoverability implies that your subsystems will take steps to re-establish contact with other systems if required. As is the case with many of these services, there's an implied negative impact on system complexity as a result of this consideration. If subsystems are associated with maintaining transient business data, recoverability may also indicate a need for data persistence within your system.

Support for data persistence is essential if you want to ensure continuity of your business model in the face of transient system failures. Typically, it involves developing a system that supports caching and write-back operations to persistent storage in the event of system failures. It tends to be most prevalent in distributed systems, which usually require such capabilities for an application to be considered as highly reliable. Naturally, data persistence and recovery capabilities tend to increase the complexity of code and lead to additional failure scenarios in their own right. In addition, data caching often implies a need to track data conflicts over a longer period of time. A recovered business operation may very well conflict with an action that was subsequently performed within the system. In such cases, conflict resolution becomes a vital part of application functionality, and generates an additional set of business scenarios.

Support for testing and debugging requires that you develop your code so that it accommodates easy validation and checkups during runtime. At the most basic level, this means that it's important for code modularity to be a design priority, so that it's easy to identify and isolate test points. Of course, the needs of a product often mandate a much more rigorous approach when developing tests for software. In some cases, you may have to explicitly define test points or validation behavior within your code. Modern methodologies, such as agile development methods, have championed such practices. Such testing support ultimately has benefit during code development and after the code has been deployed. In some systems, architects explicitly develop a system to support a detailed "debug mode" of execution. In cases where post-release support is an essential requirement, it may also be important to explicitly make remote testing a system capability, so that it's easier to validate a deployed system's behavior.

Manageability of a system can mean many things to many people. In the context of this discussion, it's useful to think of it as global control over a system's exception behavior. Typically, this has impact on the flexibility of a system, and implies an architectural model that supports global configuration or swapping. It's appropriate to save this service for last, since global management often involves the ability to globally configure many of the earlier services mentioned. A few common areas that you might target for global management include:

- handling and propagation strategies of a system
- reporting and logging capabilities
- system recovery policy
- evaluation of system health

Conclusion—Robust Java

What does it mean for a system to be robust? There are many different definitions, just like there are many definitions of architecture itself. One part of a working definition might be that a robust system is one that effectively addresses trouble spots in a software system. Such a system has a well thought-out approach to deal with problems as they occur in code. Most applications cannot address all their problems internally,[123] but applications can adopt a reasonable strategy that allows them to remain stable if possible, and that minimizes the negative impact of critical failures if and when they occur. Most importantly, a robust system follows its strategy in a predictable way.

If you accept that as part of a working definition of robustness, it's vital to use architectural and design practices if you want to create a robust software system. The strategic and tactical choices made for handling problems in an application represent your best chance to define a globally consistent model, and so to handle problems in a proactive rather than a reactive way.

The Shape of Things to Come

In the chapters that follow, we examine three topics that have global impact on the exception model of a system. They touch exception and error handling at many levels, from architecture to design and code development. In the next chapter, we discuss patterns in the context of exception and error management. It's been fairly well-established that patterns provide substantial benefit to both architecture and design activities. They allow you to develop a system around certain established solutions to well-documented types of problems. They allow you to solve common issues with a clear picture of the kinds of tradeoffs involved and the kinds of problems you might encounter. In the context of our discussion, patterns can be effectively used to promote effective exception behavior within a system. In Chapter 12, we look at the application of

---

123. By definition, some failure scenarios within a system require broader communication with an associated system. Additionally, some problems have multiple handling strategies, and require some intervention in order to determine what action to take.

both architectural and design patterns. We see how they can be effectively used to promote better, more consistent, and more reliable exception handling within a system.

Chapter 13 focuses on the subject of testing. Testing involves validating that a system provides accurate, consistent results over time. In addition, testing can verify that a system performs acceptably under specified conditions of use. From the perspective of exception handling, testing allows you to verify that trouble spots and failure scenarios in your code have been adequately addressed. Additionally, testing can be extremely valuable in ensuring that your system responds appropriately to unexpected usage conditions, or to violations of its fundamental requirements for execution.

Chapter 14 is devoted to debugging. Debugging refers to the process used to identify, isolate and correct errors in a system. From a system perspective, support for debugging means that a system will allow you to easily isolate and correct problems. In a well-designed system, you can repeatably, consistently, quickly, efficiently and accurately isolate a problem to a specific part of your system. You can verify problems in your code according to a repeatable set of test criteria. And you can ideally correct and verify a code fix with a minimum amount of disruption to the system as a whole.

Clearly, the practices of testing and debugging are related to one another. Though the disciplines are not one and the same, a system which has good support for testability more effectively supports debugging. What's more, all three of the upcoming chapters contribute to the broader goal of providing for a more effective overall handling strategy within your system. Ultimately, patterns, testing and debugging all help to reinforce the goal of providing a system that responds well to failure scenarios, a system that is resilient and robust.

chapter 12

Patterns

Introduction

Patterns have gained substantial popularity since they were first introduced to the software development community. It's easy to see why patterns are so useful—they provide a straightforward way to apply complex object-oriented concepts to software. Patterns abstract and generalize a solution to a common problem. They can subsequently be applied many times over to solve specific problems in your projects with known results. Many early generation patterns helped developers apply core language features more effectively:

- object-oriented concepts, such as encapsulation and polymorphism
- language capabilities, such as abstract classes and interfaces

More recently, patterns have evolved into the realm of specific technologies and architectural frameworks. It's become popular to use patterns as a way to improve the overall flexibility or stability of a specific type of Web application, thanks to books like *Core J2EE Patterns* and the J2EE *Blueprints*. Recent publications in books, articles and Web sites have highlighted the benefits of patterns when applied to domains such as J2EE and Web services.

It's also become common to apply patterns in nearly every development role. For software designers and programmers, patterns represent an effective way to promote effective coding practices, and provide good structure in their systems. For architects, patterns provide a way to establish a framework that naturally tends to promote desired capabilities such as modularity and flexibility. In addition, an entire development team benefits from the conceptual abstraction of patterns, since they provide a common language to describe complex implementation concepts. A team can effectively use a pattern name to describe their implementation choices in a clear, concise way.

How can patterns help you to manage exceptions in a system? Actually they provide an effective way to plan for specific exception management strategies in your code. Patterns can provide you with structure that you can use when planning for exception handling or propagation. They provide ways for you to effectively manage global exception-related services, or to support propagation throughout your system.

It's natural for us to talk about patterns when we talk about building a robust architecture. In the last chapter, we described some key high-level exception handling decisions—some of the choices you make to ensure that your system satisfies its basic responsibilities for exception and error handling. It's not surprising that you might reasonably want to have some assurance that your system handles these tasks well—that it manages exceptions effectively, in a way that can be maintained. Patterns and best practices seem like a natural fit, since they tend to promote the development of software that has such desirable characteristics. In the exception model for a system, patterns tend to manage the standard components used for exception management, such as:

- the propagation and handler infrastructure
- exception object creation and management
- global services related to the exception model

In this chapter, we look at how to use patterns in the exception model. Since we've been talking about how to plan a system for effective handling, we focus on how to introduce patterns while a system is being developed. Of course, it's equally valid to use patterns as you refactor an existing system, adding them to your application as a way to improve code structure.

We talk about three groups of patterns in this chapter. The first group was presented in the book *Pattern-Oriented Software Architecture—A System of Patterns*. These patterns are often used to set up a handling infrastructure for your system. The second group was first described in the book *Design Patterns—Elements of Reusable Object-Oriented Software*. These patterns have traditionally been applied during software design to solve specific development problems. The third group of patterns was introduced in the book *Core J2EE Patterns*. These patterns represent strategies that you can apply in J2EE, to realize both architectural and design benefits for standardized tiers of your J2EE system.

The intent of this chapter is to show the application of common patterns, not to describe the patterns themselves. We discuss what's sometimes called the "realization" of patterns—pattern implementations used to promote manageable exception handling within a system. We look at strategies that can be used for certain patterns at the architectural and design level to make your applications manage exceptions more effectively.

Architectural Patterns (Pattern-Oriented Software Architecture, POSA-ASOP)

From the perspective of exception and error handling, architecture-level patterns can be used to define a global structure to manage the exception model. These patterns help ensure that your system processes all exceptions, and help you organize the major exception-related functions in your handling infrastructure. We look at two common patterns in this section: Layers and Model-View-Controller.

1. Layers

The layers pattern is one of the most frequently used in software architecture. Layering has become so common that many of us use it without even thinking of it as a pattern. The basic principle is straightforward: you divide a complex application into well-defined "layers"—software modules each of which has a specific purpose in the system. Each layer is responsible for handling some part of application's functionality. Typically, layers are based around a common technology, such as database communication, or a common service, such as caching. Layers provide services to each other, allowing you to build more sophisticated code that uses the lower-level layers.

You can use layering in a complex system to set up a universal exception handling model layer. You typically do this because you want a centralized capability that can coordinate a system's response to failure scenarios. In addition, you often want to provide a global capability to manage dedicated handling services such as logging, testing and recovery. An example of layer implementation is shown in Figure 12-1.

A layered handler tends to provide a number of benefits to your system. Some of the common advantages are:

- **Uniformity:** A dedicated handling layer tends to be better at enforcing a global handling policy than if the work is done locally.
- **Integration:** A layer can bring together dissimilar systems and unify them under a common handling strategy.
- **Blanket Coverage:** A handling layer can ensure that you handle *all* exceptions and errors. Layers can guarantee that unchecked exceptions aren't accidentally dropped or propagated outside of a system.
- **Centralization:** A handler layer lets you avoid duplication of handler code within your system.
- **Manageability:** This kind of system architecture tends to increase manageability of the system, since a universal service is managed centrally within your code.

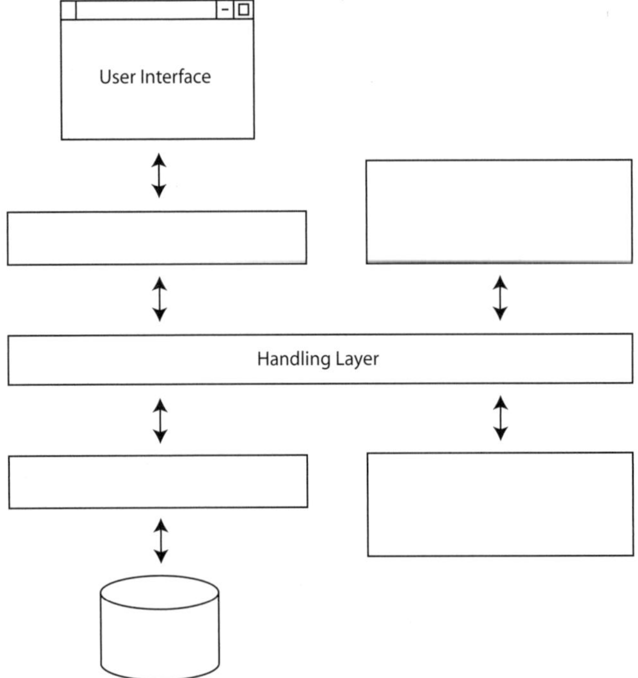

A handling layer represents a call-through part of your code. You can set up a handling layer to perform global actions for your code, including handling, propagation, conversion and logging.

Figure 12–1
Layer Pattern Implementation.

On the downside, a handler layer can be a resource bottleneck. This is especially true if you use it in a multithreaded system and your handler layer depends on shared stateful resources. In addition, the very fact that a layered handler enforces a global policy works against you in some cases. You have to be careful to avoid accidental blanket handling in your system. A handler layer implies universality, meaning that it's usually harder to set up a customized response in a specific part of your system. Finally, it's usually difficult to return to a caller from a global handler layer. This implies that you may need to combine a handler layer with some localized handling, at least for some types of handling.

2. Model-View-Controller (MVC)

The MVC pattern has been used for decades[124] to partition a software component or system into well-defined parts to increase its overall manageability. The basic strategy

---

124. The earliest documented use of the MVC pattern was in Smalltalk during the 1970s. Although it is a frequently used pattern, it actually predates the field of design patterns. In some ways, it's a primitive ancestor of patterns— sort of a pattern trilobite.

is to break a complex system into three parts. The Model represents the component state and the means to change the state. The View presents the model to callers, representing the data in a usable form. The Controller receives and acts on input from the outside world, updating the model or the view as required.[125] At a basic level, the pattern defines the requirements for a well-coded software component. The model represents the component's implementation, the view its outbound interface, and the controller the inbound interface.

It's been well-documented that MVC applies just as effectively to enterprise systems as it does to simple components. MVC is a popular pattern to organize enterprise applications in general, and Java Web applications in particular. From an exception handling perspective, MVC can be used to differentiate the major error-processing responsibilities in your system. The standard exception processing responsibilities and how they map to MVC are summarized in Table 12-1.

Table 12–1   MVC Responsibilities for Error Handling

Module	Exception Handling Responsibility
Model	**Produce:** The model produces low-level exceptions that represent violations of the core constraints of the model resources. It may also convert these exceptions to a standard form for use within the system.
View	**Adapt and Present:** The view receives and interprets errors, showing them to the caller in an understandable way. It converts exceptions propagated by the model or controller so that a caller can understand and act upon them.
Controller	**Qualify and interpret:** Since the controller is typically associated with business functionality, it can handle an exception, propagate it, or convert it to a "business" exception.

The typical structure of an MVC system, with the added exception management responsibilities, is shown in Figure 12-2.

In many ways, MVC partitioning simplifies what was formerly quite difficult to manage: the key parts of an enterprise application, and how they communicate with each other. By decoupling responsibilities, you can make exception management easier to apply when the system is reused.

For example, what would happen if you had to convert an enterprise application so that it presented data in XML? In many applications, you'd have trouble managing the transition and you'd have to rewrite a lot of code. With MVC, you could swap out the View and replace it with one that converts the data model to XML. In addition to data conversion, an MVC with exception handling would allow you to convert error information for presentation to an XML client. What's more, you could do this without rewriting the underlying exception management layer for your system. MVC differentiation

---

125. Though it isn't a core requirement for MVC, some systems define multiple views for a given component. In this case, the controller has the added responsibility of view selection.

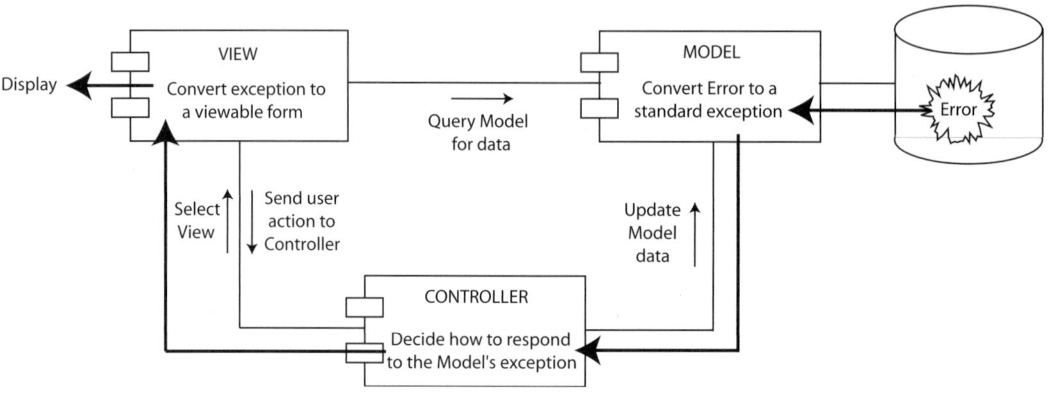

Figure 12–2
The MVC Relationship with Exception Handling.

helps you to focus your efforts on standard management considerations for an error model.

Of course, MVC also has its drawbacks. It can increase the amount of overhead for exception propagation and conversion within a system. It naturally tends to produce a non-localized exception management model, which often increases the overall complexity of your system. Since the pattern tends to focus on exceptions that originate from the model, you have to be careful that unchecked exceptions don't go unnoticed in a system.

Design Patterns (Design Patterns, GoF)

Traditionally, design patterns have been used during system design and implementation. In recent years, it's become more common to see some of these patterns used to define the architectural mode of a system as well. We present a few of the more commonly used design patterns, discussing their relevance when applied to the exception model of a system.

We follow the practice of breaking the patterns down according to standard object usage, using the categories originally set down by the GoF authors: creational, structural and behavioral patterns. Creational patterns manage the process of object creation or initialization. Structural patterns help to define and manage the static relationships between objects within a system. Finally, behavioral patterns focus on dynamic communication between objects in a system.

Creational Patterns

1. Builder

The Builder pattern helps you to manage object creation. Some objects have complex needs for resource setup and configuration. A Builder helps you to centralize these functions and avoid the overhead of managing object creation from many different parts of your code. Among its other uses, the Builder pattern can promote effective localized handling within a system. Specifically, the pattern makes it easier for you to correct for instantiation and initialization problems when creating a complex object. If you use a Builder in this way, you can correct for some setup-related problems of your product, rather than propagating exceptions to callers. What's more, you can use the Builder to throw a more generic exception to your caller, if critical errors occur when creating the builder's Product. The following code sample shows a Builder implementation with support for exception conversion. The `DataSourceConnectionBuilder` (a concrete implementation of the generic Builder interface `ConnectionBuilder`) manages the JNDI lookup and JDBC connection retrieval from a `DataSource`. If there's a problem with either of these operations, the code converts the exceptions to the custom exception `BuilderException`. This is shown in Code 12-1.

Code 12-1: Builder implementation with Exception Management

```
1    import java.sql.*;
2    import javax.sql.*;
3    import javax.naming.*;
4    public class DataSourceConnectionBuilder implements ConnectionBuilder{
5      private DataSource dataSce;
6      private String dataSourceName;
7
8      public java.sql.Connection getConnection() throws BuilderException{
9        Connection connection = null;
10       if (dataSce == null){
11         dataSce = lookUpDataSource();
12       }
13       try{
14         connection = dataSce.getConnection();
15       }
16       catch (SQLException exc){
17         throw new BuilderException("DataSource cannot obtain" +
18             "a Connection", exc);
19       }
20       return connection;
21     }
22     public void setDataSourceName(String n){
```

```
23        dataSourceName = n;
24     }
25     private DataSource lookUpDataSource() throws BuilderException{
26        DataSource sce = null;
27        if ((dataSourceName == null) || (dataSourceName.equals(""))){
28           throw new BuilderException("Unable to perform JNDI lookup: " +
29                "Specify name of DataSource");
30        }
31        try{
32           Context ctx = new InitialContext();
33           sce = (DataSource)ctx.lookup(dataSourceName);
34        }
35        catch (NamingException exc){
36           throw new BuilderException("JNDI lookup failed for DataSource " +
37                dataSourceName, exc);
38        }
39        catch (ClassCastException exc){
40           throw new BuilderException("Cannot cast result of JNDI lookup " +
41                "for DataSource " + dataSourceName, exc);
42        }
43        return sce;
44     }
45  }
```

A Builder allows you to effectively handle localized problems during object creation. Provided that you encapsulate exception and error management within the Builder, this tends to promote the overall flexibility of the system. If you choose, you can also propagate exceptions to a builder's caller. Of course, exception propagation has some risks associated with it—if you aren't careful, you can make the exception model *extremely* complex. If you throw a number of exceptions from your `build` method, you effectively force your caller to maintain additional logic to deal with them. This complexity translates directly to the caller's handling responsibilities, so it's likely that a detailed propagation model will cancel out all of the original benefits of the Builder pattern.

2. Singleton

A Singleton allows you to ensure that there is a single, universally available object resource in a running system.[126] In Java, this means that you have a single object for a JVM or class loader. In the exception model, Singletons are commonly used to provide globally accessible services or handlers. In addition, you could make an exception

---

126. Though it wasn't a part of the original pattern, the Singleton is also used to manage a global resource pool—a number of instances in a system.

object a Singleton, allowing it to be repeatedly thrown and processed by your system. A few common services in the exception model that are possible candidates for a Singleton include logging, recovery and management. You could also use a Singleton to maintain a globally accessible collection of exceptions, or to represent a global handler module for the system. The following code provides a simple example of how a Singleton might be used to provide a global capability; in this case, the Singleton provides a centralized exception queue for the system. This type of Singleton would provide a globally accessible collection used to store and retrieve Exceptions produced while the system ran, as shown in Code 12-2.[127]

Code 12-2: Exception Queue Singleton

```
1   import java.util.*;
2
3   public class ExceptionQueueSingleton{
4       private static ExceptionQueueSingleton instance = new
ExceptionQueueSingleton();
5       private ArrayList exceptionQueue = new ArrayList();
6
7       private ExceptionQueueSingleton(){ }
8
9       public static ExceptionQueueSingleton getInstance(){
10        return instance;
11      }
12
13      public synchronized void addThrowable(Throwable exc){
14        exceptionQueue.add(exc);
15      }
16
17      public Iterator getExceptionQueueIterator(){
18        return exceptionQueue.iterator();
19      }
20  }
```

Since the Singleton provides its object resource through a static getter method, it's much simpler for parts of a system to use a global resource. However, since the Singleton is globally shared, there's a potential concurrency risk, especially during the setup or initialization of the global resource.[128]

---

127. A more sophisticated Singleton might provide advanced logger capabilities such as remote reporting or filtering.
128. For a good discussion of this topic, take a look at the Sun Java Developer Connection Tech Tips article at the following URL: http://java.sun.com/developer/JDCTechTips/2003/tt0422.html#2

Structural Patterns

1. Adapter

The Adapter pattern is used to convert between dissimilar interfaces in a system. It acts as an intermediary, translating the services of one class so that they can be used by other classes. The basic structure for this pattern is shown in the class diagram in Figure 12-3.

This pattern's conversion capability can be useful for managing exception propagation, since the Adapter can translate exceptions from the Adaptee into a form that's usable in the calling framework. The Adapter is especially helpful if you need to convert an API-specific exception model into one that is more useful for your callers. For example, an adapter could convert the SQLException of JDBC into a standard business exception used by the rest of your system. A simple technique that you can use for this practice is to wrap the original exception as the root cause of a new exception object. The following code example shows how this might be done; in this case, the Adapter (represented by the class CustomerDAOAdapter) wraps the underlying SQLException (produced by the Adaptee) in an application-logic specific exception, the CustomerException, as shown in Code 12-3.

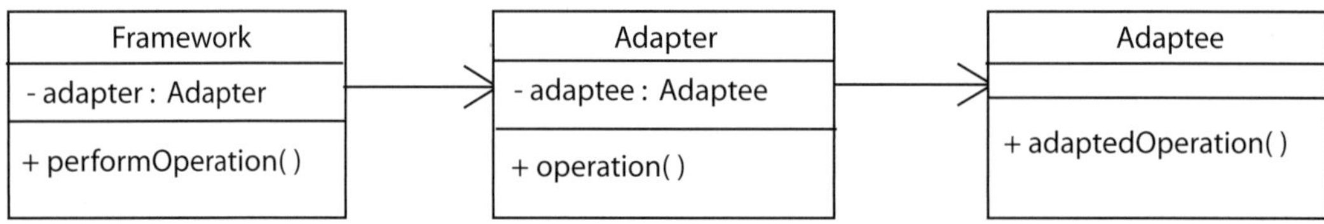

Figure 12–3
Adapter Pattern class diagram.

Code 12-3: Adapter Implementation that provides Exception Conversion

```
1    import java.sql.*;
2    public class CustomerDAOAdapter{
3       private CustomerDAO adaptee;
4       public CustomerDAOAdapter(){
5          adaptee = new CustomerDAO();
6       }
7       public CustomerVO lookUpCustomer(String id) throws CustomerException{
8          CustomerVO rtnValue = null;
9          try{
10            rtnValue = adaptee.getCustomer(id);
```

```
11        }
12        catch (SQLException exc){
13            throw new CustomerException("Cannot locate Customer " + id, exc);
14        }
15        return rtnValue;
16    }
17    public void updateCustomer(CustomerVO cust) throws CustomerException{
18        try{
19            adaptee.updateCustomer(cust);
20        }
21        catch (SQLException exc){
22            throw new CustomerException("Unable to update Customer", exc);
23        }
24    }
25 }
```

The adapter pattern helps promote reuse within software without forcing you to rewrite code. Its application to the exception model is particularly useful, since you can avoid many of the common problems traditionally associated with the conversion. The primary difficulty for an adapter applied to an exception model arises when there is no natural mapping between the failure modes of the Adaptee and the Framework. In this case, there's a danger of trying to force an exception into a form that's not really compatible with the underlying framework. If you see this situation, it's usually better to use a custom handler for the new code failure scenarios rather than trying to force the model into the Adapter.

2. Composite

The Composite provides a flexible way to create a hierarchical tree structure of arbitrary complexity, and to providing a uniform calling interface for each element of the tree. You can use a Composite to define operations that can be handled at a local component, or propagated down the tree as required. The pattern provides an effective way to perform global notification operations related to the exception model, to propagate global handling and to send recovery commands to a system. In addition, this pattern can make it easy to collect information about a system's global health and well-being. The code example provided in Code 12-4 shows a Composite implementation with a structure that allows management of global, service-based resources. In this case, the HandlerComponent interface defines methods that can be called on any part of the system to check resource "health," and to start and stop a system if there's some problem. More advanced implementations could additionally provide handler methods, methods to provide detailed information about service availability, and more advanced ways for the system to manage recovery.

Code 12-4: Composite Pattern applied for Exception Propagation

```
1   public interface HandlerComponent{
2     public boolean isHealthy();
3     public void stop();
4     public void start();
5   }
```

```
1   public class HandlerNode implements HandlerComponent{
2     private Resource managedService;
3     public void setManagedService(Resource rsrc){
4       managedService = rsrc;
5     }
6     public boolean isHealthy(){
7       return managedService.isHealthy();
8     }
9     public void stop(){
10      managedService.stop();
11    }
12    public void start(){
13      managedService.start();
14    }
15  }
```

```
1   import java.util.*;
2   public class HandlerComposite implements HandlerComponent{
3     private ArrayList components = new ArrayList();
4     public void addComponent(HandlerComponent comp){
5       components.add(comp);
6     }
7     public void removeComponent(HandlerComponent comp){
8       components.remove(comp);
9     }
10    public boolean isHealthy(){
11      Iterator iterator = components.iterator();
12      while (iterator.hasNext()){
13        if (!((HandlerComponent)iterator.next()).isHealthy()){
14          return false;
15        }
16      }
17      return true;
18    }
19    public void stop(){
20      Iterator iterator = components.iterator();
21      while (iterator.hasNext()){
22        ((HandlerComponent)iterator.next()).stop();
23      }
```

```
24     }
25     public void start(){
26        Iterator iterator = components.iterator();
27        while (iterator.hasNext()){
28           ((HandlerComponent)iterator.next()).start();
29        }
30     }
31   }
```

A Composite promotes extreme flexibility in a system and makes global management straightforward. Since exception handling tends to follow a fairly standardized model, it's usually easier to define exception-related Composite implementations than other forms of the pattern. The key drawback of the pattern is that it can be complex to test and debug the system. This potentially means that you need to spend a great deal of effort to validate and test the handling capabilities of your system.

3. Facade

You can use the Facade pattern to provide a simplified interface into a complex subsystem. The Facade makes it simpler to call a number of subcomponents, or to convert a number of fine-grained methods into coarser ones that are more meaningful to the core business model. The Facade can be used as a way to effectively consolidate exception handling within a system. It's particularly helpful when you want to deal with certain common categories of problems that would normally be hard to handle at a component level, such as concurrency or cache management. The example in Code 12-5 shows how a Facade could provide coordinating control as part of a business operation. In this case, the OrderFacade will attempt to complete an order, but will attempt to cancel reserved items in inventory if there was a problem with processing the payment.

Code 12-5: Facade with Exception Management for a Business Process

```
1   public class OrderFacade{
2      private InventoryService invSvc;
3      private PaymentService paySvc;
4      private ShippingService shipSvc;
5      public OrderFacade(){
6         invSvc = new InventoryService();
7         paySvc = new PaymentService();
8         shipSvc = new ShippingService();
9      }
10     public void placeOrder(Customer c, Order o) throws OrderException{
11        boolean result;
12        try{
13           invSvc.reserveOrderItems(o);
```

```
14          if (o.isComplete()){
15             paySvc.purchaseOrder(c, o);
16             shipSvc.shipOrder(o);
17          }
18       }
19    catch (InventoryException e){
20      throw new OrderException("Unable to reserve items for the order",
21            o, c, e);
22    }
23    catch (PaymentException e){
24      try{
25        invSvc.cancelReservedItems(o);
26        throw new OrderException("Problem with payment: " +
27           "order rolled back", o, c, e);
28      }
29      catch (InventoryException ex2){
30        throw new OrderException("Unable to roll back order " +
31           "in inventory; must manually roll back", o, c, e);
32      }
33    }
34   }
35 }
```

Because the Facade adds an additional coordinating layer to a system, there's often a concern that it will introduce overhead into a system and slow it down. There tends to be a reduced risk for exception handling, however. If you apply the pattern to the exception model, you can effectively build your code to avoid performance impact on the system. You typically do this by placing most of the management code in the handling blocks, where it will be run only in the case of a problem with the business process.

4. Proxy

A Proxy pattern duplicates the calling interface of another component and uses the Proxy object as a "front" for the real component. Proxies are common in programming, providing such capabilities as distributed communication, security, and lazy access to a resource. You can apply this pattern to set up proxy-level exception management for your component. The exception-handling proxy can potentially be used in many different ways: to provide global handling or propagation, to manage common exception management services, or to support testing capability with the component. The example in Code 12-6 shows a remote communication proxy, PaymentProxy. This class handles the details of managing the remote service Payment (an RMI commmunicator, in this case). If there are problems with lookup or use of the remote service, the proxy converts the exceptions to one of two custom business exceptions: Service-

`UnavailableException` (for problems with initial service lookup) or `PaymentEx-`
`ception` (for problems during payment processing).

Code 12-6: Remote Proxy Pattern to Handle Network-Related Exceptions

```
1   import java.net.*;
2   import java.math.*;
3   import java.rmi.*;
4   public class PaymentProxy implements PaymentService{
5     private Payment implementation;
6     private String serviceMachine = "localhost";
7     private String serviceName = "paymentService";
8     public PaymentProxy() throws ServiceUnavailableException{
9       lookupRemoteService();
10    }
11    private void lookupRemoteService() throws ServiceUnavailableException{
12      try{
13        String url = "//" + serviceMachine + "/" + serviceName;
14        Object lookup = Naming.lookup(url);
15        if (lookup instanceof Payment){
16          implementation = (Payment)lookup;
17        }
18        else{
19          throw new ServiceUnavailableException("Cannot look up " +
20               "remote service");
21        }
22      }
23      catch (RemoteException exc){
24        throw new ServiceUnavailableException("Error during remote " +
25             "service lookup", exc);
26      }
27      catch (NotBoundException exc){
28        throw new ServiceUnavailableException("Remote service is " +
29             "not registered with naming server", exc);
30      }
31      catch (MalformedURLException exc){
32        throw new ServiceUnavailableException("Malformed URL " +
33             "for naming lookup", exc);
34      }
35    }
36    public void setServiceMachine(String machineName){
37      serviceMachine = machineName;
38    }
39    public void setServiceName(String svcName){
40      serviceName = svcName;
41    }
42    public void purchase(PaymentVO pay, BigDecimal price)
```

```
43          throws PaymentException, ServiceUnavailableException{
44       try{
45         if (implementation != null){
46           implementation.purchase(pay, price);
47         }
48       }
49       catch (RemoteException exc){
50         try{
51           lookupRemoteService();
52           implementation.purchase(pay, price);
53         }
54         catch (RemoteException exc2){
55          throw new ServiceUnavailableException("Cannot process payment: " +
56              "remote communication problems with payment service", exc2);
57         }
58       }
59     }
60   }
```

The principal drawback of this pattern comes with the risk associated with tight coupling between the Proxy and its component. In the exception model, tight coupling implies that there's a danger that the component may become too dependent on its Proxy for exception management. In this case, the exception management is spread across two components and becomes difficult to manage and maintain. If you don't carefully plan a distribution of responsibilities, this can present problems with maintainability, and there's an additional risk that essential parts of the exception model may be omitted.

Behavioral Patterns

1. Chain of Responsibility

With a Chain of Responsibility, you set up a delegation model for a group of objects in your system. The pattern allows you to handle a method call locally or forward it "up the chain" if the object cannot satisfy the request. This can be handy for the exception model, especially if a single exception affects many related objects in a system. A Chain of Responsibility makes it relatively easy to respond to some exceptions locally, while maintaining the flexibility to delegate more critical errors to a higher-level handler. Figure 12-4 shows one example of how the pattern might work—in this case, each ConcreteHandler object could potentially handle some kinds of exception or error, while passing other problems up the "chain" to the next ConcreteHandler.

You can use a Chain of Responsibility to handle system exceptions and recovery, to manage modular testing, or to get notifications about the health of your system. Of

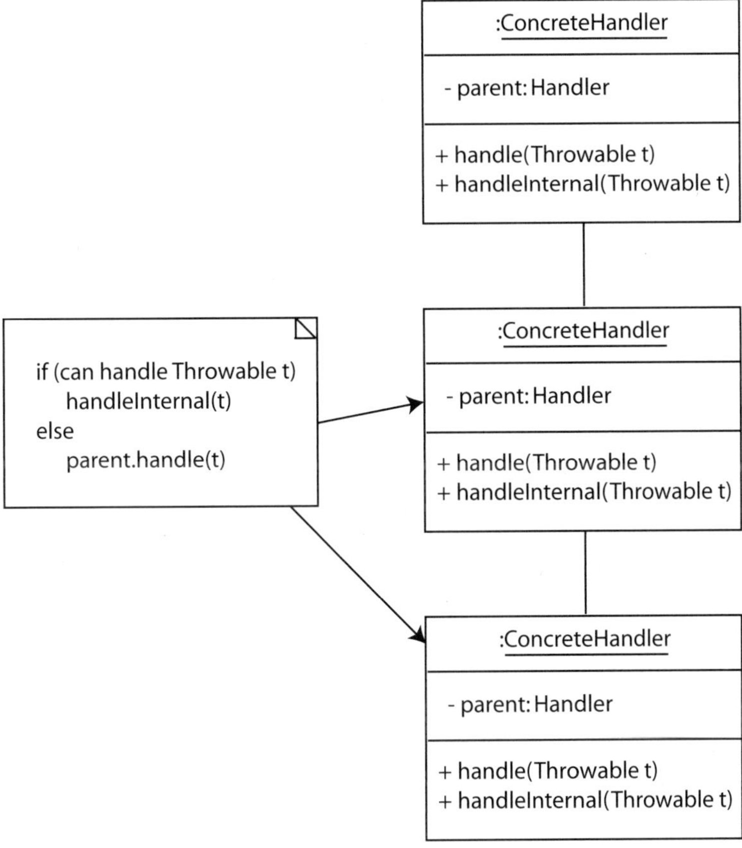

Figure 12–4
Chain of Responsibility Pattern example.

course, the very flexibility that makes this pattern so useful is also one of its greatest drawbacks. Because the Chain of Responsibility can be set up dynamically with arbitrary complexity, such a system can be extremely hard to test and debug. Additionally, you must carefully manage the volume of communication in a system if you want to avoid a potentially large impact on system performance.

2. Command

This pattern allows you to encapsulate a "command" operation within a class or class hierarchy. You subsequently have flexibility to create command objects and propagate them. This effectively decouples parts of a system, allowing you to extend commands as required and run them on generic command processors in a system. This pattern can be used in systems that require flexibility in dealing with exceptions in code. A

Command can provide an effective way to provide a standardized exception definition to be used in a handling framework. Figure 12-5 shows how this might work: the `CommandException` could be standardized in the handling framework used to process Command objects, while leaving individual ConcreteCommand objects with the freedom to follow an approach to exception management best suited for the operation to be performed.

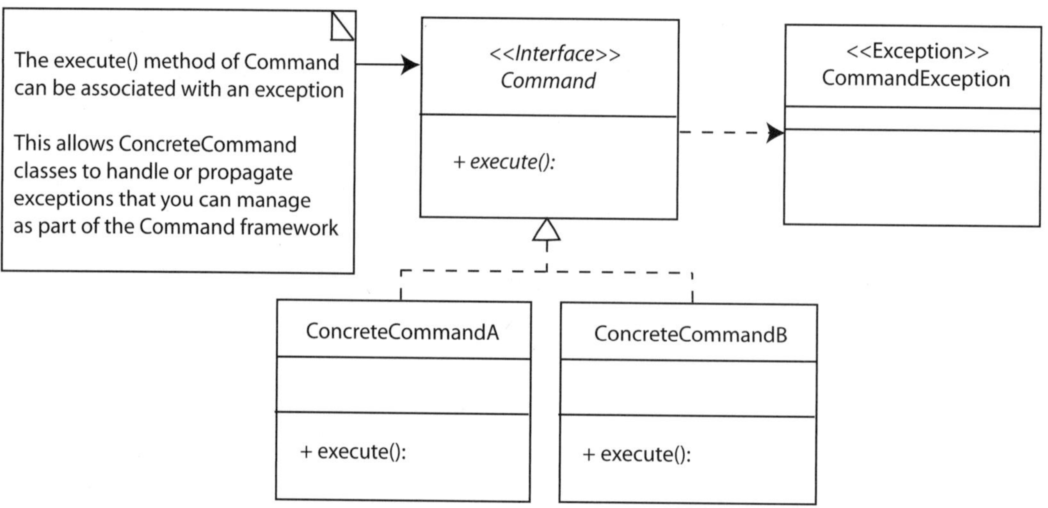

Figure 12–5
Chain of Responsibility class diagram.

This is a powerful pattern, since it provides a high degree of dynamic flexibility in applications. Of course, you have to be careful that Command objects fulfill their core responsibilities—that they perform all core actions required by the system. This is especially crucial when you're working with exception handling Command objects. Improper use of Command that is designed to handle errors in your code has the potential to introduce a large number of additional exceptions into your system without a way to effectively address them.

3. Observer

The Observer pattern allows a component to broadcast messages to any interested receivers. A receiver registers with the "observable" component, and subsequently receives method calls when an event of interest occurs. In the exception handling world, you can use this pattern to effectively support broadcasting of exceptions and errors to handlers, or to other parts of a system. This pattern is especially well-suited to model the "backbone" of an exception handling system—it can effectively represent a high-level handling model for an application or framework. The sample code in Code 12-7 shows a simple Observer model with support for the method `handleException`. If a business operation (represented here by a call to BusinessService method `businessOperation`) threw an exception, the `handleException` method would be called for all registered Observers.

Code 12-7: Observer Pattern example

```java
1  public interface ExceptionObserver{
2     public void handleException(Throwable t);
3  }
```

```java
1   import java.util.*;
2   public class ExceptionObservable{
3      private ArrayList observers;
4      private BusinessService bizService;
5      public void addObserver(ExceptionObserver obs){
6         observers.add(obs);
7      }
8      public void removeObserver(ExceptionObserver obs){
9         observers.remove(obs);
10     }
11     public void setBusinessService(BusinessService svc){
12        bizService = svc;
13     }
14     public void businessMethod(){
15        try{
16           bizService.businessOperation();
17        }
18        catch (Throwable th){
19           Iterator iterate = observers.iterator();
20           while (iterate.hasNext()){
21              ((ExceptionObserver)iterate.next()).handleException(th);
22           }
23        }
24     }
25  }
```

A key advantage of this pattern is that each Observer has flexibility in how it responds to an exception. Of course, it's important to design the Observer's callback method properly. For an Observer to be effective, it's important that listeners are able to receive and act upon the appropriate data. The exception-observer has a special advantage in this case, since the handling model is essentially set up as part of the language. As a result, the pattern tends to be easier to manage for exceptions than for other types of methods. You should take care not to overuse this pattern, since it has the potential to introduce high communication overhead into a system. For this reason, it's often useful to apply it as a communication model for major subsystems, rather than using it for low-level propagation. One final warning about this pattern: as with any pattern that involves propagation over a potentially large number of objects, the Observer can cause major problems in a multithreaded system. If you plan to use the pattern in such a system, you may need to implement a non-blocking version of the pattern in order to ensure that your system runs properly.

4. State

The State pattern encapsulates state-dependent behavior of an object in a number of classes where each class represents a well-defined state. An object can swap state objects to change the way it behaves. Ultimately, this makes an object much easier to extend and manage, especially if its state-dependent behavior is complex and variable during runtime.

This pattern represents another way to achieve flexible handling of errors within a system. If your system must have variable handling or propagation models depending on the state of a crucial object or component, you can model a series of handlers based on the component's own state. Handling behavior becomes more straightforward, since it is inherently associated with the state of the object. An example is shown in Figure 12-6.

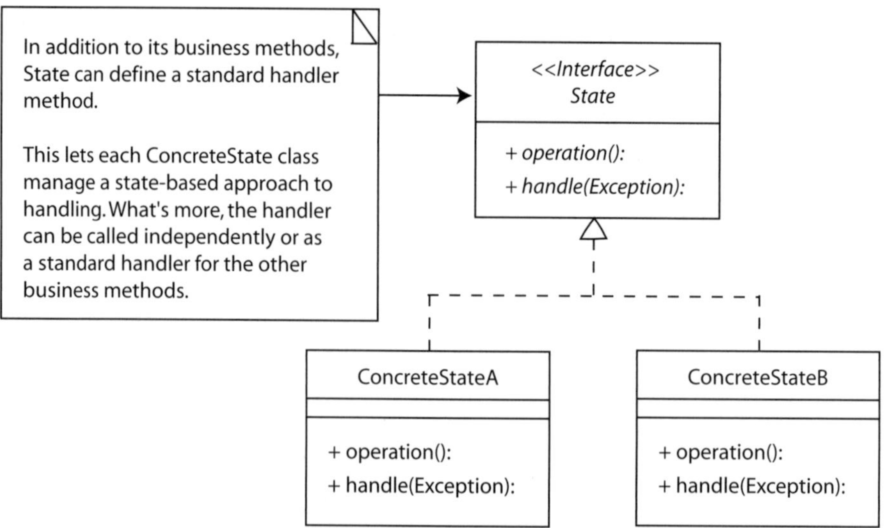

Figure 12–6
State Pattern with Built-in Handler.

Of course, the number of classes used in the State pattern can make the system harder to understand and manage. Handling code is inherently decoupled in this pattern, stored among many classes. That also means there's a real danger of code duplication. In cases where you want to centralize your handlers, you may be better off using State to branch to a global handler, rather than copying the exception management code itself.

It's important to contrast this pattern with the concept of a "state object" in an application or framework. In some situations, a global state object is defined for a system. This object encapsulates the outcome of a business process so that the outcome can be more effectively shared by objects throughout a complex system. A global state object may or may not implement the State design pattern, but it does have a definite benefit in terms of exception management. Specifically, a "status" object can be used in enterprise applications as a way to hold exceptions for a deferred reporting strategy.

5. Strategy

A Strategy defines a common method in an interface or class. The method can subsequently be implemented in a number of different ways in subclasses, providing a number of different "strategies" for the method. You can subsequently plug in a Strategy class during runtime, and change the way a system functions. This pattern represents another useful way to provide flexibility in your handling or propagation model for a system. Specifically, a Strategy allows you to dynamically define exception handling or propagation methods for a system. In the example shown in Code 12-8, the Handler-Strategy interface defines a basic handler method. This method can fully handle an exception, or throw a `BusinessException` back to the caller. Any class implementing this interface could subsequently be associated with the framework, Exception-HandlingFramework, as the handler for the `businessOperation` method. Notice that the strategy object is a blank final variable; this ensures that the strategy will only be defined for the system once, during object creation.

Code 12-8: Strategy Pattern example

```
1  public interface HandlerStrategy{
2    public void handleException(Throwable t) throws BusinessException;
3  }
```

```
1  public class ExceptionHandlingFramework{
2    private final HandlerStrategy strategy;
3    private BusinessService bizService;
4    public ExceptionHandlingFramework(HandlerStrategy strat){
5      strategy = strat;
6    }
7    public ExceptionHandlingFramework(HandlerStrategy h, BusinessService b){
```

```
 8        strategy = h;
 9        bizService = b;
10      }
11    public void businessOperation() throws BusinessException{
12      try{
13        bizService.businessOperation();
14      }
15      catch (Throwable exc){
16        strategy.handleException(exc);
17      }
18    }
19  }
```

Since each handler's behavior is maintained in a separate class, the complete system tends to be easier to maintain and extend. Of course, this pattern naturally separates handler code into multiple classes, just as the State pattern does. In many situations this is exactly what you want—you want to be able to plug in a completely different handling or propagation strategy during runtime.

Of course, you have to be careful about the fallout of behavior swapping.[129] If you dynamically change something like exception management while an application runs, the system can degenerate into chaos. To avoid this danger, some systems implement the pattern with a "set once" behavior so that the approach to exception management remains consistent during runtime.

The Strategy pattern is popular in many frameworks, where the implementation typically sets up the Strategy class to be used for a given application. There are a number of Java APIs that use this pattern to provide handling flexibility to the programmer. The Logging API uses this pattern with its ErrorManager. An ErrorManager can be associated with a Handler object to provide a flexible exception handling strategy defined by its error method.

J2EE Patterns
(Core J2EE Patterns, ACM)

The use of patterns in J2EE represents patterns applied within a specific architectural context. All patterns depend on some foundation assumptions about the environment in which they will be used. Most of the early-generation patterns, such as those defined by the "Gang of Four," depend on having a suitably object-oriented language. It's been demonstrated that you can apply the GoF patterns with the same associated tradeoffs in a number of OO languages including C++, Smalltalk, Eiffel and Java. In

---

129. If you change a strategy object used to handle exceptions during runtime, it may cause what's perceived as strange or buggy behavior in the system.

recent years, a number of technologists have carried the concept of patterns into specific computing environments and into specific high-level frameworks. The concept of patterns has the same benefits, but they are applied to a more specific scope.

One of the more popular areas within Java that involves the focused application of patterns is the Java 2, Enterprise Edition. It's been effectively shown that the use of patterns when developing a J2EE application can ultimately result in a more manageable system. J2EE patterns often adapt the core principles defined in earlier-generation patterns, applying them within the context of the architectural model.

Integration Tier

1. Data Access Object (DAO)[130]

The Data Access Object pattern defines an object that is responsible for interacting with persistent storage. This object provides standard business methods to interact with the underlying storage, such as create, retrieve, update and delete. The DAO interacts with the persistence layer and hides the technology-specific implementation from the rest of the system. In the realm of exception management, the DAO provides an effective way to translate a technology-specific exception model into a form that is more usable by calling software. Just as the DAO can define business methods to perform insert, select, update and delete operations, it can also declare business exceptions, converting API-based exceptions into a more generic format. In the DAO implementation shown in Code 12-9, the `CustomerDAO` business methods convert SQLException to the business exception `CustomerException`. The DAO also handles JDBC resource shutdown, and does *not* propagate a SQLException that is thrown when closing a ResultSet, Statement or Connection.

Code 12-9: DAO Pattern example

```
1   import java.sql.*;
2   import javax.naming.*;
3   import javax.sql.*;
4   public class CustomerDAO{
5      private DataSource dataSce;
6      private String dsName = "java:comp/env/jdbc/DBSource";
7      public CustomerDAO() throws NamingException, ClassCastException{
8          Context ctx = new InitialContext();
9          dataSce = (DataSource)ctx.lookup(dsName);
10     }
```

---

130. In fact, the DAO pattern is commonly applied to solve problems outside of J2EE today, since enterprise system integration represents such a common need in distributed systems.

```
11   public CustomerVO getCustomer(String cid) throws CustomerException{
12     CustomerVO rtnVal = new CustomerVO();
13     Connection conn = null;
14     PreparedStatement ps = null;
15     ResultSet rs = null;
16     try{
17       conn = dataSce.getConnection();
18       ps = conn.prepareStatement("SELECT * FROM Customer" +
19               " WHERE cid = ?");
20       ps.setString(1, cid);
21       rs = ps.executeQuery();
22       if (rs.next()){
23         rtnVal.setName(rs.getString(1));
24         rtnVal.setId(cid);
25       }
26     }
27     catch (SQLException exc){
28       throw new CustomerException("Unable to retrieve Customer " +
29           "because of SQLException", exc);
30     }
31     finally{
32       close(rs, ps, conn);
33     }
34     return rtnVal;
35   }
36   public void updateCustomer(CustomerVO cust) throws CustomerException{
37     Connection conn = null;
38     PreparedStatement ps = null;
39     try{
40       conn = dataSce.getConnection();
41       ps = conn.prepareStatement("UPDATE Customer SET name = ?" +
42               " WHERE cid = ?");
43       ps.setString(1, cust.getName());
44       ps.setString(2, cust.getId());
45       ps.executeUpdate();
46     }
47     catch (SQLException exc){
48       throw new CustomerException("Unable to perform Customer update " +
49           "because of SQLException", exc);
50     }
51     finally{
52       close(null, ps, conn);
53     }
54   }
55   private void close(ResultSet rs, Statement stmt, Connection conn){
56     if (rs != null){
57       try{
```

```
58            rs.close();
59          }
60        catch (SQLException exc){}
61      }
62      if (stmt != null){
63        try{
64          stmt.close();
65        }
66        catch (SQLException exc){}
67      }
68      if (conn != null){
69        try{
70          conn.close();
71        }
72        catch (SQLException exc){}
73      }
74    }
75  }
```

Presentation Tier

1. Front Controller

The Front Controller is one of the most popular patterns in J2EE frameworks. The pattern defines a single control "entry point" for a Web tier, often represented by a Servlet. This object fulfills the general responsibilities of an MVC Controller within the Web application.

Clearly, a global controller within an enterprise application offers an excellent opportunity to provide a central point from which to coordinate the exception model for a system. The Front Controller can effectively be used to manage exceptions for an application, especially dynamic handling and propagation.[131] Depending on the complexity of your exception model, this may greatly expand the size of the controller. In such cases, keep in mind that you can always refactor the Front Controller and delegate the handling behavior to a dedicated handling component within the Web tier. Code 12-10 shows an example of the Front Controller pattern.

---

131. You could also suggest that the Deployment Descriptor can provide for global configuration, but a Front Controller can provide more flexible, dynamic configuration of a handling strategy in a Web Application.

Code 12-10: Front Controller Pattern example

```java
1   import java.io.*;
2   import javax.servlet.*;
3   import javax.servlet.http.*;
4   public class HandlerController extends HttpServlet{
5     public void doGet(HttpServletRequest req, HttpServletResponse rsp)
6       throws ServletException, IOException{
7       processReq(req, rsp);
8     }
9     public void doPost(HttpServletRequest req, HttpServletResponse rsp)
10      throws ServletException, IOException{
11      processReq(req, rsp);
12    }
13    public void processReq(HttpServletRequest req, HttpServletResponse rsp)
14      throws ServletException, IOException{
15      String action = NavigateConstants.NO_ACTION;
16      try{
17        action = req.getParameter(NavigateConstants.NAV_FORM_NAME);
18        if (action.equals(NavigateConstants.NAV_LOGIN)){
19          RequestDispatcher rd =
20              req.getRequestDispatcher(NavigateConstants.LOGIN);
21          rd.forward(req, rsp);
22        }
23        else if (action.equals(NavigateConstants.NAV_REGISTER)){
24          RequestDispatcher rd =
25              req.getRequestDispatcher(NavigateConstants.REGISTER);
26          rd.forward(req, rsp);
27        }
28        else if (action.equals(NavigateConstants.NAV_LOGOUT)){
29          RequestDispatcher rd =
30              req.getRequestDispatcher(NavigateConstants.LOGOUT);
31          rd.forward(req, rsp);
32        }
33      }
34      catch (Exception exc){
35        SystemHealthVO health = HealthCheckService.checkSystemHealth();
36        LoggingManager.log("Exception occurred during business process " +
37            action);
38        LoggingManager.log("Exception stack trace: ", exc);
39        LoggingManager.log("System health status:  ", health);
40      }
41    }
42  }
```

2. Intercepting Filter[132]

The Intercepting Filter in some ways represents the concept of the Decorator design pattern applied to the J2EE Web tier. The ability to flexibly layer filters within the Web tier naturally implies the ability to add global services without disrupting the underlying application model. This is especially useful when introducing global exception services such as logging or testing. Filtering allows you to add these services on an as-needed basis in your Web tier. In addition, a filtering model allows you to perform both preprocessing and postprocessing tasks, if need be. The example in Code 12-11 shows a simple filter that tracks system health, logging it at the entry and exit points of a filtering chain. The example uses the Filter interface defined in the Servlet 2.3 specification as an easy way to manage filtering behavior. If an exception occurs during processing, the filter logs the problem and again provides a snapshot of system health.

Code 12-11: Intercepting Filter Pattern example

```
1   import javax.servlet.*;
2   import java.io.*;
3   public class LoggingFilter implements Filter{
4     public void init(FilterConfig cfg){}
5     public void destroy(){}
6     public void doFilter(ServletRequest req, ServletResponse rsp,
7         FilterChain ch) throws IOException{
8       try{
9         LoggingManager.log("Entering filter chain. System health: ",
10          HealthCheckService.checkSystemHealth());
11        ch.doFilter(req, rsp);
12        LoggingManager.log("Leaving filter chain. System health: ",
13          HealthCheckService.checkSystemHealth());
14      }
15      catch (Exception exc){
16        LoggingManager.log("Exception thrown in filter chain", exc);
17        LoggingManager.log("System health: ",
18          HealthCheckService.checkSystemHealth());
19      }
20    }
21  }
```

---

132. The Servlet 2.3 specification introduced Filters, which duplicate the behavior of the Intercepting Filter.

Business Tier

1. Service Locator

A Service Locator represents a delegate for a specific task within the business tier. Typically it handles JNDI lookups and caching tasks. This effectively allows the rest of the business tier to avoid the coding details associated with management of this enterprise resource, and to use it as a more coarse-grained service. Since JNDI has its own fairly complex set of exceptions and failure modes, there's a lot of sense in using this pattern to encapsulate the handling associated with the naming and directory operations in a J2EE system. Beyond its regular responsibilities of naming lookup and reference management, a service locator can fairly easily be extended to enforce a standard handling and exception conversion strategy for its naming operations. In the example in Code 12-12, the locator converts exceptions into a generic format (the custom exception class LocatorException) while providing additional messages that help to qualify the problems that can occur during the lookup.

Code 12-12: Service Locator Pattern example

```
1    import javax.naming.*;
2    import java.rmi.*;
3    import javax.sql.*;
4    import java.sql.*;
5    public class DataSourceServiceLocator{
6      private Context context;
7      private DataSource source;
8      private String dataSourceName;
9      private void lookupDS() throws LocatorException{
10       try{
11         if (context == null){
12           lookupContext();
13         }
14         source = (DataSource)context.lookup(dataSourceName);
15       }
16       catch (NamingException exc){
17         throw new LocatorException("Problem with JNDI lookup." +
18             "Unable to access naming services", exc);
19       }
20       catch (ClassCastException exc){
21         throw new LocatorException("Unable to convert JNDI" +
22             "lookup to DataSource", exc);
23       }
24     }
25     private void lookupContext() throws NamingException{
26       context = new InitialContext();
```

```
27     }
28     public Connection getConnection() throws LocatorException{
29        Connection connection = null;
30        try{
31           lookupDS();
32           connection = source.getConnection();
33        }
34        catch (SQLException exc){
35           throw new LocatorException("Unable to obtain a Connection" +
36                 "from the DataSource", exc);
37        }
38        return connection;
39     }
40     public void setDataSourceName(String n){
41        dataSourceName = n;
42     }
43   }
```

2. Session Facade

As its name suggests, the Session Facade is a Facade implementation for the J2EE
business tier. The application of a Facade in J2EE systems has a number of substantial benefits, including a fairly important role in exception management.[133] A Session Facade can effectively consolidate your exception model in the EJB tier. Just as
the Facade can unify a number of EJBs, so it can also unify your exception handling
model. It can act as a central handling point for converting exceptions into a form
that allows manageable propagation to another tier. In addition, it is an excellent
location to manage exceptions that relate to the whole tier, such as those that relate
to transactional behavior or the failure to locate objects. Typically, it's difficult for
EJBs to manage these exceptions locally; the Session Facade can deal with these
more complex exceptions and organize them in a more global, consistent manner.
As the diagram in Figure 12-7 suggests, you can manage global exceptions in a more
controlled manner in the Facade, handling problems locally or providing more
meaningful exceptions to the caller.

---

133. Take a look at *Core J2EE Patterns* for full details about this pattern and its substantial benefits to the EJB tier.

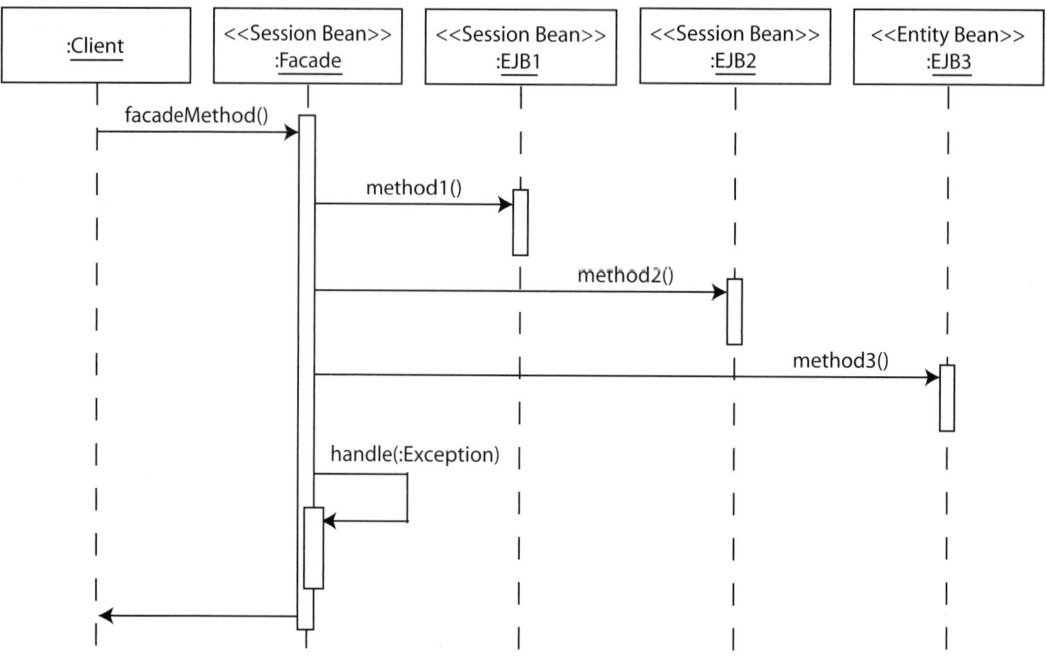

Figure 12–7
Session Facade sequence diagram with Exception Handling Behavior.

Conclusion

In this chapter, we have taken a look at a number of standard patterns. We showed some of the ways that they can be used to manage the exception model of a system. Patterns provide substantial benefits to you when you use them to handle exception management for your system. Better still, most patterns can be applied effectively by developers, designers or software architects. They can effectively provide localized benefits to your exception handling, or be applied to a software system as a whole. Whichever approach you use, it's clear that patterns can provide an effective, manageable structure to manage exceptions in your code. In the chapters to come, we talk about some other global considerations related to the exception model—testing and debugging. To a degree, both of these tasks depend on a solid core architecture for your system and depend on a good morel for exception management. You could contend that both of these practices can be improved by the use of patterns as well.

chapter 13

Testing

What's the Purpose of Testing?
Why is it so Important?

Testing. One of the most misunderstood subjects in software development and one that many programmers love to hate. Testing is a vital part of any software project, but we often don't associate nearly enough importance with it. To get an idea of how vital it is, compare it to testing something like an automobile. Is it a good idea to build a car without providing any way to check inside of it? If you have no testing capabilities, you might have to replace the whole car each time something went wrong![134]

Put another way, would you feel happy getting into a car if you knew that it hadn't been tested and shown to have such desirable automotive qualities as mobility or safety? Would you be comfortable buying an untested car? One thing's for certain—automotive repairs would take a lot longer than they already do.[135] Even though it seems crazy to build something like a car without test capabilities, development teams still make this mistake in their applications. Even today, a lot of teams don't adequately test their code. Worse still, some groups release under-tested code into the wild, letting their users find the "features" in their systems.

What exactly is the purpose of testing? Almost anyone you talk to will agree that it's important to test an application, but it's a bit harder to get a clear answer about what the effort is supposed to accomplish. One of the most basic answers is:

1. **Testing verifies that an application does what it's supposed to do.**[136]

That's a good starting point, but it doesn't cover all of the motives for testing. Let's expand the list a bit:

---

134. I have owned a few cars like this.
135. There would probably also be a lot more people riding bicycles.
136. Of course, it's often more useful to show that a system *doesn't* do what it's supposed to do.

2. **Testing establishes that an application responds appropriately to use and misuse.**

3. **Testing helps you identify bugs in an application.**

4. **Testing helps you ensure that changes to an application don't introduce new bugs.**

5. **Testing evaluates system behavior under conditions of use and load.**

6. **Testing determines the limits of an application under stress.**

With this list, it's easy to understand why testing is so crucial. There's a lot that's directly relevant to every job role in software development. Without effective testing, you have no real guarantee that software development is complete. Many of us have been involved with projects that have run much longer than originally scheduled. Without an effective way to validate the functional and architectural characteristics of software, we have no way to ever really verify that a product is ready for distribution—and, therefore, no way to effectively finish a project.

This chapter focuses on testing from the perspective of software architects, designers and developers. We talk about common misconceptions about testing and present some thoughts on the kinds of tests developers should perform. We describe how you can write tests for your code, and present some of the commonly-used APIs and software that support testing in Java. We also show how developers can work with testers to effectively meet the shared goal of creating a high-quality software product.

Common Misconceptions about Testing

Software testing has traditionally been the subject of many misunderstandings. This is due in part to the fact that software development has some features that set it apart from other forms of engineering. Many common testing practices used in other engineering disciplines have seen only limited success in software development. In a field like mechanical engineering, a tester can operate within the constraints of physical laws, content in the fact that they'll ensure you don't try to circumvent the forces holding the universe together. In software engineering, there are almost no constraints—and that means there's a lot more for you to test.

We've made plenty of mistakes in testing to get to where we are now. Some of these errors in practice or judgment have been popular enough that they survive even today. As a result, there are still a lot of piranhas swimming around in the fish tank of software testing. With that in mind, here are four of the most common fallacies about testing.

Misconception #1: Developers should do "no" testing for their code.

Thanks to the agile software methodologies, and to eXtreme Programming in particular, this misconception is well on its way to extinction. Early development methodologies tended to define a programmer's responsibility rather loosely—they were supposed to write code and ensure that it "worked". Many projects made one of two mistakes. They either provided no guidance about how programmers were supposed to verify their code, or they defined verification too narrowly, in terms of basic compilation or code reviews.

A common problem in most early-generation software development models was a lack of testing standards. There was basically no yardstick to determine whether a programmer effectively tested their code, or to see whether the right kinds of tests had been performed. Although a good team of testers can work wonders when uncovering problems in code, their effectiveness is severely hampered if a development team has no formal way to validate and test their own work. Lack of a formal approach to ensure a certain baseline "correctness" means that it's highly likely that any coding—bug fixes included—will introduce more problems into an application. For this reason, it's vitally important for a development team to incorporate a test strategy into their projects.

Misconception #2: Developers should do "all" the testing for their code.

This misconception is a bit more controversial than the first. It's a seductive viewpoint, especially for projects operating under severe time and budget constraints. It's easy for an organization to adopt the mindset that testing can be entirely performed by developers as they write their code. "After all," the argument goes, "they know their code better than anyone. Why shouldn't they be the ones to test it?"

Actually, that's precisely the reason that developers shouldn't be the only ones to perform testing. Effective testing requires a team to look at a product from many different perspectives. It's true that developers have a detailed understand of their software, and that makes them excellent candidates to perform *some* types of testing. However, that familiarity works against developers when they have to test boundary conditions of an application, or evaluate software from a user's perspective. It's a rare programmer who can get enough distance from his or her code to perform all kinds of required testing.

The mindset of testers is fundamentally different from that of software development. In order to do their job, testers must usually try to get code to fail, which involves looking at things most developers don't spend much time on. Specifically, testers tend to focus on ways that people might misuse an application, and on assumptions (especially implicit) that could lead to code failure. This emphasis tends to allow testing professionals to perform some types of software testing more effectively. As a result, it's usually better to share responsibilities between both roles to ensure more comprehensive test coverage.

Misconception #3: You only need to do "one thing" to test an application.[137]

This idea is fundamentally based on a development team operating in its comfort zone. If a group becomes comfortable with a certain type of test, it's easy to focus on that single area to the exclusion of all other forms of testing.

When you direct all your effort toward one specific type of testing, your tests inherently neglect other aspects of your software and quality suffers as a result. Here's a simple example. Most of us can create a throwaway prototype that looks quite good. To an outside observer, the prototype appears to meet a customer's needs. With a little ingenuity, you can probably design it to pass basic user acceptance tests. Does that mean the software product is complete and correct? Of course not—it's a throwaway prototype, a facade designed to illustrate application structure and flow. This example is a little extreme, but apply the principle to the broader field of testing. If a development team only performs unit testing, does that necessarily guarantee that the code will meet customer expectations? Does it ensure that the individual code modules will work together correctly? Of course not—you need to diversify testing in order to prove such things. At the foundation, we have to perform a combination of static and dynamic tests, low-level and high-level tests, to establish an accurate picture of how a software system actually performs.

Misconception #4: You can fully test an application.

This misconception brings endless trouble into the lives of both testers and developers. "Make sure the product is completely tested" is a terrifying directive unless it's heavily qualified. Is it possible to fully test an application? If by "fully tested" you mean evaluate an application under all possible conditions, the answer is probably not. For an application that has even a moderate degree of complexity, there are an infinite number of runtime permutations for the code. In his 1979 classic *The Art of Software Testing*, Glenford Myers showed that a simple program[138] could have over 100 trillion test paths, making it effectively impossible to test completely.

---

137. In this context, "one thing" can be any form of testing taken in isolation. The key point is that any single form of testing only covers a small part of a software system's overall behavior.

138. Myers' sample program was based on a loop with a few if statements. To this day, it provides an excellent illustration of both the power of programming languages and the challenges that such languages pose to effective testing.

Given that complete testing is basically a myth, you must focus instead on test adequacy. In other words, you must ensure that the tests you perform provide an acceptable level of coverage. Normally, you associate some kind of concrete measure with tests, some kind of meaningful benchmark or metric. Without that measure, you're essentially guessing about when you're finished with testing. Later in this chapter, we talk about testing strategies and how they can be linked to measures of code completeness.

Types of Testing: Thinking Outside (and Inside) the Box

What's in the Box? Types of Testing

Because there are many different ways to evaluate a system, there are many different kinds of testing. Typically, a well-tested software product uses several kinds of testing and several different test strategies. A mixed approach to testing allows a development team to achieve a good balance for their tests in terms of level of abstraction and code coverage. We describe some of the more common forms of testing with brief definitions. This list isn't comprehensive—there are many more categories of testing mentioned in other books and articles—but it's a good baseline.

Testing Categories

In order to relate testing to development roles, we define several high-level categories: black box, white box and architectural testing. This is by no means the only way to characterize different kinds of testing, but it's useful for our current discussion. **Black box testing** is performed without knowledge of the internal structure of an application or system. It tends to focus on evaluating the externally observable behavior of a system under various conditions. **White box testing** (also called clear box testing) requires knowledge of the internals of an application or software system. It involves direct evaluation of the system's codebase at various levels of modularity.

Architectural testing evaluates a system's architectural characteristics, qualities such as performance, reliability and security. As software has become more complex, it's become popular to evaluate the non-functional as well as systemic requirements. Some enlightened testing groups have been doing this for years, but the practice has become more universal over the past decade or so. Many kinds of architectural testing can be considered subcategories of black box testing, since they abstract an application's functionality.

Black Box Tests

Black box tests evaluate how a system works based on how it looks from the "outside." Since they are meant to evaluate the externally observable behavior of a system, it's often considered important that a tester *not* know too much about how the system works to avoid biasing the test results.

Many forms of black box testing examine a software product from a user's point of view. They attempt to duplicate, or at least mimic, various actions that a real-world user would perform. User acceptance testing—verifying that a product met its functional requirements—falls into this category. Likewise, real-world product tests within the user community, such as alpha or beta tests, represent types of black box tests.

Black box testing also includes techniques that are less effectively performed by end users. Some of these tests focus on evaluation of a product at an abstract level to uncover problems that would otherwise not be apparent to a development team. Exploratory testing, recovery testing, compatibility testing, risk-based testing, installation and uninstallation testing can all be considered to be black box techniques.

White Box Tests

White box methods formally check the internals of a software product to evaluate correctness and compliance to coding standards. Broadly speaking, you can subdivide white box testing into static and dynamic tests. Static white box tests check to see whether source code is correct and follows certain established requirements, conventions or guidelines. Code compilation is the most common form of static test. Code validation is another, used to verify more complex dependencies and coding rules that you can't check through compilation. Most EJB development tools perform code validation, since Java compilation alone can't verify the correctness of the components.[139]

Dynamic white box tests check to ensure that parts of the software system perform as expected during runtime. The most common types are unit and integration tests. Unit testing involves direct, low-level evaluation of code. In object-oriented development, this usually means checking individual classes. Integration testing is a higher level form of white box test. While it verifies the same things as unit tests, integration testing focuses on components or subsystems. Teams that perform unit or integration tests often bundle them together, automating them so that they can be performed every time there's a milestone or major product build; this is commonly called regression testing.

Architectural Tests

The final category includes a number of tests that evaluate a product's high-level architectural qualities. Though essentially unrelated to each other, these tests share a

---

139. Though it isn't called a validator, the popular C-language tool called "lint" or "PC-lint" has a similar purpose.

common characteristic that they all focus on evaluating a system as a whole with respect to its non-functional characteristics. Some of the more common architectural tests are summarized in Table 13-1.

Table 13–1   **Standard Architectural Tests**

Type of Test	What It Does
Load Test	Evaluates a system's behavior under conditions of heavy use. This test is normally intended to evaluate system degradation based on loading.
Performance Test	Evaluates system performance under specific conditions of use or load. This test is normally used to verify that a system's response time meets application guidelines or requirements.
Security Test	Verifies that a system meets established guidelines for crucial elements of security: authentication, authorization, encryption, non-repudiation and auditing support. This type of test also checks for system and data vulnerability.
Stress Test	Evaluates system behavior and performance degradation as the loading increases. This is often used to identify the breaking point for a system.
Usability Test	Validates that a system conforms to user expectations and requirements for effective use. Though this can be considered an architectural test, it is usually conducted using black box techniques.

Notice that load, performance and stress testing use similar techniques, but measure different system characteristics. These three kinds of tests are often used in tandem to provide measures of system availability, performance and reliability.

Roles and Responsibilities for Testing

Developers are from Mars, Testers are from Venus

There's a substantial amount of literature that suggests that testing is most effective when performed by developers, testers and users. Each group brings a different perspective that tends to make certain types of testing easier. Programmers, designers and architects are strongly focused on application development. They're associated with coding and integrating the parts of a software product, and may even have been involved in design. This makes them effective at tests that involve the direct evaluation of code structure and performance, including most forms of white box testing. In addition, software designers and architects tend to be well-qualified to perform higher-level integration and architectural tests.

End users represent the best authority on how the product is perceived and how it is "supposed" to work. As the intended audience for a software product, they normally have a vision of how it should behave. In most projects, users don't have a lot of direct involvement with software internals. Instead, they're focused on functional requirements and practical use of the software. This makes them ideal candidates for activities such as alpha, beta and user acceptance testing. They're also excellent candidates for usability testing.

Testing professionals are experts in the field of product evaluation and assessment. As such, they're ideally suited for most forms of black-box testing, and for many kinds of architectural testing as well. Testers are also excellent authorities on test evaluation. They're often the best choice to plan the overall testing effort, to manage metrics and to help determine when testing has been successfully completed. Table 13-2 summarizes the forms of testing commonly performed by each of the three groups.

Table 13–2   **Development roles and the kinds of testing they do best**

Role	Effective Types of Testing
Developers	**White-box**: Static and dynamic tests, including unit, integration, smoke and regression testing **Architectural**: most forms of testing, though usability tests are often more effective when performed by users
Testers	**Black-box**: most forms of testing, especially exploratory and risk-based testing **Architectural**: most forms of testing
Users	**Black-box**: Alpha, beta and user acceptance tests **Architectural**: usability tests

Given the definitions above, we can better define testing responsibilities of software developers. What can we do to support the overall testing process? Basically, there are three things that software developers can do to support testing:

1. Developers should perform the types of testing they do best as part of normal product development. At a minimum, development teams should perform both static and dynamic white-box tests.
2. Developers should write code that is easier for others to test. This is more complex than the previous concept, and implies that the team should do the following:
   • develop an architecture and design that promotes testability
   • define an application so that it provides explicit test points[140]
   • build explicit testing behaviors and methods into code
3. Developers should help integrate their test results. They should ideally provide output from their tests in a form that can be easily incorporated with the work done by testing professionals. It's especially important to be able to associate metrics with all forms of testing, to provide a good indication of test completeness.

---

140. Practically speaking, defining clearly defined test points implies promoting code modularity.

If It Were Easy, We'd All Be Doing It. What Makes Testing Hard in Java?

When it comes to testing, every programming language offers a tradeoff—some language features promote testing, and some make testing more difficult. Naturally, Java technology is no exception. We begin by talking about general object-oriented language features, and progress to capabilities that are specific to Java technology.

The very features that make object-oriented languages attractive for developers both help and hinder testing. Advanced object-oriented features such as inheritance and polymorphism tend to increase testing requirements because there's so much room to misuse the concepts. Misuse of a language feature can often cause substantial problems in an application during runtime.

It's well-documented that OO languages support a wide variety of ways to reuse existing code. However, code reuse doesn't eliminate the need to retest code. In fact, it usually suggests a need for increased integration testing. Even if the component itself remains unchanged, the context is different when it is reused. This requires you to completely re-test a component if you want to verify its behavior when it is used in a new system.

Object-oriented languages also support a greater degree of modularity than many other languages. This is another characteristic that works both for and against testing. While modularity itself promotes testability, the increased complexity can offset the benefit. Typically, designers compensate for the drawbacks of increased complexity by organizing their code hierarchically, building classes into components and components into subsystems.

The interface is a Java language feature with the potential to support the testing effort. Interfaces provide an excellent way to decouple functional definition and implementation. When used properly, this can provide a good way to manage test points formally within your system. They can be easily associated with stub code and test harnesses, allowing you to more easily test parts of your system in isolation.

In addition to its object-oriented features, Java provides a number of higher-level technologies that support reuse. Examples include complex APIs (such as Swing), component APIs (Servlets, EJBs) and frameworks (J2EE). While these technologies provide substantial value to Java developers, they also present greater challenges to testing. Higher-order reuse technologies abstract a more complex infrastructure, making it available to a programmer through a smaller, more manageable group of classes and interfaces. Of course, a programmer still has to know quite a bit about a technology in order to use it properly. If developers don't adequately understand the APIs that they intend to use, there's a risk that they will incorrectly apply them, causing non-obvious errors during runtime. The result—you have to test the component's integration with the complex system more carefully if you want to identify problems caused by misuse of an API or framework.

A further challenge comes from the fact that technologies such as component APIs must be run within a code framework or container. To effectively test such code, you must be able to evaluate it within its intended runtime environment. Ideally, you want to test the code in the same environment that will be used during runtime. If that's not possible, you need to emulate the framework or container if you want to properly test your component. The obvious downside is that there's more setup and configuration work required to manage your tests. What's more, it can be difficult to evaluate your test results if you're running your code inside of a container.

If you're developing a high-level API or framework from scratch, you need to be especially diligent in your testing. In general, any code that is intended for frequent reuse requires a thorough test cycle that includes both success and failure scenarios, in order to provide confidence that it will perform properly under conditions or use and misuse.

Testing Practices

If you believe in the value of testing during software development, the next reasonable question is how to manage the testing process. This is actually a two-part question. How can you make testing a part of your standard development process? How can you organize and structure tests in your system to maximize the return on investment of your time and effort? We answer both questions in the sections that follow.

How to "Institutionalize" Testing

How can a team make testing a standard part of their software development process without it disrupting their work? For most groups, the real challenge lies in integrating dynamic tests. Most software development teams are fairly comfortable performing static white box tests as a regular part of software development. Frequent, incremental compilation tests, validation tests and compile checks are usually a standard part of software development. Periodic code reviews require some discipline from the team, but are also fairly easy to institutionalize as a part of a software project.

Dynamic testing is generally more of a challenge. Unlike static testing, it's usually harder to formally set down rules for your tests. Metrics for completeness and correctness are notoriously hard to pin down. These days, there are two general approaches used to incorporate dynamic testing in the development process: **test-driven development** and **design for testability**.

Test-Driven Development (TDD)

Test-driven development (TDD) has been popularized as a best practice associated with agile software methods. Specifically, it owes a great deal of popularity to eXtreme

Programming and the work of Kent Beck. Since TDD is readily adaptable to any software development methodology, it's become common throughout the industry.

The basic tenants of TDD are straightforward and easy to apply at a grass-roots coding level. It is essentially a "bottom-up" process for test integration.[141] Applied in its most pure form, TDD requires you to test your code—all of your code—as you create it. You accomplish this goal by developing tests before you write code for a feature. The basic process is as follows:

1. Design a test for a new capability or feature.
2. Run the test and ensure that it fails.
3. Code the minimum functionality to ensure the test succeeds.[142]

You repeat this series of steps throughout your development cycle. There are a number of obvious advantages to this approach. First, it requires you to think about tests up front, as you write your code. Second, it ensures that at any given moment, you have full dynamic test coverage for all of your code features. Finally, the practice of TDD focuses on producing code errors, then correcting the source of failure. This is significant. By focusing tests on practical problems caused by code features, TDD helps ensure that the tests will be related to meaningful error scenarios.

There's a common misconception that TDD covers "all" of the testing for a project. As mentioned, TDD as a practice is focused on dynamic white box testing. It's an extremely effective way to support unit and integration tests. TDD is a developer-focused test model, and doesn't explicitly promote or advocate support for other forms of testing. It doesn't formally set down what you should test in your code, or how you should check for code failure. This means you should be a bit cautious about how you evaluate test completeness, since it only ensures that you have test coverage—TDD does not formally or explicitly define what you should check in your tests. If you aren't careful about how you apply TDD, you can write tests for all of your methods but miss code failure scenarios. The success of TDD is partially dependent on an understanding of how code can break in the first place—the "failure modes" we discussed in Chapter 6. The XP practice of pair programming, combined with test code reviews and mentoring, helps you ensure adequate test coverage.

---

141. This does *not* imply that TDD can only be performed at the unit test level, Indeed, the process can be very effectively applied to integration tests. TDD tends to cause tests to be developed as the code is created, which often means that it is developed along with low-level code functions and built "up" to higher-level modules.

142. An additional concept of TDD is integration with a standardized test tool to automate test execution. Though it isn't a formal part of the process, it is usually considered central to test-driven development. Later in the chapter we talk about JUnit as a commonly-used tool for TDD.

Design for Testability

Design for testability has never been formalized as a process, in part because it's so dependent on the forms of testing you plan to use for a project. Design for testability basically advocates formally planning for tests as part of the OOD process. This means that a team creates test methods, harnesses and code integration points along with application code. It also implies that developers explicitly write their code to support black box as well as white box tests. At its foundation, design for testability is quite simple:

1. Establish testing requirements as part of software project analysis.
2. Develop test code as part of the standard OOD process along with the application code.

As you can see, design for testability tends to be especially well-suited to structured development methodologies. Tests are usually organized around use cases or business functions. For this reason, it can generally be characterized as a "top-down" process—tests are planned using the business model and then carried down to code. A benefit of this process is that tests can be made to integrate fairly easily with black box tests that are more directly meaningful to end users. Formal test planning often makes it easier to coordinate test metrics as well, improving the odds that you can comprehensively evaluate test completeness in a project.

One of the greatest drawbacks of design for testability comes from the fact that it's so planned and regimented. If not properly managed, this approach cannot easily accommodate change within a project. It takes careful planning to ensure that tests will be dynamic enough to handle fundamental changes in test strategy. For this reason, some teams choose to base their systems around good foundational OO principles that naturally tend to contribute to testability, rather than planning for tests during OOD. An obvious advantage of such an approach is that it can be standardized within the development process and subsequently adapted to testing requirements. At the foundation, a few basic software development principles tend to dramatically improve testability.

1. **Modularization or componentization of code.** This makes it possible to isolate units and segment that must be tested.
2. **Use of encapsulation and interfaces.** This provides defining limits on what's accessible outside a component and, therefore, limits the component's test points.
3. **Definition of services.** This qualifies the software to test, making it easier to relate components to meaningful business behavior.
4. **Definition of methods to capture state and flow.** These methods can subsequently be flexibly adapted for use in a variety of contexts, including test harnesses and frameworks.

Bridging the Gap between Unit and Integration Testing

Regardless of the approach you use to incorporate testing with development, there comes a point when you have to make a transition between unit and integration tests. This is typically an awkward time for a project. It naturally implies a shift in emphasis and therefore in priorities and requirements. Three of the most common challenges are listed below:

1. Integration tests usually require modules from different developers to be combined. As a result, variations in coding style and test support become much more significant during testing.

2. Abstraction and encapsulation increasingly become a factor in your tests, hiding parts of your underlying system. Although this can be a good thing, you have to be careful to ensure that you focus some effort on testing the implementation of your system. If not, there's a risk that they can introduce unpredictable "glitches" into your system.

3. Context and order of invocation play an increasingly important role in dictating how—or whether—code works. Because of this, you have to put more thought into how you organize and conduct tests, and you usually have to spend more effort managing test method sequence.

Ultimately, an effective integration test depends on the low-level stability of its classes and components. Therefore, unit tests can be viewed as a prerequisite for effective integration testing. This leads to an interesting question: what kind of association, if any, should exist between your unit and integration tests? Generally speaking, you can define the association in your project as a point along a spectrum, as shown in Figure 13-1.

The results of your decision are predictable. As you increase integration test dependency on unit tests, you tend to encourage the need for a formal testing framework or some way to manage test integration more easily. Codependency also promotes code reuse, which tends to reduce development time for your integration tests.

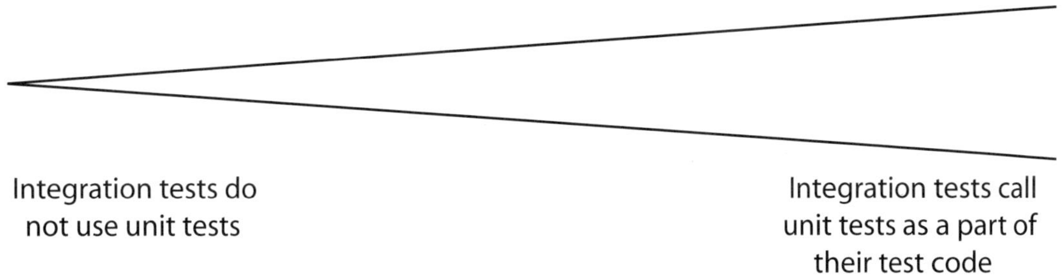

Integration tests do
not use unit tests

Integration tests call
unit tests as a part of
their test code

Figure 13-1
Relationship between Unit and Integration Tests.

Of course, you have to wait until your unit tests are complete and stable to actually perform integration tests with this approach. If you choose close association between your tests, you must be even more careful to verify completeness of your unit tests. Since they provide a foundation for higher-order testing, a minor omission of unit tests can have serious consequences for a project.

At the other end of the spectrum, you can manage testing models independently of each other. While you can develop your integration tests at the same time as unit tests, you have to build them from scratch. This ultimately increases the time you have to spend on testing unless you automate test creation.

How to Organize and Structure Testing

Regardless of the approach you use to integrate tests with your software, you'll need to define a strategy for test design and integration. Where will you put test code, and how will you design your white box tests? For the question of test organization, there are two conflicting principles at work. On one hand, you'd prefer to reuse test code throughout development. Potentially, you might even use it to perform debugging after your software has been released. On the other hand, you'd like to avoid choosing an approach that causes code to become bloated, harder to understand and maintain. Figure 13-2 shows some standard locations for test code.

As you can see, the choice of code location involves a tradeoff between level and modularity. Though it may not be immediately obvious, a team's decision can have far-reaching consequences in a project. Beyond the impact on testability, the choice of

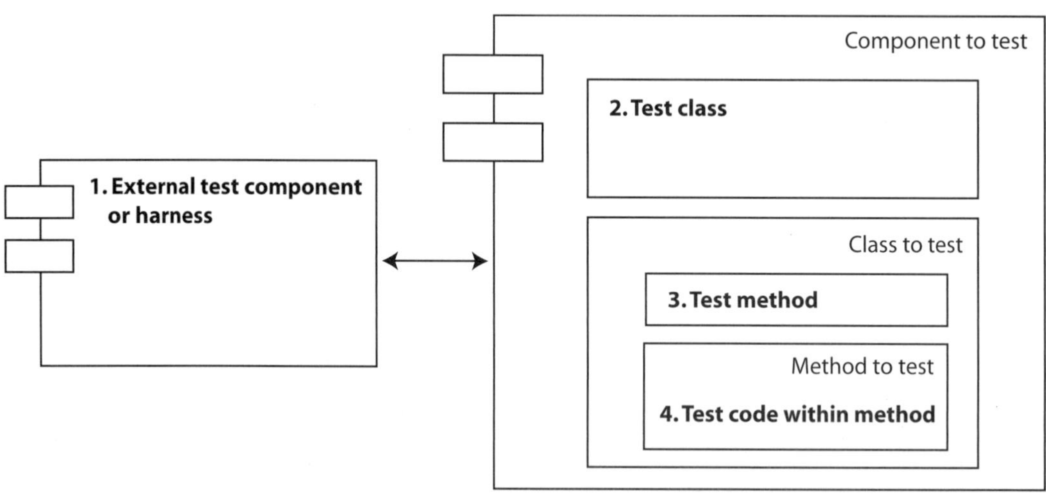

Figure 13–2
Choices for Test Code Integration.

how to structure test code impacts such features as reuse, manageability and maintainability. It's even possible for global characteristics such as application performance to be affected by a team's choice.

Now that we've talked about where you might put your tests, think about what we should test. At the foundation, dynamic white box tests should verify code correctness. Tests should verify that state and flow of code behave according to expectations, given standard conditions of input and use. Two less obvious testing objectives are code consistency and exception model behavior. For consistency, you need to verify that results remain as expected when some part of a system is used in context. For the exception model, you need to ensure that you fail predictably that the exception model works the way you want it to. Both goals tend to become more vital as you move "upward" toward integration testing. How should you design your dynamic white box tests? Fundamentally, all testing is based around behavior—you'll need to write one or more methods to test your software. However, the way that you organize and manage your tests depends on a few basic design choices. Apart from code level, there are four key ingredients that go into test code design.

1. Modularization

Modularization refers to the association between your test code and the code you want to test. **Code-resident tests** are bundled with your source code—the tests become a part of your system. They're generally useful when you want to establish a standard baseline check for code stability that can be used after software deployment.[143] **Separate tests** exist independently of your codebase. They typically test your system's calling interface, though they can also be temporarily bundled with application code to test your non-public implementation.[144] Separate test modules are used to integrate with test frameworks and to perform higher-level integration testing. Some Java-based test systems link to separate test modules through interfaces for greater flexibility.

It's become popular to see teams modularize their test code in recent years. Test modularization offers the benefit of code independence—it's easier to modify tests and test structure without affecting the overall stability of your product. You can even remove tests written as separate classes or components during runtime, allowing you to address concerns about the impact they might have on performance. Test methods, classes and components can also be more easily standardized within a project. You can create standard interfaces to enforce unit test in your projects. Test classes or

---

143. It's common to provide code-resident tests to support post-release debugging in a system.
144. In object-oriented systems, private members of a class can only be directly evaluated by code-resident tests. Protected and package-private elements can also be checked by separate test modules, provided they're included in subclasses or in the same package. In such cases, classes can be bundled with the system during testing and easily removed during runtime.

components can likewise be based around standard classes or interfaces, providing easier integration into testing frameworks.[145]

2. Mode of Interaction

The mode of interaction describes the way tests are run, and their effect on application runtime. Tests are either active or passive, and may additionally be preemptive. **Active mode tests** are ones that you explicitly invoke—you call specifically designed test methods to run your code. Because they aren't part of your regular application flow, active mode tests must be called by some coordinating code, usually another method or test harness. **Passive mode tests**, on the other hand, generate test information indirectly, as part of your regular runtime. There's a way to disable passive mode tests in code, either through a compiler option or runtime switch. **Preemptive test code** halts runtime execution when conditions are violated. In Java, this would usually be done by throwing an exception or error.[146]

3. Test Code Observables

Test code observables represent the output produced as a result of test execution. They may be directly provided to the user as method output, or be indirectly available as logged information. There are four basic types of data you can provide when running tests:[147]

- **Boolean**: a test represents pass/fail data or healthy/unheathly state.
- **State**: a test returns data for all or some part of a system, at varying levels of abstraction.
- **Flow**: a test provides sequence of method invocation, with or without calling arguments.
- **Exception or error**: a test generates an error condition if the system violates core requirements.

Boolean output provides an easily managed check on system stability or health. State and flow-based observables present you with a way to track the changes in a system as it runs. Some systems allow you to selectively filter the data provided by these methods. Some qualify flow by including calling arguments with the logged data. This

---

145. It's fairly rare to see testing encouraged inside of a method. While it's easy to develop and run such tests, they can't be effectively standardized or managed within a project. What's more, they effectively rule out test reuse—tests can only be run within their method.

146. Another alternative for some software systems would be to force the VM to halt by calling the `System.exit()` method. The drawback for this approach is that it doesn't provide explicit information about the reason for runtime termination.

147. Of course, more complex testing systems may wrap several pieces of data in a common object. Additionally, some tests may present "before-after" data, or perform basic data analysis. The four categories refer to basic types of information that are commonly sent during testing.

lets you see the data associated with flow in a system. Exceptions or errors provide a way to support code-resident, preemptive tests. Additionally, if they are triggered through assertions, errors can easily be removed from your codebase during runtime.

4. Testing Strategies

The final part of test design is the most fundamental—the test strategy itself. Strategies describe what type of testing you plan to perform in a system. They govern the code that you write, and can be used as a guide to determine when test design is complete. We talk about some common strategies for white box testing, describing their intended focus and design. Bear in mind that most development teams use a combination of strategies to test their code. For example, they may provide methods to check component state and coordinate the use of the methods through behavioral tests. They may additionally make limited use of invariants for crucial failure conditions in their code.

Behavioral testing evaluates a system's core behavior. At the foundation, this type of testing usually checks for correct order of invocation (flow) and key data elements (state) as a method is run. Behavioral tests are often designed around use cases or services. Another simple form of behavioral test directly evaluates application flow by recording method entry and exit. TDD is based around a more general form of behavioral testing that you could think of as **feature-driven testing**—for each new behavior (or "feature") you develop in code, you design a test. Projects that use UML diagrams often base their behavioral tests around use case, sequence, collaboration and activity diagrams.

State-based testing verifies that data behaves according to your expectations during runtime. Tests verify that state transitions occur only when they are supposed to and only in meaningful ways. A simple form of state-based method indicates resource "health" when it is called—it performs a state continuity check of an object or component. Since you frequently make this type of check multiple times in your code, you often write encapsulate this type of test in a method. A more detailed test provides a snapshot of state at a given moment in time, returning a summary of data to the caller.[148] A third type of test compares state over time, evaluating the delta to ensure that a system remains stable. More advanced state-based tests usually have to be qualified according to application flow, and often require higher-level, coordinating code. You can use state transition diagrams or collaboration diagrams to guide development of state-based tests.

Invariants represent a more detailed test strategy. They provide a test of state based around key occurrences during system runtime. In a sense, you can view them as state-based tests qualified according to method or system behavior. These tests are based around the five standard types of invariants.

---

148. Many systems plan for state-based test support by providing one or more getter methods for key system data.

Internal: an assumed outcome for method-level behavior, such as an if-else structure that checks for a range of values.
Control-flow: a location you assume will not be reached in a method, such as a try-catch block that you always expect to return to the caller.
Precondition: a behavioral or state condition that must be true on method entry.
Postcondition: a condition that must be true when a method completes.
Class: a condition that must always be true throughout an object's lifetime.

Invariant testing usually requires substantial forethought and planning. Because they can involve a substantial effort, you may see invariants limited to certain crucial methods or objects in a system. They typically tend to be managed as a part of structured system analysis. For example, you might see results for a method organized in a table like the one in Table 13-3.

Table 13–3   **Managing Invariants in a Project**

	State	Behavior
Internal		
Control-flow		
Preconditions		
Postconditions		
Class		

Risk-based tests focus state and behavioral evaluation on key "trouble spots" within code. Since they depend on identifying key risk factors in the first place, they have traditionally been managed as a part of black-box testing. However, the practice of failure mode analysis we described in Chapter 6 helps you identify key trouble spots in your code. Applied during development, failure modes represent the key technology-based risks for your tests.[149] Risk-based tests must usually be customized according to the type of risk, so they're harder to design than other types of testing.

Exception model testing involves ensuring that failure scenarios in code cause expected, controlled results. These tests have been largely ignored during much of the history of software development. Basically, we'd like to ensure that the system performs as expected for cases that should result in code failures as well as success. At the simplest level, this involves simulating errors through invalid inputs and verifying that the failure scenarios are appropriately managed within code. Managed this way,

---

149. There's still substantial value in performing black-box risk assessment, since a testing professional will bring a different perspective to the problem of risk analysis and will tend to check different failure modes for an application.

exception model testing can use the same infrastructure as behavioral testing, so it doesn't have to require a substantial amount of additional effort.

J2SE 1.4 provides assertions to help you standardize exception-based testing. The assertions feature allows you to easily convert a problem in code into the standard AssertionError, halting code when a problem occurs. If you additionally need to preserve detailed exception information, you can wrap the original exception or error in a standard exception class. This is especially effective when you want to standardize the exception you throw within a test harness.

Tactics & Technologies: How Do You Manage and Run Tests?

We're fortunate that software engineering has taken some major strides forward in the field of test management. A decade ago, we had little choice but to rely on test code written from scratch. Today, we have a number of freeware technologies and tools that support a variety of software test strategies. Commonly used test management methods include homegrown tests, test frameworks, Integrated Development Environments (IDEs), and benchmarks.

Homegrown Tests

Homegrown tests provide you with the ultimate degree of freedom for the white box tests you perform. You can implement any of the testing strategies we've talked about using test code you create from scratch. Of course, it takes much more planning to manage tests, since there's no infrastructure for them. If you want test standardization, you have to build your own test classes and interfaces. If you want to run tests independently of your application code, you have to develop your own test harness. You can manage tests using a number of techniques, since you can use any conveniently available API. A few commonly used technologies for output generation include:

- **Logging:**[150]
  You can perform logging using I/O, the logging API or methods from a component API.[151] An advantage of this approach is that it's easy to provide fine-grained, customizable control. Additionally, some APIs (the logging API) are easy to disable or filter.

---

150. Traditionally, legacy code has also used `System.out` or `System.err` for testing. These methods are not generally recommended, since they aren't easily portable or configurable in software systems.
151. One example includes the `java.servlet.GenericServlet` method `log(String msg)`.

- **Standard method output:**
  Methods that are designed to provide standard output are extremely flexible. As with logging, it's fairly easy to provide fine-grained, customizable control.
- **Exceptions or errors:**
  Part of the role of the exception model is to provide early, preemptive warning of problems within a system. As such, exceptions and errors are a good incidental source of test data. As previously mentioned, they're well-suited to passive mode, code resident, preemptive tests.
- **Assertions:**
  A flexible extension of exception and error capability, assertions are preemptive with additional ability to selectively enable them during runtime. This makes them effective lightweight vehicles for more in-depth, comprehensive code evaluation models.

There is basically only one case where you must use homegrown tests—when you want to directly test the private members of a class. Beyond that, you can effectively use them any time you want to provide code-resident test support. Common examples include state or flow reporting, system health checks or baseline stability tests for a product. This type of test is also often used for post-release test support and integration with other types of testing. Homegrown tests may be modularized, and are sometimes designed so that they can be selectively enabled.

Test Frameworks

A testing framework is a software system designed to explicitly support one or more types of testing. Frameworks are typically used to partially automate black or white box test techniques. Many of these products support test management and automation, making it easier to organize, manage and run a series of tests. Frameworks effectively make regression testing practical for complex systems.

When you use a test framework, you write code that integrates with the product. This usually means that your test code must conform to the model set down by the framework. It's possible that this may constrain your test code, or limit the integration you can perform with other testing models. Depending on their design, frameworks may require code-resident tests, or support modular test classes.

Today, test frameworks are available as both commercially available and freeware products. Commercial products normally support a wide range of test activities and models—it's common to see products that allow you to perform a range of black and white box tests, up to and including architectural testing. Additionally, such products often automate test runs and metric collection. They're sometimes associated with tools to perform numeric or statistical analysis, and they may even integrate with project management software.[152]

---

152. Because the array of products is in constant flux, I don't feel qualified to single out a specific tool. An excellent source of information is the testing Web site, http://www.stickyminds.com.

Probably the single most popular freeware Java testing framework is a product called **JUnit**. Part of the reason for its success is the fact that JUnit is used to support test-driven development. TDD implicitly requires the support of a tool to automate testing, and JUnit was designed to meet that need.[153] The framework provides support for white-box testing, specially focusing on unit and integration tests. It's a fairly open test framework, allowing you to automate something as simple as a single test method, or something as complex as a multithreaded, multi-pass sequence of tests.

The Apache Software Foundation has also been active in the development of testing frameworks. Two notable projects have been developed to test Java Web applications: Cactus and JMeter. **Cactus** provides a framework for managing J2EE unit tests with Java Web technologies. The project implements an in-container test model, extending your existing runtime environment to accommodate JUnit-style test cases. Cactus was explicitly developed to support the automation of integration tests—to test the interaction between J2EE components. **JMeter** is a product designed for architectural testing of Web applications. It was specifically designed to manage load testing and performance evaluation, though it can also be used to manage regression testing.[154] JMeter can be associated with your servers (locally or remotely), automate queries, and collect data on performance and response under conditions of load.

HttpUnit is another commonly used test framework hosted on SourceForge. It's primarily a black box framework used to test Web applications. Unlike the other frameworks, HttpUnit emulates browser behavior, allowing you to simulate client interaction with a Web server and compare your output against an expected result. Since this test famework emulates software, you may well need to expand testing for your supported browsers prior to release.[155]

IDEs

Originally designed to promote visual programming, IDEs have matured considerably over the past few years. Java IDEs are an excellent example of the progress that visual programming tools have made in recent years. One of the most useful developments to programmers (based on our current discussion) has been the integration of testing and debug capabilities. Today, many IDEs integrate easily with testing frameworks, providing an easy way for developers to leverage test capabilities. Since IDEs primarily exist to standardize and automate programming tasks, the test tools tend to support white box or limited architectural tests.

---

153. JUnit is actually an implementation of the more generic XUnit testing framework. There are a number of XUnit implementations to support other programming languages. JUnit was developed by pattern and programming luminaries Erich Gamma and Kent Beck, and is hosted on the freeware project site SourceForge.
154. You can optionally include assertions in your JMeter tests to verify that you receive the results that you expect from a Web application.
155. There have been substantial differences in browser technologies, and in Web server capabilities, over the years. As a consequence, it's prudent to test application capabilities over a number of browsers to identify potential compatibility issues as early as possible.

Two popular open source Java IDEs are Eclipse and NetBeans. Both products are based around a "pluggable" architecture—you can add modules to your base IDE to extend the tool capabilities. As you might expect, both tools have standard plug-ins to support JUnit

In addition to test integration, IDEs typically provide debugging capabilities to developers. Though IDE debugging tools can be used to support the overall testing effort, they weren't ever intended to support structured, repeatable testing. As you might expect, these tools are really more helpful when you want to observe runtime health, or drill down to specific, focused problems. You can use them for localized, case-by-case evaluation of invariants or boundary checks. They typically don't allow you to record these checks or repeatedly run them in support of regression testing.

Benchmarks

Benchmarks are typically designed to measure the architectural characteristics of a system. The most common tests measure load, system performance, and capacity. To a lesser extent, tests may profile characteristics like system reliability and availability. By their nature, benchmarks tend to be generic, based around certain core assumptions of technology or resource use. For this reason, benchmarks normally provide only a rough estimate of a system's performance. It's common to see them used to evaluate hardware, system infrastructure, or the performance of server software, given a certain scenario. The J2EE performance benchmark ecPerf provides an example of a common software benchmark that can potentially be used for architectural testing.[156]

When Is Testing "Done"?

General Testing Metrics

Perhaps the hardest question to answer about testing is when it should be considered complete. It's even harder to qualify this question for black box testing, since tests usually don't directly tie into the codebase. In part, a satisfactory answer depends on having clarity about precisely what testing is supposed to accomplish. Testing, especially high-level application-wide black box testing, must ultimately be conducted with a clearly established set of goals. The criteria can subsequently be used to establish and maintain a useful set of metrics that provides a rough indication of completeness, perhaps even of progress toward a goal. Traditionally, testers have defined and man-

---

156. As always, the most meaningful evaluation of a system's architectural characteristics comes from the direct evaluation of the system itself. Any benchmark only provides a rough estimate of a system's operating characteristics, since it will probably *not* duplicate the operations that you will perform in your system.

aged such metrics. A few commonly-used ways to check for testing completeness include:

1. **Raw coverage metrics:**
   This metric measures completeness based on the percentage of code, functions, use cases, or scenarios tested. It tends to be one of the easier elements to measure, and is frequently used by project teams to estimate completeness.

2. **Bugs found over time:**
   This metric is tied into product debugging, since it involves identifying discrepancies within a system. As a result, test completeness is usually identified by a roll off in reported bugs, either in specific code functions or in bugs of a certain severity.

3. **Risk-based metrics:**
   This model bases test assessment on coverage of identified "risk areas." It's based on categories identified by risk assessment techniques. Typically, completeness is based around raw coverage or bug-based metrics based around specific risk categories.

4. **User acceptance criteria:**
   This metric bases test success on customer satisfaction. This metric usually involves a measure of project completeness based on user acceptance testing.

5. **Mutation metrics:**
   This is one of the most complex metrics. It's usually based around bug-related metrics combined with controlled introduction of errors into the codebase. If a system has a low incidence of reported bugs and is able to identify the new errors, a project is considered to be complete.

Of course, plenty of organizations manage their testing without metrics at all. For better or worse, some groups scope their test efforts around project management parameters such as fixed schedule or budget. In situations such as these, testers must make the best possible use of the available time and budget and perform tests that will provide the greatest possible coverage, cover all the crucial risk areas, or find the most bugs within the allotted time frame.

Developer Testing Metrics

On the surface, it seems easier to define "success" for black-box testing. The key advantage is that a team can qualify its tests in terms of the codebase. After all, it's possible to get a rough estimate of unit test coverage by looking at your code. If you have a way to test every key behavior in a system, you know that there's basic test coverage, right?

Actually, there are a couple of problems with that perspective. First, code is never run in isolation, and the context of invocation has a significant impact on the way that code runs. The behavior of a method often cannot be fully tested until it's used as part of a component. Raw coverage metrics often ignore this fundamental reality. More importantly, such metrics provide no guarantee that tests check for all significant error scenarios. As a result, you must be cautious not to associate too much importance with the amount of code covered. One advantage of using coverage evaluations for unit tests and integration tests is that the results can be easily merged with other testing metrics. In other words, it becomes easier to correlate black box and white box tests.

What other metrics can you use for white box tests? Of course, there's no perfect way to evaluate *true* code coverage. In many cases, a team has to compromise by providing the greatest assurance possible with limited time and resources. Static metrics provide a good baseline for completeness.

- Compilation tests to check general code conformance
- Build tests, which test for system-wide compatibility
- Static integration tests to check for complex component dependencies[157]
- Validation tests to verify detailed conformance to specifications

Beyond these checks, reviews of test code can provide a more in-depth check for completeness. An advantage of applying the code review process to test evaluation is that it can be adapted to your test strategy. For instance, if you build unit tests around invariants, you can base test reviews that are based around group evaluation of the invariants. The XP practice of pair programming is also invaluable in this regard. Ongoing evaluation by a peer can provide an excellent way to ensure that you're not overlooking obvious test cases.

Dynamic evaluation can often be based around coverage metrics, then extended to cover a team's specific test strategies. After all, each approach to test design is based around certain code assumptions; group evaluation of those assumptions is often as good a metric as any when trying to obtain a measure of completeness. Part of the beauty of TDD is that it tracks very closely with the development process. At any given time, if you're faithfully following the principles of TDD, your tests are up to date and consistent with your code.

---

157. Some consider these tests to be a subcategory of validation. The key difference is that static integration tests are project-specific and so cannot be easily automated for code validators.

chapter 14

Debugging

Introduction

One of the earliest recorded stories about software bugs comes from the journals of the renowned Admiral Grace Hopper. According to popular legend, she came into her office at Harvard University one day in 1945 to find that one of her computer operators had taped a moth into their log. Underneath it, scrawled in pencil, was the entry "First actual case of bug being found."[158]

Debugging is one of the most appropriate terms I know in software. When you think about it, bugs in an application are a lot like bugs in the real world: If you see one, there are probably a lot more hidden away somewhere in your code. Debugging is one of the hardest skills of software development to learn. In many ways, it seems to be more closely related to intuition than to logic. Even after many years of programming, it's practically impossible for most of us to define a series of steps that we go through when debugging code.

With that rather daunting reality in mind, our final chapter focuses on software debugging. We begin by talking about what bugs are and how they find their way into code. Following that, we discuss the foundation principles behind debugging—core skills for anyone who intends to effectively debug a system. We talk about a number of practical strategies you can use to help you debug a system. After that, we discuss various testing approaches that you can use in support of the debugging effort. We close by talking about a few special debugging challenges in Java—tasks that tend to be tricky or high risk.

---

158. The insect in question was retrieved between the points of relay #70 in panel F. This knowledge will hopefully help someone win a trivia contest some day.

Demystifying Debugging: "It's not a bug, it's a..."[159]

What's a bug? The simplest answer would be to say that a bug is anything in a software system that doesn't behave the way it's supposed to. Given that definition, debugging is the process of identifying the root cause of a bug—usually with the intent to fix your system and subsequently test it to ensure that your changes have resolved the problem. Debugging implies an understanding of both how a software product works and how it should work. What's more, it requires applied problem-solving skills so that you can trace a problem to its source based on observable symptoms and tests.

There are many different ways that software can be perceived as "broken," and so there are lots of ways that bugs can manifest themselves in code. Bugs can be represented by exceptions and errors propagated from your application to the user. This type of bug represents a problem for which you *already* have a detection mechanism, even if the handler code is buried somewhere deep within your code. What's more, exception-based bugs provide a starting point for developing a bug fix, since they're based on Java's preemptive notification mechanism.

Of course, you can also encounter more subtle bugs—bugs that don't necessarily cause an application to crash. Mistakes in code can lead to inaccuracies in your calculations that can only be observed indirectly, as discrepancies in data over time. Bugs can cause inconsistent behavior within an application, or short-circuit a part of your business process. These kinds of bugs tend to be harder to identify, track down and subsequently correct.

Of course, the problems we've mentioned are still based around problems within source code. They represent only one of many ways that bugs find their way into software. If debugging were just about the code you wrote, life would be a lot easier. If "bugs" were limited to directly observable failures that only occurred in your source code, it would be straightforward to identify and correct them. Unfortunately, life is rarely that simple. There are lots of ways for your system to fail, and many of them aren't directly related to your source code at all. Here are four categories of external problems that are often reported as bugs. If you have maintained a software product over any length of time, the odds are good that you have encountered a few bug reports related to these causes.

1. Misunderstandings about Desired Business Features

The act of software development implies a translation from the business domain to a software model. The success of software design depends in part on the ability to map business requirements into features of the software product. As anyone who has worked on an OOD project can tell you, this can be a difficult task. There can easily be misunderstandings about how a business process is supposed to work, or the way a

---

159. . . . feature, of course. *Everything* is a feature to someone.

technology should be used to fulfill business needs. What's more, a lot of business problems are not fully understood at the beginning of a software project. This becomes a major point of contention in projects, and a major source of bugs, of course.

2. Assumptions about Architectural Capabilities

Any software system is based around certain core architectural requirements. Ideally, these requirements are explicitly identified and incorporated as a part of the development process. No matter how architectural needs find their way into a software product, any system has limits in terms of its response time, maximum sustainable load, and so on. When you exceed the limits of a software system, the resulting behavior is often reported as a bug.

3. Limitations or Bugs in System Infrastructure

Most modern software is built on top of a substantial infrastructure. Whether your software uses an underlying protocol, framework or complex API, the value of "infrastructure reuse" is well established in our field. Unfortunately, there's no guarantee that the infrastructure you use will be perfect. It's entirely possible that weaknesses in the underlying framework will propagate up to your system. In such cases, problems in the framework are often classified as bugs in the software product itself.

4. The "No Code is an Island" Effect

Almost every application has complex dependencies in its codebase. Most modern systems integrate software, systems or services to provide more advanced functionality. Any code or system dependency requires your code to behave a certain way if it is to correctly use the target system. You can expect problems to surface in your code if it doesn't use the other API, framework or system correctly. This type of bug can be very hard to track down, since you may have to drill down into other software products to diagnose the problem. What's more, it's quite possible that such bugs will surface in some other part of code than the part that first produced the error, or at a different point during runtime.

Debugging Principles, Debugging Practices

Can anyone actually define the process of debugging? More to the point—can anyone do so in a way that will be consistently useful? There's no doubt that debugging tends to be one of the most highly complex and personalized activities in software development. You probably can't define how the process "should" work. There are a few foundation principles that tend to be important for *any* debugging effort, however.

Regardless of the specific approach you follow when you identify and locate a bug, you normally base your efforts around a core set of debugging requirements. Without them, you're essentially fumbling around in the dark. You may eventually be able to identify and correct bugs in your system, but it will be a random process, not terribly efficient or reproducible.

What are these principles? They're actually fairly simple—you may even consider them intuitively obvious. They are vital to the debugging process, however. In many cases, fundamental issues with bug location, identification and resolution trace back to deficiencies in one or more of these areas. The four key principles are:

1. Know your system.
2. Repeatability, repeatability, repeatability.
3. Understand the differences between the bug and your system.
4. Debugging usually requires testing.

1. Know your System

You can't effectively debug what you don't understand. Though seemingly self-evident, this principle requires you to have a surprising breadth of knowledge. In order to debug your system, you typically need to understand your application code, the system architecture, the problem domain and the failure modes of the system. Of course, you don't have to keep all of this information inside your own head. Effective debugging may require you to use documentation[160] or rely on subject matter experts.

2. Repeatability, Repeatability, Repeatability

It's virtually impossible to correct what cannot be reliably observed. Notice that this principle does *not* necessarily require a developer to reproduce a bug, though that's always helpful. At a minimum, you must be able to repeatedly observe the behavior that's been reported as a bug and collect data related to the error. Ideally, you should be able to follow an explicit series of steps to reproduce the problem.

3. Understand the Differences between the Bug and your System

If you don't understand how a reported bug differs from current system behavior, it's hard to identify the source of the problem or even know where to look for it. What's more, you won't really understand what changes you need to make to fix the problem—if and when you find it. At a basic level, this principle implies that you need the ability to observe a system and to compare its actual behavior with expected system behavior for the reported bug.

---

160. I'm a fairly typical engineer—documentation is usually my last resort. There's no denying the value of accurate, up-to-date documentation to support the debugging process.

4. Debugging Usually Requires Testing

Without some way to test your system, you're severely hampered when you perform debugging. If you can't interact with your application, you're an armchair detective, guessing about the nature of a problem. Although you can debug without this capability, it becomes vital when you need to evaluate the results of a bug fix within your system. Ideally, you can observe the state of the system and its infrastructure. You can introduce controlled input into the system, and observe the system's state and behavior during runtime. Finally, you can modify your codebase and observe the results of the changes you have made.

In addition to these principles, developers often use a few standard software tools to support debugging. Though teams differ on their exact debugging practices, most rely on a version control system, bug tracking system and testing tools.[161] A **version control system** (also called a source code management or software configuration management tool) stores and manages code versions. It's typically important for debugging because it makes it possible for a team to identify changes made to a system and to revert to earlier versions of code, if necessary. A **bug tracking system** is used to store and organize information about bugs; it allows teams to effectively track, prioritize and manage bug-related data over time. **Software testing tools**, such as IDEs, harnesses or frameworks, allow a development team to perform detailed evaluation of a system. Such tools ultimately make it possible for developers to identify bugs within code, to collect data from the system and to verify that changes to code have actually fixed a bug.

Debugging Strategies

A lot of books spend a substantial amount of time describing the debugging process. They present a series of steps that outline the "right" way to debug your code. I'm going to follow a slightly different approach in this book: a one-size-fits-all approach to debugging just doesn't seem to work, given the range of problems that you can encounter in a project. If I give you step-by-step directions to perform debugging, the process won't work for most of you. Debugging is very personalized and what works for me won't necessarily work well for you. What's more, I'd be lying if I told you I always use the same approach to debug my own code.

Most of the effective debugging that I've seen tends to boil down to the four principles we discussed earlier. Beyond those principles, developers use different techniques based on the kind of problem they're trying to solve. Most developers have a

---

161. Normally, bug tracking systems are the only software directly associated with testing. However, the other tools are often vital for the more in-depth debugging efforts, even if they're not explicitly identified as debugging requirements to begin with.

"debugging toolbox" with a number of different problem solving approaches they can use. So instead of describing a process, we discuss eleven strategies that you can follow when debugging a system. Hopefully, this will give you a head start as you develop your own debugging toolbox.

1. Reproduce the Bug

This technique is frequently used when a bug has been reported to a developer by a third-party source, such as a tester or end user. Basically, you try to identify a specific series of steps that repeatedly produce the bug. The benefit of this approach is that the act of reproducing a problem often provides insight into the actual cause of the failure. What's more, if you can combine the practice with application monitoring, you've got a good chance of finding the source of a bug in code. On the downside, this technique can be inefficient if you don't have a reasonably good idea of how the bug was produced in the first place. For this reason, this process is most effective if you have a solid staring point. The more detailed the information about how the bug was encountered, the easier it will be to recreate the scenario that led to the bug.

2. Test around the Bug

In this approach, you use focused black box test techniques to build a better understanding of the bugs in a specific product capability. It's an effective way to collect additional information if you have a general idea of the location in code, or the operation associated with a bug. This tends to be a useful way to get an idea of the extent of problems with a business function or risk area, if you're already know about one bug in a feature. This technique gives you good insight into the shortcomings of a particular part of your system, and so is more often used to measure stability of a product feature. It's frequently used to determine the extent of corrections required when a high priority bug has been identified.

3. Look for System Deltas

This approach involves comparing a system with the reported bug to one that doesn't exhibit the buggy behavior. In order to use this approach, you must be able to reliably reproduce the bug. What's more, you must have a healthy system to use for the comparison. Here are two commonly used approaches:

- **Compare between installed systems**: This approach uses the same software version, comparing a "sick" system to a "healthy" one. It's often used to identify problems with system installation, configuration or setup. It can also expose problems with the environment used to run the system, such as the operating system or JVM.[162]

---

162. You could argue that this technique actually tends to support troubleshooting rather than debugging. The distinction is a valid one, but often makes little difference when a developer is supporting software in production.

- **Compare between build versions**: This approach identifies changes in the codebase between software builds. It's a useful way to track down bugs that have been introduced as a result of code modifications.

Clearly, delta analysis depends on having an easy, reliable way to perform the comparison and to identify differences between two systems. If you can pinpoint the differences between the target and a healthy system, you've got a good start on tracing a problem to its source.

4. Narrow the Problem Scope

This debugging approach tends to be useful for systems that are highly modular, very complex, or organized around multiple tiers. Narrowing involves performing a series of tests that progressively zero in on a bug's location. Narrowing is based around the principle of layering in a system. If you base tests around services or business functionality, you're vertically narrowing. If your tests focus on protocols, servers or systems, you're horizontally narrowing.

There are two common approaches used for narrowing. **"In or out" testing** checks modules within a system, trying to determine whether the bug is produced in a given part of the system. By doing this, you progressively zero in on your bug. **Elimination testing** follows a slightly different approach. Instead of testing areas where a bug might be, it attempts to rule out large parts of the system as candidates for the bug. By doing this, you narrow the scope of the bug by ruling out services or subsystems.

Narrowing relies on a good understanding of your application code. What's more, you must be able to detect when a bug first manifests itself in a system. Without that understanding, you may be able to pinpoint the spot of visible code failure, but you won't necessarily know where the bug first occurred within the system.

5. Identify the "Point of Departure"

This technique is based around observing the system as it runs. It attempts to locate a bug by identifying the spot where a system's behavior deviates from the expected norm. If you plan to use this technique for debugging, you clearly need to have a *very* good understanding of the system and its behavior. In addition, it's difficult to use this approach effectively unless you have the ability to monitor application state and flow extensively. This often translates into detailed logging requirements, access to a high-level testing tool or the ability to dynamically monitor a system as it runs.

6. Brainstorm with a Group

In this approach, you get a bunch of people to help identify the cause of the bug. This approach can be effectively used with pair programming techniques, with a project team, or in conjunction with a user's group or special interest group. What's more, there are lots of ways that you can manage the brainstorming process. For example, you can easily incorporate a voting system with a group to determine how to proceed with debugging.

"Blue sky" brainstorming is typically managed as a single time-boxed session where any and all ideas from the group are collected and evaluated, used to guide future debugging activity. A more focused model is **"failure mode" brainstorming** , where group thinking is directed over time toward identifying possible causes of code failure, or tests for a bug. Clearly, any brainstorming session benefits from diversity of experience within a group. It has limited value if the group doesn't have product familiarity, or the group's experience is too narrowly focused.

7. Look for Reports of Similar Problems

If a system has been around for awhile, there may be a repository of reported bugs. This source of data can be exceptionally valuable to a developer. It can help you to identify possible causes of bugs, stimulate your thinking about ways to check your system, or even provide suggestions for fixes or workarounds. This approach obviously depends on the existence of a knowledge base with information about reported bugs for a product. For this reason, this technique is typically useful for commercially available products—programming languages, APIs, servers or frameworks.

8. Look for Patterns in System Behavior over Time

In cases where a bug can be repeatedly observed in a running system, you may be able to identify a link between the bug and something that's going on in the external environment. If a recurring problem is always associated with recognizable symptoms, they can often provide valuable clues about the underlying cause of a problem. This often involves looking beyond the application code itself, monitoring things like system load, business activity, or external process activity on a computer.

Profiling system behavior over time can also help you identify system problems that occur with broader scope. Many traditional debugging approaches are of limited value when trying to pinpoint problems associated with resource use or system saturation; analyzing system behavior can provide valuable insight into such areas. This approach clearly depends on a way to collect higher level data that what is traditionally available within an application. As a result, you must frequently rely on test harnesses, or tests for the operating environment, to collect such data.

9. Filter your System's Output

Sometimes, the principal challenge for debugging is that you have too much data generated by your system. Some software produces a great volume of information from many different sources—usually in a haphazard, disorganized form. This is especially true for enterprise software, where the application is often an aggregate of half a dozen different products. Effective analysis of data for these systems can be extremely challenging, since each subsystem typically has its own logging mechanism. Successful debugging in such cases often depends on removing extraneous information, then combining error data from each of the sources to build a composite picture of what's going on in the system. Since each subsystem may have its own way to represent data, you'll frequently have to interpret the data in the context of the entire software system.

10. Simulate System Behavior

Sometimes the best way to identify the source of a problem is to artificially reproduce the symptoms that led to the bug in the first place. This is a useful approach if the actions that produced the bug are well-documented but hard to trigger. It's also an effective way to work on a bug when you aren't able to directly test for the reported bug on an installed system. There are many different kinds of simulation that you can perform in a system. A few common examples include:

- direct API interaction simulation
- failure mode simulation
- user input simulation
- load simulation

An obvious advantage of simulation is that it makes it much easier for developers to vary the test conditions. When you've set up a system for simulation, it's usually easy to run a number of different scenarios and evaluate the system response. The principal drawback of this technique is that it normally takes some effort to set up a simulation. At a minimum, you typically need a testing tool or custom code to debug your system in this way.

11. Monitor the System

In cases where little is known about the cause of a bug, the best strategy may simply be to gather more information. This can be as simple as enabling logging within your system or increasing the level of logging detail. It can also be more involved, requiring you to use other technologies for data collection. In cases where the information available from the application isn't enough to diagnose a problem, you may need to perform additional system monitoring. There are two ways you might need to monitor your system. If you don't have enough detail about what's happening inside your application code, you can introduce a component to act as an information gatherer.[163] At a higher level, you may need to externally monitor your system as it runs, collecting data about CPU usage, thread state or network traffic. Monitoring helps you to supplement what you already know about a system's shortcomings. The principal

---

163. You can effectively use structures such as proxies or filters within your system to perform this function.

drawback of monitoring is that it usually requires additional setup work, and can impact the runtime efficiency of a software system.

Debugging Observables and Methods

At some level, all debugging techniques depend on the availability of data from the system. You ultimately need something that you can look at when trying to identify and locate defects. You can think of system observables in terms of how they are developed and used to support debugging.

User interface observables are those that can be seen from the "skin" of your system: bug-related data that can be directly observed by an end user. UI observables aren't usually considered the optimal way to collect or represent bug data. There are two major drawbacks that prevent them from being effectively used for debugging. First, it isn't convenient or easy to store the data associated with a system's UI. Barring screen capture technologies, it's difficult to enter information describing the bugs—the process tends to be time-consuming and error-prone. Second, the data provided from the system interface is by definition a translation of what's going on in the system. This means that there isn't always a straightforward link between the data and the underlying problems in the application.

Test observables represent a more popular source for debugging data. They represent data that can be directly obtained from system software, servers or infrastructure. When available, such data is normally directly relevant to software developers and the debugging process as a whole. The greatest drawback of test observables is that it may not be easy to get at the data, or to obtain it at the time or in the form required.

The sort of debug data produced from tests is widely varied. For testing the foundation of a system, you can often reuse the methods developed for unit and integration testing. As mentioned in the previous chapter, such methods typically provide you with data such as:

- health of a module, system or resource
- component or system state
- process or application flow
- data flow through a business process or application
- exceptions or errors produced during runtime

Beyond this set of observables, debugging may involve broader evaluation of an application's environment. In Java, this involves examining the runtime characteristics of the virtual machine. Examples include:

- memory and object use
- threads and thread state
- class or component versioning, capabilities and availability
- common resource health, loading and availability

Finally, some test observables focus on system infrastructure—the hardware, software and firmware that enables your application to run. This group of data is extremely broad, and includes things like:

- server health, loading or availability
- resource health, loading factors and activity
- CPU utilization, disk space
- operating environment: security, service availability, configuration
- network availability

How can you collect data about all these different types of observables? You can broadly categorize approaches according to level. Low-level approaches are typically static, code-resident data collection methods. Many of them use the same types of methods we talked about in the chapter on testing. Mid-level techniques are often based around dynamic, non-invasive testing within your system. Many of these solutions are built using patterns or pattern-based frameworks. High-level testing involves using other software or systems to check the environment around your code. This may involve running your system within a specially designed debugging environment, or running an independent process to periodically check parts of your system.[164] The following list highlights some common approaches to support debugging in Java. In the next section, we discuss each approach and how it can potentially be used to support debugging.

Low-level: Code-resident techniques
- Logging APIs
- Exceptions and errors
- Dedicated test methods

Mid-level: Pattern and framework techniques
- Collectors (passive data collection)
- Monitors (passive data monitoring)
- Emulators (active called behavior)
- Simulators (active calling behavior)

High-level: System techniques
- Architectural test methods and frameworks
- Infrastructure collection methods
- JPDA, the Java Platform Debugger Architecture

---

164. The distinction between testing levels is admittedly somewhat arbitrary. It seems reasonable to differentiate between method-based, pattern-oriented and external testing and collection. However, you might not associate each approach with a definite "level" of debug testing.

Low-Level Testing Techniques

1. Logging APIs or Systems

As we discussed in earlier chapters, Java now provides a standard API to support logging. In addition, open source projects such as Apache's log4j provide a good alternative for cases where you must run with an earlier generation JVM that doesn't have the Logging API.

Both APIs offer a number of advantages for debugging. They allow you to filter logging messages, ignoring messages below a defined level of severity. You can design a system that allows you to enable or disable debugging output, and adjust the volume of log messages produced. The APIs also allow you to control the amount of data reported, so you can develop applications that allow you to switch on "detailed debugging," if desired. Finally, the APIs give you flexibility in how you format the output, and where the data can be sent. Taken together, these features make logging APIs attractive for cases where you plan to provide test support in your code for long-term debugging.

The principal drawback for logging isn't related to the APIs themselves, but to the fact that they must be hard coded throughout your system if you want broad coverage. Unless you've been consistent in your logging, you can't handle debugging well—there will be sections of code without logging calls, and those sections will not be effectively testable.

If you *do* provide logging throughout an application, you often encounter another problem: it becomes harder to understand and maintain your code because of all the logging messages in your code. If you plan to use logging to support debugging, you must carefully design your application for code maintainability. This tends to steer you toward a modular, centralized logger for practical reasons of code maintainability.

2. Exceptions and Errors

In a sense, throwable objects represent the ideal way to support debugging. The kind of information that they provide is more or less exactly what you need: an error message, stack trace, and root cause exception. What's more, Java generates these objects only when there's an identified problem within the system.

Of course, there are a few drawbacks for the use of exceptions and errors in debugging as well. A lot of these drawbacks can be avoided by following the best practices we've described. At the foundation, you need to make sure that the really important exceptions are reported, and that the location (and reason) of code failure is readily available in the throwable object.

Handlers for exceptions and errors often use a logging API to record problems. When you log exceptions or errors, it's worthwhile to consider how to present the information effectively. You don't want to simply provide the exception name, or developers will have to guess when and how it was produced. On the other hand, you don't want to spit out an unqualified stack trace, or developers will have to sift through a mountain of data to determine what went wrong. To effectively use a throwable object for debugging, you usually have to evaluate data from its properties.

Exception message: Basically, you get out what you put in. If you add real information when generating an exception, the detail message can be enormously useful. If not, it will be virtually worthless.

Stack trace: In many cases, you're really only interested in a small subset of the call stack. Knowing the failure point in code is often enough to understand (or at least guess) about the problem. In a few rare cases, the next few levels in the stack provide a calling context and qualify how your code failed.

Root cause exception: In situations where you convert your exceptions, you may need to trace back to the exception that originally caused the failure. The usefulness of a root cause exception is often linked to how effectively you converted the exception to an understandable form in the first place. Ideally, the class type of the root cause is enough to provide context of a problem.

For exceptions that you create in your system, you must have the forethought to design them so that they will really be useful during debugging activities. Creating simple, "no-data" exceptions can be useful as a placeholder during development, but they actively hamper your progress when you subsequently try to debug your software.

For exceptions that are automatically generated by your code infrastructure, you need to effectively filter them and make them meaningful to developers. Without effective filtering, you'll have trouble sorting out the relevant exceptions from the ones that don't have real impact on your system. Without translation, you'll potentially be faced with trying to make sense out of a generic `RuntimeException`, `IOException` or `SQLException`.

Throwable objects have one key drawback: they're absolutely no use when you want to track down bugs in a system that doesn't actively cause code failure. If you're trying to find out why a calculation isn't accurate, you probably can't rely on your exception model to provide you with information.

3. Method-based Test Support

As we saw in the previous chapter, standard data-gathering methods provide a developer with a great deal of power to support testing. In many cases, it makes sense to create methods that check health, state and flow during testing. These methods are also a substantial benefit when you debug software, since they can be called at any time while a system runs. A lot of debugging techniques depend on having a flexible query capability for a system; data gathering methods give you low-level information any time you need it. What's more, such methods don't bog down your code when it runs – you can call them as needed to track down problems in code.

Unit and integration test methods can also be a great help during debugging. If they're well designed, they can provide you with a convenient way to drill down into your system and verify that it is running properly. Of course, you may have to explicitly "re-integrate" your test methods into your software. Some tests are independent of your code, so you have to load them into a system to use them for debugging. Explicitly designed unit and integration test methods usually fall into this category, since it's popular to modularize them for code maintainability.

Like the previous approaches, the effectiveness of this low-level technique during debugging depends to a large degree on how consistently you implement it within your system. Beyond that, you need some way to run the code. To effectively use any test methods for debugging, you have to coordinate their use in a system. To do this, many developers turn to the mid-level testing techniques: pattern or framework approaches that allow you to flexibly manage debugging calls within your system.

Mid-Level Testing Techniques

Sometimes you don't have the luxury of working with code-resident tests. Bugs don't just confine themselves to the parts of your code with dedicated logging or test methods, and it may be impractical to refactor your code to add such behavior. In these cases, you can benefit from the use of mid-level approaches: lightweight testing frameworks and design patterns can provide substantial benefit when evaluating a system.

There's a lot of diversity for this type of debugging support. Components can be simple or complex. They can be focused or quite broad in their coverage. They can be run independently, or integrated into a testing framework. Many mid-level techniques are based around dynamic modification—adding components to check your system while it runs. There's a lot of value in testing your code from the inside, and Java's dynamic class loading capability ensures that you don't have to recompile an application when you use these techniques.

Broadly speaking, you can classify mid-level test models as either passive or active. **Passive mode tests** observe system behavior while it runs; they don't actually perform direct API calls themselves—they simply watch your system. There are two kinds of passive test models: collectors and monitors.

A **collector** is a component that retrieves data from a system while it runs. It's typically used to check the state or flow of your system when business operations are performed. In many cases, it is implemented as a "pass-through" component which retrieves and logs data for the system. A collector doesn't act upon the data; it merely records what's going on. Collectors are often implemented using the Decorator, Proxy or Facade design patterns.

A **monitor** is typically introduced to "watch" parts of an application on an ongoing basis. Monitors usually check for things such as resource health or availability. They typically do not store ongoing information about the thing they observe; instead, they report if there's a problem. Most monitors have some measure to determine when the resource they're observing becomes unhealthy. When that happens, a monitor logs the problem, or it halts the system by throwing an exception or error. Some monitors are implemented as independent threads in an application, while others use filters or design patterns such as Facade.

Active mode tests plug into your software and evaluate your system's response to specific calling sequences or data values. Two common types of active tests are emulators and simulators. An **emulator** is a component that represents called behavior in a system. It's designed to stand in for part of your application code and feed back sample data values in response to various calling scenarios. Emulators are often implemented as stubs; they provide you with a way to control the data provided to a part of your system that you want to test. A **simulator**, on the other hand, is a component that's designed to call behavior within your system. It allows you to control the sequence of calls you make as well as the data you feed into the system. Simulators and emulators represent complementary parts of a whole; Figure 14-1 shows how the two concepts fit together in software.

Simulators can be used to log unexpected results, while emulators must typically be used in tandem with some kind of logging model or a passive mode component in another part of the system. Unlike passive mode tests, the active tests require a bit of

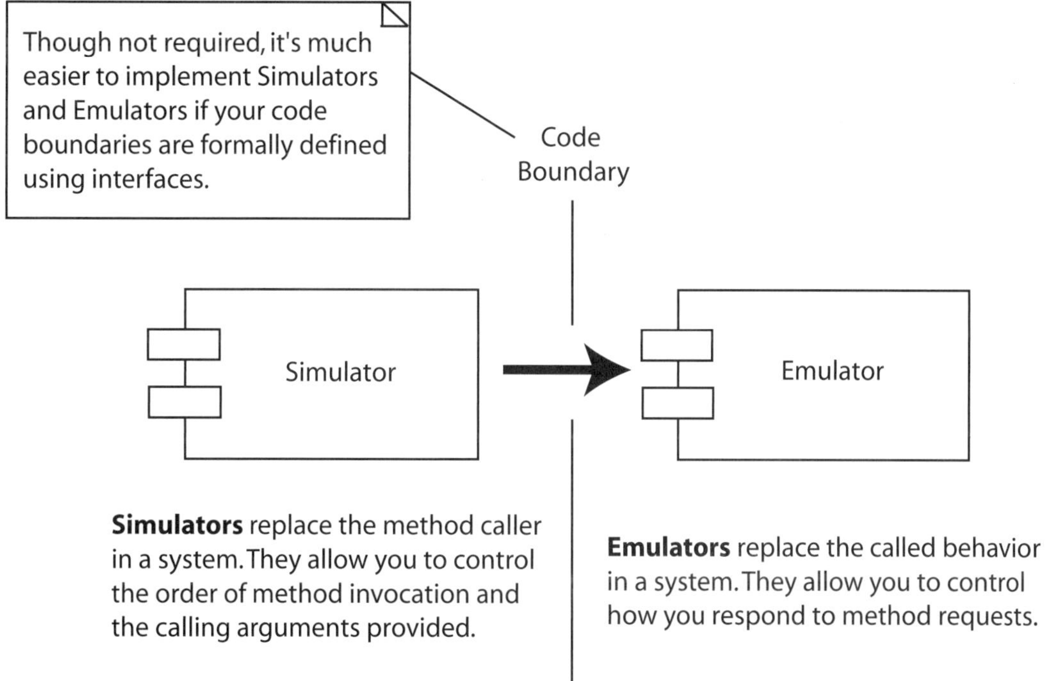

Figure 14-1
Simulators and Emulators.

initial design if you want to use them painlessly in a project. Although it's possible to use OO techniques such as subclassing to incorporate them into a system, it's often easier to dynamically add them if you design your system for modularity in the first place. In particular, technologies such as interfaces and patterns such as the Template Method provide a very convenient way to plug these components into your system with a minimum amount of hassle.

High-Level Testing Techniques

High-end testing models give you a way to check the environment in which a system runs. As mentioned earlier, developers either run a system within a "test environment," or run a separate "test process" to check the system. This type of testing is typically used to do one of three things:

- Enable a developer to flexibly query the Java runtime environment.
- See how the Java system behaves under real or simulated conditions of use; to see whether the use of APIs or frameworks results in any problems.
- Ensure that the outside environment provides the resources required by the Java system; to see whether conditions of use or load cause problems in the external environment.

If you're testing this high up in a system, you often have a specific failure scenario in mind.[165] You often use a testing technology based on a need to evaluate specific external measurable characteristics, or to collect system-wide data. A big challenge with some of the high-level techniques is that they often require you to run in a simulation environment. In particular, if you want full freedom to test architectural scenarios or to check anywhere in your runtime environment, you probably aren't running your tests on an installed product anymore. As a result, there's a risk you may bias your results.

Systemic testing is a little more forgiving. You can usually collect static data about external parts of your system, such as the operating environment or hardware platform, without disturbing the installed software. You can also probably run a lightweight monitoring process without compromising a system's runtime efficiency or integrity.

If you want to directly query your Java runtime environment, you're in luck. In many ways, your greatest ally in the process of performing high-level code debugging is already a part of your JVM, easy to integrate with an external tool such as an IDE. The **Java Platform Debugger Architecture (JPDA)** was developed to provide a flexible way to query a Java Virtual Machine during runtime.[166]

---

165. Admittedly, many developers use IDE debuggers as the preferred way to debug a software system. The technologies have become very sophisticated, and certainly support many of the techniques presented earlier in the chapter.

Conceptually, JPDA is a standardized architectural model that allows an external tool such as an IDE or debugging console to flexibly interact with any JVM. The external tool can control the "debug mode" behavior of the VM, performing actions such as stepping through code, halting threads, or pausing at breakpoints. The tool can also query the VM for data about objects or the runtime environment itself. The principal parts of JPDA are shown in Figure 14-2.

As you can see, JPDA provides standard interfaces so that any JVM and debugging tool can coordinate around a standard debugging model. The system also defines a wire protocol, so that you can perform local or remote debugging. The good news about JPDA is that it's a standardized technology—it's already a part of the JVM and is available in many Java IDEs. That means that you and I can use its capabilities, rather than studying yet another set of APIs.

There's relatively little modification required to your software development process if you want to use JPDA. During compilation, you will typically use the `javac` option `-g` to generate debugging information for your code: line numbers, code reference, and calling variables. When you run a Java application, the java command-line option `-Xdebug` will start the JVM with debugger support enabled. Of course, if you're managing debugging with an IDE, the tool usually handles the debugging setup for you.

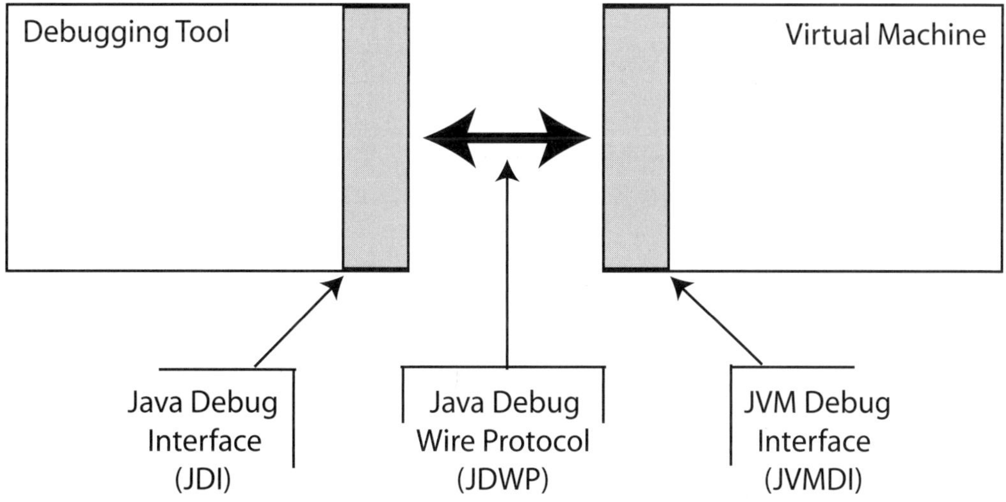

Figure 14–2
Java Platform Debugger Architecture.

---

166. JPDA was integrated into J2SE in version 1.3, though you could download a version for J2SE starting with version 1.2.2

Special Challenges for Debugging

Given how widely Java technology is used today, it's probably no surprise that you encounter a few special issues with debugging every now and then. There are two challenges that merit specific discussion: debugging non-Java technologies and dealing with exceptions thrown from within a framework.

Debugging Non-Java Technologies in Java Applications

As Java has grown, it's acquired a few hybrid APIs—ones that are based around scripted content that is subsequently converted back into Java code during compilation. The most familiar example is JSP technology. When you write a JSP, you're creating scripted content. The JSP page is then converted into a Java class during runtime.

Naturally, JSPs can present you with challenges when you debug a Web application. The code is clearly part of a Java application, so you'd like to be able to debug it along with the rest of your source code. However, the Java file produced for the JSP isn't terribly meaningful to the JSP creator. After all, one of the motivations for using JSPs in the first place is to avoid writing and maintaining a large amount of Java code to manage a limited amount of dynamic content.

For cases like this one, you need some way to correlate debugging actions with the JSP source, cross referencing the debugging position with the scripted content. That was precisely the rationale for creating Java Specification Request (JSR) 45: Debugging Support for Other Languages. JSR45 is a Java Community Process initiative introduced to make it possible to integrate debug support for languages that are translated into Java. This support was added to JPDA in J2SE 1.4, so it is now available to debugging tools. The basic concept behind this capability is that a language processor[167] will create a file that maps between sources. The mapping file is then integrated into the class file produced from the source. The class file can then be used by JPDA (or more to the point, by a debug tool using JDPA) to trace output back to the original source.

Exceptions Thrown within a Framework

This kind of exception presents a special problem for debugging. The use of a framework often adds layers of complexity that can make underlying troubles *difficult* to find. J2EE provides a perfect example. When a component throws an exception, the container typically protects itself (and the caller) by handling the exception. This is totally appropriate—you wouldn't want an exception thrown from a Servlet or EJB to crash your J2EE server. However, there can be two fairly major problems with this approach:

---

167. A language processor is software that translates source code from form to another. Language processors are a standard part of APIs such as JSP and SQLJ.

1. The container may absorb your exception, hiding it from you and making it harder to debug the system.
2. The container may wrap your exception, adding layers of unrelated container code to the stack trace and making it harder to see the true cause of code failure.

The resulting stack trace that appears in log files can be quite complex. Often, you don't see the actual source of component failure until you reach the end of the stack. Root cause exceptions can also prove challenging in the enterprise. In a complex multi-tier system, wrapping an exception can actually obscure the source of an error if you aren't careful about how you add details about the nature of a problem. Ideally, you want to wrap an exception to qualify a problem and to make it more easily understood in its new context.

Profiling Test Results for Handle-Declare

In Chapter 3, we talked about a test to compare the relative cost of handling or declaring an exception. This appendix summarizes the test and its result. The test was intended to evaluate the cost to a JVM of performing error handling operations; therefore, I avoided associating a large stack trace or volume data with the exception. The basic evaluation code was the Profile class shown below. Profile is really just a wrapper around a timer that can "clock" the execution time of an operation or operations. Since this test focused on basic execution time, this class is a simpler version of Profile as discussed in Chapter 3.

```
1   public class Profile{
2      private long startTime, stopTime, timeElapsed;
3      public void startTimer(){
4         startTime = System.currentTimeMillis();
5      }
6      public void stopTimer(){
7         stopTime = System.currentTimeMillis();
8         timeElapsed += stopTime - startTime;
9      }
10     public void clearTimer(){
11        startTime = stopTime = timeElapsed = 0;
12     }
13     public long getTimeElapsedMillis(){
14        return timeElapsed;
15     }
16  }
```

The test subject was `BytecodeExample`, a class that parses a primitive integer value given an input String. The class has three basic methods:

`readInt`, which has no exception handling,

readIntTryCatch, which handles the exception,
readIntDeclare, which declares the exception.

```
1  public class BytecodeExample{
2    public int readInt(String input){
3      int returnValue = 0;
4      returnValue = Integer.parseInt(input);
5      return returnValue;
6    }
7    public int readIntTryCatch(String input){
8      int returnValue = 0;
9      try{
10       returnValue = Integer.parseInt(input);
11     }
12     catch(NumberFormatException exc){}
13     return returnValue;
14   }
15   public int readIntDeclare(String input) throws NumberFormatException{
16     int returnValue = 0;
17     returnValue = Integer.parseInt(input);
18     return returnValue;
19   }
20 }
```

Three classes were used to run the test: Run_Declare, Run_Handle and
Run_NoHandle. All three classes perform the same test: they step through 1,000,000
iterations and call the appropriate method of the BytecodeExample class. Each
class is a command-line driven Java class that accepts an input value for parsing.
Depending on the value passed, the harness classes will either run successfully or generate a NumberFormatException.

```
1  public class Run_Handle{
2    public static void main(String [] args){
3      if (args.length >= 1){
4        String input = args[0];
5        BytecodeExample testCode = new BytecodeExample();
6        System.out.println("\tInput was " + input);
7        Profile profile = new Profile();
8        for (int i = 1; i <= 1000000; i++){
9          try{
10           profile.startTimer();
11           testCode.readIntTryCatch(input);
12           profile.stopTimer();
13         }
14         catch (RuntimeException exc){
15           profile.stopTimer();
```

```
16                }
17              if (i == 100000){
18                System.out.println("  Response time is " +
19                 profile.getTimeElapsedMillis() + " ms for 100000 iterations");
20              }
21              if (i == 250000){
22                System.out.println("  Response time is " +
23                 profile.getTimeElapsedMillis() + " ms for 250000 iterations");
24              }
25              if (i == 500000){
26                System.out.println("  Response time is " +
27                 profile.getTimeElapsedMillis() + " ms for 500000 iterations");
28              }
29              if (i == 1000000){
30                System.out.println("  Response time is " +
31                 profile.getTimeElapsedMillis() + " ms for 1000000 iterations");
32              }
33          }
34        }
35      }
36  }
```

Notice that I stop short of calling this test a benchmark. I had no intention of designing a benchmark, simply developing an illustrative test. It's intended to give you a good ballpark estimate of the effort spent by a JVM in performing basic exception handling functions. On a personal note, I'm not a great believer in most benchmarks. Most are not developed with enough attention to detail or to factors which can influence the benchmark results. As a result, they are primarily useful in identifying order of magnitude differences in efficiency. Ultimately, I tend to believe that the best benchmark is a software prototype.[168]

For this specific test, there are a number of factors that can influence the outcome of the test. For your convenience, I've summarized them below:

External Factors: Computer or Operating Environment
- Process load on the computer used to run the test
- Accuracy of the test computer's system clock, or of the library call used to retrieve the system clock's value
- Service activity performed by the test operating environment

Internal factors: JVM-specific Services
- Garbage collection
- Class loader activity
- Code optimization and interpreter behavior

168.In other words, the best benchmark is the one that tests what you were planning to do anyway!

This type of test will yield different performance results depending on factors such as CPU, RAM, Operating System and JVM. As such, you shouldn't think of the results as absolute or unvarying. To attempt to minimize the variation in test results, I ran the tests with the same JVM on the same system with a minimum external process configuration. In other words, I did my best to ensure that system load was minimal, and that the JVM run was consistent across the tests. I also averaged each test run over a large number of iterations. The output of Profile provided raw execution time for the test, which in this case provides a reasonable estimate of execution time. If you'd like a more detailed breakdown of where the JVM spent its time, you could also run this test application with the Java command-line flag -Xprof. This flag runs an application with a CPU profiler. As a result, the JVM writes a summary of the time spent on each method to the standard output stream when the application ends.[169]

Figures A-1 through A-4 summarize the results of the profile tests. Figures A-1 and A-2 show the results for the "no exception" scenario, while Figures A-3 and A-4 show the results for the scenario where a `NumberFormatException` is produced.

Summary of profiler results with no exception produced:

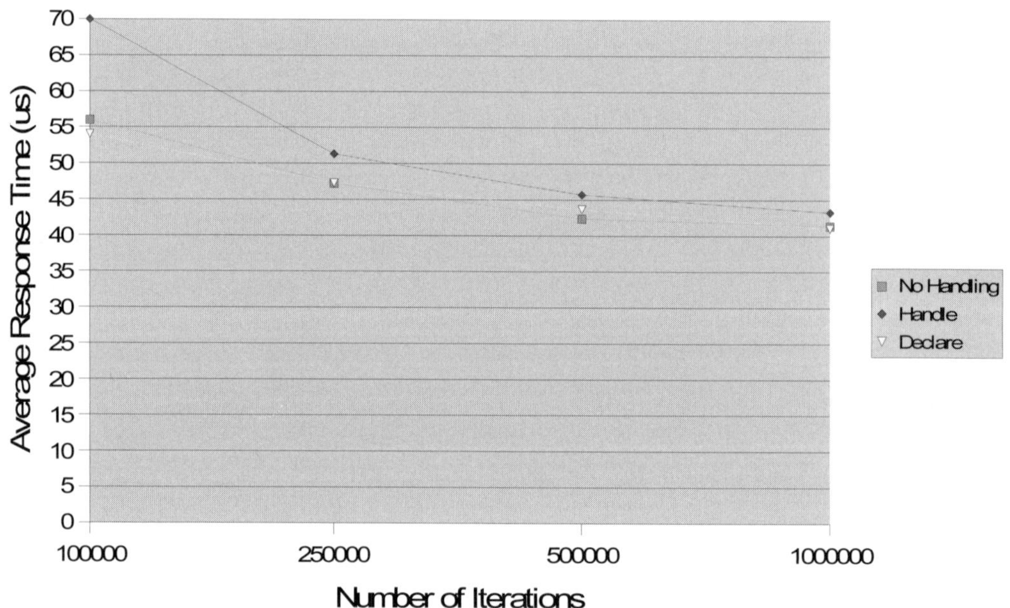

Figure A–1
Total response time, no exception produced.

169.Note that -X options are not officially supported and may not be available in every JVM version. You can get information about which options are supported by a JVM by running the command `java -X`.

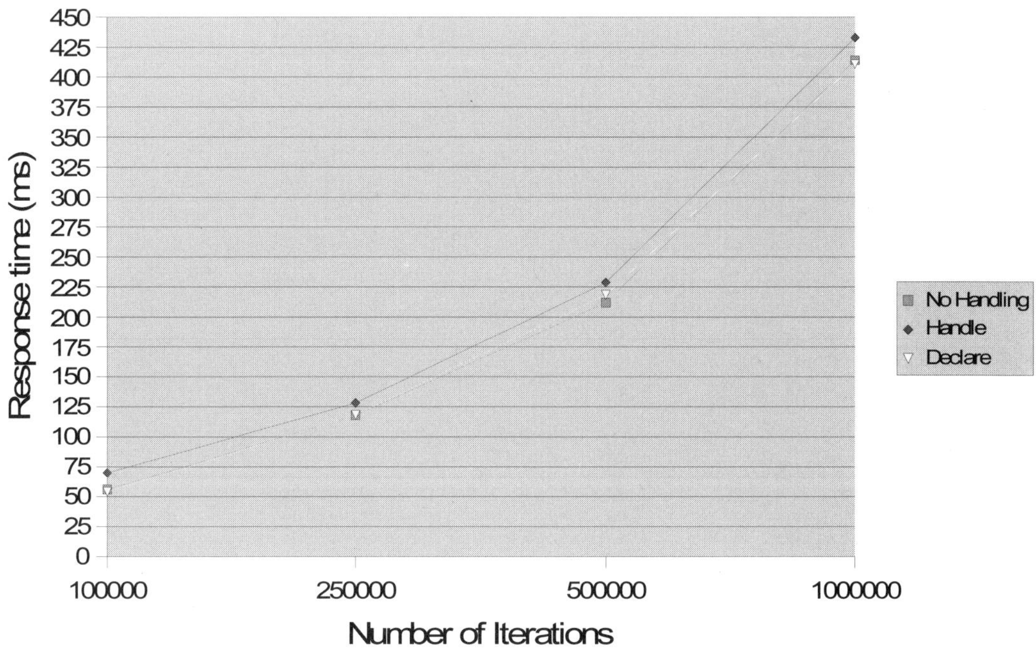

Figure A–2
Average response time, no exception produced.

Summary of profiler results with a `NumberFormatException` produced:

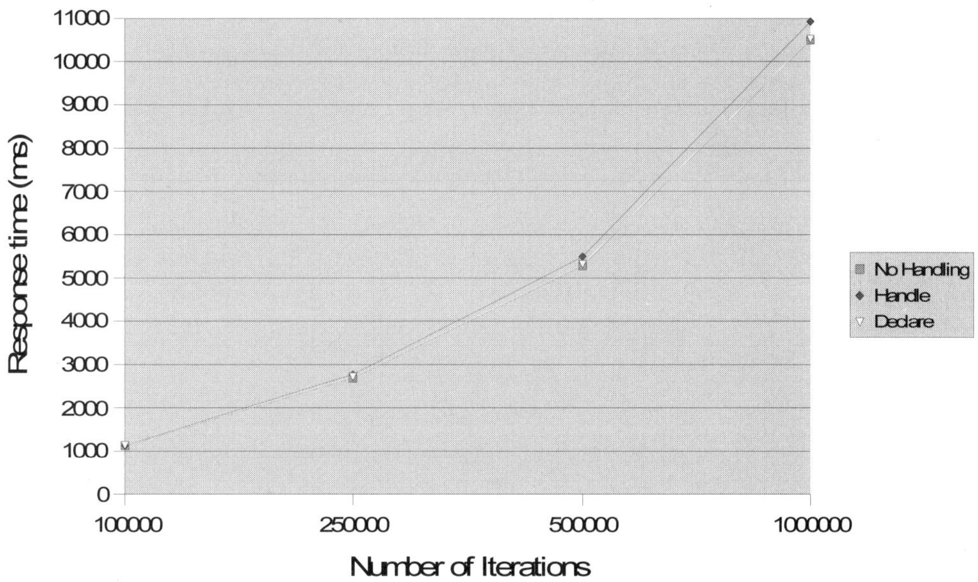

Figure A–3
Total response time, `NumberFormatException` produced

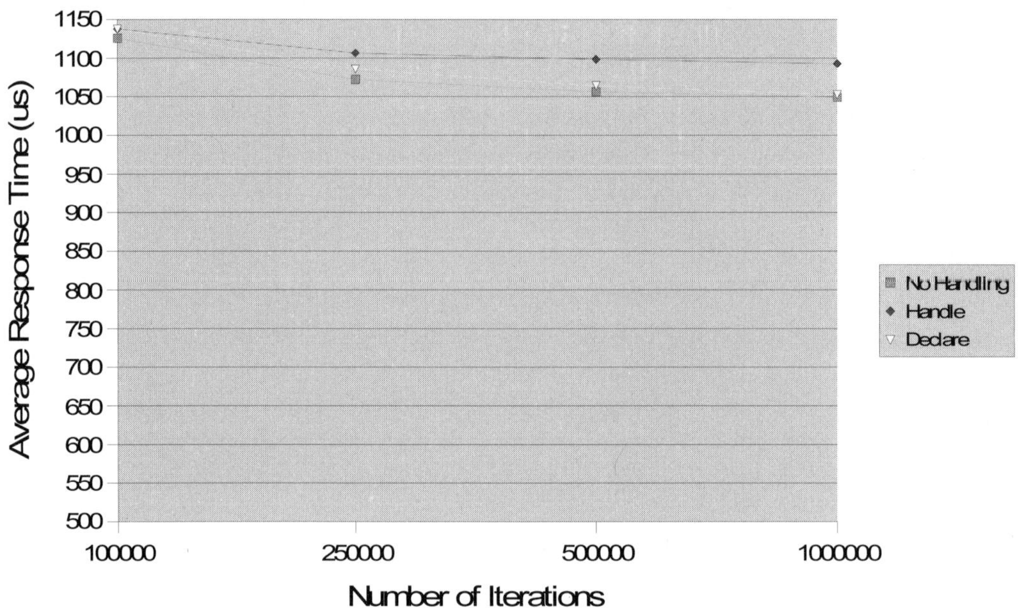

Figure A–4
Average response time, `NumberFormatException` produced

The most interesting point to notice is the relatively small variation between exception management options. Although exception handling does require additional effort from the JVM, the exact way you deal with exceptions probably won't substantially degrade an application's performance. Of course, there is a substantial difference between the scenarios where no exception is generated and ones where an exception is thrown. This emphasizes that it's important to avoid throwing exceptions unless you really need to.

Naturally, there are other exception handling factors that become important when you want to design high-performance applications. For example, you'll probably see noticeable performance degradation if you propagate an exception across a network connection, or process it in many layers of code. The good news is that the continued evolution of JVM technology seems to have narrowed the gap between exception handling options. You don't have to feel obligated to choose your exception management option based solely on the cost of the operation in the JVM.

A Short, Friendly Tutorial for JUnit

This section presents a brief, practical introduction to JUnit. It's intended to be a quick, "get you started" tutorial rather than a comprehensive discussion about how to use the framework. There are some excellent resources on the market for those who want to explore further. In particular, the Addison-Wesley books by Kent Beck (especially *Test-Driven Development by Example*) provide a good explanation of test-driven development using JUnit. For a thorough, broad overview that covers a number of Java technologies related to testing and code management, I'd recommend the Wiley book *Java Tools for eXtreme Programming* by Richard Hightower and Nicholas Lesiecki. JUnit also has excellent online documentation. The JUnit references, distributed as part of the testing framework, make especially good reading for anyone who wants to build a solid understanding of the tool and how it works.

Basic Information

Web site	http://www.junit.org (Source Forge project)
Creators	Erich Gamma, Kent Beck
Licensing	Open source, under the Common Public License Version 1.0
JDK version	JDK1.1.x or later
Installation	Include the file junit.jar in your CLASSPATH
Usable as	Standalone product, Apache Ant, various IDE plug-ins
Purpose	JUnit is a Java framework that supports unit testing

Installing JUnit

JUnit can be used as a standalone product, as an IDE extension, or as a task for Ant. Product installation is straightforward; you need only unzip the JUnit file (the software comes bundled in a .zip file) and add the **junit.jar** file to your CLASSPATH environment variable.

339

Some advanced Java IDEs, such as Eclipse and NetBeans, provide a JUnit plugin module. For these systems, you typically download the module from the tool's Web site (such as www.eclipse.org or www.netbeans.org) and install it using the standard method for installation in the IDE.

Running JUnit

1. Command line

There are three types of command-line execution. All would be run from a terminal window. For simple text-based execution, you would type:

```
java junit.textui.TestRunner [TestClass]
```

You can also run an AWT or Swing UI.

```
java junit.awtui.TestRunner [TestClass]
```

or

```
java junit.swingui.TestRunner [TestClass]
```

For UI mode, the test class argument is optional, since you can test multiple classes as the UI runs.

2. IDE

Typically, you run a JUnit test in an IDE by using a standard control or code template. For example, NetBeans provides wizard tools to automate the creation of a JUnit TestCase. It subsequently provides a link under the tools menu that allows you to create, open or run tests. The Eclipse project likewise provides a menu option that allows you to use a template to define a TestCase for one or more classes in your project.

3. Ant task execution

Ant defines a JUnit test tag that can be included in build projects. Depending on the format used, you can run a single TestCase or perform a batch run. JUnit test would be defined in the XML tag <junit> and placed within the Ant build file. A few examples follow.

```
<junit>
   <test name="SimpleTest">
</junit>
```

Further details are available in the Ant online reference manual at

```
http://ant.apache.org/manual/index.html
```

JUnit Test Framework Architecture

The JUnit framework is built around the `junit.framework.Test` interface.
When you perform testing using JUnit, you're always running tests on a class that implements this interface. Specifically, the framework executes the method run(`TestResult`) when you run a test. Like most frameworks, you don't use this interface directly. Instead, you base your tests around one of several classes that implement Test. The current group of classes defined for the JUnit framework is shown in Figure B-1.

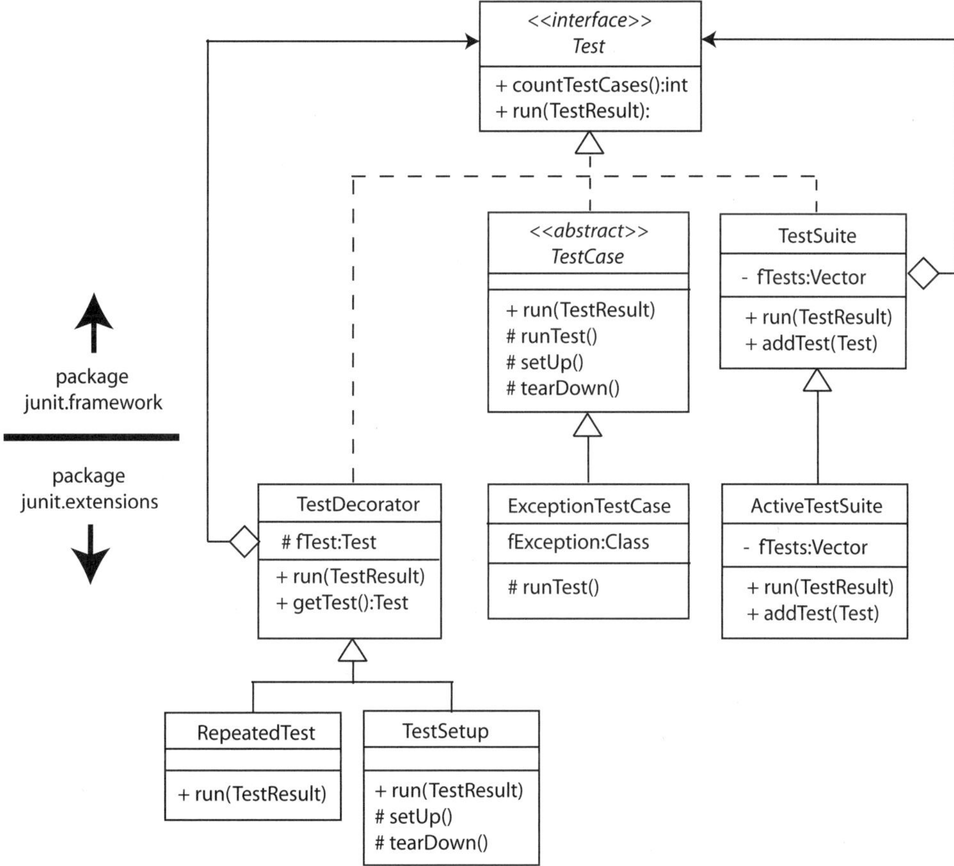

Figure B–1
Key JUnit Classes and Interfaces for Test Design.

The framework is designed to collect the results of a test run in a `TestResult` object and report the results to a developer. If a test method throws an `Assertion-FailedError`, the framework interprets the result as a test case failure. The framework intercepts any other exceptions and errors and treats them as "errors" in the test, and reports them as such.

Writing JUnit Tests

1. Simple Tests

A lot of basic test design can be managed by the abstract class `TestCase`. At the simplest level, you can create a single JUnit test if you perform the following steps:

1. Subclass `junit.framework.TestCase`.
2. Create a method called `test<`**Name**`>` to perform a desired test.
3. Inside your `test<`**Name**`>` method, perform your test by calling one of the `assert<`**Condition**`>` methods.

As a simple example, let's say we wanted to test an object used to model an order. Among other things, the Order would reference our customer and the items the customer wanted. An easy test of the Order constructor could be written like the `SimpleOrderTest` class shown below. The `testCreateOrderNotNull` method calls `assertNotNull` to verify that an Order was actually associated with a Customer object when the Order was created.

```
1   import junit.framework.*;
2   public class SimpleOrderTest extends TestCase{
3     public void testCreateOrderCustomerNotNull(){
4        Order o = new Order();
5        assertNotNull(o.getCustomer());
6     }
7   }
```

2. Multiple Tests in a TestCase

You can use this foundation to run multiple test cases, if you want. All you need to do is define multiple methods with the `test<`**Name**`>` signature. In the example above, the `testCreateOrderCustomerNotNull` method only verifies that we create a Customer when we create an Order object. It makes no promises that the object is actually valid. We might expand on the previous test by writing a series of test methods. The method `testCreateOrderCustomerNotNull` would check that a customer existed for the newly created Order, and the method `testCreateOrderItemsNotNull` would verify that there was a non-null `OrderItems`. The new form of the test harness might look like this:

```
 1  import junit.framework.*;
 2  public class MultitestOrderTest extends TestCase{
 3    public void testCreateOrderCustomerNotNull(){
 4      Order o = new Order();
 5      assertNotNull(o.getCustomer());
 6    }
 7    public void testCreateOrderItemsNotNull(){
 8      Order o = new Order();
 9      assertNotNull(o.getOrderItems());
10    }
11  }
```

The JUnit framework uses Java reflection to find and run all methods beginning with "test." In the `MultitestOrderTest`, JUnit would run all three of our test methods one after the other. If any of the assert<**Condition**> methods returns a false value, the test method throws an `AssertionFailedError`, causing the test to fail.

Where can you find the assert<**Condition**> methods? In `junit.frame-work.Assert`, a class used to manage test behavior. `TestCase` is a subclass of `Assert`, so you can freely call any or all of the assert<**Condition**> methods. There are quite a few different assertion tests you can perform: Table B-1 lists the different test methods that are available to you.

It's worth mentioning that earlier versions of JUnit performed the assertion check using a method called `assert()`. When JDK1.4 introduced assertions into the Java language, the `-version 1.4` switch caused compilation problems with JUnit test code. The framework fixed this problem in version 3.7 of the product by replacing the `assert()` method with the various assertion methods listed in the table.

Table B–1   **Test methods for a JUnit TestCase**

Method	What it does	Arguments
assertEquals	Fails if two elements are not considered equal	assertEquals(boolean b1, boolean b2) assertEquals(byte b1, byte b2) assertEquals(char c1, char c2) assertEquals(double d1, double d2) assertEquals(float f1, float f2) assertEquals(int i1, int i2) assertEquals(long l1, long l2) assertEquals(Object o1, Object o2) assertEquals(short s1, short s2) assertEquals(String msg, boolean b1, boolean b2) assertEquals(String msg, byte b1, byte b2) assertEquals(String msg, char c1, char c2) assertEquals(String msg, double d1, double d2) assertEquals(String msg, float f1, float f2) assertEquals(String msg, int i1, int i2) assertEquals(String msg, long l1, long l2) assertEquals(String msg, Object o1, Object o2) assertEquals(String msg, short s1, short s2) assertEquals(String msg, String s1, String s2)

Table B–1   **Test methods for a JUnit TestCase** *(continued)*

Method	What it does	Arguments
assertFalse	Fails if a condition evaluates to true	assertFalse(boolean b) assertFalse(String msg, boolean b)
assertNotNull	Fails if an object reference is null	assertNotNull(Object o) assertNotNull(String msg, Object o)
assertNotSame	Fails if two references point to the same object	assertNotSame(Object o1, Object o2) assertNotSame(String msg, Object o1, Object o2)
assertNull	Fails if an object reference is not null	assertNull(Object o) assertNull(String msg, Object o)
assertSame	Fails if two references do not point to the same object	assertSame(Object o1, Object o2) assertSame(String msg, Object o1, Object o2)
assertTrue	Fails if a condition evaluates to false	assertTrue(boolean b) assertTrue(String msg, boolean b)
fail	Fails and generates an AssertionFailedError	fail( ) fail(String msg)

3. Initialization and Clean-up for TestCases

Some tests require some type of initial setup. There may be standard objects used throughout a series of test methods, standard services that will be used in many tests, or APIs or frameworks that require initialization. The `TestCase` method provides two convenience methods that you can use for this purpose:

- Override `setUp()` when you need to initialize resources to be used in your tests.
- Override `tearDown()` when you need to clean up after you run a `TestCase`.

The `setUp()` and `tearDown()` methods are guaranteed to be called only once during the run of a `TestCase`. This makes them ideal when you want to manage resources that are assumed to be a part of your system, available as a precondition for your unit testing. In the `SetupOrderTest` class shown below, the class uses the methods to set up an `OrderProcessingService` object that performs an order processing check on the test Order created in the `testOrderProcessing` method.

```
1   import junit.framework.*;
2   public class SetupOrderTest extends TestCase{
3     private OrderProcessingService orderService;
4     public void setUp(){
5       orderService = new OrderProcessingService();
6     }
7     public void tearDown(){
8       orderService.serviceCleanup();
9     }
```

```
10    public void testOrderProcessing(){
11       Order o = new Order();
12       assertTrue(orderService.processOrder(o));
13    }
14  }
```

Of course, you'd run this test along with a number of other unit tests in a project. You'd probably design a series of JUnit tests for `OrderProcessingService` as well as the Order object. Notice that `SetupOrderTest` uses a variable to hold the initialized service object. It's common for a `TestCase` to use instance variables to hold objects used in multiple JUnit test methods.

4. Fixtures: Running Tests on Multiple Objects

So far, all of the examples have shown test methods that used a simple Order object—an object created with a default, no-argument constructor. In many cases, you want to run one or more tests using several different objects, objects that hold different state or configuration data.

In JUnit testing, (and testing in general) the objects used by a test are referred to as a **test fixture**. You run tests using different fixtures when you want to check that your system behaves as expected under various input conditions. For example, you might want to check Order behavior using a new customer order, an order for an existing customer account, and an order with incomplete information.

There are a few ways to manage fixture-based testing in JUnit. We talk about two of the most common. In both cases, you manage your fixture objects in the methods `setUp` and `tearDown`. Usually, you also store your fixtures in variables of the `TestCase`.

If you plan to perform the same test on all of your fixtures, you can write a test method that iterates through your objects, testing each one in turn. An easy way to do this is to store your fixtures as a collection. You can then set up your test method to iterate through the collection and run a test on each object. The example `Uniform-FixtureOrderTest` shows how you can do this.

```
1   import junit.framework.*;
2   import java.util.*;
3   public class UniformFixtureOrderTest extends TestCase{
4     private ArrayList orders = new ArrayList();
5     public void setUp(){
6        orders.add(new Order());
7        orders.add(new Order(new Customer(), new OrderItems()));
8        orders.add(new Order("Sample order"));
9     }
10    public void tearDown(){
11       orders = null;
```

```
12      }
13      public void testValidOrderCustomers(){
14        Iterator iterate = orders.iterator();
15        while(iterate.hasNext()){
16          Order orderToTest = (Order)iterate.next();
17          assertNotNull("Failed validity test for " +
18               orderToTest, orderToTest.getCustomer());
19        }
20      }
21    }
```

Notice that the test method `testValidOrders` uses an Iterator to run the test for `testValidOrderCustomers` on each Order object. Also notice that we use the form of the `assertNotNull` method with a detail string to provide information about which Order failed the test.

One drawback of this approach is that it will cause an entire test method to fail when the first fixture fails. You won't be able to test subsequent fixtures until you fix the problem that caused test failure in the first place. Another reason why you might not want to use this type of test is that you want greater control over how you perform your tests. In such cases, you can write test methods for individual fixtures. The class `MultiFixtureOrderTest` shows how you might modify the tests to check for validity of each of the three types of order configurations.

```
1   import junit.framework.*;
2   public class MultiFixtureOrderTest extends TestCase{
3     private Order noArgOrder;
4     private Order cfgOrder;
5     private Order namedOrder;
6     public void setUp(){
7       noArgOrder = new Order();
8       cfgOrder = new Order(new Customer(), new OrderItems());
9       namedOrder = new Order("Bob's order-mart");
10    }
11    public void tearDown(){
12    }
13    public void testValidOrderNoArg(){
14      assertNotNull(noArgOrder.getCustomer());
15      assertNotNull(noArgOrder.getOrderItems());
16    }
17    public void testValidOrderConfig(){
18      assertNotNull(configOrder.getCustomer());
19      assertNotNull(configOrder.getOrderItems());
20    }
21    public void testValidOrderNamed(){
```

```
22          assertNotNull(namedOrder.getCustomer());
23          assertNotNull(namedOrder.getOrderItems());
24      }
25  }
```

5. Testing Exception Behavior

So far, we haven't really talked about the way that you can test for exceptions and errors in your code. It's important to verify that your classes perform as expected when properly used. It's also important to verify that classes respond appropriately when they are improperly used! JUnit treats any Throwable object other than the `Asser-tionFailedError` as an error in the test rather than a test case failure. The framework catches any Throwable produced by your test methods, so you can continue to run tests even if one or more of your methods throws an Exception or Error. Because of this, a simple way to test for an exception is to look for an error when you run your tests. The `ValidOrderTest` class is a variation of the `SetupOrderTest` class shown earlier; the only difference is that the `testOrderProcessing` method now declares the `OrderException`.

```
1   import junit.framework.*;
2   public class ValidOrderTest extends TestCase{
3     private OrderProcessingService orderService;
4     public void setUp(){
5       orderService = new OrderProcessingService();
6     }
7     public void tearDown(){
8       orderService.serviceCleanup();
9     }
10    public void testOrderProcessing() throws OrderException{
11      Order o = new Order();
12      assertTrue(orderService.processOrder(o));
13    }
14  }
```

If the method threw the `OrderException` while running the test, you would now see the result as an error. The following shows the output from running the JUnit command-line UI if an exception were thrown:

```
.In setUp()
In tearDown()
E
Time: 0.01
There was 1 error:
1) testOrderProcessing(ValidOrderTest)OrderException: No OrderItems in Order
   at OrderProcessingService.processOrder(OrderProcessingService.java:18)
```

```
    at ValidOrderTest.testOrderProcessingValidOrderTest.java:18)
    at sun.reflect.NativeMethodAccessorImpl.invoke0(Native Method)
    at sun.reflect.NativeMethodAccessorImpl.invoke(NativeMethodAccessorImpl.
java:39)
    at
sun.reflect.DelegatingMethodAccessorImpl.invoke(DelegatingMethodAcces
sorImpl.java:25)


FAILURES!!!
Tests run: 1,  Failures: 0,  Errors: 1
```

You have several options available if you want to treat an exception as a normal, non-error outcome in a test method. One simple way to accomplish this is to wrap the exception in a try-catch block and return normally. The code shown below is a rewrite of the `testOrderProcessing` method with exception handling for the `OrderException`:

```
10    public void testOrderProcessing(){
11      Order o = new Order();
12      try{
13        assertTrue(orderService.processOrder(o));
14      }
15      catch (OrderException e){
16        return;
17      }
18    }
```

In this case, an `OrderException` or any subclass would not be treated as an error because you've handled the exception within the test method.[170] This allows you to easily automate tests where you anticipate errors or exceptions, treating them as a normal outcome of the test method.

6. TestSuite: Running Multiple Tests

A key benefit of JUnit is its ability to automate test execution. Of course, you'd probably prefer to run a whole bunch of unit tests together if you plan to use the framework for regression testing. For that reason, JUnit provides the class `junit.framework.TestSuite` to allow you to easily run several unit tests without having to call the `TestRunner` individually for every one of your `TestCase` objects.

---

170. As an alternative, you could use a class in the `junit.extensions` package called `ExceptionTestCase`. This class allows you to set up tests that expect an exception passed into the class using a constructor. The JUnit API documentation provides additional details about use, as well as additional support classes in the package.

There are a few ways that you can use a `TestSuite`. If you want to run a single `TestCase`, you can call one of `TestSuite`'s constructors that associate it with a test. For example:

```
TestSuite simpleSuite = new TestSuite(SimpleOrderTest.class);
```

This code wraps the `SimpleOrderTest` in a `TestSuite` object. You can also associate tests with a `TestSuite` by calling the methods `addTest` or `addTest-Suite`. If you want to group a bunch of tests together under a `TestSuite`, you can do it by using code like this:

```
TestSuite totalSuite = new TestSuite();
totalSuite.addTestSuite(SimpleOrderTest.class);
totalSuite.addTestSuite(MultiFixtureOrderTest.class);
totalSuite.addTestSuite(SetupOrderTest.class);
```

Since TestSuite represents a collection of Test implementors, you can make a `TestSuite` reference any other `Test`—it can even reference another `TestSuite` object. Ultimately, you could run all of the `TestSuite` objects in a project simply by associating them with yet another `TestSuite`.

A `TestSuite` runs by running all of its contained `Test` objects. If you want an easy way to run a `TestSuite`, you can simply create a `Test` class with a static method called suite that returns a `Test` implementor. The following example shows you how:

```
1   import junit.framework.*;
2   public class RealSuite extends TestCase{
3     public static Test suite(){
4       TestSuite totalSuite = new TestSuite();
5       totalSuite.addTestSuite(SimpleOrderTest.class);
6       totalSuite.addTestSuite(MultiFixtureOrderTest.class);
7       totalSuite.addTestSuite(SetupOrderTest.class);
8       totalSuite.addTestSuite(ValidExcOrderTest.class);
9       totalSuite.addTestSuite(UniFixtureOrderTest.class);
10      return totalSuite;
11    }
12  }
```

If you use any of the JUnit `TestRunner` classes to execute the `RealSuite` class, you'll see that the framework runs all of the `TestCase` objects, reporting the results as a whole. `TestSuite` objects make it much easier to organize and run a group of related tests. Likewise, they're a useful addition when you want to automate groups of tests for repeat execution.

Guidelines for Test Design

As a closing thought, let's review recommendations and best practices for JUnit test design. We've already talked about strategies to develop unit and integration tests in our chapter on testing, but it's useful to review some of the ideas in the context of the JUnit framework.

Remember that JUnit was developed to support the practice of Test-Driven Development. A basic description of the process is that you develop a test and then build the code to satisfy that test. Stated more formally, TDD recommends that you perform the following steps:

1. Design a test for a code feature.
2. Run the test, verifying that it fails.
3. Modify your code, doing the minimum work required to make the test succeed.
4. Run the test again, ensuring that it succeeds.

If you follow this practice when you write code, it tends to steer you toward writing fairly compact, focused tests. That's a major recommendation in JUnit: you should develop tests around small units of functionality. That doesn't mean that the tests cannot be sophisticated. As you continue to develop tests for your system, you can use the same approach to develop your integration tests.

A common mistake that people make when writing JUnit tests is trying to perform too many tests in a single method. There are several important drawbacks with this approach:

- If you write too much in a method, it's harder to maintain your code.
- If you test too much in a method, it's hard to isolate the source of a test failure.
- If you test too much, you risk "hiding" test failures behind other failures.
- If your tests become too complex, there's a risk that *they'll* become buggy.

JUnit recommends that you start with specific tests in your code. You can then aggregate those tests in a `TestSuite` to provide a baseline check of class or component stability. Finally, you can "build up" to more complex integration tests. If you apply this as a best practice, it suggests you should perform single-check tests in your method, or at most a *very* small set of related tests.

MyBuggyServlet—
Validation Issues with a Component

As mentioned in the testing chapter, it can be challenging to properly develop a managed component like a Servlet or EJB. A few years ago, I created a Servlet to emphasize the fact. Based on common development problems I had observed in the classroom, I created MyBuggyServlet: a class that *will* compile but is guaranteed *not* to run as the developer intended. The component is supposed to print out a table of key-value pairs based on client-submitted parameters.

Of course, I doubt you'd find all of these problems in an ordinary Servlet. I wrote this example to emphasize the fact that J2EE components need validators to ensure they are correct. Some of the problems are fairly obvious; others are much more challenging to identify. Take a look at the source code, and see what you can find. Look for outright coding errors, incorrect assumptions, poor coding practices or design problems. Above all, enjoy yourself!

```
1    import java.io.*;
2    import java.util.Enumeration;
3    import javax.servlet.*;
4    import javax.servlet.http.*;
5
6    public class MyBuggyServlet extends HttpServlet{
7       private String paramName;
8       private String paramValue;
9       private String fullFileName;
10
11      public void init(ServletConfig cfg) throws ServletException{
12         String fullFileName = getInitParameter("FileName");
13         log("Initialization has completed.");
14      }
15
16      public void dopost(HttpServletRequest req,
```

```
17        HttpServletResponse rsp) throws IOException{
18          try{
19            FileWriter output = new FileWriter(fullFileName);
20            PrintWriter httpOut = rsp.getWriter();
21            Enumeration paramNameList = req.getParameterNames();
22            while (paramNameList.hasMoreElements()){
23              paramName = (String)(paramNameList.nextElement());
24              paramValue = req.getParameter(paramName);
25              output.write(paramName + " - " + paramValue + "\n");
26              httpOut.println(paramName + " = " + paramValue);
27            }
28          }
29        catch (IOException exc){
30          getServletContext().log(exc, "Trouble with Servlet IO...");
31          }
32    }
33  }
```

Glossary of Technical Terms

Our field is renowned for its acronyms and since we've covered a lot of subjects, this book has more than usual. This section provides a quick, easy reference to the commonly-used acronyms mentioned throughout the book. In addition to defining the acronym, I've referenced the field or topic area where you'll commonly see it used.

Acronym	Where the term is used	What it means
API	General	Application Programming Interface
BLOB	Database technology	Binary Large Object
BMP	Java –Enterprise JavaBeans	Bean-Managed Persistence
BMT	Java –Enterprise JavaBeans	Bean-Managed Transactions
CLOB	Database technology	Character Large Object
CMP	Java –Enterprise JavaBeans	Container-Managed Persistence
CMR	Java –Enterprise JavaBeans	Container-Managed Relationship
CMT	Java –Enterprise JavaBeans	Container-Managed Transactions
CORBA	CORBA	Common Object Request Broker Architecture
COS Naming	CORBA	Common Object Service
DAO	Patterns	Data Access Object
DBMS	Database technology	Database Management System
DTD	XML	Document Type Definition
EIS	General	Enterprise Information System
EJB	Java –Enterprise JavaBeans	Enterprise JavaBean
ERP	General	Enterprise Resource Planning
GUI	General	Graphical User Interface
HOPP	Patterns	Half Object Plus Protocol
HTTP	Web technology	Hypertext Transfer Protocol

IDE	General	Integrated Development Environment
IDL	CORBA	Interface Definition Language
IIOP	CORBA	Internet Inter-ORB Protocol
J2EE	Java –General	Java 2, Enterprise Edition
J2SE	Java –General	Java 2, Standard Edition
JAXM	Java –Web Services	Java API for XML Messaging
JAX-RPC	Java –Web Services	Java API for XML Remote Procedure Calls
JDBC	Java –Distributed APIs	The Java Database Connectivity API
JDK	Java –General	Java Development Kit
JNDI	Java –Distributed APIs	Java Naming and Directory Interface
JPDA	Java –General	Java Platform Debugger Architecture
JRMP	Java –Distributed APIs	Java Remote Method Protocol
JSP	Java –Web technologies	Java ServerPages
JSR	Java –General	Java Specification Request
JTA	Java –J2EE APIs	Java Transaction API
JTS	Java –J2EE APIs	Java Transaction Service
JVM	Java –General	Java Virtual Machine
LDAP	General –Protocols	Lightweight Directory Access Protocol
MVC	Patterns	Model-View-Controller
NIO	Java –APIs	New I/O API
OO	Object-oriented technology	Object-Oriented
OOD	Object-oriented technology	Object-Oriented Development
ORB	CORBA	Object Request Broker
OSI	General	Open Systems Interconnect
RDBMS	Database technology	Relational Database Management System
RMI	Java –Distributed APIs	Remote Method Invocation
ROI	Business	Return on Investment
SQL	Database technology	Structured Query Language
SQLJ	Java –Distributed APIs	Structured Query Language for Java
TCO	Business	Total Cost of Ownership
TCP/IP	General –Protocols	Transfer Control Protocol/Internet Protocol
TCC	Testing	Test-Driven Development
UDP	General –Protocols	User Datagram Protocol

UI	General	User Interface
UML	General	Unified Modeling Language
URI	Web technology	Uniform Request Indicator
URL	Web technology	Uniform Request Locator
UTF	General	Universal Character Set Transform Format
VM	Java –General	Virtual Machine
XML	XML	Extensible Markup Language
XOPEN	General	X/Open Common Applications Environment
XP	General - Methodology	Extreme Programming

Bibliography

The resources in this section provide supplementary references to some of the technologies and topics presented in this book. I have grouped references according to topic area to make it a little easier to decide what references might be useful to you as you continue to explore the topics we've talked about.

Books

Debugging

Debugging: The Nine Indispensable Rules for Finding Even the Most Elusive Software and Hardware Problems
David J. Agans
© 2002, AMACOM
ISBN: 0814471684

Java Technologies, APIs and Frameworks

Bitter EJB
Bruce Tate (Editor), Mike Clark, Bob Lee, Patrick Linskey
© 2003, Manning Publications Company
ISBN: 1930110952

Bitter Java
Bruce Tate
© 2002, Manning Publications Company
ISBN: 193011043X

Core Java 2, Volume I: Fundamentals
Cay Horstmann, Gary Cornell
© 2002, Prentice Hall PTR
ISBN: 0130471771

Core Java 2, Volume II: Advanced Features
Cay Horstmann, Gary Cornell
© 2001, Prentice Hall PTR
ISBN: 0130927384

Effective Java Programming Language Guide
Joshua Bloch
© 2001, Addison-Wesley
ISBN: 0201310058

Head First EJB
Bert Bates, Kathy Sierra
© 2003, O'Reilly & Associates
ISBN: 0596005717

Head First Java
Bert Bates, Kathy Sierra
© 2003, O'Reilly & Associates
ISBN: 0596004656

Head First Servlets and JSPs
Bryan Basham, Bert Bates, Kathy Sierra
© 2004, O'Reilly & Associates
ISBN: 0596005407

Patterns

Applied Java Patterns
Stephen A. Stelting, Olav Maassen
© 2001, Prentice Hall PTR
ISBN: 0130935387

Core J2EE Patterns: Best Practices and Design Strategies, 2nd Edition
Deepak Alur, Dan Malks, John Crupi
© 2003, Prentice Hall PTR
ISBN: 0131422464

Design Patterns
Eric Gamma, Richard Helm, Ralph Johnson, John Vlissides
© 1995, Addison-Wesley Pub. Co.
ISBN: 0201633612

Pattern-Oriented Software Architecture, Volume 1: A System of Patterns
Frank Buschmann, Regine Meunier, Hans Rohnert, Peter Sommerlad, Michael Stal
© 1996, John Wiley & Sons
ISBN: 0471958697

Software Testing

The Art of Software Testing
Glenford J. Myers
© 1979, John Wiley & Sons
ISBN: 0471043281

Java Testing and Design : From Unit Testing to Automated Web Tests
Frank Cohen
© 2004, Prentice Hall PTR
ISBN: 0131421891

Java Tools for Extreme Programming: Mastering Open Source Tools Including Ant, JUnit, and Cactus
Richard Hightower, Nicholas Lesiecki
© 2001, John Wiley & Sons
ISBN: 047120708X

Testing Computer Software, 2nd Edition
Cem Kaner, Jack Falk, Hung Q. Nguyen
© 1999, John Wiley & Sons
ISBN: 0471358460

Test Driven Development: By Example
Kent Beck
© 2002, Addison-Wesley Pub. Co.
ISBN: 0321146530

Unit Testing in Java: How Tests Drive the Code
Johannes Link, Peter Fröhlich
© 2003, Morgan Kaufmann
ISBN: 1558608680

Java Technology Specifications

Technology	Specification URL
Java language	http://java.sun.com/docs/books/jls/index.html
Java virtual machine	http://java.sun.com/docs/books/vmspec/index.html
Java Blueprints	http://java.sun.com/reference/blueprints/index.html
J2EE	http://java.sun.com/j2ee/1.4/download.html#platformspec
EJB	http://java.sun.com/products/ejb/docs.html
JSP	http://java.sun.com/products/jsp/download/index.html
Servlet	http://java.sun.com/products/servlet/download.html

index

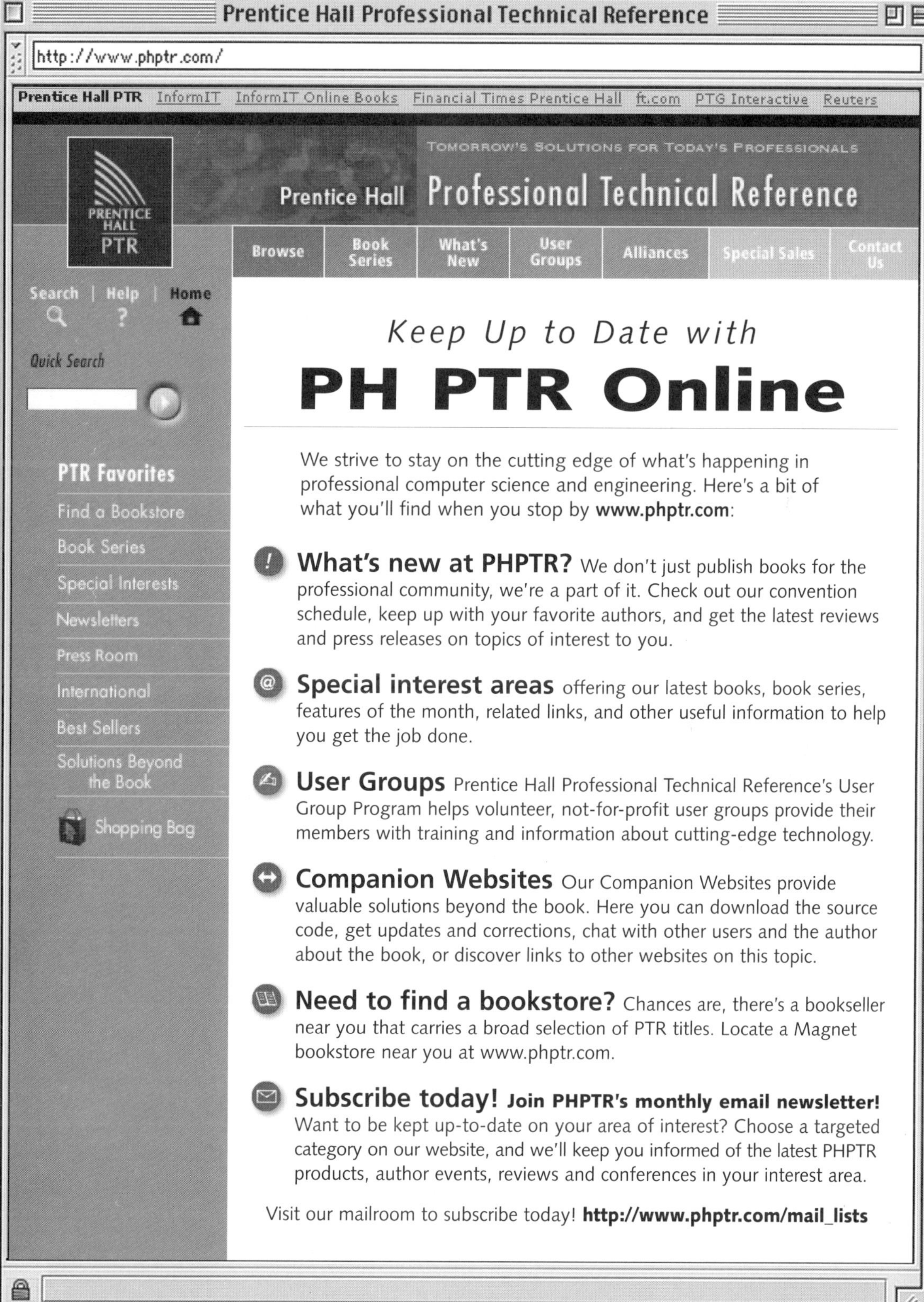